ACTING
WITH STYLE

ACTING
WITH STYLE

John Harrop

University of California at Santa Barbara

Sabin R. Epstein

PRENTICE-HALL, INC., ENGLEWOOD CLIFFS, N.J. 07632

Library of Congress Cataloging in Publication Data

HARROP, JOHN.
　　Acting with style.

　　Includes bibliographies and index.
　　1. Acting.　2. Drama.　I. Epstein, Sabin R.
　II. Title.
PN2061.H33　　　792′.028　　　81-17939
ISBN　0-13-003061-9　　　AACR2

Printed in the United States of America

10　9　8　7　6　5　4　3　2　1

Editorial production
　　and interior design by Joyce Turner
Cover design by Diane Saxe
Manufacturing buyer: Edmund W. Leone

ISBN 0-13-003061-9

Prentice-Hall International, Inc., *London*
Prentice-Hall of Australia Pty. Limited, *Sydney*
Prentice-Hall of Canada, Ltd., *Toronto*
Prentice-Hall of India Private Limited, *New Delhi*
Prentice-Hall of Japan, Inc., *Tokyo*
Prentice-Hall of Southeast Asia Pte. Ltd., *Singapore*
Whitehall Books Limited, *Wellington, New Zealand*

Contents

Preface

John Gielgud has said "Style is knowing what kind of play you are in." Young actors don't always instinctively know what kind of play they are in, or how to recognize the clues of style. One reason for this is the limiting way in which being "natural" or "honest" has been used as a touchstone of acting: An actor should do nothing that cannot be perceived as consistent with his own emotions and personal sense of identity. Thus, in this century actor training was dominated until quite recently by "naturalistic" technique, a concentration upon inner process and the generation of personal emotion. This served the dominating perception that realism in drama demanded a one-to-one relationship between the actor and his role—becoming the character in a real-world sense rather than "playing" the character within the framework of the theatrical event. While theatre continued to speak of a "play," "playing," and "players," the relationship between the acting process and the concept of play tended to be lost beneath the emphasis upon the "reality" of theatre.

The necessity for truth, honesty, and responsibility (Stanislavski's sense of the art in oneself, not oneself in the art) must work hand in hand with the recognition that a complete actor has to be able to play many parts within the full range of the dramatic repertory—from Aeschylus to Artaud—and that his character is a *dramatis persona*, a mask of the action, rather than a "real" person. The emphasis of this book is upon mask and play—acting seen as the choice, adaptation, and performance of physical actions. This is not to ignore the place of emotion: emotion is both stimulated and communicated by action. At one time it was believed that if an actor felt an emotion intensely enough, it would automatically be communicated to the audience. This turned out not to be the case; emotion is intangible and must be manifested through a recognizable action.

"Play" presumes action, and "mask" requires the adaptation of action to the inherent stylistic demands of different plays, so that the player will adopt the right mask for the right event and not give every performance generally in the style of Tennessee Williams, or vaguely like Arthur Miller. Sophocles, Shakespeare, Molière, Beckett, Brecht—each has his own identity, his particular demands—in a word, style. The clues to style are in the text. To recognize them the actor must know something of the world in which and for which a text was written: its theatrical space, society, and politics; its architecture and clothing; its social and theatrical conventions—all the flavor and physical quality of a period that informs the sensibility of a playwright.

Actors are rightly more concerned with doing than reading or intellectualizing, but without a certain understanding it is not always possible to make the right instinctive connections between the nature of a text and the manner of its performance. This book is aimed at helping the actor discover what kind of play he is in—to identify the stylistic clues—and then to come to a physical awareness of how it should be played. This is not in order to perform plays as historical curiosities, but to avoid that bland homogenization of style that obscures the inherent quality of a play and stifles its vitality. "Nonrealistic" plays are too often dismissed as artificial, irrelevant, and boring because the actors lack sufficient understanding of the play's demands and thus fail to bring them to life.

The book deals with seven styles. Its method is first to examine the intrinsic given circumstances of a style—what exactly distinguishes its sensibility from that of other styles—then to show how this intrinsic quality requires certain physical responses from an actor, and finally to suggest a workshop structure of games and exercises that help the actor get into the physical skin of the style. The more than one hundred exercises in the book use the "game playing" format with which most young actors are familiar and comfortable, an approach that employs the actor's own potential for "playing" as a bridge between textual demands and the physicalization of a performance style.

This book on style, part of an ongoing collaboration between the authors, was written by John Harrop; future work will lay emphasis upon Sabin Epstein's theory of process. Throughout the text the words *actor*, *performer*, and *player* refer to both sexes. The male pronoun has, for convenience, also been used—simply to avoid the complexity, clumsiness, and extra paper involved in saying *he/she* and *her/him*. The word *man*, when used in its broader perspective, must likewise be taken, to use Winston Churchill's charming phrase, as "embracing woman."

J. H.
S. E.

ACTING
WITH STYLE

"The Importance of Being Earnest," by Oscar Wilde.

Photo by John Vere Brown, Citizens' Theatre Company, Glasgow.

General Approach

BASIC PROCESS

Though this book doesn't set out to teach basic acting technique, but to show how an actor's method may be adapted to the creation of various styles, it might help actors better understand our discussion and get the most out of the exercises if we briefly set forth our concept of the basic process of acting.[1] This process is common to all styles of theatre: impulse leads to action, and action leads to event. Every act of creation starts from an impulse. It may be an idea, it may be an image; it may derive from pure imagination, or, as is the presumption of this book, it will be the actor's response to a play text. An impulse is a movement towards action: if an actor wants to communicate his impulse he must *do* something—play an action. Playing allows the body to respond to an impulse, to clothe the impulse in physical form—which is much stronger and more tangible than either an intellectual idea or a feeling.

The actor's focus, then, is at all times upon doing—making physical choices that express the intention of the impulse. The interrelationship of all the choices of all the actors creates the event. On stage the event, or score of actions, is a constant—the result of choices made in rehearsal. However, the way in which the score is "played" will vary somewhat at each performance: there is always a margin in performance that allows the actor to respond to the immediate rhythms of the event as they reach him from fellow actors and the audience. It is this aspect of "playing" that keeps the vitality in a performance.

SENSIBILITY AND STYLE

We have shown how the playing of physical actions deriving from impulses leads to the creation of an event. But where does style come in? Style is what distinguishes one event from another. The impulse for action is found in a text. The text also contains the given circumstances of the event—the rules of the theatrical game. (To pursue the game analogy for a moment, it is the rules that tell us how, with the same deck of cards, to play bridge rather than gin rummy, or how, with similar implements, to play tennis rather than racquetball.) So the text not only provides the impulse to action but, through the given circumstances, determines the shape of the actor's physical choices and the form and sensibility of the event.

What are the given circumstances that catalyze the impulse and shape the style? Most actors are familiar with the idea of given circumstances such as place, climate, dialects, and the physical type, age, and occupation of a character. These clues may distinguish qualities of character and situation, but they do not necessarily determine the style of a performance. The basic question is: why do a character in a comedy by Noel Coward and a comic character in Molière require different approaches from the actor? Or, what makes the quality of a play by Tennessee Williams different from that of a play by Samuel Beckett, and why are neither like a play by Bertolt Brecht or a Restoration playwright? Stanley Kowalski in *A Streetcar*

[1] An excellent discussion of the acting process, one with which we are in full agreement, is to be found in Robert Benedetti's *The Actor at Work* (Englewood Cliffs, N.J.: Prentice-Hall, 1981). Based upon the performance of physical actions, Benedetti's work essentially leads into our own.

Named Desire and Horner in the Restoration play *The Country Wife* are both highly physical men with strong sexual drives—cocks of their respective middens. But the muscular T-shirted, bowling-alley directness of Stanley and the elegant, beribboned, drawing-room subtlety of Horner could hardly be more dissimilar outward expressions of similar inner drives, and the difference is reflected in the tone of the two plays. The same actor could play both parts—differently. But how does he recognize the difference and learn to play it?

The clues are in the text: given circumstances of a much more comprehensive kind than those that indicate the nature of a character. These broader clues derive from:

theatrical conventions of the time in which the play was written—spaces, equipment, the physical manner of the actors;

language rhythms and forms;

dramatic conventions such as the use of verse, the employment of neoclassical or epic structure, and the mask approach to character;

social, political, moral, and other perspectives of the age in which the playwright was working, and his response to them.

It is only by understanding these built-in clues that an actor can hope to approach a true awareness of the stylistic demands of a text. All of this we are calling the sensibility of a time—the theatrical, social, and personal values a playwright inevitably writes into a play. An understanding of the sensibility makes possible an assumption of the physical style.

To some degree style reflects the fact that theatre holds a "mirror up to nature." Joseph Chaikin has noted that "theatre styles are interrelated with living and thought styles—everything we see carries a recommendation to be seen within a given system of perception."[2] It is this system of perception—the

reflection of a particular social reality at a particular time—that an actor must appreciate in order to avoid imposing his own contemporary sensibility upon a text and limiting or warping it.

Style might be said to be the realism of a particular time as communicated through the theatrical conventions of that time. For much of this century, the influence of realism as a genre and its "naturalistic" approach to acting tended to limit the stylistic expression of theatre. The imitation of the mannerisms of twentieth-century humans, the outward manifestation of their inner psychological process acted out within the peep-show theatrical spaces of the time, created a style that proved valid for certain plays. There was, however, a vast corpus of drama that did not respond to this approach. And for good reason: the "naturalistic" approach tried to impose a quite different reality upon these plays—one based upon a psychological interpretation of character and a contemporary concept of behavior quite foreign to the given circumstances of the text. Charles Marowitz, an early proponent of the naturalistic acting technique known as "the method," and one who came to realize its limitations, wrote, "There is some commonly experienced continuum in a work of art which we are prepared to accept as *its* truth. A truth nurtured in a very special way by the material and *its* conceptions which, if they are consistent, pursuades us to accept, even if only temporarily, someone else's coherent view of life."[3]

An actor must come to terms with the inherent truth of each text, and not impose his own sense of truth upon it. While inner process is necessary, the simple manifestation of personal feeling by an actor will not communicate the totality of a play. It is physical actions—signals and signs—that communicate, and these must take on a particular shape, create a particular style, in

---

[2] Joseph Chaikin, *The Presence of the Actor* (New York: Atheneum, 1972), p. 128.

[3] Charles Marowitz, *The Act of Being* (London: Secker & Warburg, 1978), p. 35.

accordance with the given circumstances of a text.

MASK AND PLAY

Theatre is the creation of an illusion of reality. As Lee Simonson has observed, "The reality of a performance has no inherent connection with the degree of fidelity with which it reproduces the facts of actual life." [4] For an actor there is a distinction between simply expressing the self and using the self, to express the truth of the event as found in the given circumstances. Emphasis upon "honesty" has sometimes been taken to mean that all an actor has to do is project his feelings through the role, turning every character into a carbon copy of himself. Dion Boucicault once wrote, "If actors' and actresses' minds be employed upon themselves and not on the character they aspire to perform, they never really get out of themselves. Many think they are studying their character when they are studying only themselves." [5] An actor must consider all the given circumstances in order to create the mask that the truth of the event requires. He must be aware that a character may be constructed as much out of the rhythms and images of its speech and its structural function in the play as out of imagined biological or biographical data; that a playwright may deal in broad humors as much as in detailed psyches; and that the "artificiality" of manner written into some plays must be recognized as representing the physical reality of its time, and must be reproduced if the quality of the play is to be truly served. If an actor creates a valid mask and plays it truthfully within the demands of the script, then he is being honest.

We should take a moment to clarify our use of the term *mask*. The use of masks may be traced back to primitive peoples who wore them in their rituals. Greek theatre adopted the practice in both tragedy and comedy, in order to define essential attributes of character. Mask continued to be part of theatrical convention, and in the sixteenth century the five main characters of the commedia dell'arte (see Chapter 5) not only wore masks but were referred to as "masks." In the seventeenth century Molière used masks in some of his more farcical work, and since that time the term has been generally applied to any well-defined theatrical character type, though it may no longer wear a physical mask.

More than this, however, *mask* may be used to describe the structural function a character performs in a play—which points to the fact that theatre is not "reality," but an illusion of reality. As Richard Schechner has written, "Great errors are made because performers and directors think of characters as people rather than as *dramatis personae:* masks of dramatic action. A role conforms to the logic of theatre, not the logic of any other life system. To think of a role as a person is like picknicking on a landscape painting." [6] Thus, a mask consists of everything a character is required to do in order to discharge a valid function within a play. It is a set of physical choices that includes everything from hair style, vocal quality, costume, and physical rhythms to kind of shoes and manner of walk. These choices will differ with the different demands of each text. Robert Benedetti has put it well: "Mask is a set of postures, gestures, sounds and actions performed by the actor . . . different kinds of acting, having different purposes, require different relationships of actor and character." [7]

[4] Lee Simonson, *The Stage Is Set* (New York: Theatre Arts Books, 1963), p. 46.

[5] Dion Boucicault, Constant Coquelin, and Henry Irving, *The Art of Acting* (New York: Dramatic Museum of Columbia University, 1926), p. 42.

[6] Richard Schechner, *Environmental Theater* (New York: Hawthorn, 1973), p. 165.

[7] Robert Benedetti, *Seeming, Being and Becoming* (New York: Drama Book Specialists, 1976), p. 24.

Mask is physical rather than emotional. Stanislavski, whose name is sometimes exclusively associated with inner process and the discovery of emotion, was, in fact, highly conscious of the primacy of physical actions and mask choices: "The *typical* gesture helps to bring a player closer to the character he is portraying, while the intrusion of personal movements (i.e., those not demanded by the mask) separates him from it and pushes him in the direction of his *personal* emotions." [8]

There is no fundamental contradiction between the demands of mask and playing and the need for inner process. Gestalt psychology teaches the close relationship between physical and emotional response, and Grotowski, together with many practitioners of modern theatre, feels that the articulation of the physical part of the role actually leads to the inner support. [9] If the actor plays his physical mask strongly he will find that the emotion demanded by the character's function within the text responds in sufficient strength to support the action.

FROM GIVEN CIRCUMSTANCES TO STYLE

The discovery and playing of the correct mask is, then, the actor's fundamental task in approaching the style of a theatrical event. Whether the character is perceived of as "realistic" (someone you might bump into on the street today) or is removed from a contemporary perspective by time or social environment, the task of coming to terms with it does not differ. In the theatre the one

[8] Constantin Stanislavski, *Building a Character* (New York: Theatre Arts Books, 1964), p. 76. Through no fault of Stanislavski, play and mask tended to be lost at the height of the influence of "naturalistic" acting theory. The potentiality of character tended to be limited to the actor's own personality. The attempt to produce an exact correspondence of actor to character in minute physical, psychological, and emotional detail—in other words, a correspondence of "being"—predominated over the idea of playing within a mask—as does a child who puts on a paper crown, carries a wooden sword, and becomes, for himself and his audience, a king.

[9] Quoted by E. T. Kirby, "The Delsarte Method: Three Frontiers of Actor Training," *The Drama Review*, 16, no. 1 (March 1972), 69.

character is just as "real" as the other: both are a function of, and serve, the play's demands. Stanley Kowalski is no less a mask of Tennessee Williams's dramatic action than is Oedipus of Sophocles', or a Restoration fop of, say, Congreve's. The actor discovers the needs of the character mask, as determined by the circumstances of the event, in the text.

When we speak of the actor playing a character mask we certainly don't mean to imply that there is anything hollow or surface about this. The actor inevitably invests himself in the part—gives it life off the printed page and transmits it to the audience. The character's feelings are the actor's feelings and the character's gestures are his gestures, in the sense that the actor is the material out of which these feelings and gestures are created. In the mask sense, however, they are not his in that the choices are selected, adapted according to the total transactions of the play, and shaped by the demands of the given circumstances. Thus, although an actor uses himself and plays from himself in creating a character, he does not simply project his own personality; he plays his character mask, but with absolute personal conviction. Just as no two actors are quite the same, so will no two masks ever be quite the same, although responding to the same demands.

Again, style is not an attempt to serve empty historical re-creation or to ape dated conventions. We are aware that life is constantly moving and that reinterpretation is an inevitable function of that passage of time. We can never come precisely to terms with the sensibility of another period, but we can equally never hope to understand the theatre of a period other than our own if we don't make some attempt to discover the inherent truth of the text. That truth will depend upon some appreciation of the playwright as an individual of his time, a person influenced by particular social, philosophical, and theatrical conventions.

We are not saying a particular kind of play must or can be done only in *this* way. We are saying this is a reasonable idea of how it was intended to be done; it is worth understanding; and it is at least a starting point for actors in approaching a text that doesn't fall into their contemporary time span or immediate social background. It helps them to discover what kind of a play they are in. We are aware that interpretation is a director's prerogative: this issue has already been addressed by one of the authors.[10] But, to take an extreme example, even if an actor is involved in a modern dress production of a Greek play in a small theatrical space, he will be better able to make appropriate and intelligent choices if he understands the inherent conventions of the play and has some idea of how the action is structured by the manner in which it was originally intended to be performed.

A play is a highly structured context or game, as Robert Cohen emphasizes, with absolute rules that heighten and intensify its action.[11] The actor must know the rules (the given circumstances) of the game (the text or theatrical event) in order to understand and play the action. The actor must adapt his process of playing to the different circumstances. In baseball, football, tennis, and other sports, similar skills are called for—timing, coordination, flexibility, balance, speed—but the rules are quite different. In the same way an actor brings his skills and technique to a play, but the rules for comedy of manners are different from the rules for Brecht or Shakespeare: they are different games. We have to understand the rules before we can play the game well, and the rules are in the text, the given circumstances that are the clues to the way in which the actor plays the style.

OUTLINE

In each chapter of this book the actor is given an understanding of the intrinsic demands of a style, and then shown how those intrinsic demands (or given circumstances)

determine the performance demands and lead to the physical style. For simplicity and clarity we have used similar categories to discuss both intrinsic and performance demands. The essential difference between the two is that the intrinsic demands set out the givens whereas the performance demands show how the actor gives physical shape to the givens. Finally, intellectual understanding is converted into physical experience through exercises that attune the actor's body to the physical demands of the style—what the sensibility feels like in action. The exercises are game-oriented so that the actor will learn to use his potential for playing to explore the style from within, rather than putting on the style as a series of artificial mannerisms. The exercises may be used during a rehearsal to help actors physically explore a text, or they may be the basis of workshops focused on gaining the physical feel of a style.

WORKSHOPS

Here are a few general ideas on getting the best out of a workshop. These are addressed both to individual players and to those who might lead workshops based upon this book.

Workshops, like a performance itself (and indeed any human activity), have their own rhythms. The pace of activity varies; there are climaxes and periods of quietus; there is a need for variety as well as depth of approach, for discipline as well as freedom to explore and grow. Begin a workshop with warm-up exercises. These have various purposes:

1. They tune up and limber the body and avoid accidents due to cold muscles.
2. They release tension.
3. They get the player's mind and body together in a balanced center.
4. They concentrate and focus upon the work to be done, expunging all thoughts of quarrels with friends, lack of money, or the next meal.

Many of the exercises suggested throughout this book may be used as a warm-up, but

[10] Robert Cohen and John Harrop, *Creative Play Direction* (Englewood Cliffs, N.J.: Prentice-Hall, 1974).

[11] Robert Cohen, *Acting Power* (Palo Alto, Calif.: Mayfield, 1978).

here is a short sequence that might begin any workshop:

Sit on the floor, knees loosely drawn up towards the chest. Gradually let the back roll down upon the floor, touching it with each vertebra, starting with the lowest one, until the back is flat upon the floor, the shoulders down and the neck elongated with the chin down towards the chest.

In this position take a breath into each part of the body in turn, tensing the part while breathing in and relaxing on the outward breath. Start with the scalp, move down through a clenched jaw, expand and tense the chest, move to each arm in turn, and so on down the body, finishing with clenched toes. Finally, place the fingertips lightly on the diaphragm and breathe in and out deeply ten times, feeling the breath come in with the fingertips and exhaling upon a "haaa" sound.

Stand with the legs comfortably apart and, beginning with the head, roll each part of the body in turn. After the head, which should be dropped as far back and to each side as possible, roll each shoulder forward, up towards the ear, back, and down, and then do the same with the elbow and the wrist. Roll each leg within the hip socket, then each knee and ankle. Now roll the pelvis to the side, forward, the other side, and back (the traditional burlesque grind). From the waist bend the body forward, to the side, back and to the other side; do each roll about twelve times. Drop the chin upon the chest and let the weight of the head carry it towards the floor until the body is hanging loosely from the waist. Now bring the body into an upright position, carefully placing each vertebra on top of the one below as you come up. Finally, stand as if there is a piece of string going up the spine and out through the top of the head and held taut, but not too much so, by the great actor in the sky.

Standing comfortably, take a deep breath and exhale on a "hmmmm." Move the hum into the chest where it can be felt, vibrating, with the fingertips. Then let it fill the oral cavity where it makes the lips tingle. Finally, move it up into the head where it may be felt in the cheekbones and forehead.

Standing comfortably, take a deep breath and let it out on a "mi, ma, me, mo, mu." Repeat on a "bi, ba, be, bo, bu." Now take each syllable in turn and, with the image of an elevator in mind, let it climb on a breath from the feet into the top of the head /and go back down.

A useful game to conclude a warm-up is for the players to think of themselves as karate experts and move through the space—which must be big enough to accommodate this—kicking out and slashing at the other players, punctuating each kick or slash with a "hah!" This encourages energy while focusing and controlling it.

A workshop should always have a shape and a focus: know what you are trying to achieve. Work up to the main problem or exercise with smaller exercises that build the capacity to deal with it; don't use a series of unconnected activities. A workshop shouldn't last less than two hours, for it isn't possible to warm up (fifteen to twenty minutes), build up to the main focus (thirty to forty minutes), work on the main problem (forty-five minutes), and warm down (fifteen minutes) in less than this amount of time. A three-hour workshop could have a similar shape, but with an expanded build-up period and the addition of a further problem—possibly a textual one to test the application of the exercises.

If you are running a workshop, be flexible. Pay attention to the rhythms of the participants. Be aware when an active game is needed to build up energy and when the rhythms are scattered and need a concentration exercise. Have an outline, but don't stick to it rigidly if it isn't working. Don't be afraid to stop and find out what the problem is, but normally talk as little as possible, apart from side coaching during exercises—a workshop should be a physical and not a verbal experience. Always be on the lookout for boredom or lack of effort, realizing that the fault may be in the way you are approaching the work, not in the participants. Try to get at a problem in different ways. Vary exercises—running, sitting, standing, lying, physical, vocal, mental. Add props for greater interest. Don't allow participants to come late: apart from bad theatre discipline, it disrupts the concentration of other players. Always use the working space. If it's a stage, don't let participants sit in the audience seats. Keep a good flow and allow participants freedom to explore and play within the controlled structure: a workshop should be hard but enjoyable work.

ENVOI

We began by suggesting that the acting process moves from impulse to action, and from action to event. This parallels our method for discovering style: moving from sensibility to mask, and then to play. In giving the actor a feeling for the sensibility underlying style and, through exercises, for how that sensibility may become a physical reality, we have concentrated more on essence and physical flair than on small detail. Rather than say an actor must take snuff in this or that way, for example, we have tried to show the reasons for snuff taking, and how it can be made part of the actor's mask. In other words, the actor should be allowed to make informed choices within the stylistic framework.

Joseph Chaikin has commented, "The most articulated performances are those which have been pared away: all that's non-essential, all that's outside the center has been dropped, and what remains is a spare language of tasks which speak of life and nature." [12] This "language of tasks" is the mask that communicates the action. The actor finds both the impulse for its creation and the sensibility that articulates its style in the givens of the text: "Remember you are an actor in a drama of such kind as the author pleases to make it. . . . For your business is to act well the character assigned to you: to choose it is another's." [13] That was written by a Greek critic, Epictetus, two and a half thousand years ago, and it holds true today.

We would not go quite as far as Oscar Wilde's contention in *The Importance of Being Earnest* that "in really serious matters, style is more important than sincerity;" we believe that the two reinforce each other. In this book we hope to give the actor some understanding of the nature of style—so that he will know what kind of a play he is in—and an approach that will help him create and skillfully perform the many masks of the theatrical repertory.

[12] Chaikin, *The Presence of the Actor*, p. 64.

[13] Quoted by J. J. Mayoux, "The Theatre of Samuel Beckett," *Perspective*, Autumn, 1959, p. 142.

part

PLAYING TRAGEDY

It is not our purpose to discuss the aesthetics of tragedy or become involved with nuances of literary criticism. We are going to deal with the physical demands that tragic drama puts upon a player. Performing tragedies presumes the use of similar acting tools but requires their adaptation to different specifics. As examples of these specifics we are using Greek and Shakespearean tragedy. These forms of drama not only have their own strongly recognizable characteristics, but provide a basis of understanding from which the intelligent and discriminating actor or actress can make the adaptations necessary to work on other forms of prerealistic serious drama—Jacobean and French neoclassical, for example, with which we are not dealing directly.

Tragic dramas tend to have certain common characteristics. A tragedy presumes a world in which the possibility of godhead exists. It deals with human emotions rather than intellect, with passions rather than humors. Traditionally regarded as the most noble and legitimate form of drama, it is usually written in elevated language and deals with macrocosmic issues and superhuman crises. Tragedy confronts humans with their own enormity—the original sin of being born—and pushes them to the limits of their existence before they are broken by fate—broken but unbowed, for in the fact of their suffering lies humanity's claim to dignity. The fusing of grief and joy at the end of tragedy harrows us and hallows us; it leaves us with a renewed sense of human possibility, a testament to the ultimate triumph of the human spirit.

chapter 2

National Archaeological Museum, Athens.

Greek

BACKGROUND

Evolution. The form of serious drama known as Greek tragedy and associated with the names Aeschylus, Sophocles, and Euripides is not only the historical starting point for a discussion of theatrical style, but is a perfect example of the way dramatic form relates to the society that creates it. Greek tragedy is quintessentially the product of the sensibility of the Hellenic race: its evolution is a function of the political, social, and cultural history of the Greeks from pre-Homeric times to the Periclean age of the fifth century B.C. It is history, religion, entertainment, social enquiry, and moral discussion all in one event—an example of the essential sense of wholeness of the Greek ideal. The form, environment, spirituality, and moral purpose of tragedy equals the physical, ethical, and intellectual life style of the Greeks.

The dynamic of the drama derives from the strongest of human impulses—the drive for survival. Precivilized tribes fought nature from season to season to wrest a living from the soil. Fertility was essential to survival. Fertile soil made successful farmers, and fertile women produced brave warriors. Forces of nature such as the sun, rain, the earth, and human sexuality thus determined the welfare of the tribe. To make these forces if not explicable at least accessible to him, and if not controllable at least conscious of his wishes, man transformed them into gods. The Greeks gave their gods human forms the better to understand them, and soon these personalized forces of nature became, by the flight of human imagination, the physical ancestors of the tribe. The tribe cast these ancestors in the mold of heroes, and a whole mythology of events grew up around them and was passed on and added to from generation to generation. For the Greeks it was the great epic poet Homer who structured and codified the ancient legends (compare the English tales of King Arthur and Robin Hood) that became the accepted history of the race. The history was also the religion, for the people were to worship and propitiate the gods to ensure continued good fortune. All the seasonal facets of man's life—birth, death, marriage—had appropriate gods celebrated by festivals in due season.

The strongest of man's needs is fertility—good harvests of grain and children—and spring is the time of rebirth. The dead hand of winter melts from the land with the snow; the sap rises; a "young man's fancy lightly turns": it is time for sowing the seed. A spring festival of fertility—sometimes associated with the death of an old king and the birth of a new—is one of the oldest of primitive rituals. The Christian festival of Easter, with its connotations of rebirth, suffering, and the promise of eternal life, is held in the spring. We might also note the phallic symbol of human fertility—the maypole, around which on a spring day, T.S. Eliot tells us, "danced Miss Prism, unconscious of the symbolism."

The Greek god of fertility and wine was Dionysus, himself the descendant of an earlier Egyptian myth, that of Osiris, god of vegetation and fertility, about whom a death-and-rebirth rite had been enacted for many centuries. The name Dionysus means "twice-born," and one of the myths concerning his birth suggests that he was the son of Zeus, king of the gods, and Persephone, one of his daughters. Hera, Zeus's wife, was angered by this and had Dionysus killed by her bodyguard of Titans. Zeus then gave Dionysus rebirth through Semele, daughter of Cadmus, the founder of Thebes.

This version of the myth corresponds to the ritual form of the worship of Dionysus, who, while attempting to escape from Hera's wrath, adopted the body of a bull and a goat. His worshipers acted out this odyssey, sacrificing a bull and a goat, eating the flesh and drinking the blood, and believing they were thereby achieving an identification with the god. (Note the similarity of the Christian mass to this ritual.)

Dionysus was god of fertility, wine, and divine inspiration, and his worshipers spared no means to excite themselves, inspire their imagination, and arouse their senses. The ritual was an intoxicating one: torches at night in secret woods; the music of drums, cymbals, and flutes encouraging uninhibited dancing; devotees sexually stimulated by the power of wine. The wearing of horns and snakes added to the animalism of the occasion, and satyrs and nymphs provided the train of the processional god. The ritual is highly physical, as befits its seminal origins, yet its frank sensuality contains that spiritually passionate desire to transcend the limits of human reality and achieve creative ecstasy, that is at the mystical base of all religions.

As the Greek race became more sophisticated politically and socially, as it moved from a tribal to an urban society, so the primitive rituals became more structured and formalized. Finally, the Dionysian festival was established on what had earlier been the occasion of the spring fertility rites in honor of Dionysus. The festival took the form of a competition among poets, whose versions of the traditional myths were acted out in song, dance, and story in the theatre dedicated to Dionysus, before an audience of the whole society. Thus was born what we call Greek tragedy. The very name *tragedy*, which means goat song, is derived from the most sacred roots of history, ritual, and religion: the sacrificial goat that personified the god Dionysus. Art and culture developed out of the society's myths and rituals. The shaman and the folk singer were replaced by the priest, philosopher, and poet. Man moved from the purely practical questions about his ancestry, sustenance, and survival to the moral questions of how he should live in company with his fellow man in a more complex society.

Greek tragedy engaged actor and audience in an all-embracing experience that touched both their primitive roots and their sophisticated perceptions. The playwright used the history and heroes of the race as his stories and characters to enquire into the fundamental moral purposes of man and how he should relate to the gods and to society. This was done in poetic form at a religious festival. Thus, ritual and religion, art and philosophy, were all encompassed within the dramatic event: at the very beginning of what we know as drama, the total sensibility of a people was organically linked to the nature and style of their theatrical performance.

The Polis. The political sense of the Greek was integrated with the rest of his life activities. The central nucleus of his life was the *polis*—the city-state. His function as a citizen—participation in community affairs—gave focus and meaning to his life. The affairs of the community were the affairs of all. Every citizen discussed and voted on all issues concerning the welfare of the state, be they military, economic, legal, or cultural. His role was not limited just to discussion, but extended to the practice of affairs. Any citizen could become part of the ruling body—indeed, many offices were filled by lot. All citizens were soldiers and could be called upon to defend the state. Such responsibilities were not regarded by the Greeks as we tend to regard the draft or jury duty—as onerous or vexatious—but instead were viewed as a privilege of citizenship. Those members of society who neglected their service to the community in favor of their private affairs were known as *idiotes*, from which we derive our word *idiot*. The realization of the self in the whole is a crucial aspect of the Greek sensibility. Life was participated in, not experienced secondhand on television or through the window of a Winnebago. There was a manysidedness to Greek life, and the citizen assumed many masks—performed many functions—which were all integrated into the one mask—the primary function—of man as citizen.

We do not mean to make negative comparisons here between contemporary society and Greek society but rather to stress a difference in sensibility that may be somewhat difficult to appreciate. The difference in scale and complexity between a small Greek city-state and the vast "global village" that is the modern world makes it impossible today to have the discrete and rooted relationship to society that was possible for the Greeks; width has tended to compensate for depth of experience. Also, we are aware that we are projecting a somewhat ideal view of Greek society, and that certain aspects of that society, such as slavery—which freed citizens to perform their public duties—and the circumscribed position of women, are morally unacceptable to us today. But this awareness simply underlines the need for our discussion of the Greek sensibility. The Greek way of looking at life was different from our own, and this must be understood if we are to come to terms with Greek drama.

Permeating this life style, in fact central to its sense of wholeness, was the spirit of religion. The family, the *polis*, the whole race traced its ancestry back through the heroes of mythology to the pantheon of the gods themselves. Every facet of life had its godhead. The gods were often capricious, but they were understandable. They could be appeased, the enmity of one compensated by the friendship of another. Religion was highly practical and tangible: the "church" was not an abstraction but a living, dynamic force. One of the celebrations of this religion—a function of the *polis* in which all the citizens were involved—was the dramatic festival of Dionysus.

The action of the drama concerned the history of the society: it was bound up with broad values and contemporary problems, and was illuminated by the poetic mythology of the race. The dramatists were not removed artists, but were citizens in the fullest sense of the word. Aeschylus fought at Marathon. Sophocles commanded a fleet. Their work was not preciously artistic or intellectually remote. It was active and direct, befitting their place in and understanding of society. The playwright was *didaskolos*—a teacher, not just of his chorus but of all society, in the understanding of life and the exploration of virtue. The central role of the drama is illustrated by the location of the festival—below the parthenon (the city's chief temple), in the society's midst. Those who could not afford to go were paid for by the state. Each year certain wealthy citizens were required to pay for a chorus of one of the plays. This was regarded as a privilege rather than a duty of citizenship, and any *choregus* who won the competition would raise a monument to commemorate the victory. The choruses, too, were not professional but made up of the citizens themselves—one further social function to add to those of soldier, politician, and wage earner. It was citizen performing for citizen, celebrating their pride in their society and participating in a festival whose very form and sensibility exemplified the spiritual and physical oneness of that society.

Sense of Life. There is a tendency to view the Greek in two contradictory ways: as an Olympian being living a world of profound and tranquil thoughts in an Athens filled with statuesque, well-draped men pacing reposedly through life, or as a passionate pagan, dressed in horns and vine leaves and indulging with Naiads and Bacchantes in an ecstasy of abandonment to every desire and instinct of the flesh. The truth, as always—

and particularly befitting the Greek sense of the middle way—lies somewhere between, in an integrating of the sensual and the calmly intellectual.

The Greeks lived a life outdoors in contact with the earth and warmed by the sun. To them light was associated with life itself.[1] The enjoyment of light and sun manifested itself in the cherishing and exercising of the body. Hard work and physical exercises, and the athletics, dancing, and festivals in which these could be indulged, formed an important part of the celebration of the physical act of living. As Aristophanes tells us in *The Clouds*, "Come to the splendid land of Athens and see a country rich in loveliness, rich in men. Here are processions, sacred, blessed and through every season of the year crowned feasts and festivals of gods. Here as the Spring advances comes the glory of the wine-god, and the musical delight of dancing." This sense of the importance of physical well-being and this passion for physical beauty were matched by an energy and curiosity of the intellect: the two were inseparable in the Greek sense of the whole man.

The modern mind divides, specializes, thinks in categories. Not so the Greek. Justice, courage, government, war, house building, athletics, indigestion—all were part of the totality of life and all were subject to the same purview. Athletics, education, philosophy, religion, and drama were all necessary interests of the whole man. The Olympic games were a religious festival, and the most important event was the pentathlon—a combination of five events—and not a specialized contest such as our metric mile or hundred meters. The dramatic festival was equally all-embracing. Today we have to go to a church service, play, concert, ballet, or art exhibit to achieve the same experience. (Once again, of course, modern society compensates by breadth—a much wider availability of distinct cultural events.) Our sense of beauty is also categorized: we expose ourselves to it at exhibitions, in museums, and even in the ephemeral enticements of TV commercials. We tend to switch beauty on and off rather than finding it in our day-to-day lives. For the Greeks a sense of beauty—physical, spiritual, and moral—ran through their whole approach to life, and was as applicable to how someone lived as to a sculpture or a tragedy.

In interpreting the Greeks to the Romantics in his "Ode on a Grecian Urn," John Keats said, "Beauty is truth, truth beauty,—That is all/Ye know on earth, and all ye need to know." The aesthetic and moral spheres were never sharply distinguished by the Greeks. Virtue, as defined by Aristotle, was "a health and beauty and good habit of the soul." Morality was practical: "to grow into good and noble men and learn how rightly to conduct themselves to their households and servants, their relations and friends, their country and fellow countrymen," to quote Xenophon. The proper balancing of the physical and spiritual elements of life was attained by the reasonable exercise of the mind. Courage, for example, was regarded as a virtue, being a reasonable mean between foolhardiness and cowardice. In this scheme of things anger found its place: if a citizen had been affronted, then he had a right to reasonable response—not the unbridled exercise of passion such as Clytemnestra's revenge on Agamemnon, but due recourse. Turning the other cheek—the meekness of the Christian creed—was not reasonable to the Greek mind. Nor did they, like the Puritan, abjure the pleasures of the senses—only their excess, as in Euripides' *The Bacchae*.

"To see life steadily and to see it whole" was the sensibility of the Greek. This involved acceptance of the good with the bad. Failure was not admired, but neither was it disguised; it was a part of life. There was no

---

[1] The very name of the god of the dead, Hades, means "he who is blind," and by blinding himself the protagonist of *Oedipus the King* is not only gaining ironic insight but is inflicting a living death upon himself.

romantic belief in the attainment of some abstract happiness or some mystical human perfectability. What you saw was what you got—something neither overvalued nor belittled.

The dichotomy between the pleasurable experience of life, full of striving and possibility, and the apprehension of it as subject to unalterable laws leading finally to death produces the passionate tension found in Greek tragedy. The tragic poets could see man as both capable of free choice and yet subject to determining powers. The crime of *hubris* was to overdo the one and discount the other. We define ourselves through our striving, though knowing we shall be struck down. Achilles was offered a long, mediocre life or glory with an early death. For the Greek there was only one possible choice. Choices determined character and character determined destiny. Everyone was subject to the laws of the gods—and to *Dike*, the retribution that fell upon the *hubris* of man when he deluded himself into thinking he could ignore them.

This sense of life is foreign to the romantic age, which believes that science, technology, or money can achieve anything: beat mental illness now; cure cancer now; whip inflation now. Surprise and disillusionment follow when the desired result doesn't occur. The Greek would have not entirely expected it to, but that didn't obviate the necessity of trying. Today, the gods and fate tend to have given way to environmental determinants and behavioral psychology. We are relieved of free choice and responsibility. The Greeks had to accept the consequences of their fate: the gods may dispose, but man was still responsible. After he has learned the truth about himself and put out his eyes, Oedipus says, "It was Apollo, friends, Apollo, that brought this bitter bitterness, my sorrows to completion. But the hand that struck me was none but my own."

All of the basic qualities that constitute the wholeness of the Greek ideal—balance, directness, simple truth, intellectual curiosity, spiritual passion, physical power—will be found operating within the physical and textual givens of Greek tragedy.

INTRINSIC DEMANDS

We must preface our discussion of the physical nature of Greek theatre with a general caveat. As the authority Oscar Brockett has observed, "What is known with certainty about the theatre of the 5th century will not fill half-a-dozen pages."[2] Although there is a certain amount of scholarly consensus on the nature of Greek theatre, there are still areas of significant disagreement—particularly on the extent to which the qualities of the fourth-century theatre (for which there is more evidence) may have been present in the fifth century. Much of what we detail is conjectural, but it is based upon the works of leading scholars, especially the most recently published studies, such as Oliver Taplin's *Greek Tragedy in Action*. If we lean to the side of the fully built and embellished fifth-century theatre—as opposed to the simple arena advanced by some authorities—we are encouraged in this by Taplin's feeling that "drama was, in the fifth century, one of Athens' greatest cultural showpieces, and its accoutrements will not have been barely utilitarian."[3] We believe there is enough evidence to support our conclusions about the nature of Greek theatrical style, and that these conclusions make good sense in the context of the Greek sensibility and the demands of the plays themselves.

Space. It is generally accepted that the Greek theatre contained a circular dancing area some sixty to seventy feet in diameter called the *orchestra* and used primarily by the

[2] O. G. Brockett, "Producing Greek Tragedy," *The Classical Journal*, 56, no. 7 (April 1961), 322.
[3] Oliver Taplin, *Greek Tragedy in Action* (Berkeley: University of California Press, 1979), p. 11.

Ruins of the theatre at Epidaurus.

chorus. Two-thirds of the circumference of the *orchestra* was surrounded by an auditorium—that part of the amphitheatre in which the audience sat—which could accommodate upwards of 15,000 persons. To the rear of the *orchestra* was a scene house some fifty to sixty feet long, fronted by a somewhat elevated platform. The distance from the stage to the back of the auditorium was approximately 300 feet. On either side of the scene house was a *parados*, an entrance used by the audience to reach the auditorium and by the chorus to proceed into the *orchestra*. These specifics are important for a bald understanding of the environment of Greek theatre, but what is more important to the performer is an appreciation of how the space relates to the spirit and style of the event.

The first thing to notice is that the performance took place—as did the normal life of the Greek—in the open air, under the eye of the gods. Little artificial scenery was used, the natural environment forming the background. The largest space is given to the *orchestra*, around which the audience sits, embracing the event. This emphasis on the *orchestra* connects the drama with its past—its evolution from the choral dance within the threshing circle, a ritual thanking of the gods for the harvest. The physical form of the dramatic event connects religion with reality, spiritual and cultural well-being with physical sustenance. The *thymele*, the altar at which offerings to Dionysus are made, is present in the middle of the *orchestra*—at the heart of the dramatic event.

Despite the size of the amphitheatre, the relationship of the actors to the audience is very direct. This is due not only to the spirit of the occasion, which touches both actors and audience, but also to the physical form of the event. All citizens participated in the festival. The chorus was itself a group of citizens trained especially for the event, but not professionals, who would return to their day-to-day activities when the festival was over. Thus, a body of citizens sit around a chorus of citizens, who are close to the actor/heroes, who are dealing with the gods on issues concerning the moral and spiritual life of the society as a whole. This direct line from citizens to gods, each in their place but all interconnected, was a physical manifestation both of the Greeks' hierarchical sense of life and of its spiritual wholeness. Here, as everywhere in Greek life, the practical, cultural, and spiritual are integrated.

Although the event was of religious origin, the audience was robust and responsive, out to enjoy itself in every way. Though aware of the spiritual significance of the occasion, it was not overawed or formalized into the sepulchral hush associated with the Christian churches. There are records of showers of stones and olive pits being thrown at the actors, and on one occasion Aeschylus had to take refuge at the altar of Dionysus to escape the wrath of the crowd. Nor was the audience afraid to leave during less than dynamic passages, as Aristophanes tells us in *The Birds*:

> There's nothing like wings to get fun out of things;
> When you're bored with a play long and tragic,
> You can fly from your seat to get something to eat,
> And be back in the benches like magic.

Magnitude, both physical and spiritual; directness of approach and response; harmony, passion, and power—these are the intrinsic givens suggested by the physical environment of Greek tragedy.

Text and Language. Within the space the text is performed. The structure of the text is related both to the shape of the space and to the ritualistic and religious nature of the event. There are five parts to this structure: *prologue, parados, episode, stasismon,* and *exodus.* The *prologue* is expositional, and the *episodes* involve the actors and the action of the piece.

The other three parts involve the chorus, and are directly connected with the ritual basis of tragedy and the shape of the amphitheatre. The *parados* is a processional part. It takes its name from the entrances on either side of the stage through which the chorus sings its way into the *orchestra*. The *stasismons* (which alternated with the actors' episodes) pass general comment upon the situation or reflect upon the issues. They are chanted, sung, and danced by the chorus within the *orchestra* itself. The music and rhythms of the dance reinforced the ritual atmosphere. The *exodus* is the final part of the textual structure. Usually summarizing with a pithy moral or a restatement of the philosophical burden of the drama, it serves to remove the chorus from the orchestra. Thus, the chorus directly connects the physical shape of the event (the theatre) with its dramatic shape (the text).

If the physical environment of the tragedy and the structure of the plays can thus be shown to have evolved from ritual and religion, the structure of the tragic action no less embodies ritual and religious form.[4] Action consists of an *agon,* or conflict; a *pathos,* or suffering; a *threnos,* or lamentation; and finally an *epiphany,* or revelation of the godhead or spirit.

This structure not only follows the essential quality of the ritual worship of Dionysus, but may be compared with the spirit and rites of the Christian religion—especially in its Roman Catholic form. The Christian service begins with a procession of the priests and the choir. There are choral songs, there are prayers, there are invocations and responses among priest, choir, and congregation. There are readings of well-known texts from the Bible—the repository of the history and myths of the religion. There is a sermon in which the priest draws from a biblical text a moral that applies to the contemporary life and mores of the society. There is often a communion in which the priest acts out an offering and makes a ritual sacrifice in which

[4] Oscar Brockett, in "The Greek National Theatre's Staging of Ancient Drama," *Educational Theatre Journal,* 9, no. 4 (December 1957), 285, emphasizes that the Greek National Theatre sees the ritual character and religious atmosphere of the plays as central to its style of performance. Taplin, in *Greek Tragedy in Action,* agrees that the plays use the form of ritual, but suggests that the festival was not itself a ritual as much as a party, a celebration, and a holy day.

the congregation participates. There is a final choral hymn and exit of the choir. Note too the shape of the event: the priest is usually raised above the congregation, and thereby positioned nearest the Godhead; the choir is between him and the congregation—the citizens. The congregation, however, does not surround the event, which reflects the more hierarchical spirit of the Christian religion, as opposed to the more democratic wholeness of the Greeks. But the similarities are very close, and the specific point for the performer is that an appreciation of the form and the spirit of an event will reveal its style to him.

The form of Greek tragedy derives from:

1. the structure of religious ritual
2. the shape of the theatrical space where that ritual takes place
3. the mythic plot/action, which manifests the philosophical attitudes of the playwright

The Greek sensibility informed and interrelated all of these elements to create the style of Greek tragedy.

If the form and structure of Greek tragedy are organically linked to its spirit and the shape of its performance, the language is no less so. The drama sprang from the ancient rituals of celebration and lamentation, and its language was rhythmical and lyric so as to create a sense of special occasion. Greek tragedy is sung, danced, and declaimed. The spirit, action, and moral purpose of the drama are wholly united to the verse form; the truths of mythology or religious experience do not submit to prose form. It is upon these truths, contained in tragic legend and the human imagination, that Greek tragedy is founded.

This sense of elevation of spirit and idea requires language that fits the dignity of the characters, the occasion, and the magnitude of the issues. The festival and the worship that takes place within it may be democratic, but there is nothing democratic in the vision of tragedy. Gods and heroes may be accessible to mortals through religious experience, but they are not on the same level as mortals. Their style of utterance reflects their elevated stature and the significance of the issues in which they are involved. The reverberations are cosmic. Here again there is an analogy with Catholic church services, in which the priest chants certain prayers and invocations and the congregation responds in a similar fashion.

Apart from creating a sense of exaltation and making a direct emotive contact through rhythm, the consistent structure of verse clarifies and focuses the action, which in turn intensifies the moral and intellectual issues and places them in high relief. The formality and dignity of the verse does not necessarily mean dullness, or limit the expression of human emotion. Formality means the acceptance and use of form; it does not mean stiffness. Greek society was both verbal and extremely open. All issues were subject to public debate, and oratory was an important technique for influencing political decisions. The Greek language allowed for broad, vigorous, and imaginative emotional expression. Rhetoric becomes dull only if it is pompous and divorced from an active purpose.

In Greek tragedy language appears in at least five forms:

1. choral odes, which have an essentially lyric function
2. long passages of narrative description couched in active, colorful, and imagistic language—often spoken by messengers as a means of expounding events from the past or action that has taken place offstage
3. speeches between the protagonist and antagonist dealing with philosophical issues and using language with a powerful intellectual appeal
4. highly emotional speeches by the protagonist dealing with inner torment or conflict with the gods

5. *stychomythia*—a series of one-line statements and responses conveying argument, anger, and sharp enquiry

All of this—the gamut of verbal communication—takes place within the formal structure of the verse. The emotive and imagistic qualities of the verse elevate the dramatic form without losing the direct, intellectual appeal of prose.

Costume. The costume of Greek tragedy reflects the magnitude and elevation of its space, form, and language. Iris Brooke tells us that "at the time when Greek drama was at its finest the costume was also at its most decorative and splendid."[5] She adds that theatre employed an even "grander style" than real life. This would seem to be supported by Oliver Taplin's sense of the magnificence of the occasion, which we noted earlier, and by the logical presumption that a certain larger-than-life impression would have to be conveyed in the large theatrical space. So, we may assume that theatre garments were grander and richer versions of everyday wear.

The basic body garment was the *chiton*, a cool and simple tunic pinned at the shoulder and falling to the knee or ankle. Over this was worn a short cape, the *chlamys*, or a long mantle, the *himation*. The latter tended to be a mark of status, and as such it was suited to the characters of tragedy. The emphasis of these garments is upon vertical line, simplicity, and flow, all of which create a sense of dignity, substance, and authority. The *himation* especially, with its color, weight, and manner of being draped across one arm, suggests physical strength and control.

The tragic actor also wore a *kothornos*, a laced-up boot peculiar to the stage. There is some controversy as to whether or not it had a raised sole. Current scholarship tends to reject the notion of a raised-sole boot in the fifth century, but there is evidence that it existed in the fourth century, and Brooke tells us that a thick-soled sandal was a fashionable item of Hellenistic dress.[6] Obviously, a high sole would have the advantage of increasing the height and visibility of the wearer, and it is perhaps worth asking why a boot was worn at all if it did not have some such purpose. It must at least have been intended to lend a sense of importance to the actor's costume.

Two other items of costume particular to the Greek tragic actor were the *onkos* and the mask. The *onkos* was an ornate headdress worn with the mask. Brooke notes that ornate coiffures were a feature of fifth-century dress,[7] and it is reasonable to presume that this might have been carried even further on the stage. There is some disagreement about the height and calculated artificiality of the *onkos*: it is known to have become highly exaggerated in later centuries, as did the mask. If one accepts a certain height for the *kothornoi* in the fifth century, then the *onkos* is likely to have been the higher to balance this. In any case, it is fairly certain that a highly styled coiffure was worn as a means of adding to the impressiveness of the character. Though not supporting a heavily exaggerated headdress, Brooke believes that a clearly defined head with a distinct style would have been needed in order for the character to be easily distinguished at a distance.[8] Further, as all actors were male, the color and style of the headdress would help in identifying the sex, age, and status of the character. For example, the Bacchantes of Euripides wore snakes and vine leaves in their hair. So, the *onkos* probably fulfilled a practical function in increasing the actor's visibility and impressiveness, and an aesthetic

---

[5] Iris Brooke, *Costume in Greek Classic Drama* (London: Methuen, 1962), p. 3.

[6] *Ibid.*, p. 74.

[7] *Ibid.*, p. 82.

[8] *Ibid.*, p. 78.

Face of Poseidon, fifth century, manifesting strength and reflecting the simplicity of the mask of the period.

National Archaeological Museum, Athens.

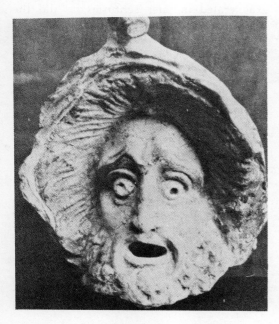

Later mask strongly delineating the spine of the character. Also note the headdress.

Antiken Museum, Berlin.

function in lending dignity, social stature, and spiritual elevation to the character.

The *onkos* was closely related to the mask in assisting character definition. Though the essential quality of the mask was dramatic, and though the mask was more organically related to the roots and spirit of tragedy than either *kothornos* or the *onkos*, it also had several practical functions:

1. It was a further source of identification for the audience of the sex, age, and general sensibility of the character.
2. It enlarged the features of the face, making it more easily seen.
3. It enabled an actor to play more than one part.
4. It added resonance to the declamation of the verse, and probably aided audibility—though the acoustics of the Greek theatre were excellent.

More than this, however, the mask is the very heart of the event. From primitive times man has, in his rituals of worship, attempted to assume the mask or attributes of the revered object (animal, god, or whatever) so that its spirit will enter the wearer. The shaman assumed the masks of the tribal gods, and was transported into a divine state of possession in which the god's spirit could be put to the benefit of the tribe. The mask struck awe into the audience, and gave the movements of the wearer, whoever he was, a certain unearthly quality.

Similarly, in the worship of Dionysus, from which the tragic festival traces its descent, the horns of bulls and goats were worn—attributes of Dionysus, who adopted them in his flight from Hera's wrath. The connection between adoption of mask and assumption of spirit runs throughout human religious symbology. The mask permits that assumption of otherness while remaining oneself that is an essential quality of the actor's art.

This idea is fundamental in Greek tragic performance, and is focused in the mask. The mask connects the religious and spiritual nature of the event with its dramatic form. It integrates the direct dramatic connection among audience, actor, character, and story with the underlying (or supervening) spiritual connection among citizen, shaman/priest, and godhead.[9] As such the mask is the very core of the event. Indeed, *prosōpon*, the Greek word for mask, also means face, aspect, person, and stage-figure.

The mask is the core of the event in a more specific sense as well: it is the impulse and the focus of both the poet's and the actor's creativity. There is some indication that the playwright wrote for the mask, that the choice of mask prescribes what is to follow. We have sculpture of Greek playwrights seeking inspiration by gazing at a tragic mask, plus Aristotle's suggestion that the playwright had particular gestures in mind while writing speeches for his characters. In this way the language would conform to the mask, as would the nature of the character. This is, of course, the basic attribute of the mask—its definition of an attitude.

In this sense the mask is the character. It is not for the actor to determine the nature of the character—the playwright in his choice of mask has conveyed that essence both to the actor and the audience. Rather, it is for the actor to live up to the character, to fulfill what has been written into the mask. This does not mean, of course, that the character is one-dimensional; he may run a gamut of emotions and attitudes. That I am basically a prideful and angry person, does not mean I have no moments of humility and humor. But it is my pride and anger—my dominating characteristic (or, to use Stanislavski's term, the through line of my character)—that will determine my basic reaction to life, and my fate. This idea of the essential attribute of a character is consistent with the large theatrical space, in which small detail could not be seen. Thus, the essential attribute, which denotes the part a character is to play in the

Playwright seeking inspiration from a mask.

Lateran Museum.

outcome of the tragedy, is a given. It does not have to be sought, for it is there. More than that, it is writ large on the character's face.

The overall impression of the costume, then, is one of stature, dignity, direct communication, clarity, and emotional force. Those attributes are present in the space, form, and language of Greek tragedy, and are also to be found in its action.

Concentration of Action. So far we have dealt with the tangible intrinsic qualities of the tragedies: space, costuming, text structure, and language. It remains to look briefly at the issues dealt with by the playwrights and the scope of the action in which they were treated. An actor will inevitably be influenced by the values he discovers in a script, and the way in which those values are given shape by the action.

Dramatic action is not the same as movement or activity. Activity can illustrate ac-

---

[9] After a successful performance a Greek actor sometimes dedicated his mask. Compare this with the retiring of one's number at the end of a successful athletic career.

tion. A character opening a door and going offstage may be representing a dramatic action of leave-taking, or he may simply be going to the bathroom. Apparent lack of activity can also be a strong dramatic action: two persons sitting silently in a room may be denoting a dramatic action of sorrow at the death of a friend. Action may depend upon the incidents that make up the plot of a play. Even an essentially plotless play such as Samuel Beckett's *Waiting for Godot* (described by one critic as a play in which nothing happens—twice) can have an extremely dynamic and tension-filled dramatic action—waiting. The dramatic action of a play is, then, the essence of what happens in the play. It is created by activity and stillness, speech and silence, thought and emotion. It is the "idea" of the play manifested through its total structure and distilled from all of its parts.[10]

In Greek tragedy the playing out of this action is highly concentrated. Unlike romantic plays and melodramas, whose interest lies mostly in events largely peripheral to the action (such as the car chases, gunfights, overdoses, and abortions of our modern TV fare), Greek tragedy focuses upon the logical revelation of the action; anything irrelevant to that purpose is avoided. More than this, the action of the play tends to take place in one situation and within a restricted time period. Rather like in a courtroom situation, information necessary to the action of the play is brought to us by witnesses or messengers. We hear descriptions of exciting events that have taken place, but we don't see them, for the focus is not on the events themselves but on the significance they may have for the unfolding of the action. In *Oedipus the King* we get vivid descriptions of the deaths of Laius and of Jocasta, but we do not see the

deaths, for our concentration is meant to be upon Oedipus. This play is, in fact, the classic example of the Greek method of logic and condensation. Its action may be said to be to find and expel the guilty party, or, in terms of ritual, to seek and purge. As such it follows the logic of a detective story, but only the final scene, when the detective calls everyone into the parlor, recapitulates the events and evidence, and points to the guilty party. We do not—as we tend to in Agatha Christie's plays—see all the events leading to the murder: the creation of false motives, the footprints in the flower beds, the shots in the dark. We simply see the detective gathering facts, cross-examining, and letting the logic of the evidence lead him to the culprit, which in *Oedipus*, with splendid irony, turns out to be the detective himself.

This concentration (which is sometimes called the unity of time, place, and action) puts the characters in an extremely intense relationship with one another. Like boxers in a ring, they cannot escape each other. The action is "to win," and there is no place for activity not geared to that end. The action is contained, economic, and direct, and there is nothing to distract the attention of the audience from its playing out. There are no cheerleaders to distract from the action of the game, as it were. In Greece this concentration was further enhanced by the space in which the action took place. The embracing amphitheatre with the play at its center was the very hub, in fact, of the Greek world: it was between heaven and earth, gods and citizens, the past and the future. The magnitude of the issues compressed within this compact form completes the intensification, rather like the engraver's feat of inscribing the Lord's Prayer on the head of a pin.

The Issues. At the heart of the dramatized myths from which comes the action of Greek tragedy lay the question of how man is to live his life—not whether it is preferable to be a rock star or a skateboard champion, but

---

[10] This is the definition of dramatic action used by Francis Fergusson in his *The Idea of a Theatre* (Princeton, N.J.: Princeton University Press, 1949). It may be compared with Stanislavski's through-line of action into which the moment-to-moment actions are fitted—a concept more practical in its application to acting.

what it means to be Man, in the fullest sense of that word. The religious, moral, and political aspects of life were all connected in the Greek sensibility. One could not be a good politician yet an immoral, irreligious person. The limited sense of "good" as "successful" that we sometimes employ was foreign to the Greek mind. Goodness was all-encompassing. It was physical, spiritual—any property that enabled a man to live as a virtuous citizen in harmony with his neighbor and in accordance with the gods' laws.

It is not surprising, therefore, to find a religious issue having political significance in the tragedies, or both being involved with the making of moral choices. Nor is it surprising that the punishment of *hubris* should be a theme in almost every Greek tragedy, for goodness, virtue, beauty, and a sense of proportion were all closely linked in the Greek sense of life. Man must never forget that he is mortal and vulnerable: he is subject to laws that have meaning and purpose even though he may not understand them. A necessary humility must temper necessary pride.

Oedipus is the classic illustration. Through no conscious fault of his own he killed his father and slept with his mother. But these sins polluted the society in which he lived, and had to be purged through his expulsion. He had transgressed the laws of the gods, and his pride blinded him to his sin. He lacked self-knowledge. Only by blinding himself to the outer world, therefore, could he gain knowledge of the world within. Man's pride in his personal, material achievements often blinds him to the larger demands of the world of the spirit. The gods will find a way of humbling the prideful, and man's spirit is both purified and elevated by his suffering.

This suffering, which produces emotion, is united with meaning in a context of social, intellectual, theological, or moral conflict. *Antigone*, for example, deals with the conflict between the laws of the gods and those of society, and the moral choice this involves. In contemporary terms this issue would be expressed as the rights of the individual versus the power of the state, or civil disobedience versus law and order, and is one of the most acute problems for modern society worldwide. *The Oresteia*, a trilogy of plays, shows how civil law and justice based upon a moral balance, evolved from an earlier, more ritualistic sense of justice that called for an eye for an eye—a self-perpetuating structure of revenge. *The Bacchae*, a play based upon the very worship of Dionysus in which the tragic festival originated, is concerned with the balance between passion and reason and with the necessity of self-knowledge—that understanding of what it means to be a man that teaches humility, compassion, and moral goodness.

The essential point is clear: the issues dealt with by Greek tragedy have macrocosmic significance. They are not the concerns of any one individual, family, or social group, but of Man and human society as a whole, and they reflect upon the very essence of humanity. It may underline our point to compare *Oedipus the King* with a modern play about a man driven to his death by social pressures—*The Death of a Salesman*. In this play Linda, the wife of Willie, the play's hero, says of her husband, "He is a human being, and a terrible thing is happening to him. So attention must be paid." Compare this with the last lines of *Oedipus*:

> You that live in my ancestral Thebes, behold this Oedipus, him who knew the famous riddles and was a man most masterful; not a citizen who did not look with envy on his lot—see him now and see the breakers of misfortune swallow him. Look upon that last day always. Count no mortal happy till he has passed the final limit of his life secure from pain.[11]

[11] Reprinted from *The Complete Greek Tragedies*. David Grene and Richmond Lattimore (eds.), by permission of The University of Chicago Press. Copyright 1953.

In the first play we have a strong sense of romanticism—things shouldn't be like this; somebody ought to do something. And that somebody is likely to be the sociologist, to whom Willie is a statistic, or the psychologist who will deal with his personality problems. Willie, if he is a victim, is a victim of the American Dream rather than the human condition. Oedipus is a sacrifice to the gods. His suffering connects him both with the ancient rituals of the scapegoat who dies for a society's sins, and with the Christian passion of Jesus' sacrifice. The King suffers and dies that we may live. No sociologist or psychologist can alter God's laws. The sacrifice may be a cruel necessity, but it is the way things are. It tempers our pride in human capacity and achievement with a necessary humility and awe at the magnitude of powers beyond our comprehension. It leads us to the compassion that accommodates us to our fate and that of our fellow men.

The issues dealt with by Greek tragedy have great magnitude, directness of impact, a powerful effect upon the emotions, and a central significance for society. These qualities are equally manifested by the space, text, language, costume, and action of the theatrical event; they are a reflection of Greek sensibility. The performance style of Greek tragedy is that sensibility expressed through the physical givens of the theatrical event.

PERFORMANCE DEMANDS

Body. Size, simplicity, and selectivity are basic qualities required of the Greek actor. There are some technical reasons for this, in that the costume makes certain physical demands:

1. The *onkos* and mask prevent sharp or sudden movements, and require the head to be held upright.
2. The mask restricts peripheral vision, which suggests that care must be taken with movement.
3. Movement is further refined by the holding of the *himation* across the arm.

Note the dignity of posture and the simplicity, line, and flow of costume in this statue of Sophocles.

Lateran Museum.

Note the similar dignity, simplicity, and strength in this modern production of *The Trojan Women*.

Alley Theatre, Houston.

These technical reasons suggest that the physical presence of the actor is upright, controlled, and dignified. The need for such qualities is supported by the nature of the event—what Taplin calls "the measured pace and large-jointed construction of ancient tragedy."[12] If the actor stands still and doesn't shuffle, or moves strongly with clearly defined strides rather than short steps, he does so because this is required by the costume and because small movements blur the action and weaken the character. Size of movement is always relative to size of space.

The posture of the actor's head is upright so that he can communicate with the gods and the audience, both of whom are situated above him. Such a posture also helps show off the mask and *onkos*, elevating and dignifying the character, and enhances direct communication with the audience. The modern actor should remember that direct com-

munication is achieved by the forceful projection of the action through space—by voice, gesture, and emotional power. It does not require leaning towards the audience or any other attempt to make physical contact.

Gesture is the most flexible part of the Greek actor's body movement. But its use is entirely consistent with that movement: gestures are full, extended, and sustained. Not only are large gestures needed to communicate meaning over a large space, but the emotional force of the occasion depends on them. Commanding presence demands commanding gesture. Gestures must fill the space and be filled by the emotional force that catalyzed them. Small, quick, loose-wristed gestures are meaningless, and lessen the strength of the character and the situation. "There is no place in this theatre for fidgeting, for the idiosyncratic twitch and reflex: stance, large use of the arms, and the whole style of movement must convey both the ethos of the characters and the significant

[12] Taplin, *Greek Tragedy in Action*, p. 32.

action of the play."[13] When larger gestures are employed they will be less frequent and each will have greater significance. The frequent small gestures we observe in the daily behavior of individuals have no place in Greek tragedy. As Oscar Brockett suggests, "The actor appears to have searched for the one essential detail which will convey his meaning, and to have suppressed all irrelevancies."[14] In the playing of Greek tragedy, gestures communicate emotional states and advance the action rather than detailing a character's personality.

If gesture is highly selective, it can still be varied. One of the demands upon the actor's imagination is to discover meaningful gestures that powerfully convey the emotional force of the action. Gestures should be connected with and extend from the center of the body—the actor's emotional core—and not just come from the shoulder. They should have a clear beginning, middle, and end, and not blur into each other. The body should not be swung into gestures, nor should gestures be pushed. The emotional idea should be allowed to lead the gesture, which should flow strongly and fully from the body and fill both the space and the emotional time demanded by the action. The actor should not be afraid to hold gestures as long as they are filled with present meaning. An incomplete or abrupt gesture weakens the force of the moment and disrupts the fullness of the rhythm.

Flow is important. There is a always a danger that an actor may become stiff and mechanical when attempting to put on a formal posture and assume dignity. But Greek tragedy flows, as any theatrical event must flow. The rhythm is like that of a wide, full river rather than that of, say a, mountain stream darting and jumping over rocks and spurting through falls, which one might associate with farce. Tragedy has a strong, continuous flow with virtually no scene changes or other intervals. The processions, dances, and flowing costumes adding to the unbroken rhythm.

The actor must flow with the theatrical event. This doesn't mean looseness; it means working comfortably within a particular formality. Looseness often means lack of clarity and focus rather than ease and flow. The latter will come to the actor in Greek tragedy just as they would in any other dramatic style—through understanding, familiarity, and concentration. Playing the action relaxes and releases the actor so that he does not think about moving in a stately manner or extending his gesture, but rather is engaging his inner emotional force with an outer practical objective. In this way the intrinsic and performance demands reveal and communicate the action, and create the style of the event.

Statue of Poseidon, fifth century, expressing fullness, strength, and extension of gesture.

National Archaeological Museum, Athens.

[13] *Ibid.*, p. 15.
[14] Brockett, "Staging of Ancient Drama," p. 285.

Even in a modern dress production of *Hippolytus*, note the fully extended, firmly body-purchased gesture of actor Patrick Stewart.

Royal Shakespeare Company.

Mask. Control and impact are two givens of the mask: it is well defined and unchanging. The mask enables the audience to see a facial characteristic over the large space—changes of expression and small emotions communicated by the face would be lost in the Greek amphitheatre—and immediately indicates the part the character is to play in the action. The mask has the further effect of taking the event out of everyday reality and investing it with an otherworldliness.

The effect of the mask upon the actor is to remove him from his own personality and the detail of his daily life. It inevitably calls for movement larger than life—you simply can't put on a mask and then go about your ordinary business. Facial immobility puts greater emphasis upon verbal and physical gesture, which the mask by its very nature invests with larger-than-normal significance. A mask, because of its incredible stillness, idealization, and clarity of outline, tends to fill time and space, to charge the surrounding air with the electricity of its presence. The actor who accepts this quality of the mask will gradually eliminate nonessen-

Stillness and intensity created by masks in Guthrie Theatre Company production of *The House of Atreus.*

Courtesy of the Mark Taper Forum.

tial movement and allow the mask to do its work.

All these are highly practical effects the mask will have on the actor who is willing to assume it. And these effects are, as we have seen, crucial qualities in the performance style of Greek tragedy. The actor who does not fight the mask will find that it will do much of his stylistic work for him. There is an impulse to identify with the mask. The actor's face assumes the expression of his mask, and his body posture and gestures will be drawn into harmony with it. (Even if in a modern production a director chooses not to use masks, the wearing of them will be a useful part of the rehearsal process.)

Given this adaptation of the actor's body to the mask, a further important effect takes place: a direct relationship between the physical characterization suggested by the mask and the interior emotional and spiritual response. The mask takes over not only the body but also the feelings of the actor. This gives the actor a very strong purchase upon the spine, essential characteristic, or active through-line of the character. What the actor should look for is not the psychological detail of the character, but the essential actions and emotions. The character is both more and less of a man than we understand. He is less in the sense that he has no life outside the play. For the purposes of Greek tragedy, heroes never had indigestion or went to the bathroom. Their anger or pride was not a result of their car being smashed up or their child winning a little-league baseball game. It was a function of their fate, who they were—it defined them. More than defining them, it defined their part in the action of the play—indeed was a part of that action, for it was geared to making the

Note the masklike facial attitudes of Mike Gwilym and Lynn
Dearth in the Royal Shakespeare Company production of *The
Greeks*. Note also the strength and stillness of their body
positions.

Photo by Donald Cooper.

play work. The mask is the character, the
motivation, the action—and the action is the
play.

A character's mask has all the characterization the situation requires; character drawing for its own sake is not a dramatic virtue.
For example, when Hippolytus, in Euripides'
play, expounds upon the virtue that prevents
him from responding to Phaedra's passion,
we could easily regard him as a prig. But this is
to misinterpret his function in the play. He is
not a "character" but a tragic figure. His
purity is the basis of his tragic function. An
actor who played him as a prig, or a homosex-
ual, would be quite wrong in doing so. The
mask of Hippolytus is chasteness, his character is chasteness, and his tragic function is
to be chaste and be destroyed for it.

From Aeschylus to Euripides Greek drama
moved toward somewhat more domestic and
personal concerns. However, the physical
givens of style—environment, space, and
costume—remained constant and although
Euripides may be as much concerned with
human as superhuman passions, the way in
which the actor approaches the playing of his

mask is unchanged. The mask still delineates the dominant characteristic: characters are still archetypes more than individuals. As Stanley Glenn suggests with reference to *Medea*, "Euripides is far more concerned with examining capacities for pride, jealousy, and barbarism than in presenting a 'well-rounded' depiction of a woman scorned. Archetypal characters are less complex psychologically than particularized ones."[15]

The actor must play what the playwright has given; he should not get caught up in self-examination and become so involved with his character that he develops detail not demanded by the action. There is no need for anything other than the essentials, highly focused and powerfully communicated. This is not to say that a tragic character cannot run a gamut of emotions. It is, though, the dominant passion or trait—the mask—that informs all the emotions and that brings about the tragic fate as necessitated by the action of the play. The mask directs attention not to inner, subtextual thought but to the heroic figure whose constant ethos it portrays. As Taplin points out, "passion and suffering are not introvertedly wrung out through tiny intimate gestures and facial movements; but put directly before the audience's consideration. . . . the emotions of Greek tragedy are presented openly in word and action, not inferred or guessed at."[16] The mask is a function of and reinforces this broad explicitness of emotion, and matches the size of the space, the occasion, and the issues.

Voice. Much that has been said of the demands upon the actor in terms of body and mask applies also to voice, the final element of the stylistic integrity of the performance. As the action of the tragedies is communicated not as much by activity as by language, the voice attains special significance as an actor's tool. The spoken language had to reach an

audience 200 to 300 feet away. This would not necessarily require loudness, but rather strong, precise enunciation and projection to match the language, which is itself direct, uncluttered, and powerful. The rhythms and structure of the verse must also be respected, as they are essential parts of the ritual sense, the spiritual scope, and the emotional impact of the drama. "Naturalistic" delivery, breaking of rhythms, deliberate working against the verse, introduction of verbal mannerisms for "character" definition—these have no place in Greek drama.

Within the discipline of its form the language spans the entire human emotional and descriptive palette. There is nothing dull or restricted about it, and it places tremendous demands upon the actor's vocal capacity. In our discussion of text and language earlier in this chapter we mentioned five particular forms of language in the plays. For our present purposes, the two most significant are the messenger or witness speeches and the protagonist speeches.

First we will examine an example of the latter, a brief section of a speech by Oedipus after he has discovered his crime and blinded himself:

1392[17]

> Cithaeron, why did you receive me? why
> having received me did you not kill me
>   straight?
> And so I had not shown to men my birth.
> O Polybus and Corinth and the house,
> the old house that I used to call my father's—
> what fairness you were nurse to, and what
>   foulness
> festered beneath! Now I am found to be
> a sinner and a son of sinners. Crossroads,
> and a hidden glade, oak and the narrow way

---

[15] Stanley Glenn, *The Complete Actor* (Boston: Allyn & Bacon, 1977), p. 187.

[16] Taplin, *Greek Tragedy in Action*, p. 14.

[17] This apparent discrepancy in line numbering is explained by Richmond Lattimore as follows: "Various editions of Greek drama divide the lines of lyric passages in various ways, but editors regularly follow the traditional line numbers whether their own line divisions tally with these numbers or not. This accounts for what may appear to be erratic line numbering. . . ." (David Grene and Richmond Lattimore, eds., *Greek Tragedies, Volume 1* [Chicago: University of Chicago Press, 1960], p. 3) By permission.

at the crossroads, that drank my father's blood
offered you by my hands, do you remember
still what I did as you looked on, and what
I did when I came here? O Marriage, marriage!
you bred me and again when you had bred
bred children of your child and showed to men
brides, wives and mothers and the foulest
   deeds
that can be in this world of ours.
1407

The general quality (or mask) of this speech
is lamentation and self-hatred. Pride has become despair, and Oedipus flagellates himself with the powerfully evocative memory
of his life and the circumstances that have
led him to his present condition. The speech
is highly compressed, which increases its
emotional charge. In seventeen lines he
recalls his childhood, his parents, his killing
of his father, and his incestuous marriage.
Pain, self-hatred, despair, and remorse are
all contained within the short compass of
the speech. It is extremely direct, nothing is
wasted, and the memories fall like blows upon Oedipus' head.

Together with this active function of the
speech, there is a ritualistic sense of invocation. Oedipus calls upon the memories and
the events of the past as if they were the
godheads responsible for his doom, as indeed they were: "O Polybus and Corinth;"
"O Marriage, marriage!" The image in lines
1400-1401 of the earth drinking his father's
blood offered by his hands has a strongly
sacrificial and ritualistic quality. The lines
"you bred me and again when you had
bred/bred children of your child" (lines
1404-5) have a rhythmical quality strongly
evocative of the casting of a spell.

The language itself creates the emotion
and action of the character's situation. Lines
1396-97 oppose fairness and foulness and
use the explosive alliteration of "foulness
festered." Line 1398 contains an alliteration
of sibilants, "sinner and a son of sinners."
that causes the actor to spit out these hateful
words. In this way the playwright helps the
actor achieve the sense of the line, the

character's emotional state, and the direct
force of the action being played out. The
emotion, the form, and the action are one.

Whereas powerful emotion and direct involvement with the action are dominating
features of the protagonist's speeches, the
messenger or witness speeches make somewhat different demands upon the actor.
Here is part of a messenger speech relating
what took place after Oedipus had learned
of his sin and Jocasta, his mother/wife, had
killed herself:

1253

He burst upon us shouting and we looked
to him as he paced frantically around,
begging us always: Give me a sword, I say,
to find this wife no wife, this mother's womb,
this field of double sowing whence I sprang
and where I sowed my children! As he raved
some god showed him the way—none of us
   there.
Bellowing terribly and led by some
invisible guide he rushed on the two doors,—
wrenching the hollow bolts out of their
   sockets,
he charged inside. There, there, we saw his
   wife
hanging, the twisted rope around her neck.
When he saw her, he cried out fearfully
and cut the dangling noose. Then as she lay,
poor woman, on the ground, what happened
   after,
was terrible to see. He tore the brooches—
the gold chased brooches fastening her robe—
away from her and lifting them up high
dashed them on his own eyeballs, shrieking
   out
such things as: they will never see the crime
I have committed or had done upon me!
Dark eyes, now in the days to come look on
forbidden faces, do not recognize
those whom you long for—with such impreca-
   tions
he struck his eyes again and yet again
with the brooches. And the bleeding eyeballs
   gushed
and stained his beard—no sluggish oozing
   drops

but a black hail and bloody rain poured down.
So it has broken—and not on one head
but troubles mixed for husband and for wife.
The fortune of the days gone by was true
good fortune—but today groans and destruc-
    tion and death and shame—of all ills can be
    named
not one is missing.
1286

The general quality of this speech is de-scriptive. It has a strong active and emotional atmosphere, but does not directly communicate the emotions of the character. There is no conflict implied in the speech, no personal passion. The messenger who is speaking has no direct emotional involvement in the speech; it has no effect upon his life. It does, however, have a strong effect upon the purpose of the play's action, and by extension upon the audience. Messenger speeches in general contain narrative. They report events, actively describing them in colorful terms. There may also be an element of personal comment, sometimes a philosophical reflection upon the event, and, in exceptional cases, a direct conversational remark to a character on stage. The main functions, however, are to provide information necessary to the action but not available to the other characters and the audience, and to evoke a strong response in them. The purpose of the messenger speech we have quoted is quite clearly to evoke part of the pity and terror, the cathartic effect, that is the purpose of the action.

As with the protagonist speech we looked at, we find that the way this speech is constructed shows the actor how it should be performed. It is full of actively descriptive and onomatopoeic words. "Bellowing," which if given full value by the actor suggests that very sound, "wrenching," "dashed," "gushed," "oozing"—all are active, colorful words that suggest, through their sound, the concept they are depicting. The actor should be aware of the function of these words; their choice is not accidental. He

should also be aware of the rhythms and build of the speech, as, for example, the quiet moment of comment by the messenger in lines 1266-67. This sentence brings us down from the climax of the previous lines in order that full effect may be given to the coming main climax of the speech—the description of Oedipus dashing out his eyes. It is, as the French say, *reculer pour mieux sauter*, a step back to get a better jump.

The active description in the speech also gives the actor strong images that help him in his choice of gesture. Though parts of the speech are obviously narrative and do not call for physical embellishment, such images as "tore away the brooches," "dashed them on his eyeballs," and "struck his eyes again and yet again" certainly suggest gestures to the actor, if not, indeed, demand them. There is perhaps no better example of the language, the gesture, and the sense of the line being one than in "he struck his eyes again and yet again." The rhythm of this line is di *da* di *da* di *da* di *da* di *da*—a series of iambs—which is the rhythm of lifting and striking. It is the only line in the speech with such short, sharp rhythms.[18]

As for the "character" of the messenger, as much as is necessary is contained in the speech. We are not concerned about who the messenger is, whether he is married, or even whether he has any particular concern for the events he is describing. What the playwright wants us to know of him he has given us. The messenger's function defines him. He plays his part in the action and that is enough. The last thing the actor should be concerned with here is embellishing his part in "character" terms—like the bit actor described by Michael Green who, for a walk

---

[18] It should be mentioned here that the actor is very much at the mercy of the translators. It is difficult to find a translation that is both faithful to the original and beautiful in its new form. The best translations are those that convey the active spirit of the play, and actors and directors should be aware of this when selecting a text. The Grene and Lattimore edition, published by Chicago University Press, from which we have quoted by permission of the publisher, has the virtues of being close to the original, poetically valid in its own right, and highly actable.

across the stage, assumed a limp, an eye patch, an arm sling, and a toothless grin.[19]

We are not suggesting that an actor play generalities. Rather, he should play the specifics given to him rather than those of his own invention outside the play. When he approaches the mask of the messenger, the actor has the given circumstances of the situation: he knows where he is, who he is, and whom he is addressing. He knows his objective as a messenger: he wants the king to receive and to understand his information. If he needs to justify the detail gone into by the playwright, it can be because the king needs all the available information so that he may make valid decisions as a ruler. All of this helps the actor to play the action of the messenger—the reporting of the information. But the actor needs to know no more than what the situation and the action demand. He has a strong action to play, and the playwright has given him highly descriptive images to play it with. This descriptive action is the function and the focus of the actor; not the feelings or sensibility of the character. The actor knows the given circumstances of the mask, knows what action he is playing as the messenger, and uses the poetry given him by the playwright to manifest the action in a way that will engage the audience. It is what the audience feels that is the test of the effectiveness of the character's actions—and, thus, of the actor's performance. The actor who is prepared to explore and give full value to the poet's language—and not get stuck in an artificially assumed emotional tone—will find that the reality and purpose of the action is communicated by the form of the speech.

Sense of Occasion. By way of brief summation and to focus discussion back on the sense of integration and wholeness we have stressed as a crucial part of the Greek

[19] Michael Green, *Downwind of Upstage: The Art of Coarse Acting* (New York: Hawthorn, 1966), p. 44.

sensibility, we should confirm that all of the performance demands are embraced and informed by a strong sense of occasion. Bourgeois audiences at contemporary performances of plays are sometimes criticized for their approach to the event: dressing up, having drinks and dinner before or afterwards, and so forth. The critics believe that their sense of occasion is a hollow one—that they are more concerned with being seen than seeing, with being involved in the trappings rather than the core of the event. It is not our intention to make judgments, but simply to show that a sense of occasion is strongly present in the rhythms of human activity. The celebration of a cultural identity and the instinct to involve oneself in activities of larger significance than offered by everyday life seem to have been human needs since time immemorial.

For the Greeks, the dramatic festival was a momentous occasion. More specifically, it was a religious occasion: a ceremony descended from ritual, it celebrated the history of the race, discussed its moral purposes, and praised its continuance. Played within the sight of the gods, it was lent both its structure and its passion—a control, balance, clarity filled with tension, and spiritual excitation—by its ritual base. Dionysus restrained by Apollo—this was the eternal dichotomy, the essential dramatic conflict in Greek tragedy. To create an equivalent sense of occasion today, we would have to combine the qualities of a Roman Catholic mass, a football game, a rock concert, and a session of the Supreme Court.

The actor must be aware of this; he must be willing to rise to the occasion, to be filled by the eloquence and grandeur of the event. In general, we contemporary actors are used to underplaying. We choose and judge in terms of what we see around us; small persons performing small tasks. Contemporary dramatists, mirroring contemporary life, mistrust the large gesture, the blatant assertion. They see "honesty" in terms of everyday actions: the men and women of the stage must seem to behave and speak like their audience. We dare not make a grand noise in this age when the chatter of empty voices fills our space. Everyone is ordinary now. But the Greek heroes were descended from the gods, or at least were significant enough to suffer their wrath, and the issues and emotions were momentous. We must not be afraid of filling these; we should not, as actors, accept T. S. Eliot's observation that "this is the way the world ends, not with a bang but a whimper." The end of the tragic hero caused cosmic reverberations, and our gestures, voice, and passion must be consistent with this occasion.

EXERCISES, GAMES, TECHNIQUES

Isolation/Plastique. This is an exercise in body control and body awareness. As with any exercise of this nature, its application and utility in the training of actors and actresses is wholesale, but it provides a good starting point for acting in the style of Greek drama.* The essence of the exercise is to work upon one part of the body at a time while the rest is relaxed but focused. It is best to start from the top of the body and work down, or from the foot and work up.

Standing in a comfortable, balanced, and centered position, move the top of the head in all directions; continue with the nose, the jaw, each shoulder, each elbow, and so forth down the body until all parts have been worked upon separately. This is not simply a warm-up exercise, although it serves that purpose; the intention is not just to roll the jaw or shoulder, but to move it in as many ways as possible, isolating the part and extending its potential. It is important to keep

* The emphasis upon control and clarity that is fundamental in playing Greek tragedy is also extremely useful training for an actor in any style. It is our experience that when an actor returns to a realistic style after having worked on Greek drama, he is the better actor for it. His economy and selection are much heightened, and this lends force to the adage that the better the actor the less he does to achieve the same effect.

a strong point of concentration during this exercise. The mind should be focused in the part of the body that is being worked upon. Be aware of what is happening to that part of the body. Do not let the mind drift off into thoughts of this morning's breakfast or tomorrow night's date. At the same time, do not let the mind control the exercise. The parts of the body should follow their own course, with the mind supporting the activity.

An extension of this exercise is to allow the body to follow one specific part with complete plasticity through 360 degrees of space. Start, say, with the shoulder—it is better not to use arms or legs until the exercise is well under way—and move it in any direction, leading the rest of the body with it. Then transfer the leading point to the head, the pelvis, the hip, the knee, and so on. The change is not abrupt, but the plastic energy flows through the body from one leading point to another. The body follows, and the center of balance is constantly adjusted to remain the fulcrum of whatever position is taken up from moment to moment in the adjusting flow. The feet may be moved, but it is better to keep them firmly planted until some skill has been gained at finding and adjusting the center of balance. The exercise should never jerk; the body should never overbalance; all parts of the body should lead at some time, and a full 360 degrees should be employed. This is an exercise in control, flow, extension, and discovering and moving from the center.

Space Walk. This is fairly simple exercise that gives players a consciousness of filling space with their body. Start by having the players simply walk around the workshop area in a neutral manner, conscious of the space within which their body moves. Coach the players to make the space concrete. Let them discover where it supports them—the chin, the underarms, the crotch, and so forth. Coach them to lean on it; let it fill their body. Then throw images at the players and coach them to explore each one fully. For example, tell them they are wearing stilts that make them ten feet tall. Then take the stilts away and coach the players to remain ten feet tall with all parts of their body in proportion. Coach them to experience the body rhythms of this situation and how it makes them move and react: there will be a greater sense of size, and movements will be fuller and slower. When the players are comfortable with this, ask them to add sounds and words while they are moving and to note the distance the sound travels in their body and the fullness with which it is projected. Other images that may be used to achieve this effect: the players have their head in the clouds; the players are working on top of a high mountain.

There are two further images, but these must be used with care as there is a danger that the players may adopt a stiffness of movement, which is to be avoided. First, the players are coached to become an oversized puppet with the gods controlling the strings. A string from the top of the head is essential, as it will tend to extend the posture, and strings to the arms—shoulders, elbows, wrists—legs, and so on, should lead to extension and control in those areas. Being controlled by the gods is a useful image for players to have as they explore the sensibility of Greek tragedy, and not just its physical style. The second image is that of an automaton, or astronaut on the moon. Care must be taken here to coach the players away from stiffness of movement and toward experience of body control and size in space.

Passing Action. The players should stand in an open circle with working space between them. One player pantomimes a simple activity and develops it into a rhythmical action. The next player copies the activity in the same rhythm. When the two have been working in unison for a few moments, the first player returns to rest. The second

player now extends each of the movements that go into the activity and reduces them by one. Once again the two players work in unison for a few moments, and then the second player returns to rest. This process continues until a player feels he cannot reduce the movements any further without destroying the activity, and stops. Discuss as a group whether the activity could have been reduced further. Then continue the exercise with a new activity. For example, suppose the chosen activity were digging. Movements associated with digging may include thrusting, levering, lifting, throwing, wiping the forehead, rubbing the back, and scraping the shovel. Players could probably reduce these to thrusting and lifting without destroying the communication of the action. This is an exercise in the extension of gesture and the reduction of an activity to its absolute communicative essence.

Explosions. Players should begin as in the space-walk exercise—by becoming conscious of their bodies in the workshop space. On a signal (a hand clap or a drum bang) they explode out of themselves, fill the 360-degree space around them, and remain completely still in whatever position they land. Have the players hold the position for a few moments, and then coach them to release slowly back into themselves, from the fingertips and toes back to the center. Repeat this three or four times, coaching the players to explode from the center—not to think about the position they are going to adopt (that is, "how" they will explode), but to let it happen spontaneously upon the signal and to fill the 360-degree space around them. At first the players will tend to use just their arms and legs, and either adopt a standing explosion with arms thrust into the air or land flat on the floor. Both ways avoid a full commitment to the exercise. Coach for a total explosion from the center.

Once the players are committing themselves fully to the exercise and discovering interesting positions, extend the exercise: when they have come to rest after the explosion, have them hold their position for a few moments and then coach them to begin a simple rhythmical movement suggested by that position. Let this movement continue until it is well established, and then coach the players to turn it into any simple activity it suggests. For example, a movement of the spine up and down could become digging with a pick, chopping wood, casting a fishing rod, or picking apples and putting them in a basket. Coach the players to let the movement develop out of the position and the activity out of the movement without imposing a thought process. Coach them to avoid balletic motion and to make their movement strong, simple, and extended. This exercise focuses upon dynamic flow from the center and, once again, upon economy, extension, and control.

Neutral Mask. Work with the neutral mask has a general validity in the training of actors. Some of the qualities it encourages are, however, especially useful to the player concerned with Greek drama. Use of the neutral mask focuses the player upon fundamental and universal actions—whatever is necessary to execute a given task, and only that. By dispensing with all personal mannerisms and irrelevant responses, use of the neutral mask reinforces what is communal among human beings and identifies the essence of their actions. It emphasizes the expressiveness of the whole body by removing the expressiveness of the face, and it leads the player to the simplest, minimal physical ways of dealing with activities and situations. The player should let the mask tell the body what to do and not impose upon it, in the same way the athlete or gymnast lets the body respond to the rhythmical demands of the activity—skiing, playing tennis, performing a somersault—and does only what is necessary. The mask demands only what is necessary to perform with highly focused energy and economy. This combination of economy and energy gives an experience of size and clarity that we have suggested is part of the performance of Greek drama. The neutral mask helps the player to discover this experience organically, and not impose magnitude by an attempt to play "nobly" or "grandly."

Put on the mask with a certain reverence. Focus upon this act, aware that something is about to happen to you. Once the mask is in place, do not touch it or relate directly to it as an object, except to remove it from your face. Do not relate to another person as yourself with the mask in place—push the mask up onto the head to talk directly to others, and then reabsorb the mask when ready to go back to the exercise. With the mask in place, look at your whole body in a mirror until you feel the neutrality of the mask informing your whole body—this will start with the face and work down. The relaxed, serene, neutral features of the mask will help the body to achieve a neutral posture—neither sloppy nor stiff, but well-balanced and centered with a relaxed but powerful energy ready to be discharged in a highly focused way into whatever activity is asked of it. This is positive neutrality, player's neutrality. It is not the amoebic neutrality achieved by transcendental meditation, where energy is dispersed rather than focused, or a neutrality that denies human qualities. It is a neutrality that puts the wearer in touch with the universal in yourself: your inner core.

Exercises may be done in the mask, such as mirror exercises with a partner—copying gestures as a mirror would do. You may extend this exercise by suggesting objects, elements, or colors to the players, who allow their response to these suggestions to inform the gestures and physical positions the mirror game encourages. Individual exercises are best geared to the performance of simple activities such as lifting and carrying; picking a flower and smelling it; making a bed; and building a fence. Coach the players to avoid naturalistic cliches and any stylistic imposition upon the activity, such as mime: all actions should derive from the reality of the situation as transmitted through the mask. Coach the players to focus upon the physical demands of the object, action, or situation.

Psychological Gesture. This is probably one of the most useful and important exercises for a player approaching Greek tragedy.[20] It is based upon the principle that the more you repeat any simple gesture, the stronger it will become and the more it will induce supporting emotion in your body. The nature of the gesture made will also give the emotion of a definite focus: it will animate a specific desire, want or wish. The strength of the movement activates the emotion; the quality of the movement focuses its intention.

To put the principle into practice, choose any strong quality—greed, lust, pride or despair, for example—and explore it physically until you discover some configuration of the body that communicates your sense of the quality. Work for strong gestures and total involvement of the body; avoid small detail. Once you have discovered the gesture, repeat it both to clarify and strengthen it and to encourage the supporting feeling that will have developed in your body.

In working on a character, determine the main desire of the character—in Greek drama this will be the mask—and use that as the starting point for the psychological gesture. Start very simply with the foot, hand, or arm—note the connection here with the isolation/plastique exercise—and let your discoveries extend to involve the whole body. For example, your character may have a defiant, arrogant mask, and you might start with sweepingly dismissive or strong punching gestures. For a character who is more humble and submissive, a downward movement of the head or an imploring, open-palmed gesture might be a useful starting

Psychological gesture as illustrated in Michael Chekhov's *To the Actor*.

Drawing by Nicolai Remisoff. Copyright 1953 by Michael Chekhov. By permission of Harper & Row, Publishers, Inc.

point. Each player will of course choose his own starting point. The important thing is to start simply with a strong focus upon the mask, and explore without imposing until you have discovered the sense of rightness and the gesture extends to involve the whole body.

Having discovered the psychological gesture that communicates the main desire or mask of the character, you may refine it by working to encompass other attributes. For example, prideful ambition may be a dominating characteristic, but the character will at

[20] We are indebted to Michael Chekhov, who originated this exercise on the basis of Stanislavski's theory of physical actions. Those who wish to go into the exercise in more detail should refer to Chekhov's book, *To the Actor* (New York: Harper & Row, 1963), Chapter 5.

times be subject to other emotional states—uncertainty, pain, and anger, perhaps. These may be explored in the context of the basic psychological gesture, which will influence the way in which the other emotions are manifested. To discover a psychological gesture is to encompass the physical essence of the character. It is like a charcoal sketch done broadly and simply with the least possible number of strokes.

Explosion-Emotion. This is an extension of the explosion exercise; here it relates to the psychological gesture. Begin as in that exercise, moving fairly quicky to where the players are exploring a physical action suggested by the position they fall into after the explosion. Make sure the players are committing themselves fully to the exercise. Coach them to extend and strengthen their action until it suggests some emotional response such as pain, anger, despair, or futility. Have the players make any adjustments necessary to clarify the action and strengthen the relationship between it and the emotion. Have them return to neutral by concentrating upon lessening the action until the emotion drains away, and then relaxing the gesture from the extremities back into the center. Repeat the exercise several times, then extend by coaching the players to support the action/emotion with enough given circumstances to give it a real focus—to create a reason for the despair, an object of the anger. Coach the players to keep the action strong, clear, and simple; do not allow unnecessary detail to creep in with the given circumstances. Then have the players return to neutral as before.

Primal Scream. Be careful with this exercise: it is possible to lose control of it. It is not recommended for inexperienced players or a group that the coach is not quite familiar with. Nor should it be attempted by a relatively inexperienced coach.

Start from a horizontal floor alignment. Have them concentrate upon listening to and deepening their breathing. Coach them to drain all muscular definition and energy into their stomach as water, and then to pull the plug and let it drain out completely. Give them the image of the amoeba—formless and breathing. Coach the players to develop slowly from an amoeba into a child and continue forward until they hit/remember a moment of pain or emotional tension. It should be early and deep. Coach them to allow this moment to develop and to be taken into their whole body. Coach them to absorb and intensify it, but to keep it in their body until the last possible instant, when they allow it to burst out with whatever physical movement and sound it has catalyzed. Allow the moment to peak, and then coach the players to become aware of their gestures—this will remove the emotional intensity—in order to control and clarify them into a rhythmical and repeated gesture. Have them relax back into their center and drain. Now coach them to rediscover the gesture, slowly until their whole body is involved. Then coach for strong and intense repetition until the emotion previously associated with the action returns. Have the players allow the emotion to peak, then control it, relax, and drain as before. Discuss the discoveries made, in terms not of psychological significance but of intensity and utility for the actor. Discuss also how successful the players were in restimulating the emotion by repeating the action.

It is important to proceed slowly through this exercise, keeping control of the rising emotion until the moment for it to burst. Players will, of course, develop at different paces, and it is better to cut off the slower boilers at first than to allow some to boil for too long.

Emotional Mask. Start from a floor alignment and have the players concentrate on their breathing. Ask them to think of a sentence expressing a strongly emotional attitude, such as "I hate people," "I want to be alone," "Nobody loves me," or "I refuse to give in." Have the players repeat this quietly to themselves and then more strongly until a facial expression develops that epitomizes the attitude. When this becomes established, coach the players to stand and walk around the space, concentrating upon the phrase and the facial mask. Coach them to let the mask inform the body rhythms, so that the facial expression is absorbed into the whole body and the posture and rhythms of movement become one with the facial mask. When this has become well established, coach the players to repeat the original phrase more and more strongly, and to develop a gesture that focuses the emotional idea the body now also manifests. Coach them to repeat the gesture as strongly and fully as possible. Coach them to focus upon the physical gesture and allow emotion to drain away. Then have them return to their center and rest.

Animal Dance. Choose a speech with strong images. Either of the messenger speeches in *The Bacchae* would be suitable, as would the messenger speech or some of Medea's speeches from Euripides' play. Work with the images in the manner of the psychological-gesture exercise, having the players discover strong physical gestures that communicate the essential quality of the images. Have them gradually build up the momentum and rhythms of the gestures until a dancelike movement has evolved. Have the players concentrate upon the physicality of the dance and the emotional rhythms now produced. Coach them to develop more intense, primitive, and animalistic gestures and rhythms. Throw animal images to the players to help their imaginations work; make the animals strong or predatory. Allow the dance to reach a peak of intensity, then bring the players to rest by giving them relaxing images of evening, sunset, cooling breezes, and so on. Now have the players go back to their original speeches and perform them with no movement other than the absolutely necessary gestures. Players will find that their vocal range and their gestures are now strongly supported by a physical emotion emanating from their body's center and associated with the physical images kinesthetically implanted in their body memory.

Domestic Activity. Choose domestic activity that is not too complex—for example, making a sandwich, shaving, cleaning your teeth, or painting a door. Pantomime it as a normal, everyday activity. Repeat the exercise, this time clarifying the activity—that is, removing unnecessary movements. Repeat the exercise again, this time performing the clarified activity for a special purpose— shaving before going out with a special girl; painting the door because you want to sell the house; making a cake for someone's birthday. Repeat the exercise with the added dimension that there is to be a prize for the best cake, painted door, or shaved face. Repeat the exercise a last time, competing for a prize with the judges sitting fifty yards away from you. You have probably already discovered the purpose of this exercise. Starting from your own experience, it moves toward clarifying and strongly focusing an action, investing it with a larger significance, and finally bringing the size of the action to match both its significance and a large acting space.

Operatic Scene. Have the players pair off and then decide upon some simple situation with a potential for conflict, such as playing cards, ending an affair, or arranging furniture in a room. Then have them create a simple improvisation upon their theme. Repeat the exercise as if the situation were part of an opera. Initially the players will tend to impose their idea of operatic style upon the exercise and lose touch with the basic reality of the situation. Coach them to focus upon the reality they discovered in the realistic improvisation, but to project it through an operatic event. Repeat with groups of three players.

This is one of the very best exercises for coming to terms with the demands of a Greek style—indeed, any style that has presentation demands. It is an exercise players can have a lot of fun with, and it leads to high energy and dynamics. Take care that this energy is always focused within the exercise; it should not become an end in itself. The game re-creates all the necessary qualities of playing in a large manner—economy, clarity, getting to the essence of the action without unnecessary detail. Players begin to relate more strongly to each other, to focus energy through the simpler gesture, to be directly connected to the pulse of the action. More than this, the whole quality of approach changes, in speech as well as gesture: "Sure, man, I'll do it" becomes, without coaching, "It shall be done," because that is what now feels right to the player. The players gain a strong sense of language as a total part of the event—the cadence, rhythm, and weight of the line, which convey meaning as much as the words. They learn a very important lesson: "truth" is what is right for the given situation, and what is right will also be comfortable to the player—the style feels both right and necessary. This understanding is related to the players' experience of feeling comfortable as players: the style begins to feel both right and necessary to them. The players discover that the "truth" of the realistic improvisation is projected through new dynamics to create a different but equal truth for the new event. This is an essential lesson for understanding the playing of style.

Verbal Coloring. Start with a simple mirror exercise: players in pairs opposite each other mirroring movements. Throw images for the players to explore with their physical movements: "yellow," "ice cream,"

"peaches," "rough blanket," and so on. Coach the players to move out of the mirror relationship while continuing to explore individually and adding sounds that the images and movements suggest. Continue the exercise, presenting more potent images taken from the Greek tragedies—again, the messenger speeches from *The Bacchae* could be used, but all the tragedies have extremely dynamic images. At the end of this part of the exercise, have the players come to rest on the floor, align themselves and concentrate upon breathing.

For the next part of the exercise, use excerpts from any heroic or patriotic songs or hymn, "The Battle Hymn of the Republic," "Scotland the Brave," "Cymru" (the Welsh anthem), and "Jerusalem" are all suitable. Give sentences to the players as they are at rest and have them voice them on their outward breaths. Have them gradually deepen their breathing and voice the sentences with more power. Bring the players to their feet and move them around the space chanting sentences. Introduce music of a heroic mode—organ music is excellent, or Beethoven or Handel—and have the players continue chanting in the rhythms and the emotional atmosphere of the music. Finally, bring all the players together and chant verses in unison to the accompaniment of the music. Have them return to rest in their floor alignment. Now go back to the speeches from which the Greek images and phrases were taken, and have the players work on them. Their approach will now be informed by the physical sense of the imagery they have gained, the vocal range they have discovered in exploring the images with sound alone, and the sense of size and occasion the latter part of the exercise encourages.

Ritual. This is an excellent culminating exercise, bringing elements together and creating a sense of occasion. Start with an "orchestra" exercise: players are in a loose circle, one player in the center. He is the conductor. Start a rhythmical beat on a drum. The conductor starts a movement expressing the rhythm, and the players in the circle pick up the rhythm and movement and explore it further. After a minute the conductor goes up to another player in the circle and takes his place; that player now becomes the conductor. Change drum rhythms and tempo frequently. The exercise continues until most players have been conductor. Build up the tempo and rhythm to an intense level and coach the players to close in on the conductor. The conductor now becomes the victim, and is pressed to the ground. Change the rhythm and tempo to a steady, gentle beat. Darken the space. The victim is now raised on six players' shoulders and carried around the space. The drum leads with a solemn beat, followed by two players with lighed candles. The rest of the players follow the victim. All chant. The players process for a few minutes and then return to the center of space and place the victim on an altar (made of boxes or levels). Candles are placed at the sides of the altar, and two players bless wine and bread, offer it to the gods, and then place it at the victim's feet. The players return to the original circle and the chanting ceases. There should be a period of absolute silence. Now a new, dynamic drumbeat begins and the players begin an ecstatic chant. This raises the victim, who takes the bread and wine and gives it to each player in turn while embracing him. As the victim-become-priest moves around the circle, it closes and players put arms around each other's shoulders. The chanting and singing continue. When the victim has given wine and bread to all the other players, he stands on the altar and proclaims to the gods the opening of the festival. At this moment bring up the lights once again as dawn breaks. The players now return to their places and the festival begins.

This exercise works extremely well when the players commit themselves to it. At first there is the danger of camp and of surface reaction. Strong coaching can remove this and establish an emotional response to the situation. There will be a tendency to be overly primitive and aggressive after the killing of the victim. Coach for a sense of the religiosity of the occasion—the total significance and atmosphere of the ritual. It is an entirely serious exercise that gives players a strong sense of the ritual roots, the religious nature, and the dramatic potential of the event. Note how the citizen becomes victim and then priest and then player. The use of props is extremely important; emotion can be controlled by lighting, and the chanting and singing is a strong unifying element in the exercise. When this exercise works well, the players gain a thorough sense of atmosphere intrinsic to the Greek tragedy.

THE CHORUS

We have left our discussion of the chorus to the end not because we feel it performs the least important function, but because:

1. It has to be dealt with as an integral unit with its own demands.
2. The manner of its performance can depend more upon directorial/choreographic choices than upon the choices of any one actor.
3. Everything we have said about an actor's approach to Greek style—intrinsic demands, performance demands, exercises—can be applied to choral work.

To help the actor adapt this approach to the special demands of the chorus, we are presenting a brief summary of the chorus's function and how it relates to the dramatic event as a whole, plus some exercises geared to achieving a group identity. Again, this is not to impose a style, but to show what the inherent demands of a chorus are, so that an actor will be better able to adapt to its function within the choices made by the director/choreographer.

Intrinsic Function. The chorus is believed to have originally numbered fifty; it was then reduced to twelve, and finally settled at fifteen members for much of the fifth century.

This reflects the evolution of Greek tragedy from its early beginnings in ritual and dance, with a strong focus upon the choral element, to the greater emphasis upon dramatic action with a consequent increase in the number of actors, to three, and the lowering of the number of chorus members. The chorus probably had three basic functions:

1. It brought an atmosphere of ritual and religiosity to the dramatic event. In Greece a chorus was present at, and lent ceremony and spiritual import to, all occasions—weddings, funerals, victory celebrations, and so forth.

2. It had a lyric function, setting a mood or tone that enveloped the drama. In this the rhythms of dance and chant were probably more important than the content of the lines;

3. The chorus was a unifying element; it provided both a physical and a spiritual thread, or through-line, to the performance, connecting the episodes and uniting music, dance, and speech in a consistent whole.

As an extension of its lyric function, the chorus reinforced the passions of the dramatic action with its song and dance. The chorus also connected the audience and the actors, both physically, in that they were closer to the event and could draw the audience into it, and dramatically, in performing the function of an ideal audience—making responses and asking questions.

This raises the question of how the chorus is to be viewed structurally. Aristotle felt that it should be "regarded as one of the actors; it should be an integral part of the whole, and share in the action."[21] In this sense the chorus might be thought of as a collective character. The part it plays in the action of certain plays would support this notion. In *Oedipus Rex*, for example, the chorus represents the people of Thebes, reinforcing the presence of the plague and emphasizing Oedipus' social responsibility. In *Agamemnon* the chorus represents the city elders, and in *The Bacchae* it carries the central action of the play in representing the maddened followers of Dionysus. But, as Aristotle goes on to point out, the function of the chorus is not always strongly related to the action of the play: "As for the later poets, their choral songs pertain as little to the subject of the piece as to that of any other tragedy."[22]

In those plays where the chorus does not seem structurally integrated into the dramatic form in the sense that it could be perceived as an actor, it may be that its full significance comes across only in performance, where the visual and aural effects, while not directly furthering the action, add enormously to the dramatic impact of the event as a whole. Thus the function of the chorus in any play must be taken on that play's terms. It may range from rhythmical dance and singing to chanting and movement patterns to simple use of collective gesture and the dramatic rhythms of the verse.

Performance Demands. Even when the chorus's function has been determined, it remains to the contemporary director to decide to what extent it will work as a unit. If dancing and singing are emphasized, then the chorus will probably function as a homogeneous unit making a strong visual and rhythmical impact with identical costume, mask, and movement. If the chorus is regarded more as an actor, a collective character, this leaves the choice as to how far each member of the chorus might be individuated within the collective idea: do all the people of Thebes wear identical costume and mask and use unison gestures, or are there variations within the choral group, in the cause of greater "realism" of effect? This, again, will depend upon how much of a formal impact the director wishes to make with

[21] *Aristotle's Poetics*, trans. S. H. Butcher, New York: Hill & Wang, 1961, p. 92.

[22] *Ibid.*

the production as a whole. Whatever the director's choice, there are certain constants:

1. The movement of the chorus should be consistent with the style as a whole.
2. The choice of gesture and movement should arise from an organic sense of the play's action, and not be arbitrarily overlaid.
3. "The movements and gestures which the chorus members employ," Oscar Brockett reports, "are not basically different from those used by a single actor."[23]

This confirms our feeling that stylistic determinants for the individual actor also apply to the actor in the chorus—given the extra demands of working in a group, and the choreographic choices.

Brockett observes that choral gestures and movements "by being done in unison have great impact and stylized effect."[24] This supports our own opinion that even when the chorus is a collective character there should be a strong unison of movement and gesture. Iris Brooke also believes in chorus uniformity, suggesting that "the wandering eye or facial peculiarity could be a distracting element when the main purpose is to produce a sense of rhythm into the whole production."[25]

Insofar, then, as an actor in the chorus is part of a collective character, his approach to the style will be pretty much the same as his approach to an individual character: the same givens of size, sensibility, directness, clarity, and so on, will apply. He must adapt to the further demand of working in unison with a group. Thus, rhythmical response is extremely important, and the actor will have the help of music, with its inherent rhythmical discipline, to assist the unifying process.

[23] Brockett, "Staging of Ancient Drama," p. 284.

[24] *Ibid.* Another good discussion of the chorus is to be found in Brockett's "Producing Greek Tragedy," *The Classical Journal*, 56, no. 7 (April 1961), 317–23.

[25] Brooke, *Costume in Greek Classic Drama*, pp. 80–81.

The impulse for choral movement and gesture is discovered in the action and given circumstances. It may be evolved by a director or choreographer and given to the chorus. In this case the individual actor must relate the rhythms to the meaning and assimilate the ensemble identity. As we shall show in the exercises that follow, there are also ways in which the individual actors can organically arrive at and share movement and gesture developed from the action. Whatever method is employed there are a few guidelines:

1. It is just as well not to imitate or create rituals unrelated to the text and then try to integrate them with the action. However, modern icons or patterns that relate to the action can usefully be employed. In one recent production, for example, the chorus performed a dance for peace and used the pattern of the international antinuclear sign—a Y within a circle.
2. Movement should arise, as far as possible, from the textual circumstances, in the form of patterns illustrating the persona of the chorus and its function in the action.
3. Movement may run the gamut from dance to walking patterns, and singing, chanting, and speaking may all be employed. But the movement should be consistent with the givens of the action—it is probably inappropriate for stately and dignified elders to dance around like young nymphs.

Exercises. All the exercises previously presented will be useful to chorus actors. Those we set out below are particularly adapted to the ensemble nature of the chorus. Again, the intention is to help the actor understand physically the demands put on a chorus, to absorb a feeling for the style that will come through in performance.

Getting Together. Basic ensemble games such as "Machine" (Chapter 7) and "Conductor" (Chapter 8) are a useful start for chorus work. Tag games in which players join hands when tagged until all players are in a connected line make players aware of joint physical rhythms. These games can be varied with added demands such as hopping on one leg, putting one arm behind the back, or moving in slow motion.

Passing Rhythms. Rhythms are developed and passed around the group with voice, hands, drums, pieces of wood, and so on. This may be done in various ways:

1. A leader begins and other players join in in any order.
2. A rhythm is passed from player to player, each adding his own adaptation.
3. All players start together, and by listening to the person on either side gradually adapt their own rhythm until a group rhythm is evolved.

The exercise may be done with pure rhythms, or a coach may give ideas or themes to the group as a basis for rhythms. These rhythms may be of a joint character, such as the rhythms of the elders of Thebes or of the Bacchantes, or of a more abstract quality, such as despair, hope, or joy.

Follow My Leader. Players sit in a circle (they may stand when they are more adept), with one player outside, back turned to the group. The players in the circle agree upon a leader, who begins a rhythmical movement with some part of the body. All players follow until the whole circle is performing the movement together. From time to time the leader changes the movement and rhythm and the other players adapt. After a couple of minutes the outside player turns towards the circle and tries to identify the leader. The trick is for the players in the circle to follow without looking directly at the leader—they come to develop a 180-degree sense of connection and rhythmical flow. Coach the leader to use large expansive gestures. Play the game several times with different leaders. Players get a real sense of pleasure and achievement at being able to defeat the observer with the unity of their movements.

Melting Sculptures. Players stand in a circle and number off. Numbers are then called and the numbered player runs to the center and adopts any physical posture with a dynamic tension. Other players, as called, attach themselves to the developing group until all players are in contact and form a dynamic but immobile sculpture with their bodies. Numbers continue to be called, and each player must adjust his position, keeping in contact, so that the sculpture is constantly melting and reforming. The game may be played with a theme for each sculpture, which will give the players a stronger sense of focus. This exercise trains players to be aware of others while working physically in a group, and to become part of a larger physical pattern.

Group Mirror. Two players face each other and begin a simple mirror exercise. Each player is joined by two more players standing slightly behind and to each side. The mirror exercise continues. Each group of three is joined by two more, again slightly to the rear, and so on until all players are involved as two equal groups facing each other. The mirror game continues with each group keying off its leader. The origination of gestures can change from group to group, and themes may be introduced.

Expanding Explosion. This is an elaboration of the explosion exercise presented earlier in this chapter. Start as for that exercise, with players exploding out of their centers and adopting frozen 360-degree positions. Have players explore their position and begin a simple rhythmical movement suggested by it. Now each player turns to a partner, and by a process of offering and taking the two adapt their individual movements into a joint movement that incorporates part of each. When these joint movements are well established, each pair turns to another pair and offers/takes once more until a joint four-way movement develops. The process is continued—four, eight, sixteen, and so on—until the whole group has developed one united rhythmical pattern of movement. The coach can elaborate the exercise by introducing a theme as a basis for movement once the explosion has taken place.

Ideographs. Players explore aspects of a collective character, or a chorus theme from a text. This is done individually, each player evolving a simple pattern of movement and gesture. Now the two–four–eight process of the preceding game is adopted, players attempting to clone each other's patterns. Gradually a joint pattern of movement and gesture will develop that shares part of each player's impulse and connects them all. Players should be coached away from small detail and towards simple, large, essential patterns. A rhythm beaten out on a drum during the exercise can help players achieve a joint response.

Cheering Chorus. Divide the players into two even groups and have them occupy areas at different sides of the workshop space. Set up a small platform in front of each group. Have the groups agree on a theme that has social, political, or moral overtones. As a simplistic example, if the groups are one of men and one of women, the theme may be the battle of the sexes. The idea of the game is for the men to propound male superiority and the women female superiority. First a male player mounts his platform and declaims an assertive phrase—for example, "Men are physically stronger" or "Men are more intellectual." At the same time, he performs a strong physical gesture that illustrates the point. His chorus picks up the gesture and joins him in declaiming. The opposing chorus denies the proposition: one of the female players mounts her platform and makes a gesture and declamation asserting female superiority: "Women sustain the race," "Women are more artistic," or whatever. When this happens the male player rejoins his chorus, which discovers a

gesture denying the female proposition. And so the game continues, male and female players making assertions and denials in turn.

Strong coaching will be needed at first to keep a joint focus upon idea and gesture, and to encourage each chorus to work as a unit. Energy runs high in the exercise, which gives players a strong sense of the demands of group gesture and vocal rhythms. The exercise also acquaints players with the dynamics of give and take present in the strophe/antistrophe choral structure, and with the relationship of chorus to both protagonist and antagonist.

SUGGESTED READINGS

ANDERSON, M. J., ed., *Classical Drama and Its Influence*. New York: Barnes & Noble, 1965.

ARNOTT, P.D., *Greek Scenic Conventions in the Fifth Century B.C.* Oxford: Oxford University Press, 1962.

BIEBER, MARGARETE, *The History of the Greek and Roman Theatre*. Princeton: Princeton University Press, 1961.

BROOKE, IRIS, *Costume in Greek Classic Drama*. London: Methuen, 1962.

HOPE, THOMAS, *Costumes of the Greeks and Romans*. New York: Dover, 1962.

KITTO, H.D.F., *Greek Tragedy*. London: Methuen, 1961. _____, *The Greeks*. Chicago: Aldine, 1964.

PICKARD-CAMBRIDGE, A. W., *The Dramatic Festivals of Athens*. Oxford: Oxford University Press, 1953.

TAPLIN, OLIVER, *Greek Tragedy in Action*. Berkeley: University of California Press, 1978.

WEBSTER, T.B.L., *Greek Theatre Productions*. London: Methuen, 1956. _____, *The Greek Chorus*. London: Methuen, 1970.

chapter 3

Albert Finney as Hamlet.

National Theatre, England.

Shakespeare

BACKGROUND

Introduction. As Greek tragedy was an expression of a civilization at its cultural zenith, so was the work of Shakespeare the finest cultural manifestation of an age of equal dynamic and distinction—the Elizabethan age in England. In Greece the drama reflected the almost perfect integration of society in a "classical" harmony of balance and proportion. In England Shakespeare's drama expressed a more "romantic" sensibility whose various, vigorous, and contradictory elements, held in a state of dynamic balance during the time of Elizabeth, led to the verve and creativity of the period. "Dynamic balance" might well describe both periods, but if the Golden Age of Greece was a balance of centripetal forces, that of Elizabeth was an equilibrium of centrifugal forces. This quality marks not only the life style of the Elizabethan period but the theatre of Shakespeare, who (born just six years after Elizabeth came to the throne and dying thirteen years after her) was entirely a product of the social, political, economic, and cultural forces at work during Elizabeth's reign.

Elizabethan Age. The coming of Elizabeth to the throne brought England a significant degree of political solidity, which was reinforced by the events of her long reign. During the sixty years before she became queen, England was racked from within by civil war—the Wars of the Roses—and threatened from without by Catholic Europe—a result of Henry VIII (Elizabeth's father) breaking with Rome. Just before Elizabeth became queen, her sister Mary, a closet Catholic, caused further instability by conspiring with Spain to return England to the Roman Church. Elizabeth's accession brought political stability to England and confirmed the independence from Rome of the newly founded Protestant Anglican Church. The defeat of the Spanish Armada in 1588 is the political high point of Elizabeth's reign, as it confirmed in one blow the military security, political integrity, and religious independence of England.

In a sense, England became a prototype of the values of independence and vigorous effort associated with Renaissance humanism. Breaking with Rome was an assertion of individual rights in the face of old traditions, an event showing the desire and willingness of the nation to pursue its personal destiny. Elizabeth, as head of both state and church, was no longer in political or moral fee to any foreign power. This was, of course, a disruption of the medieval sense of a hierarchical religious order based on the concept of the chain of being: the chain stretched from the foot of God's throne to the meanest of inanimate objects. The angels were nearest to God, followed by man and the lesser living creatures—the pope, of course, being at the head of this class. Then came vegetables and finally inanimate objects such as metals and liquids. The function of all classes was to come nearer to God, but without disrupting the given progression of the chain. Henry VIII, in breaking with Rome, had disrupted this natural order of things,[1] and his daughter Elizabeth confirmed the break by becoming head of the Church of England. But, in a sense that is typical of the period, Elizabeth had not so much disrupted a natural order as re-

---

[1] Shakespeare asserts this sense of life in a speech by Ulysses in Act I, Scene iii of *Troilus and Cressida*:

The heavens themselves, the planets and this centre

Observe degree, priority and place,

Insisture, course, proportion, season, form,

Office and custom, in all line of order;

focused it. The sense of hierarchical political and religious order was to a considerable degree retained in Elizabeth's England: she simply replaced the pope's authority and place in that scheme of things with her own. Thus, past traditions were not so much broken as reoriented, or subsumed into a new sense of life's purposes. New social structures were built upon old foundations, which were not obstacles to progress but provided a firm base for it.

Integration of Medieval and Renaissance. This flexible sense of the integration of the past with the possibilities of the future was typical of the Renaissance and of the reign of Elizabeth, and informed the sensibility of Shakespeare's work. There was a balancing of the tensions between medieval roots and modern attitudes, which is well exemplified in the nature of the Anglican Church: firm in its beliefs, yet not dogmatic; broadly based and flexible enough to encompass differing Protestant opinions; excluding only the most radical of Puritan or Roman beliefs. This balancing of potential tensions, which was the prime achievement of Elizabeth, brought political and religious security, and a dynamism that created great economic and cultural wealth.

From an economic point of view, the period saw the establishment of that commercial base that in the eighteenth and nineteenth centuries was to make the middle class the power center of England and England itself the commercial, industrial, and colonial power center of the world. A new spirit of commercialism and profit incentive was applied to land, which became a commodity, and the making of money led to the investment of money in an age of optimism and ambition. The securing of the seas to English ships, a result of the defeat of the Armada, led to an expansion in the export trade—to match and support the expansion at home.

While politics and economics went hand in hand, capitalist entrepreneurship was being supported by the new spirit of Protestantism. Humility on this earth and trust in the priest to intercede for you in the better life to come was replaced by material self-reliance. The counting of sheep and money replaced the counting of beads and lighting of candles. One could buy one's way to heaven as well as enjoy material goods on this earth. Priestly faith could no longer control a world of economic fluctuations; an assertive self-interest could. When the merchant of London looked into his heart he found that God had planted there a deep respect for the principles of profit and private property. Productive economic activity, after all, could be construed as a charitable good work:

> A servant with this clause,
> Makes drudgery divine;
> Who sweeps a room as for Thy laws,
> Makes that and the action fine.

The Elizabethan period was also one of dynamic conflict in its philosophical outlook on life. A God-oriented sense of life whose rewards were in eternity was opposed to a man-oriented, humanistic outlook stressing achievements on earth. Humanism suggested that man could define his own nature: "What a piece of work is Man. . . ." Hamlet's words express the humanism of the day, in which the dignity rather than the humility of man is paramount. The hierarchical and unchangeable sense of religious and social authority was giving way to secular individualism. But the earlier traditions died hard. They formed part of the vocabulary and sensibility of Shakespeare's time while providing a framework upon which the new ideas of the Renaissance were grafted.

Humor and Personality. Medieval concepts of the universe and of man himself are present in Shakespeare's work. The medieval world was God-oriented and earth-centered. The sun, the planets, and the rest of the known universe moved around the earth,[2] and produced the "music of the spheres." It was an age of "belief" not only in God but in the magical, mystical, and alchemical. The

---

[2] As we saw from Ulysses' speech in footnote 1.

medieval world was made up of four elements: earth and water, which were personalized as having a tendency to fall; and air
and fire, which were given a tendency to rise.
These elements also became the humors of
living bodies: earth was cold and dry and cor-
responded to melancholy; water, cold and
moist, to phlegm; air, hot and moist, gave rise
to a sanguine temperament; fire, being hot
and dry, was choleric in bias. As a harmonious balance of the elements was necessary to the world, so a balance of humors was
necessary to the functioning of the human
body. The humors were related not only to
the general health of a person, but also to his
personality traits. Overbalance of a particular
humor was thought to determine his basic
sensibility. The four elements entered the
body as food, went to the stomach, and then
journeyed to the liver, which was regarded as
the seat of the humors, or personality.

The concept of a dominating personality
trait was a fundamental principle of medieval thought, and it persisted well into the
eighteenth century. The behavior of an individual was determined by his predominant
humor—phlegm, melancholy, and so on. This
attitude went hand in hand with the concept
of the seven ages of man, which forms the
basis of Jacques's speech in Act II, Scene vii of
As You Like It. People were expected to
behave as their humor, station in life, age, and
sex dictated. The "lean and slippered pantaloon" would not be expected to play tennis
or go jogging with his wife.

Character "Typicality." It cannot be over-
stressed in our age of individualism and self-
determination, where everyone is to be
regarded as a separate and unique "person"
in his or her own right, that a sense of
"typical" behavior—determined by such
variables as class, race, sex—was common in
the Elizabethan period. Nor should we make
value judgments about this if we wish to
understand the sensibility of the time. Such
concepts were not regarded as anti-
democratic, sexist, racist, or any of the other

terms we would now apply to them. They
represented the social and intellectual structure of that time. Not only were they perfectly
acceptable, they were a way of looking at life
and understanding people that the playwrights of the time inevitably reflected in
their work.

While humanism was introducing the
sense of individuality that was to lead to the
more sophisticated psychology of the twentieth century, two other concepts of the
Renaissance tended to reinforce the idea of
typicality: decorum and verisimilitude. Decorum dictated that behavior should be
appropriate to rank, place, sex, and other
qualities. Verisimilitude required that actions
be true to life. But the truth was not a private
and individual one—it was an ideal or universal truth. Kings should be "kingly"; they
should behave in a formal manner, carry an
air of authority, be brave and honorable, and
never, certainly in public, be seen to pick their
noses, belch, or appear to be capable of any of
the coarser bodily functions that are the appropriate actions of lesser mortals.

The combination of the concepts of decorum and verisimilitude reinforced the idea
of appropriate actions based upon universal
truths. Although they may not be applicable
to every individual of a given class or group
at all times, such actions are seen to be
typical of the group. A book of the period on
the art of rhetoric set down some of the
received character determinations of the
time: a man of good years is sober, wise and
circumspect; a young man, wild and careless; a woman, babbling and inconstant; a
soldier is a great bragger and vaunter of
himself; a scholar simple; a courtier flatter-
ing. The English are known for feeding and
changing apparel, the Dutch for drinking,
French for pride and inconstancy, Spaniards
for nimbleness and disdain.

Lest we be too quick to dismiss this simple
view of character, we might remember that in
our day certain generalizations are held about
national and ethnic identities: Latins are
regarded as hot-blooded, emotional, and sexually dynamic; the British as phlegmatic and

aloof; Germans as proficient technicians and heavy beer drinkers. One could go on. The point is not how true this is of any individual, but that it is a received attitude based in very generalized observation and truth. It serves as a reference point if one wishes to characterize a people or group as a whole. This is what many playwrights regarded as the function of character before the nineteenth century. Their main concern was with action and events, and a recognizable shorthand of character saved a good deal of time that could be devoted to the main purpose of the play: dramatic action.

Verbal Society. While talking of the approach to characterization we should look at the sensibility of people as a whole in the Elizabethan period: what social events and attitudes characterized the time. It was predominantly an aural and verbal society. Less than fifty per cent of Shakespeare's audience would have been able to read or write. But it would not have regarded itself as deprived by this inability, for reading and writing was yet to be a general expectation among society. Communication was geared more to the tongue and ear and to broad visual panoramas than narrowly to the printed page. Remember, Shakespeare was not concerned that his plays should be printed— this was not completely done until some seven years after his death. The people of the time were used to listening: they had an ear for language, used not just as a means of information but embellished with rhetorical imagery and emotionally stimulating phrases. It was a time of long speeches, sermons, stories told of a winter evening. The town crier, the night watchman, the itinerant tradesman all added their sounds to a daily life that included church bells and bird song as part of its music. People were accustomed to listening and glad to hear. Education had a verbal tradition. One of the basic principles of instruction in the grammar schools and universities of the day was learning by heart and repeating aloud. With the Renaissance came renewed interest in Greek and Latin

plays also read aloud, which accustomed the students to an atmosphere of public performance. The teaching of rhetoric supported this sense of performance. Students were taught to recognize and understand the emotional function of many poetic structures: how the quality of certain words and the nature of their arrangement in particular images and structures—alliteration, onomatopoeia, apposition—can produce a particular effect upon the ear and human emotions. The aim of rhetorical speaking was clear enunciation, fitting modulation, and the conveying of proper emotion. Speech came close to performance as students learned appropriate gestures that would fit particular rhetorical structures and enhance emotional effect.

Ritual and Rowdiness. As well as being verbal, the Elizabethan period was an age of activity, color, and enormous contrasts. A time of ritual, ceremony, and processions saw the formal dignity of the Mass side by side with the celebration of pagan festivals such as May Day, with its Morris dancing, phallic maypole, and "country matters" in the woods. Elizabeth's "progresses" through the country, surrounded by her court, from one dignified mansion to another—in itself an enormously theatrical act—took place next to country fairs with their bearbaiting, exhibiting of cretins, and tooth breakers who removed teeth with pliers, to the great amusement of the crowd. It was an age of rugged physicality; it was closer to its pains and its passions. Criminals were not only hanged in public but cut into quarters. It was not uncommon to see the heads of traitors on the spikes of city walls. The poetry and the physicality, the formality and passion, the blood and thunder, the perfume and music, the folklore and the classical rhetoric: all the colorful diversity of the society of the day found its way into Shakespeare's work.

A Popular Theatre. Theatre itself played an important part in the social life of Elizabethan people. Fynes Moryson, a sixteenth-century traveler and writer, after confirming the tremendous number of games and sports played by the Elizabethans, goes on to say:

> All Cittyes, Townes and villages swarme with Companyes of Musicians and Fidlers, which are rare in other Kingdomes. The City of London alone hath four or five Companyes of players . . . they all play every day in the week but Sunday, with most strange concourse of people. . . . There be, in my opinion, more Playes in London than in all the partes of the worlde I have seene, so do these players or Comedians excell all other in the world.

Theatre had always been a part of the social tradition of England. Mystery plays flourished in the streets of medieval cities such as Coventry and York. Troupes of itinerant actors—still regarded on a level with "vagabonds and sturdy beggars"—presented morality plays and interludes in market squares and the halls of country mansions. A whole tradition of popular theatre was alive in England in the sixteenth century, when the cultural influence of the Renaissance and the economic prosperity of Elizabeth's reign led to the professionalization of theatre and the development of permanent companies, permanent theatres, and permanent audiences. The rediscovery and teaching of classical playwrights such as Plautus, Terence, and Seneca in schools and universities provided for a greatly expanded repertory of plays. These neoclassical models were integrated, especially by Shakespeare, with conventions, characters, and forms taken from the native stock of farces, religious plays, and moralities to create the unique quality of the Elizabethan drama.

The Elizabethan theatre was not a break with, but a continuation and sophistication of, a popular tradition. As it progressed from the streets, market squares, inn yards, and bear pits to the permanent theatres of Shakespeare's day (such as the famous Globe), theatre took its popular sensibility with it. The audience at the Globe would be socially, economically, and educationally heterogeneous, made up of every rank and class of society—artisans, craftsmen, shopkeepers, petty gentry, nobility, and respectable women in company with whores, pickpockets, students, and apprentices. A good deal of flirtation went on as well as some pushing, shoving, and drinking among the bustling throng that had come to enjoy itself in an emotionally open way.

There was something for everyone in the plays. Middleton's prologue to his *No Wit, No Help Like A Woman's*, asks:

> How is't possible to suffice
> So many ears, so many eyes,
> Some wit, some in shows
> Take delight, and some in clothes;
> Some for mirth they chiefly come,
> Some for passion—for both some.

The appreciation of different elements—wit, passion, blood and thunder, perfection of poetic form—was obviously at different levels for different parts of the audience, but the involvement was total—the audience participated in the event. An audience used to listening would admire and enjoy the language; an audience used to a coarser, more passionate, less squeamish life would accept the violence of deaths and enjoy the physicality of fighting, wrestling, and dancing. The music of trumpet and drum, the splendor of the costumes—all would add to the eloquence of the plays and re-create a colorful panorama of daily life.

It was in a sense a secular festival, to be compared with the religious festivals of the Greek theatre. Tracing its descent from the popular tradition of the mystery and morality plays, and incorporating many of their conventions, the Elizabethan theatre is a celebration of man and his attempt to define himself, discover a moral structure, and come to terms with his own nature. God was still present in this world, but the heroes were earthbound, dealing with each other in human terms. As with the Greek theatre, the themes of Elizabethan drama have significance for the audience of the time—how man should deal with the challenges of living—but the answers were to be found more in the woods, heaths and throne rooms of England than upon Mount

Olympus. And, again in common with the Greeks, pride and curiosity in the historical evolution of the race is a significant element in the drama. Shakespeare's chronicle plays trace the history of England from the time of Henry IV through the Wars of the Roses to the accession of Elizabeth's ancestors, the Tudors. This, for Shakespeare and England, was equivalent to the Greeks' use of the Homeric legends in their tragedies. Both bodies of drama reflected a dramatic use of the historical mythology of the race to underscore its achievements, create pride in ancestral roots, and place a heroic mantle around rulers. It also reinforced a sense of the special potentiality for human action and leadership that people in the Golden Age of Greece and the Elizabethan age believed they possessed. Religious or secular, the theatres of the two periods shared in the universality of the common culture and traditions of their day—whether this was the Greek sense of wholeness or the dynamic diversity that typified the Elizabethan period.

Dynamic Contrast. The Elizabethan age was, then, a period of flux, flexibility, and contrasts. The solid, structured rhythms of the Middle Ages were being penetrated and improvised upon by the humanism of the Renaissance. The conflicts between the old and the new, in every area of life, produced dynamic accommodations, a creative fervor in which curiosity, ambition, private enterprise, and initiative abounded, but always with a rooted sense of continuance, structure, and popular form. Ambition was given scope but absorbed into existing structures, in this way ensuring social stability without inhibiting the upward mobility of talent. Shakespeare's own social ambition was to buy a small estate and carry the title of "gentleman"—which he achieved.

Elizabethan architecture: Bramall Hall, Cheshire.

Countrylife. *Reproduced by permission.*

Popular tradition and new values cross-pollinated, jostled each other, and found expression in the drama. Vigor, credulity, virtuosity, and imagination rubbed shoulders with convention, formality, ritual, and lyricism. The theatre was a union of classical artistry with a romantic sweep of energy, color, and exuberance; of classical verbal form with romantic insistence upon action.

Embracing and juxtaposing the contradictions of his age, Shakespeare made an artistic virtue of this dialectical dynamic. The integration of contrasting ideas gives the clue not only to the understanding of the Elizabethan period and the theatre it produced, but to the style of Shakespeare's drama and how it should be acted. Contrast informs Shakespeare's dramatic structure, which is compounded of accepted conventions yet allows for an experience of the crosscurrents, whirligigs, and "mingle-mangle" of life. Contrast is in the nature of his language, where poetry and prose, elaborate imagery, and simple, active speech all find their place. Contrast is at the heart of his characters, where "typical" attitudes and a conventional core support the more subtle and sophisticated actions and emotions of unique individuals. And, finally, however elevated may be the emotion or idea, the superhuman is always firmly anchored in the everyday.

Shakespeare's was truly "el gran teatro del mundo," combining classical plots, rhetoric, moralizing, and blood and vengeance with his native tradition born of Christian

A historical re-creation of an Elizabethan playhouse based upon the architecture of the time, at the Ashland, Oregon, Shakespeare Festival.

Photo by Hank Kranzler.

religion, morality types, clowning, pagan dances, royal processions, and the virile and acrobatic physicality of a passionate age. His own life typified the contrasting values of his time. His ambition and his success in London did not lead him to sever his connections with his native town. He embodied Renaissance drive and medieval structure. Nurturing his roots, he brought the profits of his talent back from the dynamic activity of London to the earthy solidity of Stratford, where he died. He was a poet with a strong sense of everyday reality. Though his head may have been in the clouds of inspiration, his feet were planted firmly on the ground. It is these qualities of contrast and integration, the dynamic created by the balancing of multiple tensions, that we shall discover as we examine Shakespeare's theatre and its acting style.

INTRINSIC DEMANDS

Space. The theatre where most of Shakespeare's plays were first performed was the famous Globe, home of the Lord Chancellor's (later renamed the King's) Company, of which Shakespeare was a shareholder. In some respects we have even less concrete evidence of the Globe than of the original Greek theatres. When the Puritans came to power in the 1640s they banned play performances and razed the public theatres. However, some evidence remains: a drawing

A modern re-creation of an Elizabethan space in the Stratford, Ontario, Shakespeare theatre.

of the Swan Theatre; contracts for the building of other theatres; and references found in property lists of the time. This, together with intelligent conjecture from references found within the plays, and the inherent staging demands of the plays themselves, has given us a very good sense of what the Elizabethan public theatre must have been like.

The prologue to *Henry V* speaks of an "unworthy scaffold," a "cockpit," and a "wooden O." And it is reasonable to presume that the Globe Theatre, as befits its name, was round in shape, or at least octagonal, with the acting space, as confirmed in the Swan drawing, a raised platform thrusting into an audience that surrounded it on three sides. Here, immediately, we find a connection with the tradition of popular entertainment. The "scaffold" is directly descended from the cart or platform upon which itinerant players acted in town squares, and from the *platea* of the medieval theatre. The circular shape of the theatre recalls the pits where bearbaiting and cockfighting took place, which, together with the yards of inns, were the first homes of professional companies, before the building of permanent theatres. Like the bear pits and inn yards, the Globe theatre was open to the sky, and the performance took place in daylight. The platform is calculated to have been about forty-three feet wide, twenty-seven feet deep, and about five feet high. At the back of the platform was a permanent facade at least two stories high—to accommodate such action as the balcony scene in *Romeo and Juliet*—which may have looked like an Elizabethan mansion. At all events it remained a constant background to the play and was not used as a changeable scenic device. At either side of this facade was an entrance, and there is some evidence that in the center was a curtained recess called the "study" or "inner below," which may have been used for intimate interior scenes such as bedrooms. The second story may have contained a balcony over this lower recess—an "inner above"—and balconies and windows over the side doors, providing flexible acting areas in the facade

itself. There may have been a third-story room used for musicians or storage of certain properties. It seems certain that a canopy, known as the "heavens," stretched out from the upper level of the facade (also known as the "tiring house," probably because the actors dressed—"attired"—there), supported by two pillars rising up from the stage. There was certainly one, and possibly more, trapdoors in the stage—allowing for such scenes as the gravediggers' scene in *Hamlet*. So, the whole concept of the stage can be seen as a metaphor for the universe, with heaven above, earth on the *platea*, and hell below. At the same time, the facade of the stage was a concrete, if neutral, reminder of everyday reality: the metaphysical was firmly anchored in the mundane.

In front of the stage platform, within the open yard of the theatre, stood the groundlings, or "stinkards," the poorer and possibly less educated members of the audience (though students from the Inns of Court and apprentices would also be there). The wealthier citizens—shopkeepers, professional people, and petty nobility—sat in the galleries within the surrounding walls of the theatre. A potential audience of two thousand persons has been conjectured for the Globe, with no one member more than fifty feet from the stage—an incredible potential for intimacy with such a large audience. The audience was visible and indeed palpable to the actors. It shared common daylight, weather, experience of life. If no longer a direct participant, as in the medieval theatre, it was definitely more than a spectator: it "assisted in" the dramatic event in the true sense of the French term describing an audience's function—*assister à*.

Little stage furniture, scenic elements, or properties were used for the staging of Shakespeare's plays.[3] Although certain actions and locales were loosely defined by freestanding scenery—trees and walls are found in property lists of the day—the emphasis is essentially upon the actor, the verse, and

---

[3] In comparison with ours, Shakespeare's world was uncluttered with objects: a room furnished only with a chair and table would not have seemed particularly bare.

the audience's imagination. As the prologue to *Henry V* says, "Let us . . . On your imaginary forces work." The broad, unlocalized stage was a fluid and flexible area that through interaction of the actor and the audience's imagination, could represent whatever the playwright wished. A situation could be specific, loosely defined, or unlocalized. Eighty percent of Shakespeare's scenes simply require actors and a bare stage—not even a stool is called for in the text. In several plays Shakespeare tells us where we are—the forest of Arden, Illyria, Troy—and in many instances where the next scene is moving to. The beginning and ending of scenes are demarked by actors entering or leaving the stage. The fiction of a scene is created by the actor, and when he leaves, the "verbal scenery" dissolves with him "into air, into thin air," as Prospero tells us, "like the baseless fabric of this vision."

Shakespeare's theatre is a "vision" of life, and in one sense a baseless fabric, and "insubstantial pageant," for it is founded in inspiration and imagination. Yet because it is created by men and is compounded of their deeds, it is firmly anchored in a tangible reality. The stage is a metaphor. It stands for rather than represents a situation. Can one put Illyria, Cleopatra's Egypt, Othello's Venice, or Lear's world upon an "unworthy scaffold"? They are too large to be encompassed: concreteness would minimize them and limit the scope of Shakespeare's action. So he says "imagine," and "suppose," and in the blinking of an eye the audience is transported from England to France, from Egypt to Rome, with the exciting tension that such quick apposition of action can produce. All this magic is, of course, the responsibility of the actor. Without the help of Prospero's staff but with the aid of Shakespeare's language, he must draw the given circumstances for the audience, playing with his tongue upon the eye of their imagination.

Shakespeare's stage is a platform from which to tell a story. The action presses on swiftly—the "two hours traffic"—to its climax. There is in Shakespeare's work a constant forward sweep that requires an unimpeded presentation. The flexible unlocalized stage and the essentially neutral facade is the perfect environment. It allows for expansion, magnitude, ceremony, as well as the most direct, intimate playing. The world of Shakespeare's plays is compounded one-half of the life of man, one-half of the presence of God; one-half of history and legend, and one-half of fantasy. The result is a vision of reality twice as large as life itself. The metaphorical space could encompass this. It could physically allow for the ritual and ceremony, the splendid pomp that was part of the Elizabethan experience. Its metaphysical quality could give breathing space to the magnitude of the moral issues Shakespeare illustrates in his work. But if it could be spacious enough to imitate the universe, the stage could equally be as intimate as a conversation between two persons. An actor talking to the audience from the limit of the thrust could reduce the space, the whole world, to the simplicity and directness of one-to-one communication.

What has been called the "unlicensed geography" of the Shakespearean stage allows actor and audience to traverse the world and be wherever and whatever the imagination presumes. It is a space to tell, excitingly and vigorously, "sad stories of the death of Kings." The actions, motivations, and situations come from the text. They are as diverse as the nature of Elizabethan life, as the reality of the audience's everyday experience. Neoclassical values never had as strong an influence upon the drama or, indeed, the life style of England, as they did in Italy and France. And the unity we find in Shakespeare's work is a poetic unity, not a spatial and temporal unity that attempts (again in the service of verisimilitude—truth to "nature") to equate the use of time and space on the stage with that of "reality." Poetic unity is a unity of action; the totality of impressions makes the event whole.

It is important for an actor to accept the diversity of impressions the playwright has unified by his total vision. He will not, then, make the mistake of applying too rigid a logic to his role, but will see himself as part of the all-embracing sweep of the play. At the same time, the actor *is* the prime focus of the Shakespearean theatre. The bare stage works as the unadorned walls of an art gallery, to isolate the essential thing—the actor. It requires him to encompass and manipulate many contrasts. There is a pattern of vigorous, fluid movement: from exit to entrance; above to below; locale to locale. The doors, windows, recesses, traps allow for and demand a diverse and dynamic use of space. As opposed to the central focus of the Greek stage, the Elizabethan is constantly moving, unified and given a core by the central action of the play. Like this fluid pattern, the quality of playing is equally diverse—at once magnificent and intimate; formal, ceremonious, yet physically flexible; a world of activity, a world of contrasts, bringing both great challenge and great opportunity to the actor.

Form. In keeping with both the sensibility of the time and the nature of the stage, Shakespeare's work tends towards open rather than closed forms. The Elizabethan period had a centrifugal sense of life, of a world moving outwards from the core. It took the enquiring thrust of humanism from the Renaissance, but not the center-seeking unity of neoclassical dramatic form. The shape of Shakespeare's tragedies is a concurrence of classical, medieval, and Renaissance energies, integrated by his personal genius. The classical tradition of Seneca was mingled with the popular inheritance from medieval forms. The legacy of ritual and symbol, of clowning and witchcraft, the religiosity of the mystery cycles that took heaven, earth, and hell for their stage, lent dynamic to Shakespeare's sense of Latin forms. The epic structure of the native drama absorbed the quality of Senecan tragedy, in which the hero contemplates his suffering. This led to a nuclear rather than a linear form, unified by action but with a fine contempt for limitations of time or space. It was a pre-Cartesian sensibility, and we must beware of expecting it to be logically sequential or intellectually explicable. It is intended more to be experienced than analyzed. Stanislavski, whose linear and analytic method was splendidly useful for the proscenium-oriented, neo-Aristotelian realism of the late nineteenth and early twentieth centuries, confessed himself defeated by Shakespeare's plays, which illustrate the varied possibilities of human experience and may not mean any *one* thing. Imagery, symbolism, thought, action, character are all interrelated and cannot be viewed in isolation. Character, especially, must be seen in the context of the whole play, not as a psychological integer. There is no time, nor is there the necessity for things to be fully and minutely explored, as with Chekhov.

Elizabethan life was simpler, more external, not as privately introspective as our own—life "happened" more and was examined less. The form of Shakespeare's plays recapitulates this. There is a flux, a dynamic structure of scenes, that sweeps the action forward to a climactic crest. We compared the action rhythm of Greek tragedy to that of a broad, full, deeply flowing river. The Shakespearean is swifter, shallower, drawing tributaries into the mainstream as it flows increasingly swiftly downhill to plunge over a waterfall and find peace in a deep, tranquil pool below.

The Shakespearean form, then, is a swiftly flowing coherence of contrasts. The apposition of opposing qualities—movements and soliloquy, humor and suffering, violence and tenderness, verse and colloquial speech, formality and physical energy, philosophy and clowning—creates a sense of tension and conflict that is the heart of drama. Lacking the coolly intense compression of the best of Greek tragedy, the all-embracing unity of Shakespeare's work reflects the multiplicity, the reinforcing contrasts of Elizabethan life, integrated by the poet's own idea of human action. The form is related to the experience and finds a perfect environment in the theatrical space.

Language. Shakespeare's language is poetic—mostly blank verse, some rhymed verse and some prose—but the total effect is a poetry of the theatre. Theatrical poetry is active and functional, not simply decorative. Cocteau has said that it should not be tenuous like gossamer, but thick like the rigging of a ship and visible at a distance. Poetry, while able to express the nature of man's existence, is not limited by the details of everyday reality. Poetry both simplifies and sophisticates the portrayal of human conduct. It strips away day-to-day irrelevancies like indigestion and dandruff—if there are bathrooms in tragedy, they are for Agamemnon to be murdered in. At the same time, it extends the range and quality of human comprehension, expressing and defining patterns of thought and feelings otherwise inexpressible and indefinable. The use of verse gives the world of tragedy a certain distance from the audience. It invests characters and actions with a special magnitude. Royal and heroic characters are higher than mere men in the Chain of Being, and their style of speaking reflects their elevation. Kings speak in verse; common mortals reply in prose. George Steiner makes a splendid conceit out of this in discussing Shakespeare's tragedy *Richard II*.[4] He suggests it is a play in which two languages fail to communicate. Richard is a royal poet defeated by baronial prose. He attempted to enforce an abstract, poetic truth on a pragmatic and prosaic political reality.

Shakespeare's poetry, like the form of his drama, is essentially active, multifaceted, and sinewy. The sound supplies the meaning; the structure displays the content. The actor must be aware of the total shape of the poetry,[5] and how that shape is constructed. The technical devices—the patterns, images,

and rhythms built into the verse—contain clues to the portrayal of character and the nature of the dramatic action.

Technical Structure. The fundamental feature of Shakespeare's poetry is his use of blank verse written in iambic pentameter. Each line breaks down into five "feet," and each foot has two syllables of which the second is stressed. To take as an example perhaps the most famous line in Shakespeare: "To be, or not to be, that is the question" (*Hamlet*, Act III, Scene i). This line scans into five feet.[6] To be,/ or not/ to be,/ that is/ the question." Each foot should have two syllables, and, for the line to be a perfect iambic pentameter, the stresses would be marked as follows: "Tŏ bē,/ ŏr nŏt/ tŏ bē;/ thăt īs/ the question." The crescent demarks the unstressed syllable and the bar the stressed syllable—giving the unstressed/stressed pattern of the iambic foot. However, the line is not perfectly iambic, as it has eleven syllables. "Question" has two syllables, not one as marked above, and is a complete foot in itself. This gives the fourth foot of the line three syllables: "thăt ĭs thĕ," with stress on "that." This foot is called a dactyl (discussed below). The fifth foot, "question," will now scan "quēstiŏn," making the scansion of the whole line "Tŏ bē,/ ŏr nŏt/ tŏ bē;/ thăt ĭs thĕ/ quēstiŏn." There are several reasons for this. The sense of the line is Hamlet framing an existential problem for himself. He is working something out and has put his finger on it—which leads to a stress on *that* (what I have come to realize) is the question. In technical terms "that" is in apposition to the phrase "to be or not to be," and balances it. It is also the fulcrum of the line, balancing "to be or not to be" and "question." "Is" performs neither of these functions; being a slight word, it lacks the weight to balance the line. "That" also comes after the natural break in the line—the caesura

---

[4] George Steiner, *The Death of Tragedy*, New York: Hill & Wang, 1963, p. 242.

[5] As is said to musicians, "Don't play the notes; play the music."

[6] *Scansion* is the term given to the analysis of verse to discover the meter—the number of feet per line and stresses per foot.

(of which more below). Thus stress falls rhythmically upon the word, emphasizing the whole phrase. To stress "is" would be an artificial imposition upon the natural rhythm of the line, as would stressing "the." Either choice would disrupt the flow and balance of the line as it illustrates the ponderous, reflective quality of Hamlet's action. The fifth foot of Hamlet's line—"questiŏn"—has become a trochee. This is an inverted iamb, and is the most common form of variation in Shakespeare's verse.

Verse and Human Rhythm. Both the iamb and the trochee relate to basic rhythms of the human body. The iamb is the even, lively beat of the human heart—di dum. The trochee is the fuller, more reflective rhythm of our breathing—the long drawing in of breath and the quicker exhalation. English speech falls naturally into iambic pentameter. You may well speak the meter in your daily communication without realizing it—just as Monsieur Jourdain, Molière's Bourgeois Gentilhomme, did not realize he had been speaking prose all his life! A simple sentence such as "You came home in the middle of the night" does, in fact, scan into an iambic pentameter. This can be useful to actors who forget their lines when playing Shakespeare—it is not too difficult to improvise the verse. However, this should not be relied upon, as the average actor is unlikely to do it as well as Shakespeare!

That the natural rhythm of the English language reflects the rhythm of the heartbeat gives it a swift, strong, flowing quality that has an immediate and direct effect upon the listener. It is a romantic and visceral rhythm that befits the sensibility of Shakespeare's England. In contrast the principal verse rhythm of the French language is the Alexandrine, which is a longer line, perfectly balanced with a rational, logical structure. This reflects the more neoclassical quality of the French sensibility. In both instances it is important to note how much the rhythms of verse, as opposed to the flatness of prose, are

a reflection of and have a strong emotional impact upon human rhythms: the very sound of verse can tell us much, even when we do not understand the intellectual meaning. This is a point of fundamental significance to the actor performing Shakespeare.

Apart from the iamb and the trochee, there are four other foot structures the actor is likely to come across in Shakespeare's verse. The pyrrhic, which has two unstressed syllables, $\cup \cup$, and is the weakest foot; the anapest, which has two unstressed and one stressed syllable, $\cup \cup -$; the dactyl, which is opposite the anapest with one stressed, then two unstressed syllables; and the spondee, the strongest foot of all, with two stresses, $- -$. Scansion is not an exact science: one actor's choice will lead him to stress words or syllables that another might underplay. Again, stress is relative: the amount of stress placed upon stressed syllables will vary from foot to foot. Readings would tend to be monotonous if this were not the case. Actors should develop an instinct for reading verse, if they have not already done so. They will then feel the inherent rhythms; the line speaks to them as much as they speak the line. The more one reads verse aloud, the more this instinct will grow. It is certainly not necessary, formally, to scan every line in every part—to say "Ah yes, that's a spondee," or an anapest, or whatever.

Verse and Meaning. The basic iambic pentameter flows easily off the tongue. But, the more sophisticated and subtle the character, the more Shakespeare deviates from the iambic norm. The deviations are all there for a purpose, and are important clues to the nature of the character, his actions, and his reactions. Scanning the more complex lines not only clarifies the meaning, but can reveal the effect of the line's rhythms upon an audience. A simple example of this is the line King Lear speaks upon discovering the dead Cordelia: "Nevĕr, nēvĕr, nēvĕr, nēvĕr, nēvĕr." This is a perfect trochaic pentameter:

"Nĕvĕr,/ nēvĕr,/ nēvĕr,/ nēvĕr,/ nēvĕr." It is a mournful, falling meter, perfectly expressive of sorrow. It falls upon the audience with the sound of the tolling of a bell, as at a funeral.

The division of a line into feet will not always coincide with whole words. Scansion, the meter, is related to the rhythm of the line, not directly to its intellectual meaning. To quote a famous line from *Romeo and Juliet*: "Bŭt sōft./ Whāt līght/ thrŏugh yōn/ dĕr wīn/ dŏw breaks?" This is a perfect iambic pentameter, but "yonder" and "window" are split to achieve the meter of the line. When the natural rhythm of the line works against the integrity of the words, this creates a tension between the listener's intellectual understanding and his rhythmical appreciation of the line: it sets up some particular effect or emphasizes particular qualities. In the line quoted, "soft," "light," and "breaks"—the words that carry the weight of the action—are the words stressed by the meter. "Soft" and "light" also suggest some qualities of Juliet herself.

Punctuation. We have already mentioned the caesura. This is the major pause in the line of verse. Unlike the French Alexandrine, it will only infrequently come in the middle of the line, more often at the end of the second or third foot, but it may come anywhere. In some instances there is no major pause, as in "Never, never, never, never, never," whose regularity and pounding monotony is the effect the playwright wants. The placement of the caesura gives shape to the line. Lacking the formal precision of the Alexandrine, the pentameter has the virtue of flexibility, but this flexibility must be controlled by the playwright and the grouping of words into patterns and images by the caesura performs this function. The caesura also indicates where rhythmical pauses should be taken—thus giving emphasis to particular parts of the line—and is a possible place for the taking of a breath.

The caesura is, of course, a form of punctuation. Punctuation in the Shakespearean texts is often a tricky business. The Elizabethans had a somewhat more cavalier approach to punctuation than later ages, and this, together with inaccuracies, ambiguities, and corruptions in the early editions of Shakespeare's work, has led to much controversy. The punctuation given by scholars in the major editions of Shakespeare's plays is an intelligent guide to the actor, but, as with the caesura, sense, syntax, and rhythm are the best guide to the shaping of the lines.

Elision. In considering punctuation we notice that not all of Shakespeare's lines are end-stopped, or concluded by some kind of punctuated pause—comma, colon, period, or whatever. Often the sense and rhythmical nature of one line runs into the next without pause, to create a larger pattern of meaning. This run-on effect—enjambement—will occur very readily when lines have a "feminine" ending: the last syllable of the line is unstressed, which gives a bounce from the second-to-last syllable of one line straight into the next line. Sometimes syllables are given very little or no stress, and are not voiced at all. This process is known as elision, and is used to keep the rhythmical meter of the line. For example, a speech by Macbeth (which we will use more fully below to illustrate some of the technical qualities we have discussed) has the line "Who should against his murderer shut the door." Giving full value to all syllables, we would scan this: "Whō shōuld/ ăgaīnst/ hĭs mūr/ dĕrĕr shūt/ thĕ dōor." This would give the line one more syllable than the ten syllables of the penatmeter form, make the fourth foot an anapest, and break the rhythmical flow of the line. It is possible to argue that Shakespeare wanted to emphasize "murderer," and thus employed the "hypermetrical" (more-than-ten-syllable) line. But the anapest seems to hold up the line and interrupt the flow of Macbeth's argument, and it seems preferable to elide one of the syllables in "murderer," making it "murdrer," and the fourth foot of the line a normal iamb. In the opposite case, there are occasions in our normal speech where we would elide syllables that in Shakespeare's verse structure must be given a full value to complete the meter. An example of this comes in a famous speech by Mark Antony in Act III, Scene ii of *Julius Caesar*. The speech contains the line: "The good is oft interred with their bones." In order for this line to become an iambic pentameter, "interred," which today would be pronounced "interd," must be given three syllables, so that the line will scan: "The good/ is oft/ inter/ red with/ their bones."

Scansion and Sense: An Example. To pull together and illustrate the use of the technical attributes of blank verse, we are giving below a scanned and annotated passage from *Macbeth*, Act I, Scene vii.

If it/ were done/ when 'tis/ done then/ 'twere well

(Attack upon the speech seems to demand emphasis upon "if," which gives a trochee in the first foot. Emphasis upon "when" also makes the third foot a trochee. The caesura will come in the middle of the fourth foot, laying especial emphasis upon "then.")

It were done/ quickly./ If th'as/ sassi/ nation

(This is a hypermetrical line with either eleven or twelve syllables. It seems to flow better with eleven, which is achieved by eliding "the" in the third foot and making "th'as" into one syllable. The first foot works as an anapest, reemphasizing "done." The caesura comes with the period before "if" and emphasizes that word again. The line is mostly trochees and has a feminine ending, with "tion" running into the next line.)

Could tram/ mel up/ the con/ sequence/ and catch

(an iambic pentameter; caesura before "and")

With his/ surcease/ success;/ that but/ this blow

(The fifth foot seems to call for a spondee, "this blow"—once and for all—being the crux of Macbeth's thinking. The caesura comes before "that.")

Might be/ the be-/ all and/ the end-/ all here

(We have scanned this as an iambic line, but there are possible variations: the first foot could be read as a trochee with stress upon "might;" the last foot could become a spondee, which would give three stresses at the end of the line—"end-all here." The latter variation slows down the line and deemphasizes "here," which Shakespeare reemphasizes in the next line. So although it is a conceivable choice, we think the iamb at the end of the line, with strong emphasis upon "here" [which is reinforced by the caesura before "here"] is the better reading.)

But here,/ upon/ this bank/ and shoal/ of time

(It seems that "here" and "this" are in apposition and should both be stressed, giving a spondee in the third foot. The caesura is after "here," lending it further stress.)

We'd jump/ the life/ to come./ But in these/ cases

(This is another hypermetrical line with a feminine ending. The fourth foot could be a dactyl, which would mean deemphasizing "these," and seems to go against the sense of the speech. We cannot emphasize both "but" and "these" without throwing away "cases": the scansion would have to be "But in/ these cases." This is a good example of the necessities of scansion telling us where the emphasis must be.)

Further Technical Effects. The speech continues, and we will deal with it again more fully in the section on performance demands. The examples we have given cover most of the technical aspects of the verse. In this particular passage the deviations from iambic pentameter show a certain complexity of character and thought process that we will discuss further when dealing with approach to character. It remains here to mention a couple of further aspects of Shakespeare's use of verse: the employment of rhyming couplets and the splitting of lines between characters. Shakespeare's rhyming couplets tend to be found more in his earlier and less mature work. They are by definition more formal and less subtle and flexible than blank vese. When used within the body of a scene or in the middle of a speech, as in *Richard II*, they tend to indicate a formal, ritualistic, poetical sensibility: a character, or situation, less connected with everyday reality, but consciously "poetical" or meant to be ceremonious. The couplet is usually found at the end of a speech, and particularly at the end of a scene. Act I, Scene vii of *Macbeth*, from which we took our preceding example, ends with a couplet spoken by Macbeth:

> Away, and mock the time with fairest show.
> False face must hide what the false heart doth know.

Couplets such as this sum up or emphasize important points of action, give a strong completion as the actor moves to exit, and also indicate to the audience a change of scene. As with all Shakespeare's techniques, the couplet has specific purposes and should be given full value, not thrown away by the actor.

Shakespeare frequently shares a pentameter line with two characters. This happens consistently in the *Macbeth* scene from which we are quoting. There is an urgent discussion, not to say an argument, going on between Lady Macbeth and Macbeth. The completion of one character's line by the other character gives an impetus, an almost stychomythic quality to the scene, despite the length of the speeches. A particularly good example is:

Lady Macbeth: And dash'd the brains out had I so sworn as you
Have done to this.
Macbeth: If we should fail?
Lady Macbeth: We fail.

The last three lines are one complete pentameter shared over three speeches. The lines must be taken as one; the build shows tension, excitement, anticipation. Lines such as this and half lines completed by another character require no pause—being one line. Divided lines usually call for quick, overlapping delivery. Note how the last one hundred lines of *Lear* are broken up to reflect the turmoil of the action. However, when a half line at the end of one speech is followed by a complete line at the beginning of another, a pause seems to be indicated. The incomplete line is marked by silent beats that complete the pentameter. There are examples of this in *Othello*, Act III, Scene iii, where Iago is laying seeds of jealousy in Othello's mind. Othello has such short lines as "O misery," and "Dost thou say so?" These are followed by complete lines from Iago, and the nature of the scene suggests that Iago lets Othello stew in his juice of uncertainty before replying. Othello's lines are completed by short pauses in which he can be seen to be thinking, worrying over what Iago is saying.

Summation of Structure. Everything Shakespeare does with his verse has a purpose in furthering action and delineating character. The sense is revealed by the sound and shape of the lines. This applies equally when Shakespeare shifts from verse to prose, which we will deal with in the section on character. To sum up the technical characteristics of Shakespeare's verse that the actor should identify:

1. the scansion of the line into metrical feet, and the determination of the nature of these feet
2. the distinction between word divisions and foot divisions, and the dynamic tension this creates
3. the caesura in the line, with the emphasis this places upon words and phrases
4. such properties as elision and enjambment, which affect the rhythm of the line, and the grouping of lines into larger patterns
5. the use of rhyming couplets
6. the distribution of a pentameter line over more than one character or speech

Figures of Speech. We have already mentioned the function of rhetoric, not only in Elizabethan education but in the life of the society. Shakespeare was brought up in this tradition and inevitably incorporated it into his work. For the preachers, lawyers, teachers, politicians, and playwrights of the Elizabethan period, speech was an affirmation of man's dignity, his superiority over the beasts. It was the great civilizing force, and beauty in discourse was calculated to win men over to virtuous actions. Richness of expression and richness of life experience were equated. Rhetoric was the core of humanistic education, and the tools and disciplines of rhetoric illuminated speech and furthered its primary function, which was to play upon feelings and move men to action.

Shakespeare had an enormous vocabulary of rhetorical figures that he incorporated into his verse. It is not our purpose to give a lesson in rhetoric, but the ability to recognize some of the major figures of speech is useful to the actor. Various forms of repetition is one of Shakespeare's main devices. Repetition of words at the beginning of sequential sentences is a common form of emphasis. This may be taken further, in a form known as "parison" (remembering the name is not

important, unless it helps to identify the function), where there is an almost exact correspondence between two sentences:

Was ever woman in this humour woo'd?
Was ever woman in this humour won?

These lines from *Richard III*, Act I, Scene ii, emphasize by repetition and add an irony by the antithesis of the last words in each line. Antithesis is another figure of speech, which by opposing words and images balances them, lets each emphasize the other, and can show calculation and an ironic sensibility.

There is also a form of punning repetition, which repeats a word but with a change of meaning. This figure often reveals a sad irony, as with Othello's line in Act V, Scene ii:

Put out the light, and then put out the light.

Finally, there is a very active form of repetition, which is illustrated by the lines Henry V speaks after the Dauphin has mockingly sent him tennis balls:

For many a thousand widows
Shall this, his mock, mock out of their dear
  husbands;
Mock mother's from their sons, mock castles
  down; (Act I, Scene ii)

The repetition of "mock" gives it the feeling of a riposte, a blow. It creates the rhythm both of a tennis match and the firing of a series of cannonballs. "Mock" is also used here in an onomatopoeic manner, whereby the sound of a word suggests the sense in which it is used: "mock" becoming the sound of a ball striking a racket. Onomatopoeia is a figure of speech often used by Shakespeare, as in Juliet's famous line "Gallop apace, you fiery-footed steeds." The word "gallop" creates the sound of horses galloping, which is reinforced by the repetition of "p" in "apace."

The use of "fiery-footed" in Juliet's line is yet another rhetorical device—alliteration. This, again, is a form of repetition: of the initial sounds of words in close proximity. It is used for emphasis, and gives a rhythmical reinforcement to the words. In our example it also has an onomatopoeic value in that the repetition of the "f" sounds creates, in itself, the breathy attack of fire.

A very calculated rhetorical form that employs repetition is climax. Claudius, in Act V, Scene ii of *Hamlet*, has this speech:

And let the kettle to the trumpet speak,
The trumpet to the cannoneer without,
The cannons to the Heavens, the Heavens to
  the earth,
Now drinks the King to Hamlet.

There is a climbing ladder of degree in the speech: the picking up and repetition of "trumpet," "cannon," and "Heavens" builds to the climax of the King drinking to Hamlet. The quality of the speech builds the splendor of the ceremonial, and the hyperbole indicates the somewhat hollow pomposity of Claudius. There is a calculated formality in the speech, which indicates the sentiment is not deeply felt. Indeed, the king believes he is drinking to Hamlet's death. All of this illustrates Claudius's character in action.

The last rhetorical figure we will mention is technically known as paronamasia. It occurs when two words are used in apposition and the sense is radically altered by a change of letter or syllable. The most famous and sophisticated example is in *Hamlet*, Act I, Scene ii, in which Hamlet's stepfather calls him "son," and he replies: "A little more than kin, and less than kind." "Kind" here being used both in the sense of "like" or "relative," and "sympathetic" or "good-willed." This figure of speech lends itself to irony, or draws attention to opposing feelings within a character, as when Iago employs it in Act III, Scene iii of *Othello*:

But, O, what damned minutes tells he o'er
Who *dotes*, yet *doubts*, suspects, yet strongly
  loves.

Our intention here is not to get the actor to heavily emphasize Shakespeare's figures of speech, but simply to be aware of their presence and function. They go together with the rhythms and imagery of the verse in helping the actor create character and action.

Imagery. Painting with words. This is probably the best description of a poet's use of imagery. Whereas a journalist might have said that "Cleopatra's barge gleamed brightly as it sailed down the Nile," Shakespeare, through Enobarbus, tells us: "The barge she sat in, like a burnish'd throne Burn'd on the water. The poop was beaten gold." The appeal of imagery is total. It is not just to our intellect, but to our rhythms and emotions—the whole inner vocabulary of seen and intuited experience. In Shakespeare's great tragedies image after image envelops us, illustrating the meaning of the action and displaying the life of the characters. Through imagery the poet taps resources that are not limited by discursive thought. He can, with an image, add levels and dimensions to an inch of verse that could not be equaled by a yard of prose.

The presence of imagery is recognized more easily than figures of speech, so we will illustrate its use only briefly, and show how it plays an active part in Shakespeare's design. To take a further example from *Macbeth*, Act III, Scene ii:

            Come, seeling night
Scarf up the tender eye of pitiful day
And with thy bloody and invisible hand
Cancel and tear to pieces that great bond

Which keeps me pale. Light thickens, and the
  crow
Makes wing to the rocky wood:
Good things of day begin to droop and drowse
While night's black agents to their preys do
  rouse.

The speech is a personification of night in imagistic form. We gain the experience of oncoming darkness: "night thickens" perfectly creates the feeling of the mellowing, opaque, less distinct light of dusk. It also has the resonances of "the plot thickens," which is what is happening to Macbeth, now plotting to kill Banquo and gradually sinking into the "darkness" of sin. The image of night seen as sewing up the eyelids of the tenderer-hearted day, gives us the feel of Macbeth's desire to keep his actions secret and the brutal manner in which he must constantly kill to achieve this. The night is also the night of Macbeth's soul; he is lost to the light of goodness—good now "droops and drowses" while he pursues his prey like an animal. The experience of the speech gives us the feeling and the understanding that Macbeth has become habitually brutalized; that violence is now a way of life; that he almost welcomes the darkness into which he is sinking as a way of forgetting that he once had a conscience. It would take a great deal of exposition or activity to convey all of this. It would also both lose force in the telling—lack the intensification of the close-packed verse—and be more limited in its appeal to our senses than the total, or "holistic," effect achieved by the verse images.

Shakespeare's imagery, though it certainly embellishes his verse, is not there for that purpose alone. It plays a direct part in delineating character, establishing situation, and furthering the action of the play. The imagery is the more impressive because much of it is taken from life in Elizabeth's time and, recognizably, our own—as opposed to the more ornate mythological allusions used by the neoclassical writers of Shakespeare's day. In the passage from *Macbeth* the references to crows, woods, and sewing are everyday and countrified. Wilson Knight, in illustrating Shakespeare's use of daily experience, tells of meeting two countrymen in Shakespeare's own county of Warwickshire in the 1950s. The men were repairing hedges. Knight asked them what they were doing, and was told: "Well, I roughhew the branches, while he shapes the ends." This country expression found its way four hundred years ago into Shakespeare's verse: "There's a Divinity that shapes our ends, roughhew them how we will" (*Hamlet*, Act V, Scene ii). Perhaps the most wholesale and perfect unity of idea, action, and imagery comes at the end of *The Tempest*, "probably" (i.e., to take into account those who argue for *Henry VIII*) Shakespeare's last play. Prospero has a valediction in Act IV, Scene i:

Our revels now are ended. These our actors,
As I foretold you, were all spirits and
Are melted into air, into thin air;
And, like the baseless fabric of this vision,
The cloud-capped towers, the gorgeous
  palaces,
The solemn temples, the great globe itself,
Yea, all which it inherit, shall dissolve
And, like this insubstantial pageant faded,
Leave not a rack behind. We are such stuff
As dreams are made on, and our little life
Is rounded with a sleep.

Here we have an extended image of the stage as a metaphor for life itself. What actors create is ephemeral, as is man's life; the play comes to an end, as must man's life. Man can no more grasp his own reality than the fantasy illusions of the stage. This was Prospero's swan song, as it was Shakespeare's own. Shakespeare lived upon the stage, as did Prospero, but, for an equally little life. Here, on this globe (which was the theatre's name), on this earth, on this stage did we once live, and were illumined and aware. Now there is nothing to come but dust and sleep. There could hardly be a better example of integrated and active images.

Shakespeare's language is lyrical, dynamic, and flexible. Based in the iambic pentameter, a rhythm close to that of everyday speech, it incorporates figures from the tradition of rhetoric, and images that rose from Shakespeare's own poetic soul. The strength, color, and sinewy masculinity of its Elizabethan roots were leavened by the eloquent spirit of the Renaissance. It is essentially an active language in which shape, structure, and rhythm combine to make the required impression of character and action upon the audience. We will look more closely at this when discussing character, but may note here how the structure and the use of language create the kind of balance of contrasts and dynamic tension found in the other areas discussed. The language contains transcendental poetry and vernacular prose; formality and colloquialism; soliloquy and stychomythia; rhetorical forms and coarse humor; poetic imagery and direct information. As in sensibility, structure, and space, so we now find in speech that dynamic integration of opposing forces that typified the Elizabethan period and informed its "idea" of theatre.

Costume. Such evidence as we have from sketches, contemporary references to performance, and the plays themselves suggests that the Elizabethan actor was the "glass of fashion," wearing clothes from the everyday wardrobe of the time. There were two basic principles of Elizabethan stage costumes. First, though based in the everyday, they were more splendid that it. Second, close attention was paid to decorum and verisimilitude: the costumes should be seen as fitting the rank and station of the character. But, as we have already suggested, the verisimilitude of the day was not detailed

or precise; it was geared more to a typical expectation. Thus, although care was taken to fit the richness and splendor of a costume to the rank of the wearer—royalty would wear purple velvet, ermine and satins; friars, the simple brown habit of their calling—little attention was paid to historical accuracy or geographical variety. Julius Caesar would wear Elizabethan costume with possibly a toga over it; Othello, Elizabethan clothes with perhaps a moorish headdress. Such emblematic identification was the furthest concession to "realism" made by the Elizabethan stage.

However, the audience was not concerned about realistic detail; it accepted the conventions of the day. What the audience did expect was that the costumes should be evidently rich and expensive. This was part of the show. It was an age of splendor in dress, and this had to be outdone upon the stage. Costumes were the heaviest expenditure in an acting company's budget. It has been suggested that members of the nobility either gave their castoff clothing directly to players, or to their servants, who then sold them to the actors. In any event, the costumes were frequently trimmed with gold and pearls, and three layers of velvet were often used for a slashed doublet. Remember, the audience was close and the performance given in the light of day. The modern costumer's art of using cheap fabrics that can appear costly under lighting was not available to the Elizabethans.

The male dress generally consisted of a shirt with fancy cuffs that were pulled out to trim the sleeves of the overgarment—the doublet. The doublet emphasized the shape of the male upper body, padded in the shoulders and chest and narrowing down into the waist. This gave a sense of strength and dignity that was furthered by the ruff, worn around the neck, which meant the head was held high with a certain arrogance. Breeches were either full, like a pumpkin, or worn tight on the thigh (in which case they were known as Venetians). Beneath these

The foursquare dignity of Sir Walter Raleigh and his son in
Elizabethan clothing.

National Portrait Gallery, England.

were close-fitting hose, and flat-heeled shoes or boots for riding and rough activity. There was a strong emphasis upon the leg that suggested virility and sexual potency. Hats were decorative as well as utilitarian (in a cold, wet climate). Embellished with feathers, they added to the rakish arrogance of the set of the head. The Elizabethan male was something of a peacock in his sense of dress, but it was to emphasize a pride in showy masculinity. Because Drake wore earrings it should not be forgotten that he pirated the Caribbean or sank the Spanish fleet. The time of Raleigh, Essex, and Sydney put English ships around the globe, gained military influence in Europe, and laid the foundations of the future empire. The elaborate costumes and heavy jewelry showed anything but a lack of masculine force.

Female dress was as heavy and ornate as that of the male, but much more binding and constricting. The lower part of the body was the freest, though covered by layers of petticoats and skirts over a farthingale—a hooped construction that gave a bell shape to the body below the waist, extending the hips well beyond the normal body line. This gave the impression, when the woman moved, of a procession rather than any sense of body movement. The upper body was bound from below the breasts to the lower stomach by corsets and a "stomacher." The latter was a triangular piece of wood that pushed up the breasts and pointed down towards the

The portrait of Queen Elizabeth's sister Mary shows the ornate heaviness of female clothing and the erectness it gave to body posture.

Isabella Stewart Gardner Museum, Boston.

crotch. The gown, which went over all this, was usually highly ornamented with pearls and other gems, and of rich material. It revealed the upper breast, had large puffed sleeves, and was often slashed at the front to show the fancy petticoats. With the gown went a large ruff or a high wing-collar. Head-dresses were high, encrusted with jewels, and often topped with a small ornamental hat.

Thus, the formality, dignity, and pride of the male was repeated, but without his freedom of movement. The woman was bound into a masculine sense of uprightness (as a "good" woman should be). She showed a strength, but one that befitted her place in society. Of course, younger women such as Juliet and Ophelia would be less physically restrained—but, then, they died for their freedom! Shakespearean women who at-

Pride, power, and dignity are shown in this costume designed by Robert Morgan for a Pacific Conservatory of the Performing Arts production of *Hamlet*.

tained a certain informality are to be found in the comedies, not the tragedies. They did this by adopting masculine clothing and wearing it with the kind of pubescent virility that might be expected of the boys who played them.

In general, the Elizabethan dress worn on Shakespeare's stage was costly, dignified, and ornate, and emphasized an essentially masculine pride and strength. Note that even the feminine ideal—Queen Elizabeth herself—showed a masculine force, and was childless. The dress reflected both the sensibility of the age and the nature of Shakespeare's language: rooted in the everyday but heightened and embellished, formal yet flexible, forceful and flowing. The stage costuming also contained the kind of contrasts that we have found in all areas of Shakespeare's theatre—being both street wear yet highly glamorized, democratic yet exhalted, real but fantastical and removed.

PERFORMANCE DEMANDS

We don't, finally, *know* how the actor performed Shakespeare's plays. Future students of theatre may get a better idea of the nature of acting during the more recent past, because performances are now committed to film. But even here there's a problem, for one of two things tends to happen: the actors adopt a filmic technique, or, if a stage performance is filmed "straight," the camera alters the dimensions and perspectives of the acting performances and we cannot get from the resulting film a true sense of the theatrical dynamic that informs an actor's work. Thus, it is likely that some reconstruction will always have to be done to gain a sense of the performance style of any theatrical period.

Such reconstruction will rely upon the clues in those areas we have just discussed, which allow us now to draw some specific conclusions as to the way an actor may approach the performance of Shakespeare's work. Our enquiry into the sensibility of the period, theatrical space, dramatic form,

linguistic structure, and stage costuming has consistently identified certain qualities, such as dynamism and formality, simplicity and embellishment, muscularity and lyricism. These seemingly contrasting properties are a function of the Elizabethan period's place as a cultural watershed, in which deep-rooted popular traditions and newly discovered Renaissance values came into contact, interpenetrated, and created new forms. One of these forms was the professional Elizabethan theatre, and we can expect to find the qualities we have discovered reflected in the Shakespearean actor's work.

Dynamic Formality. The physical nature of the Elizabethan stage was geared to emphasizing the actor as the prime element in performance. The actor moves the audience with his body and his voice, and, technically, the most obvious influence upon the actor's physical movements will be his costume. The male costume emphasized masculinity—broad shoulders, full chest, strong legs—and a formal sense of self-importance, with a strong, erect carriage. The weight of the doublet and the wearing of a ruff would eliminate small turns of the head and lead to full turns of the body, giving a strong, upright emphasis to body movement. The heavy breeches and free, exposed legs indicate wide-legged stances, strong stage purchase with the feet, and long, firm strides. The actor would be very solid in his possession of his stage space, and when he moved it would be definite, with purpose—no shuffling of feet, or shifting of weight from leg to leg giving a weak, uncertain air. Muscular legs were a part of male physical attraction, and consciousness of the leg would mean the adoption of deliberate positions for both standing and sitting. Elizabethan chairs had tall, straight backs, an indication of how people were expected to sit: once again, in an erect, dignified manner with the male leg well displayed—one leg forward and slightly turned out, the other back with the knee bent, and a hand possibly resting on the thigh. This posture communicated a sense of purposeful ease, a man dignified yet ready to move quickly into action.

The corset, stomacher, and ruff give the women an even more erect, contained, and formal stance than the men. Small movements were not possible. Turning the head necessitated turning the body, and turning the body meant manipulating the large expanse of farthingale and skirts. The farthingale also prevented the arms from being held loosely at the sides of the body. Rather they were held forward, the lower arms and hands curving down towards the point of the stomacher. Walking was a smooth, even "process" so that awkward swaying of the skirts could be avoided and the corset and stomacher prevented any forward bending from the waist, further emphasizing the upright carriage. This meant women had somehow to back into chairs and sit on the forward edge to prevent the skirt from billowing up and revealing the leg. Though some of this might sound awkward for both men and women, it should be remembered that it was their everyday dress and manner, and would be comfortable to the wearer. The style of movement is precisely the physical adaptation to the nature of the costuming so that it does appear natural in both its formality and its impression of strength.

If the costuming lent an air of formality and strength to the performance, the stage space called for dynamism in movement. It

Powerful yet fluid physicality with poetic dynamic seen in this production of *Romeo and Juliet*. *Citizens' Theatre Company, Glasgow.*

was a fairly deep, wide, open stage thrusting into the audience, with entrances at the rear. The structure of the plays called for a continuous rhythm of playing. Scene followed upon scene with a rapid flow; actors often enter in mid-speech. No stopping for change of scenery; there may, indeed, have been no intermissions whatsoever. The space, then, was filled with a continuous activity: entrances and exits taken at different sides of the stage, and upper levels engaged in the action. All of this required dynamic, bold, and compelling movement from the actor. He had a lot of space to cover—space that thrust down to the audience and thrust the actor with it. The directness of much of Shakespeare demands that the actor get down front to contact the audience. He has distance to cover and must hold the audience while covering it. He has basically his own resources with which to do it: the stage is bare, he is the actor, and there

Strong leg purchase and concentrated power in this scene from *Coriolanus*.

Royal Shakespeare Company.

is the audience. The audience shared the same daylight and was aware of the ever present distractions. To impress and control such an audience required a strong and lively physical presence. The raised stage did give the actor a certain automatic dominance over the audience—and helped to reinforce the larger-than-life quality of the action—but he had to justify his position. He had to take the stage and fill it. All this is not to say that the actor was hurried or hyperbolic. Physically full, strong, bold, and masculine is a better description of the approach, and one that, again, fits what we know of the sensibility of the age.

The plays themselves contained strong passions and violent action, which lends further credence to our sense of physical dynamic in performance. The actor had to encompass the demands of the plays and live up to the expectations of the audience. As suggested, part of those expectations were based upon the tradition of the popular theatre—a tradition that the actors themselves would have assimilated, and that would have provided such training as they had received. The popular style was born in the open air—in the streets and inn yards. It was broad and vigorous and included expertise in dancing, vaulting, and tumbling. The jig was a popular addition to the tragedy on the theatre bill. It was a spectacular dance, requiring considerable physical agility and strength. However much the rough-and-ready nature of the popular tradition was refined—as companies were professionalized and joined by the rhetorically trained actors from the boys' companies—everything points to physical dynamism as one of the features of the Shakespearean theatre.

The physical dynamism was, of course, allied to the sense of formality—another tradition of the Elizabethan period. It was an age of ceremony. The ritualistic sensibility of the Middle Ages was still present in church, at court, and in the minds of much of the population. Elizabeth's "processes" through the country capitalized on this. Greetings and leave-takings were ceremonious. Bows, curtsies, hat removals, arm clasps, and "God be with you" had not yet been replaced by the offhand "Hi" of the casual present. Shakespeare's plays incorporated ritual and ceremonial entrances, which impressed the audiences by their dignity and were recognizably a part of everyday social manner. With violence and speed of action went nobility of character and elevated situation. It was a function of the time. Shakespeare's actors could integrate physical and formal qualities, just as they could dance the jig, the nimble galliard, and the stately pavane. There was no uncomfortable contradiction in this; it was all a part of the dynamic formality of the physical style.

Extended Directness. We have spoken of body movement, but what of gesture as a means of communicating action? The ability to gesture will be subject to costume limitations, and in this, once again, we find women more restricted than men. The fullness of the women's sleeves and the fitted nature of the bodice across the shoulders limit the movement of the upper arms and tend to emphasize the hands and lower arms. Such smaller, more delicate and contained gestures would, of course, be perfectly in keeping with what society regarded as women's place. Men were less restricted in this way, but the heaviness of the doublet's shoulder makes it likely that gestures did not extend the upper arm above the head. High gestures were probably made with the upper arm parallel to the ground and the lower arm extended upwards from the break at the elbow.

Large and fully extended gestures found to be a feature of the Greek theatre seem less likely in the Elizabethan. Size of gesture will be relative to space and the metaphysical scope of the drama. The Elizabethan theatre was smaller than the Greek, and the manner of performance was more direct and although aware of man's relationship to heavenly powers, not as God-oriented. The

Powerful but direct and contained gesture from actor Patrick Stewart, seen here in rehearsal.
Royal Shakespeare Company.

space of Shakespeare's theatre is less and the tempo is quicker: time flows swiftly rather than standing still, and the rhythms of the plays reinforce this. Thus, the tendency will be for quicker gestures with a powerful thrust, taken more directly to other actors and the audience. Shakespeare's characters, though elevated, are more human than the Greek; gestures will carry meaning in more everyday terms, but at the same time must fill the universality of the poetic time and space in which they are operating.

Perhaps we should mention here, although it is implicit in what we have said, that we do not subscribe to the view that Shakespearean acting is a form of recitation with a specific vocabulary of gestures based upon accepted rhetorical forms of the day such as found in Bulwer's *Chirologia* and *Chironomia*. It is certainly possible that the actors were aware of and did in fact use some of these conventional gestures. After all, all conventions (even clichés) are based at some time upon an observed reality before being heightened, refined, and finally petrified if

too far removed from the original human truth. However, if such gestures were used, they would become a part of the actor's own reality. They would be made dramatic by actors—who were not preachers or speechmakers but performers. That Shakespeare's players did use gesture and physical activity is born out by our Elizabethan traveler Fynes Moryson: "Stage players came out of England into Germany, having neither a complete number of actors, nor any good apparell, nor any ornament of the stage, yet the Germans . . . flocked wonderfully to see their gesture and action." So, without costumes or any set pieces, the actors could make the performance live by their physical presence.

There was a certain amount of recognizable "domestic" business. Pulling of beards and playing with codpieces is called for in the plays. Then there is putting on and off of clothes, gloves, and armor and the handling of swords, food, drink, etc. But for the most part, gesture will illustrate action and character, and here we should mention the importance of selectivity: "Suit the action to the word," as Shakespeare tells us in his famous acting lesson in *Hamlet*, Act III, Scene ii. But, as he also tells us, if this is overdone it will make "the unskilful laugh" and "the judicious grieve." An important fact to remember is that Shakespeare has done a great deal of the actor's work for him with language. Let the line do the work when it can. Tyrone Guthrie's comment "What do you want, a pink light?" given to an actor discussing Horatio's speech in Act I, Scene i of *Hamlet* ("the morn, in russet mantle clad, walks o'er the dew of yon high eastward hill") aptly makes the point about the descriptive capacity of Shakespeare's verse. This was further confirmed in a production of *Romeo and Juliet* in which the otherwise competent actor playing Mercutio seemed to find it necessary to physically illustrate every image in the Queen Mab speech. Leaping, prancing, mincing, swashbuckling, he managed to so overburden the speech that the audience reeled away from it like a beaten boxer, and a brilliant piece of verse was reduced to a molten mass of gestures and images. Selectivity is a watchword of all good acting, but never more so than in Shakespeare.

Selectivity and directness go hand in hand. The Shakespearean actor was strongly aware of the audience's presence. He could hardly have avoided it. The audience closely surrounded the stage in broad daylight and came to the event not with sepulchral reverence but with delighted awe. The whole popular tradition reinforced the element of direct communication between actor and audience. It was present in the street shows, mysteries, and morality plays and carried over into the professional theatres. Modern actors sometimes have a problem with this concept. Unless we are very fortunate, our first contact with "theatre" today will be either filmic or through television—totally passive forms in which no audience response is possible. Contact with "live" theatre is likely to be some form of "fourth-wall" realism in a darkened theatre where the actors are doing

their best to make us believe that they are not actors at all, but "real" people.[7] Thus, the idea of being aware of the audience's presence, and even addressing it directly, is immediately foreign to a young student's sensibility. Raymond Williams probably made the definitive comment: "It is as natural when on a stage before people to address them, as to pretend to carry on as if they were not there."[8] It must certainly be seen as natural to the actor playing Shakespeare. Not only is there a directness, a forceful activity about the plays that takes the actor down to the audience, where the emotional and rhythmical contact is strongest, but the very form of the plays contains prologues, choruses, and soliloquies made to be given directly to the audience.

The soliloquy is a special problem, as it can have different qualities and serve various functions, but it is likely to fall into four categories, each of which calls for a slightly different technique. There is what might be termed the introspective or contemplative soliloquy, in which the character is trying to resolve an issue or is reflecting upon his situation in philosophical terms. Hamlet's famous "To be, or not to be;" falls into this category, as does Macbeth's "Tomorrow, and tomorrow, and tomorrow" (Act V, Scene v). Here it is likely that the actor's focus will be inward: he will see images in his mind; there is unlikely to be any direct external focus, even in space.

Other soliloquies might be described as more actively reflective. Their speakers are basically men of action who are being troubled by a conscience. *Macbeth* has two examples of this: "If it were done when 'tis done," from which we have already quoted, and the dagger speech (Act II, Scene i). In these the

[7] On one occasion, when one of us was teaching Brecht, a student almost tearfully related that she was having difficulty with it and couldn't we please do some "real" acting. By this, of course, she meant some form of psychological realism in which she could fall back on her own emotions and mannerisms. Incidentally, she did know what she wanted, and is now successful in television soap opera!

[8] Raymond Williams, *Drama from Ibsen to Brecht* (New York: Oxford University Press, 1969), p. 14.

images will be placed in space; they are out in front of the actor, beckoning or driving him on, or forming obstacles for him to stumble over. Thus the focus will be shifting, but directly fixed upon images the character sees outside himself.

The most direct form of soliloquy is that given to the audience. Iago frequently does this, most obviously, perhaps, with his "And what's he then that says I play the villain," (*Othello*, Act II, Scene iii). Richard III also enjoys taking the audience into his confidence: the first speech of his play is almost a prologue, except that it establishes character as well as situation. *Lear's* Edmund, and indeed most of Shakespeare's villains, likes to get down and talk to the audience, telling them of his misfortunes, cunning, and witty knavery. Nor is this surprising when one remembers that the villains are the descendants of the medieval Vice characters, whose function, in the popular theatrical tradition, was to amuse the audience as much as disconcert the "good" characters.[9] Speaking directly to the audience does not mean transfixing one poor soul in the eye, but talking to the audience in general as participants—other actors—in the play.

The last soliloquy technique is the use of an objective correlative. Shakespeare provides Hamlet with one in Act V, Scene i, in what is more of an apostrophe than a soliloquy (he is not alone on stage). The objective correlative here is the skull of Yorick, which Hamlet addresses. If the playwright does not provide one, it can be useful to the actor to create one for himself in order to give a more direct purchase on or focus to the speech. Sometimes it may be an object on the stage, sometimes simply the actor's hand that seems to contain the image. A sword, or the sword hilt (which forms a cross) may also be used in appropriate circumstances. The actor's imagination and his sense of the speech must be

[9] It is a sad fact of theatre (and possibly of life itself) that unalloyed goodness tends to be bland; the titillating touch of evil is necessary to hold our interest and provide the conflict that is the heart of drama. This is one reason why the pure heroes and heroines of comedy are so often dull, and the heroes of tragedy never purely good.

his guide here. Nor will the techniques described above be discrete. The actor may wish to employ more than one in a given soliloquy. We don't wish to dogmatize, simply to show possible approaches from which the actor may determine what best suits his needs and what seems to be called for by a particular speech.

Vocal Flexibility. The vocal qualities required in Shakespearean performance match those we have discovered in discussing space, language, and body movement. We should expect an energy, directness, strong sense of action, and a certain elevation. Richard Carew in *The Excellency of the English Tongue* (c. 1595) wrote: "Our speech doth not consist only of words, but in a sorte even of deedes as when we express a matter by Metaphors; wherein the English is very fruitefull and forcible." "Very fruitefull and forcible" suggests both the straightforward vigor found in Shakespeare's language and its poetic eloquence. It is important to keep the motif, the thought line of the speech very clear and the shape of the speech as simple as possible. Do not set out to elaborate, but to clarify. Do not let the knowledge that one is speaking poetry lead you into a rhetorical style. There is a danger that actors give the speeches a "Shakespearean sound," which all actors pick up on and which lends a monotonous flatulence to the performance. Quite apart from the fact that the tone of each role is particular to the character, the essence of speaking any language is to make sense of it to the audience. Keep it as simple as the nature of the play allows.

While emphasizing the simple, direct, and forceful basis of the vocal delivery—avoiding verbal attitudinizing and overly wrapping one's tongue around and smacking the lips over the poetry—the actor must also observe the fact that he *is* for the most part speaking poetry. Control the speech, gather it rather than scatter it, speak, as it were, from the seat of one's pants; do not, on the other hand, labor the speech or lard it with pauses or interjections in the cause of clarity or "naturalness." Do not go from word to word. Go for the sense and color of a phrase or sentence. An audience may not understand all the words (but, of course, the actor must), but it will still get the sense of a line that is well delivered. Do not add unnecessary pauses, either in imitation of modern incoherence or to give the impression of thinking out a word or idea. The fact of thinking or reflection is contained in the rhythmic flow of the speech. Do not add words or expressions—this will destroy or at least alter the meter. Robert Lewis, in *Stanislavsky and America*, tells of an actor he once directed who added "Y'know" to almost every speech. When asked why, he told Lewis that it made it more "natural"; that was the way he himself spoke. To which Lewis responded: "Well, you are not going to be able to say 'Y'know, to be or not to be'!"

While adhering to the meter, don't get sucked into it (you won't if you go for the sense of the line), stressing the ends of every line in a rhythmical monotone. Yet it is verse, not prose, the actor speaks. He must give full value to the rhythms, imagery, and figures of speech. It is perfectly possible to let the cadences swell without drowning the audience; to color the images but not dwell upon them; to point the figures of speech but not hammer them into the ground. The speech must seem easy without being casual, elevated and yet "natural," suited to the total style and sensibility of the play.

Shakespeare's is a brisk, active language to be taken, as he tells us, "trippingly upon the tongue." He would not have it "mouthed," but at the same time it must be given air, allowed to take wing in the theatre. The actor must approach the language as he did the physical demands of Shakespeare's theatre. He must give the audience an experience of the lines as poetry while sounding like a man—however ennobled—with human thoughts, feelings, desires, and intentions. The vocal delivery must convey the explicit sense while manifesting the poetic values and supporting the implicit emotion.

Mask of Character. Actors who come to Shakespeare from work in modern, realistic drama often have problems coming to terms with the creation of character. They find lack of motivation, or inconsistency, or lack of biographical or physical detail on which to "build" a character. Some of these elements are, indeed, facts of Shakespeare's work, but they are problems for the actor only if he approaches the plays from the wrong perspective. Actors sometimes fail to recognize motivation through ignorance of the Elizabethan approach to human psychology, or of Shakespearean dramatic conventions. Similarly, they may look for character detail and motivations when the playwright is concerned chiefly with narrative and action and not with character at all. Shakespeare was communicating an essentially imaginative and poetic, not literal, interpretation of human action. Character is not important in and of itself, only in furthering the action of the play and illuminating the passions of the human soul. It is this soul rather than psyche, passion rather than personal feeling, with which Shakespeare is concerned.

The theatrical space and the form of Shakespeare's plays create a continuous, swift, forward-flowing sweep of action. In such a structure time is compressed. The "two hours traffic" (or even three) of the stage may encompass weeks, months, or years. Action is developed quickly: the story is always moving towards its climax, and there is little time for complex psychological exploration of character. Shakespeare does not stop to examine character; he displays it in action.

Nor would Shakespeare's actors or audience have expected detailed character analysis. We have already touched upon the concept of typicality and basic "humor" that informed the Elizabethan sense of human psychology. This went hand in hand with the dramatic tradition of the medieval theatre— especially the morality play—in which a character was defined by his function in the dramatic action. The audience did not ask why "good deeds" were good, or the Vice figure was evil; they were so by definition.

The playwrights and the sensibility of the time dealt in opposing values of good and evil, personifications of God and Devil, the seven deadly sins, and the four basic humors. To take a simple example: Jaques in *As You Like It* is melancholy. No one in Shakespeare's theatre would waste their time asking why: "Did he have an unhappy childhood?" "Is he a frustrated artist?" "Was he rejected by his first and only love?" It was his humor; it had to do with his liver. He would be expected to act in a certain way and have a particular view of life. To be melancholy was also his function in the play. He was part of a total pattern; he lent a particular poetic coloring that Shakespeare wanted. It is to these factors—his function, place in the larger pattern, and poetic coloring—that the actor must look when preparing to play Jaques, and not to his genes or childhood environment, which in any case we can know nothing of.

There is a certain relationship between the "essence" of a Shakespearean character and the mask of a Greek. The Greek mask, being physical and unchanging, is much more specific and concrete than the Elizabethan. But "essence" can serve the actor in a similar way, as a handle, a purchase, a starting point for his character. For the Elizabethan there was a direct correspondence between character type and character action, and between external appearances and internal qualities. Young men will be rash. Don't ask why Romeo falls in love: he is young, unstable, emotional; it would be expected of him. A deformed person will be evil—look at Macbeth's witches and Richard III.

The four basic character humors worked in permutations with the passions. Love, pride, lust, ambition, envy—all were accepted human temperaments whose existence in a character the Elizabethans would take for granted, without asking for specific reasons or motivations. Unpromoted men would be given to envy, as Italians to revenge, and women to lust. These passions would be expressed in a recognizable fashion, not repressed or internalized. Feelings and behavior were on the surface; the Elizabethans had yet to hear of Freud or Stanislavskian subtext. They were interested in what the character did, how the passion moved him to action.

If we are ever in danger of trying to impose a twentieth-century conception of "realism" onto Shakespeare's work, we have only to remind ourselves that his women were played by boys. An audience that happily accepts such a convention would have no trouble with Iago's "motiveless malignity" (as Coleridge called it) or Othello's sudden jealousy. That the women characters were played by boys often seemed to give them a certain masculine authority and strength. Their sexuality is boyish; they love poetically, not physically. It is as well to remember this, for too much emphasis upon the physical details of love can reduce and demean the larger qualities of Shakespeare's love relationships. The women in the tragedies are masculine in sensibility—Lady Macbeth, Reagan, Goneril—or have the strength to disobey the proprieties of a male-dominated society—Juliet, Desdemona, Cordelia. They are unusual, interesting women, whose mask of character owes not a little to their boyish players.[10]

There is, then, a tangible essence to Shakespeare's characters. In a simple sense Macbeth is ambition, Lear is pride, Othello, jealousy, Falstaff both the Roman braggart warrior and the medieval Vice, and Henry V nobility and right kingship. This gives a strong, central definition to character and insures quick recognition by the audience.[11] But, of course, Shakespeare went much further than this. He created recognizable and complex human individuals from the medieval form. He was touched both by the humanistic sense of human uniqueness and by genius. He brought his own intuition and

[10] Young women today, who pursue "masculine" freedoms, physical strength, and boyish figures should, as actors, find interesting connections with Shakespeare's "female" characters.

[11] Compare the way television news, interested in action, identifies persons it interviews: Joe Doe, "hostage"; Ann Smith, "victim"; Willie Jones, "stranded." It is the essence of the part played by the person in the action that is being reported.

observation of human passions, motives, and actions to his characters and transmitted these through language, action, and form. Once again we have that integration of traditions, of seeming contrasts that typified the age: a strong central character trait given individuality in action. Shakespeare's characters are "complete" because he gives them traits that act well. The character is built to accord with the demands of the action, so every trait is necessary and actively expressed. This gives the impression of fully rounded characters, but their human definition is only what is required to further the action and passion of the play.

If we have heavily stressed the idea of psychological typicality and motivation inspired by the necessities of the action, it is not because we do not recognize the sophistica-tion of Shakespeare's characterization, but rather to shake the actor out of his modern sensibility that acting can be "real" and "honest" only if based upon detailed psychological analysis, personal "feelings," and subtextual motivations. "Typical" human behavior was perfectly real to the Elizabethans, and Shakespeare's drama is entirely real if it is taken as a theatrical event, with its own integrity, consistent conventions, and totally believable illumination of the human condition. If we look too hard for psychological motivation and ignore the demands of the poetic structure, language, and action, we will get a rather limited, pseudomodern character who has a problem with arcane speech. It is false to treat Hamlet as a living man rather than an element in a dramatic composition. There is no Hamlet outside of

Controlled, brooding strength from actor Daniel Davis as Brutus in *Julius Caesar*, performed by the American Conservatory Theatre, San Francisco.

Photo by William Ganslen.

the play. It is equally invalid to ask how many children Lady Macbeth might have had. "I have given suck" must be taken at its value in the play: she has experienced maternal love, which lends greater force to her statement that she would dash out her child's brains before being as vacillating as Macbeth. Shakespeare does not bother to motivate when it is irrelevant to the action. In what has been described as "superb effrontery," he has Portia say in *The Merchant of Venice* (Act V, Scene i): "You shall not know by what strange accident I chanced on this letter." It doesn't matter how she got it; the important thing is she did. Finally, everything we are saying is in the hope that no actor reading this book will ever remark, as a famous black actor did, "I could never play Othello, as I wouldn't have killed Desdemona"—a perfect example of the "naturalistic" fallacy of putting one's own emotions or psychological makeup before the action of the play.

Shakespeare has given the actor all he needs in order to stimulate his imagination. If we look for subtext that isn't there or become involved with minutiae,[12] we are in danger of reducing the stature of the characters to our own petty size and diminishing the impact of the tragedy. The characters are recognizably human, but through dramatic and poetic expression. We suggested in our discussion of language that Shakespeare's verse carries the burden of the play's action and through that action depicts and displays character. Character development comes through rhythms, imagery, and verbal structure. If sound equals sense then melody equals mask. We are briefly going to illustrate aspects of this from certain tragedies, and then show how all the elements may be seen to work in a speech from *Macbeth.*

If we look at the language Shakespeare has given Hamlet, we are immediately struck by three things: significant use of soliloquy, complex nature of verse rhythms, and fre-

quent use of prose. This would indicate a self-questioning, somewhat solitary individual who operates on many levels and in his use of prose deviates from the expected norm of a royal prince. And this is precisely what we find. Hamlet's basic humor would be melancholy, which tends to solitariness and introspection. Note, too, that he is dressed in black—the "typical" costume that might be expected of a melancholy humor. In the play Hamlet adopts the mask of madness and, while wearing it, adopts prose speech, which becomes part of that mask. Madness is a deviancy, and Shakespeare deviates from the norm of verse to give it active force. Hamlet also adopts prose when speaking to Polonius, Rosencrantz, and Guildenstern—the gulls of the play. He does this at times to ridicule and demean them, at other times to show familiarity—which adds to the levels of his character and illustrates the use of language in depicting relationships.

In the same play Horatio speaks for the most part in simple, regular iambics. It is a general rule of Shakespeare's speech rhythms that the more a character uses basic iambic pentameter, the less complex that character will be. Horatio is an even, rational character—educated, dutiful, and speaking with a simple eloquence. Claudius, on the other hand, has a much more complicated mask of language. We have already suggested that his speech "And let the kettle to the trumpet speak" (Act V, Scene ii) shows qualities of hyperbole, pomposity, and hollow sham. We find these to be consistent qualities of Claudius's character. His very first speech of the play (Act I, Scene ii), which goes on for some forty lines, is tortuous, bombastic, full of pompous images, and archaic in syntax. There is an elaborate formality about it, a hyperbole that is geared to fooling people with sound. The speech builds up Claudius's sense of self-importance—it is full of rhetorical figures, antinomies, alliterations, appositions. The actor who feels the rhythms, senses the shape, and listens to the sound of Claudius's speech will find the character developed for him.

---

[12] The actor should not proceed from character analysis to a view of the character in action, but from the logic of the action as a whole, which places exactly those demands upon the character that make him "lifelike" within the total fabric of the play.

Before leaving *Hamlet* we should mention Polonius's family. Polonius himself speaks with a euphuistical formalism of imagery. It is, like Claudius's, somewhat hyperbolic, but in a much less active way. It is indirect and obfuscating befitting the politician he is. The whole family tends to speak with Polonius's sententiousness. Laertes, Ophelia, and Polonius use moralizing parables and summarize their speeches with rhyming couplets. There is about the family that quality that led Gertude to ask Polonius for "more matter and less art."

Othello is as well defined by the characteristics of his language as is Hamlet. With Shakespeare's Moor these characteristics are not so much the rhythms and the structure of the speech as the resonance, images, and word choices. In general Othello's language is not complex in structure, and as such befits a fairly simple, nonintellectual man. But there is an oratorical, baroque extravagance about it. He uses the expression "O" a great deal, as well as words containing the vowel "o." This tends to give a full-chested resonance to his speech, a sonorous, rather magniloquent sound. This is consistent with a man of large emotions and open sensibility. It also lends an air of formality and ceremoniousness, enriched with extravagant metaphors and fantastical allusions. He speaks of the "anthropophagi"—an unfamiliar word in Venice, and one that also contains two "o's"—and of men with two heads. Not only does he look somewhat strange in Venice, but he sounds like a stranger too—a man born in a simpler and more primitive clime, mysterious and somewhat dangerous to the occidental mind. To Iago's uncharitable ear, his language is full of "bombast circumstance" and "stuffed with epithets." But to kinder wit-

Strong mask of emotion from two actors playing Othello: (a) Donald Sinden in a Royal Shakespeare Company production and (b) Moses Gunn in a New York Public Theater production.

Photos by Joe Cocks (a), and Martha Swope (b).

nesses his demand for "ocular evidence" and allusions to Mount Olympus may be seen as the excessive deliberation of one speaking in an unfamiliar tongue and attempting both to seem on a par with and to flatter his listeners.

Iago, on the other hand, being calculating and unemotional, often speaks in a light, direct, easy, ironic prose. This fits both his character and his situation as Othello's "ancient"—a bluff, "honest" soldier, with no pretentions to nobility, who has made his way through the ranks. He has a good deal of direct address to the audience, which is not only derived from the medieval Vice tradition but gives him an accessibility that the more elevated characters lack. We may have more sympathy for Othello, but we seem closer to Iago.

We could go on, drawing attention to the difference in Brutus's and Antony's speeches over the body of Caesar—the first legal, scientific, and honest, the second rhetorical and calculatedly emotional. Or to the way in which the Fool's gibberish, Edmund's malice, and Lear's madness are all manifested in prose in *King Lear*. In this play, when Nature is disrupted in the storm on the heath and Lear loses his kingly mask to become a "bare, forked animal," verse is not used, no longer being appropriate to the situation. We hope the point about character being actively contained within the rhythms, imagery, and structure of the language has been adequately made. The example we give below, together with those we have discussed, however briefly, above, should enable the actor to approach Shakespeare's plays with a good perspective on characterization.

We are going to look further at Macbeth's speech from Act I, Scene vii, the scansion of which was partly discussed in the section on the technical structure of language. First, here is the complete speech with suggested scansion:

If ĭt/wĕre dōne/whĕn 'tĭs/dŏne thĕn/'twĕre
  wĕll
Ĭt wĕre dōne/quĭckly./ Ĭf thʼ ăs/sassĭ/nātiŏn
Cŏuld trăm/mĕl up̄/thĕ cōn/sĕquĕnce,/ănd
  cātch

With hīs/sŭrcease,/sŭccess;/thăt bŭt/thīs
  blōw
Mīght bē/thĕ bē-/all ānd/thĕ end-/all here,
Bŭt here,/ŭpŏn/thĭs bank/ănd shoal/ŏf time,
Wĕ'd jump/thĕ līfe/tŏ come./ Bŭt ĭn
  these/cases
Wĕ stĭll/hăve judge/mĕnt here;/thăt wē/bŭt
  teach
Bloŏdy ĭn/structiŏns,/whĭch, bĕ/ĭng
  taught,/rĕturn
Tŏ plague/thʼ invĕn/tŏr; thīs/
  evĕn/handĕd/justĭce
Cŏmmends/thʼ ingrĕ/dĭents/ŏf
  oŭr/poisŏn'd/chalĭce
Tŏ oŭr/own lĭps./ Hē's here/ĭn doub/lĕ trust:
Fĭrst ăs/Ĭ am/hĭs kins/măn ānd/hĭs/subjĕct,
Strōng both/ăgainst/thĕ deed;/thĕn ăs/hĭs
  host
Whŏ should/ăgainst/hĭs mur/dĕrer shut/thĕ
  door
Nŏt bear/thĕ knife/mўself./Besĭdes,/thĭs
  Dŭncan
Hăth borne/hĭs fac/ŭlties/sŏ meek,/hăth been
Sŏ clear/ĭn hĭs great/officĕ,/thăt hĭs/virtŭes
Wĭll plead/lĭke an/gĕls, trum/
  pĕt-tongued,/ăgainst
Thĕ deep/dămna/tiŏn ŏf/hĭs ta/kĭng-off;
Ănd pĭ/tў, līke/ă na/kĕd new/bŏrn babe,
Strīding/thĕ blast,/ŏr heav/ĕn's cher/ubĭm,
  horsed
Ŭpŏn/thĕ sight/lĕss cour/iĕrs ŏf/thĕ air,
Shăll blow/thĕ hŏr/rĭd deed/ĭn ev/erў eye,
Thăt tears/shăll drown/thĕ wind./ Ĭ have/nŏ
  spur
Tŏ prick/thĕ sides/ŏf mў ĭn/tĕnt, bŭt/onlў
Vaultĭng/ambĭt/iŏn, whĭch/o'ĕrleaps/ĭtself
Ănd falls/ŏn thĕ/othĕr.

In simple words, Macbeth wishes to kill Duncan and become king, but is afraid of being found out. His ambition wrestles with his fear, to create vacillation and uncertainty. This desire for action versus fear of consequence is clearly shown in the structure of the first line and a half. There are three sets of equivalents: the repetition of "done" is active, falling like a blow, but this is qualified by "if," "when," and "then," and by "were," "t'were," and "were." Thus, the balance of the line sets up the nature of the problem.

This is then extended by the use of imagery and rhetorical devices. We have the antithesis of "assassination" and "consequence," the repetition of "trammel up" by "catch," and the paranomasia of "surcease" and "success". To catch the consequences, bind them up, would be to catch success, to tie up the deed neatly. Macbeth returns to a series of active words in "blow," "be-all," and "end-all," but the consequences are still on his mind and he goes into a long examination of them. This has the effect of frustrating his direct action. The extended images that follow seem to "trammel up" his own ability to take action. The active words are being caught in an imagistic web of uncertainties.

Macbeth's main concern is that justice might catch up with him in this world. We have the repetition of "here" four times in the space of six lines, and the "even-handed" nature of justice means that it is likely to catch him. Duncan deserves justice, but justice to Duncan means justice to his murderer too. Once again Macbeth gets caught up in antitheses (which are, by definition, even-handed): "host" balances "murderer," and "shut the door" equates with "bear the knife myself." The balanced nature of the argument is displayed in the structure of the line.

Macbeth's fear of the consequences takes over for the next ten lines. There is a complex, hectic imagery that shows Macbeth's mind running away with him as he tries to come to grips with his confusion. Images of innocence—angels and children—are mixed with images of a headlong, screaming rush to destruction—riding a storm of keening, howling, swirling winds. The speech ends with a riding metaphor, but with a rhythmically declining fall, broken only by the image of "vaulting ambition."

Essentially Macbeth comes full circle in the speech. He starts by being unable to act quickly because of fear of earthly consequences; he finishes still anxious to kill Duncan, but even more afraid of the consequences. The images also come full circle, from "jump the life to come" to the ambition that "o'erleaps itself." "Jump" and "leap" suggest the man of action that

Macbeth is. However, he is a man of action afflicted with a fearful imagination. Thus, his will to action is opposed by imagined obstacles. The imagery and structure of the speech reveal this. It moves strongly and actively up to line 7, but is unable to complete the course of action because of the obstacles set out at lines 7, 12, and 17. To follow up the inherent riding imagery of the speech: the rider sets out wanting to complete the course but, unsure of himself and having had to clear three obstacles, presumes that he is likely to fall and decides not to go for the finish. All of this reveals Macbeth's character. He is ambitious but uncertain of himself, a man of action whose fears affect him through his imagination—later he imagines both a dagger and the ghost of Banquo. Note that the images of fear in the speech are Christian, not Freudian. The speech embodies that sense of contrast that we have suggested is typical of the Elizabethan period and of Shakespeare's work. Humanistic, human ambition is opposed by medieval Christian ethics.

Another way of looking at the shape of a speech is to phrase it as seems indicated by the demands of breathing cadences, caesuras, punctuation, and scansion emphases. With Macbeth's speech we would get something like this:

> If it were done
> When 'tis done
> Then t'were well it were done quickly.
> If th' assassination could trammel up the conse-
> quence
> And catch with his surcease
> Success;
> That but this blow
> Might be the be-all and the end-all
> Here, But here,
> Upon this bank and shoal of time,
> We'd jump the life to come.
> But in these cases we still have judgement.
> Here;
> That we but teach bloody instructions,
> Which, being taught, return to plague th'inventor;
> This even-handed justice
> Commends th'ingredients of our poison'd chalice
> To our own lips.

He's here in double trust:
First, as I am his kinsman and his subject,
Strong both against the deed;
Then as his host
Who should against the murderer shut the door
Not bear the knife myself.
Besides,
This Duncan
Hath borne his faculties so meek,
Hath been so clear in his great office,
That his virtues
Will plead like angels, trumpet-tongued,
against the deep damnation of
His taking-off;
And pity,
Like a naked new-born babe, striding the blast,
Or heaven's cherubim, horsed upon the
sightless couriers of the air,
Shall blow the horrid deed in every eye,
That tears shall drown the wind.
I have no spur
To prick the sides of my intent,
But only
Vaulting ambition,
Which o'erleaps itself
And falls
On
The other.

Setting out the speech this way will give the actor a strong physical sense of its shape and impress the phrasing and rhythms upon him. The shape of Macbeth's speech shows the strong through-line of thought carried by such words and phrases as "If t'were done," "success," "here," "even-handed justice," "besides," "pity," and "falls." It also illustrates the obstacles, in the shape of larger phrases, to the through-line—particularly the largest phrase of all, which climaxes the confusion of the speech before the declining fall from "I have no spur" to "The other."

We have by no means exhausted the many ways of approaching Shakespeare's language, but have tried simply to illustrate the point that the clues to Shakespeare's characters lie mainly in a broad understanding of the character's "humor" and function within the play, and in the rhythms, structure, imagery, and verbal melody of his speech. Sound equals sense; melody equals mask; character is displayed through language and in action.

EPILOGUE

Secular Festival. Shakespeare's theatre was an occasion. We tend to have lost the sense of occasion today; in fact we almost consciously work against it. We don't understand the social function of ceremony. We regard it as an unnecessary formality, and dressing for an occasion as some form of "dishonest" mask behavior. Because of this we have lost a feeling for eloquence, life seen as poetry. Belief in life's colors, passions, faraway places, the forces of the imagination—witches, ghosts, the irrational—has been taken away from us by science. Electric light has taken many of the fears and fantasies from life and replaced them with television. Watching television is not an occasion.

Shakespeare's theatre was still close to popular tradition, to religion, and to ritual. It had come, by way of mystery plays, morality plays, inn yards, and bear pits, to be a celebration of man's humanity and capacity for action within the cosmos and the chain of being. Theatre no longer celebrated strictly religious festivals, as in the Middle Ages. Now the festivals were more secular—but festivals they were still. As Christ was both a man and the Son of God, so Shakespeare's heroes are recognizably men and act as such, but partake of a larger cosmic spirituality. We must be aware of this suprahumanity in Shakespeare's work and not be afraid to manifest it. It is largeness not so much of manner as of spirit.

Yet for all its poetry, Shakespeare's was still a rootedly popular theatre. It may have been conscious of heaven and hell, but it

Strength with lightness and humor shown by Alan Howard and Glenda Jackson in *Antony and Cleopatra.*

Royal Shakespeare Company.

happened on this earth, in broad daylight, and between men. A direct chemistry could flow from actor to audience—a robust, curious, imaginative people eager for physical and emotional experience, and for adventure. The theatre was intimate and epic, immediate and removed. Poetic imagination was linked to physical vigor. We must, as actors, be aware of the richness and variety of the occasion and let it inform our approach to performance. We must not become so involved with technicality or detail that we reduce the stature of the dramatic effect. Nor must we become so infatuated with the poetry

that we fail to root it in a recognizable reality. If the occasion of Shakespeare's theatre can be called a secular festival, then the approach to acting might be termed lyrical physicality.

Lyrical Physicality. The actor in performance had to match both the expectations of a vigorous, virile, and somewhat violent age, and the demands of the sweeping, onward drive and powerful passions of the dramas he was performing. A direct, robust, foursquare physical approach seems the obvious response. The actor was a man among men;

yet he was more than this. Firmly on this earth, he was still halfway to heaven; his characters were touched by fate and drawn by the genius of a poet. The language the actor spoke, though rooted in human action, had transcendental power and lyrical grace.

It was a romantic form of acting—not extreme and decadent, but lively, brawny, passionate, direct. The actors were not afraid to project the stature of their characters, to deal in archetypal vices and virtues rather than peccadilloes and idiosyncrasies. There was power, poetry, and passion. A lyrical physicality: derived from the sensibility of the age, inherent in the dramatic form, reinforced by the physical setting, and communicated through language and action.

PLAYING THE STYLE

This section deals with more specifics of mask, and suggests a few approaches that tie the discussion of the physical demands of style into the exercises in the next section.

Building a Mask. In our discussion of mask and character we showed how the rhythm and shape of language reveal character in action. Taking Iago as an example, we are going to suggest ways of approaching character mask that further develop and reinforce the qualities discovered in the language.

The Facts. What are we told of Iago? He is a professional soldier, twenty-eight years old, married to Emilia. He is Othello's ancient—his third-in-command—having been passed over as second-in-command, about which he harbors a grudge against Othello and Cassio.

Self-revelation. We learn a great deal about Iago from what he tells us of himself.

He doesn't like "arithmeticians," educated men who "prattle without practice," the nonpragmatic "proper" men who assume gentlemanly airs.

He is a mask wearer: "I am not what I am"; "Show out a flag and sign"; "Not I for love and duty."

He is a man of action: "Dull not device by coldness and delay"; "Pleasure and action make the hours seem short."

He does not hold human life very highly, and has a cynical view of human nature: "Preferment goes by letter and affection"; "Virtue, a fig."

He has an equally cynical view of women's lusts and fidelity: "Go to bed to work"; "A thing for me—it is a common thing."

Other Opinions. No one has a harsh word for Iago until the end of the play, when his treachery is revealed. The term most characters use of him is "honest"; it is repeated countless times in the play. He is also remarked upon as "just" and "kind," and Othello speaks of his "honesty and love." In negative (and ironical) terms his wife, Emilia, by implication calls him "an insinuating rogue" and "a cogging, cozzening slave."

Images. The images and verbal choices are instructive. Iago uses full oaths, such as "Zounds." " 'Sblood" is the first word he speaks in the play. An especially interesting oath is "by Janus"—the Roman household god with two faces. It seems no accident that Shakespeare should give this to Iago, the mask wearer. Iago uses insidious (note again Emilia's word for him—"insinuating") images of "poison" (four times), "plague," and "pestilence." With these images go those of ensnaring or catching in a "web" or "net.". There are earthy expressions: "snorting," "scurvy," "tupping." With "tupping" are other sexual images—"hot," "prime," "act of sport."

Humor. Shadings of humor add depth to every tragic mask. Shakespeare has given Iago a nice sense of irony, letting him joke about his wife's tongue and tell Roderigo that should he drown himself, "I will never love you after." His bluff good humor is also present at the drunken party that undoes Cassio. Iago gets on well with his fellow men—he is "one of the boys."

This by no means exhausts the detail Shakespeare has provided, but is enough to confirm and expand the mask of Iago we discovered by examining his typicality, rhythms, and structural function in the play (p. 84). From the Medieval Vice comes the humor and directness—an easy relationship with the audience that lets him confide in them; they see both his faces. Looked at from one side Iago's mask is that of the good-natured soldier. His forceful, un-romantic prose suggests the man of action, and the images of sex, wine, and fighting are no more than to be expected of the soldier who makes an honest accommodation to minor venial sin. The other face shows the calculating Machiavel—another Elizabethan type—who holds life cheaply and revenge dear, whose cynicism is deep and bitter, and who uses sex and wine to commit mortal sin in a cold, unrepentant manner. The two masks are consistent: one is the warped im-age of the other.

If we were looking for further practical character images to add to the picture of a trusted man of action—bluff, physical, cool, consistent, stoical, and unrepentant at the end—we could note that the rhythms of Iago's scenes with Othello remind us of a bullfighter taunting a bull or a Roman glad-iator pricking his opponent with a spear and gradually ensnaring him in a net. There are many ways of looking at what Iago does in the play, but the point we are trying to stress is that Shakespeare has given the actor a tremendous amount of direct information, and indirect indications through imagery and language, to add to the mask elements of typicality and those created by the shape and rhythms of the language.

Nuts and Bolts. Though we firmly believe that the performance of external manner is useless if not informed by both an under-standing of sensibility and a strong sense of character, the mask does operate within a given social form. Therefore, in this section we present a few specifics of Elizabethan social manner that may help the actor become accustomed to the shape of the Elizabethan courtesies, which may then be adapted to a particular mask.

The Bow. Draw the left foot backwards, slightly turned out. Bend both knees, keeping the heels on the ground. At the same time the body bends forward from the waist with a straight spine and neck. The body weight moves partially onto the back foot, and the back knee is slightly turned out. If the bow is deep the back knee may touch the ground. At the end of the bow, the body comes erect, the weight moves onto the front foot, and the back foot is drawn in.

The Curtsy. Starting with feet together, draw the left foot back a few inches behind the right, keeping the foot flat and the body straight. Bend the knees and incline the body slightly forward with straight spine and neck. The knees turn outwards slightly and the left heel rises. At the end of the curtsy rise slowly and smoothly and replace the left foot beside the right.

Other major courtesies were as follows:

When doffed, the hat was swept down to the side during the bow (inside of hat to the thigh) or, in the presence of a superior, held under the arm.

The kissing of a woman's hand was done with a bow. The hand was never actually touched with the lips.

An informal greeting, kissing lip to lip, was quite frequent among the Elizabethans.

The kissing of one's own hand, which was then held out towards the person saluted, was used only for extreme reverence; it became more commonplace in the later-seventeenth-century court.

Arm clasps and strong physical embraces were common among men.

FIRST   SECOND   THIRD   FOURTH   FIFTH

16ᵗʰ CENTURY BOW

16ᵗʰ CENTURY CURTSEY

Detail of Elizabethan bow and curtsy.

Line drawings by ClaireMarie Verheyen.

Basic hand properties that give the feel of the period were pomanders—gold or silver balls of perfume—which, together with spice-stuffed oranges, were used to keep away the smell of human waste thrown in the street. There was also some use of fans—by male dandies rather than women—and long-stemmed clay pipes.

Exploring the Style. Having become familiar with these physical details, use simulations of costume and set up small social situations in which to explore their use further: dining, dancing, going to the theatre, court receptions, processes, a day at home in an Elizabethan house. Background for this is to be found in the following books:

GEORGE EDELEN, ed., *The Description of England* (Ithaca, N.Y.: Cornell University Press, 1968).

J. D. WILSON, *Life in Shakespeare's England* (Cambridge: Cambridge University Press, 1949).

ELIZABETH BURTIN, *The Elizabethans at Home* (London: Secker & Warburg, 1958).

ANTHONY BURGESS, *Nothing Like the Sun* (London: William Heinemann, 1964). This book is also a fascinating novel reconstruction of Shakespeare's life.

Use music to accompany your explorations. Ronald Watkins has suggested that "a strain of Byrd, Morley Gibbons or Weelkes can evoke sooner even than Shakespeare's words . . . the freshness, vigour and strength of the age."[13]

All of this is to help you act a Shakespearean play. Never forget the theatrical necessities discussed in the section on performance demands. The different approaches we have suggested reinforce each other to produce the intellectual and physical understanding of Shakespearean playing. Don't apologize for, slough over, or attempt

[13] Ronald Watkins, *On Producing Shakespeare* (London: M. Joseph, 1950), p. 68.

to homogenize the elements that give the text its distinctive flavor. Rather, underline them in your text—they are the very stuff of the style. Enjoy the classical references, the oaths of the day, the appellations and titles—"O my good Lord," "my most sacred Lady." These are part of the texture and a strong indication of social manner. Don't skimp the bows and curtsies, the kisses and embraces—they are the mettle and color of the time.

Above all, don't let the plays hang loosely upon an undersized and juiceless body of acting, because our twentieth-century social behavior is much thinner and more understated than the Elizabethan. We must embrace all the social elements Shakespeare has given us: not only do they give the audience a strong sense of distinction, but from their feel we as actors can understand their necessity and the society that required them.

EXERCISES, GAMES, TECHNIQUES

The first few exercises are of a strongly physical nature, and emphasize the necessity of leg purchase. They may be played as robustly and vigorously as the ensemble of players wishes, but they must always bear in mind that physical contact is not the purpose of the game but, as with Shakespearean acting, the necessary means to the achievement of the objective. The games are also good warm-up exercises and achieve high energy levels.

British Bulldog. Players line up at one end of the space and have to walk as quickly and purposefully as they can to the other end; they may not run. There is one player in the middle who has to intercept them and take prisoners by lifting the walking players until both legs are off the ground. The captured player now joins the player in the middle. The game continues until all the crossing players have been taken prisoner. When intercepted, players may not drop to the ground but should remain upright and try to keep both feet on the ground for as long as possible.

Red Rover. This is a variation of the previous game. Once again players line up at one end of the space with one player in the middle. All players fold their arms across their body. Now players have to hop on one leg to the other end of the space. They may change legs, but only one leg may be in contact with the ground at any one time. The player in the center has to intercept by knocking the crossers off balance. This is done with the folded arms. The center player must also hop when intercepting. The game continues until all players have been intercepted.

Shark Island. Draw a chalk circle in the middle of the space. The circle should be just large enough to accommodate all the players with a one-foot margin all round. The players all stand within the circle. They are castaways on an island, with just enough water for one person. The sea around is full of sharks. Players must try to jostle and push each other off the island. The game continues until just one player is left standing in the circle. There is an elaboration on the game whereby all the people pushed into the sea become sharks and from outside the circle try to pull the remaining castaways into the sea.

Jousting. This game may be played simply or as a ritual. Basically it requires two pairs of players. In each pair one player is horsed upon the other's back. The rider has a rolled-up newspaper as his lance. The pairs advance upon each other and the object of the game is to push or knock the rider from the horse's back, or to knock the horse off balance. The game may be played along a narrow channel or, again, inside a chalked circle. To make a ritual of the game, other players may form a medieval court with a king and a princess whose hand is being sought by the jousting knights, and who will suffer a "fate worse than death" if the wrong knight wins. Clothing props will be needed for this, and the court should "process" to the tournament field where a whole elaborate ceremony may be played out.

Cockfighting. Two players are within a chalked circle with hands clasped behind their backs. The circle should be no more than eight feet in diameter. The object is for a player to push the other player out of the circle using only his chest—no other contact may be made. The game adds nimbleness of foot and strong-chestedness to leg purchase. The game is obviously not suitable for women, but women might play it using their backs instead of chests—this would give a sense of the upright but not forward-thrusting strength of Elizabethan women.

Cock o' the Midden. This game begins to include language with physicality. Players should learn a speech from Shakespeare—say, some forty lines. The speech should be outward-going and dynamic in nature. The king's speech from Act IV, Scene iii of *Henry V* beginning "If we are marked to die, we are enow" is excellent for the purpose. Other good speeches are Hamlet's "O, what a rogue and peasant slave am I" (Act III, Scene i); Cassius's "Why, man, he doth bestride the narrow world" (*Julius Caesar*, Act I, Scene ii); and a combination of Lear's speeches on the heath (Act III, Scene ii); there are many others. Place three or four small eight-inch platforms about eight feet apart in the space. A player now stands on one of these levels and begins a speech. He has a rolled-up newspaper with him. Two or three other players approach him and attempt to knock him off the level with rolled-up newspapers. If they succeed, he retreats to the next level and continues the speech. The game goes on until the speech is finished or the player is driven off the stage. While defending his space, the speaking player must keep the sense and flow of the speech. If at any time he loses the thread of the speech, he must retreat to the next level and start again. The game is good for concentration as well as physical purchase in space.

We made a thorough examination of the approach to language in the section on performance demands. We are including below a few further techniques that should help the actor in this area.

Telegrams. We stressed that no matter how important it is to be aware of the structure, imagery, figures of speech, and other elements of Shakespeare's verse, it is still of primary importance that the through-line of thought be maintained. The intellectual sense of the speech must be clear to the audience. This won't happen unless the actor himself has gotten a strong purchase on it. There are a couple of ways the actor can clarify the speech in his own mind. One is to write a synopsis of the speech in his own words. The other is to write out the speech as if it were a telegram. The purpose of this, of course, is to reduce the speech to its absolute essentials, so that if one more word were removed it would lose meaning. Macbeth's speech in Act I, Scene vii, which we have already worked on in different ways, would look something like this in telegram form:

> If done when done then done quickly. This blow end-all here jump life to come. But judgment here. He's here double trust. Kinsman host. Besides Duncan virtues plead pity. Every eye tears. I no spur but ambition. Which o'erleaps falls.

It might just be possible to remove another couple of words—"besides" or "o'erleaps," but not much more. It's an interesting exercise to decide which word you would delete if you couldn't afford the whole telegram. But the point of the exercise is that the sense is reduced to an absolute skeleton and becomes very clear to the speaker. Now, of course, the actor must go back to the whole speech and give it full value, but with a clearer spine of sense to guide him through it.

Verbal Circle. Players sit in a circle. Some familiar lines from Shakespeare are chosen, known to all the players or quickly learned by them. One player begins the speech by saying the first word. The player on his right continues with the second, the next player with the third, and so on around the circle. The object of the first reading is to pick up the quality of the speech received from the player before you, and carry it on. Repeat the exercise, this time attempting to change the quality of the speech when it reaches you. This may be done by altering pitch, volume, coloring, rhythm, or stress. Repeat several times, mixing up the circle or starting at different places, so that all players get to handle different words and to use all the many possibilities of altering the line readings. Discuss the exercise in the following terms: which verbal qualities were most difficult to alter; what qualities, when changed, most significantly altered the speech; how far a player was swept into the rhythm of the speech as it came to him; what, in the group's opinion, became the optimum reading of the speech. Repeat the exercise, this time illustrating your word with a gesture—even prepositions and conjunctions can be physicalized. Then do the speech again with gestures alone. Discuss what gestures are unnecessary to the speech and what seem most appropriate in communicating the sense.

Playback. This is an individual exercise derived from the one above. The player needs a tape recorder. Scan a piece of verse, then record it. Listen to it. Try a different series of stresses. Record and listen. Continue with this process, exploring different possibilities of volume, pitch, rhythm, pace, and so forth. Try not to change the through-line of sense in the speech, but play with all the vocal possibilities. Compare the readings with one another for the impression made by the various vocal techniques employed. Respond simply to the sound—aurally and emotionally rather than intellectually. An extension of this exercise is to get a recording of a Shakespearean play by a professional company. Choose a scene between two actors and rerecord it, omitting one of the parts. Now play the scene against the recording, speaking the part omitted. If possible, record your scene, then play it back and compare with the original. This is in no sense to imitate the actor on the record whose part you played, but to see where your rhythms, and other vocal characteristics coincide and what possibilities you have missed. This technique has the great virtue of enabling the player to speak with an accomplished actor and to get a feeling for the way in which verse can be used.

Poetic Palette. Write out a highly imagistic speech and physically color the images. Use crayons or paint and let the feel of the images influence your choices. Avoid literalness. Forest images aren't necessarily green, nor are sea images blue. Be aware of the effect the image is trying to produce. When you have colored the whole speech see what kind of pattern has been created—it will look like an abstract painting. Look at the whole effect of the speech in visual terms. See whether the shades and tones blend, or whether there are images that stand out from the rest. This exercise, combined with the speech shaping discussed on pages 85, 86 and the telegram exercise, will give an actor a very strong and clear sense of the dimensions of a speech. Obviously, in speaking it is the active sense of the speech on which the actor concentrates, not the imagery as such, but being fully aware of the effect of the imagery will inevitably lead the actor to give the speech appropriate coloring.

Kinetic Images. Players pair off and begin with a simple mirror exercise—performing physical gestures exactly copied by the partner. When concentration and fluidity are established, the game leader should throw some simple images at the pairs, such as birch trees, waving flags, fountains. The pairs now use these as a basis for the mirror exercise. When this is working, coach the pairs to split up and give the individuals more abstract or complex images to perform—yellow, Monday morning, vanilla ice cream with butterscotch topping. Allow the players time to explore and establish an image before moving on. When the players are committing themselves fully to the exercise and exploring with the whole body (this will need some coaching), start to introduce some literary images and images from Shakespeare's plays. Keep coaching players to avoid literal interpretation, to go for the poetic meaning of an image—they should let the image speak to their body, not to their mind. The point of the exercise is not to discover physical gestures for the specific communication of images, but to experience the images so that the physical sense of them will inform the actor's speech, although he may well not use a gesture at all to illustrate an image in performance. This is an intense exercise, physically and emotionally, and should probably not be played for more than twenty minutes at a time. It is an exercise that may be developed over a long period of time; actors can come back to it at each rehearsal or workshop session.

An extension of this exercise is to create a dance out of a speech. Have the players learn a Shakespearean speech that might take two or three minutes to speak. Choose a dance style—classical ballet, modern, jazz, Spanish, disco. One player now reads the speech while the other players interpret it according to the chosen style. Repeat the exercise in different styles of dance. Make sure the players stick fairly closely to the form of dance chosen and don't go off into abstractions—the fact of the dance form gives a structure and discipline to the exercise. Finally, let the players interpret the speech with any combination of the dance forms that seems appropriate. When each player has choreographed the speech, have him perform to the other players *while* speaking the lines. This gives the players a tremen-

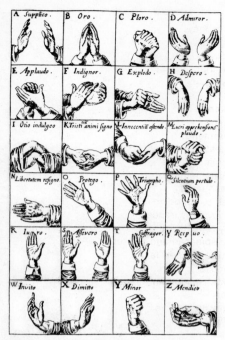

Key:
A. I beseech
B. I pray
C. I cry
D. I admire, wonder at
E. I applaud
F. I am angry, displeased at
G. I reject
H. I despair
I. I have time for
K. I show sadness of mind
L. I reveal innocence
M. I anticipate the receipt of money
N. I surrender
O. I defend
P. I am triumphant
Q. I ask for silence
R. I swear
S. I assert
T. I vote for
V. I reject
W. I invite
X. I dismiss
Y. I threaten
Z. I beg

Oxford University Press, by permission.

dous experience of the physical shape, rhythms, and dimensions of the speech.

A Day in the Life of . . . This is a soliloquy exercise. Players should sit in a half circle. In the middle are a few props, such as a chair, table, pen, paper, pipe, and cigarettes. Each player in turn goes into the middle of the half circle and tells an amusing anecdote about something that has happened to him. This will be much in the manner of the stand-up comedian. Then in turn each player gives a two-or-three-minute synopsis of the events of the previous day, in the following different ways:

1. as a report, as if he were a witness talking to a jury
2. as if he were thinking aloud about the day's events
3. as if he were writing a letter to a distant friend
4. as if concerned by the events and actively visualizing and considering them
5. as if musing upon the events, telling them to the dog or a glass of whiskey

The players may sit, stand, lean on the table, move around, or adopt any other manner, but they must keep their focus upon the events, be consistent in their chosen manner, and retain an awareness of the players sitting around them. Finally, players should do the exercise using whatever mode of delivery seems appropriate to the nature of the events being related. Thus, several modes may be employed in one synopsis. It is often useful to follow up the exercise by doing a Shakespearean soliloquy. In doing so the actor will find himself more aware of the variety of ways it may be approached. Discuss the exercise as a group, paying attention to appropriate rather than arbitrary choices, maintenance of a strong sense of throughline, and how far a player kept the audience's interest once the events were known. Remember, most Shakespearean soliloquies are known to audiences; it is the actor's performance that will make them fresh.

Chirologia/Chironomia. This exercise is based upon the rhetorical vocabulary of gestures set out in Bulwer's work in the seventeenth century. The purpose of the exercise is not to learn a set of mechanical

Oxford University Press, by permission.

gestures to employ in performance, but to get a sense of the physical manner of the period and to extend the gestural range and imagination of the players. By examining the nature of clichés we may adapt or eliminate some of our own. Players should examine the gestures in the accompanying illustrations and agree upon a certain number that should be practiced and learned. Players should now pair off, and the exercise should begin with a mirror game based upon isolations: movements of one part of the body at a time—hand, shoulder, foot, hip, jaw, nose, etc. From here move into a conversation with isolations. Once the rhythm and concentration of the exercise are working, the conversations should be continued with the agreed vocabulary of gestures. One player will try to convey his feelings or thoughts about a subject to his partner, who should respond. The coach may now give the group certain situations or subjects for discussion, and partners can be changed while they keep the conversations going. Move partners a good distance from each other in space so that the gestures achieve size and do not remain too private. Finally, a piece of text may be chosen that each player in turn tries to communicate to the group, using the gestural vocabulary. The group should discuss how far the gestures are necessary or appropriate and whether, if adapted to a more modern usage, they might be a useful extension to an actor's physical range.

Humor Game. As we have already suggested, Elizabethan psychology was based upon a set of humors, the balance of which determined the basic way in which an individual was likely to act. This was also used as a core of character or a basic mask for *dramatis personae*. The humor game accustoms actors to using the humor qualities as a foundation for the creation of character. Players should begin by walking in space, concentrating upon a good, easy body alignment. They should then be coached to perform simple domestic activities—sweeping the floor, washing windows, making a bed, and so on. The coach now suggests particular humors: melancholy, phlegm, sanguinity, choler. The players continue the domestic activities, but the work is now affected by the nature of the humor. Coach the players to become aware of how the humor is affecting their rhythms and how those physical rhythms affect the way they feel about the situation. Keep the exercise simple at first so that players gain a quick experience of the quality. Now set up a simple situation: a hotel where a party arrives to find there has been a mistake in booking and no rooms available. Let the players draw from cards that have the names of the humors on them. They must now play out the situation in a character based upon their humor. The basic humors might manifest themselves as follows:

Melancholy: We might have expected this.

Phlegm: Oh well, let's make the best of it.

Sanguinity: There's probably a better place just down the road.

Choler: Where's the manager? I'll wring his neck.

As the scene develops so will the character. And the player will make discoveries about how a person with a basic humor will act in the situation. He will develop certain rhythms and responses to the other characters in the situation. As he makes choices and decisions he will be developing a much fuller character. However, the character will be based upon the original humor and the actor will not need to know more about him than demanded by the situation. The character will be a function of his action within the situation. When the exercise is concluded, it should be discussed in terms of the discoveries made by the players about their characters' rhythms and responses, and in terms of just how much they needed to know about the character to operate within the scene. Probably the choleric player discovered abrupt, fast rhythms and quick-tempered responses. The phlegmatic player may have found steady, flowing rhythms (the element associated with phlegm is water) and a somewhat easygoing manner. Having made these discoveries, the players may test their developing character in other

situations, such as being in love or plotting a murder. The whole function of the exercise is to examine how the assumption of a particular humor will produce a set of physical responses in a situation. These responses will themselves produce feelings that will influence further physical action. A whole character may be developed in this way, with no superfluous detail but fully equipped to play his part in the action given him by the playwright. This is an economical approach to the development of Shakespeare's characters—through an understanding of their humors, their objectives, and the part they play in the action pattern of the drama.

SUGGESTED READINGS

AYKROYD, J. W., *Performing Shakespeare*. New York: Samuel French, 1979.

BECKERMAN, BERNARD, *Shakespeare at the Globe*. New York: Macmillan, 1962.

BRADBROOK, MURIEL C., *Elizabethan Stage Conditions*. Connecticut: Archon Books, 1962.

HARBAGE, ALFRED, *Shakespeare's Audience*. New York: Columbia University Press, 1941.

JOSEPH, BERTRAM, *Acting Shakespeare*. New York: Theatre Arts Books, 1960.

KNIGHT, G. WILSON, *Shakespearean Production*. Chicago: Northwestern University Press, 1964.

MUIR, KENNETH, AND S. SCHOENBAUM, *A New Companion to Shakespeare Studies*. Cambridge: Cambridge University Press, 1971.

NAGLER, A. M., *Shakespeare's Stage*. New Haven: Yale University Press, 1958.

RIGHTER, ANNE, *Shakespeare and the Idea of the Play*. London: Chatto & Windus, 1962.

STYAN, J. L., *Shakespeare's Stagecraft*. Cambridge: Cambridge University Press, 1967.

WEBSTER, MARGARET, *Shakespeare Without Tears*. New York: McGraw-Hill, 1942.

WEIMANN, ROBERT, *Shakespeare and the Popular Tradition in the Theatre*. Baltimore: Johns Hopkins, 1978.

part II

PLAYING COMEDY

Comedy does not concern itself with the grand passions, with metaphysical absolutes, with man in strife with gods, but rather with the detail of everyday existence: man in conflict with man in his more earthy and mundane circumstances. Comedy rejoices in the wearing of human masks, in playing with human posturings and shortcomings and making man laugh at himself. It is both release and accommodation, and ranges from the broadest, most knockabout form of physical humor to the most elegantly turned and carefully honed shafts of intellectual wit: low comedy to high comedy, farce to comedy of manners.

The gradations along the spectrum are not discrete; the ingredients tend to become mixed in the middle. The two ends of the spectrum represent the more distinct qualities from which the mixed forms are created, and the nature of a particular comic style will be determined by the balance of elements from the two opposing norms. We are going to deal with the ends of the spectrum—comedy of manners and farce, and within the latter include a discussion of commedia dell'arte, perhaps the purest, most atavistic expression of the comic mask. From it farce draws its dynamic physicality and comedy of manners its strong definition of social types.

Comedy uses certain fundamental elements, conventions, and techniques that create the form of any comic script: exaggeration, aggression, incongruity, reversal, automatism are but some of them. They may be expressed in verbal or physical form, and just as the building of comic structures is carefully contrived, the playing of comedy is dependent upon a high level of technical expertise: David Garrick is credited with saying, "Any fool can play Hamlet, but comedy is a very serious business." Comedy tends to flirt with the potentially painful, and the need to keep the necessary balance, the right distance from the reality of the pain—a light-footed, playful, yet absolutely serious approach—makes the playing of comedy perhaps the greatest test of an actor's ability.

Comedy has a genuine awareness of man's contradictions and incongruities, and helps to accept and reconcile them. It has a strong consciousness of mask and play. It springs from life's basic energies; it is resilient, tonic, and redemptive. With Toby Belch comedy is constantly asking all our Malvolios "Because thou art virtuous, shall there be no more cakes and ale?" and supplying its own answer with a burst of vital laughter.

chapter 4

Colley Cibber as Lord Foppington.

Courtesy of the Garrick Club, London.

Comedy of Manners

BACKGROUND

General. A form of drama that illustrates and satirizes the behavior of a particular social group, comedy of manners finds its most complete expression in the court-oriented Restoration theatre of Charles II. From 1649 to 1660, during the period of the Commonwealth, theatre had been banned in England as subversive to good moral behavior, and the robust democratic tradition of the Elizabethan theatre was almost entirely lost. When Charles II returned to the English throne, he brought with him the manners of the French court and a sense of theatre as court entertainment. These two factors influenced the nature of the two theatres licensed by Charles to William Davenant and Thomas Killigrew. These theatres were patronized essentially by courtiers, a small coterie who used them as a forum for self-display and expected to see their own attitudes portrayed on the stage.

The comedy of the day reflected the court's concern for correct form—the neoclassical obsession with rules and decorum. This placed great emphasis upon theatrical presentation of that accepted social mask by which judgments of people were made within the court itself. Unlike comedy of character (which tends to deal with eternal human traits seen in different environments), comedy of manners deals with the mores and patterns of behavior of a group of individuals whose sense of values is peculiar to the group and may have no connection with any outer reality. In such a self-involved society the matter and the manner become one and the same. The medium is the message in the sense that the external form, the mask of the group, is its values—without which it doesn't exist.

Formalized within the narrow and egocentric Restoration theatre, comedy of manners continued to be written by observant dramatists wishing to reflect or comment upon the attitudes of similarly constituted social groups who looked upon theatregoing as a prerogative of their class. The spectrum of comedy of manners from the Restoration through Sheridan, Wilde, and Coward reflects the shifting of social power and privilege. In the eighteenth and nineteenth centuries the aristocracy came to share its power with the *haute bourgeoisie* and finally with the middle class portrayed by Coward. As each group came to exercise social leadership, it took up the cultural practice of theatregoing and was itself mirrored upon the stage. Although the specific external manner of each group differed, adapting to the different physical environments of changing times, the inner attitudes and sense of values underlying that manner remained remarkably similar. Once understood, this sensibility is a key to the creation of the outer reality of the group. To take a simple example: the lace cuffs of the seventeenth century and the starched shirt cuffs of the nineteenth century play a similar part in the creation of the social mask. The flicking of the lace and the "shooting" of the starched cuff depict a like sense of self-display, although the exact manner has been adapted to the different times.

To understand both the inner reality of a particular social group and the outer expression of that reality, it is important for an actor to immerse himself, as far as time and energies allow, in the verbally and graphically expressed thoughts and manners of the period. Studying and wearing the costume is, of course, extremely informative, and this facet of understanding a character will be dealt with below. But although a costume will often tell a sensitive actor how it should be worn, it is always possible to wear a seventeenth-century costume with a twentieth-century manner. To avoid this, the actor needs an appreciation of the sensibility of the time that used a particular costume as part of the social mask of its wearers. Such appreciation will be assisted by a study of the literature and of the portraits, engravings, or photographs.

Sources. Although there are many excellent historical and critical studies of the Restoration and eighteenth-century theatres—the names of Allardyce Nicoll, Montague Summers, and J. H. Wilson come at once to mind—they are of more direct use to the scholar than to the contemporary actor who wishes to get into the skin of a part, to understand not just the theatre of a time but the social attitudes represented. More useful to the actor will be the diaries of a period, such as those of Samuel Pepys for the Restoration; biography, such as J. H. Wilson's *A Rake and His Times: George Villiers, Second Duke of Buckingham;* and collections of letters, such as Frederick Bracher's *Letters of Sir George Etherege.* Social history is excellent background, especially the work of Arthur Bryant—responsible yet colorful accounts from the Restoration (*The England of Charles II*) to the nineteenth century. For the eighteenth and nineteenth centuries, the novel gives many insights into the lifestyles and attitudes of privileged upper-class social groups. In the late nineteenth century and the twentieth century, British "society" magazines, such as *The Illustrated London News* and the *Tatler*, report these attitudes from life. An amusing source for "public-school" manners, which in the nineteenth and twentieth centuries underlay the life style of the British social elite, may be found in the stories by Frank Richards serialized in *The Boy's Own Paper*—a popular magazine of the early twentieth century.

Perhaps even more useful in understanding external manner are the pictorial sources of the periods. The portraits of the seventeenth and eighteenth centuries, together with seventeenth-century engravings such as those of Bosse and the work of eighteenth-century engravers such as Hogarth and Boucher, give an active sense of the physical style and manner of their time. The cartoonists of the nineteenth century, such as Spy, continue this active representation, and in the age of photography the society magazines depict, as to the manner born, the *beau monde* performing its social round. A useful gloss over the whole period of the comedy of manners, containing both illustrations and descriptions, may be found in Wildeblood and Brinson's *The Polite World*, the best comprehensive secondary source in this context.

Reference to appropriate literary and visual sources (and those mentioned above are merely an indication of possible lines of inquiry) is useful to an actor attempting to understand the reality of any part. It is especially the case with comedy of manners, where the focus of the drama is on the representation not so much of any individual but the manners of the group—that social mask that manifests the reality of the underlying sensibility.

INTRINSIC DEMANDS

Living as an Art. An appreciation of this concept is crucial if an actor is to understand the practicing sensibility of the social groups mirrored in comedy of manners. It is an aristocratic and somewhat Catholic attitude, which for our purpose may be traced to the outlook of the court society surrounding Charles II at his restoration. It is based in the divine right of the king to rule and, by extension, of the aristocracy to support him in this mission. In the hierarchical structure of a God-given social order it was the function of the lower classes to serve the upper, whose divine right it was not to work for a living. Thus, if a courtier did not inherit an estate (for land was the only acceptable source of income), it was important either to marry into one, to marry a fortune with which to purchase one, or to have one given by the King's favor.

The necessity of marrying an estate or a fortune is one of the principal plot devices of Restoration comedy. As with kingship, so membership in the aristocracy was conferred by birth, and a gentleman's breeding was his major asset. He might cheat (though not at cards), sponge, borrow, or even kill without losing claim to gentility, but he must not be seen to work for a living. As breeding was conferred by divine right, so the evidence of it—comporting oneself according to the accepted code of manners—must be displayed with effortless ease: "as to the manner born." To be seen to ape or copy a manner was a sure sign that one was not born to it. Thus, one of the main distinctions in Restortion comedy was between the true wit, who managed life with an effortless air of urbanity, and the false wit, who tried too hard to be thought one of the charmed circle and became a butt of laughter.

The acceptable manner of the polite code had, of course, to be learned: the art of sitting a horse, lolling in a coach, dancing a minuet, writing a poem, paying court to a woman. But it had not to appear learned, for that would give it a stiffness or an extravagance, and any form of excess was to be abhorred. The art of living had to be absorbed through the pores, as by osmosis, which could only come to one born to it. Sincerity, indulgence in emotion, were not regarded as virtues. The inner man was judged by the outer manner, which had above all to show the controlled and polished mask of the gentleman. Sir George Etherege was known as "Easy," a great compliment of the day. Congreve let it be known that he would rather be remembered as a gentleman than a playwright. To write plays was a way

to court preferment, but it was to be regarded as the exercise of gentlemanly wit—an amusing hobby rather than a profession, which smacked too much of work.

The "amateur" sensibility of the British upper class continues down through the twentieth century.[1] Professionalism was associated with having to work at something, as opposed to the assumption of being able to do it by divine right. The ruling classes had to evince effortless superiority in order to assure themselves of their God-given ascendancy.[2] At Oxford University, still something of an upper-class preserve in the first half of the twentieth century, it was important not to be seen studying. If one achieved a First Class degree it would be by innate superiority. The "gentlemanly" third was quite acceptable, but the unfortunate student was he that worked hard to achieve a "respectable" second.[3] Again, until the mid-twentieth century the English international cricket team was captained by an amateur, who did not need to be paid to play but made it a gentlemanly hobby.

The totally rigid sensibility that made ownership of land the only acceptable form of income did become diluted over a couple of centuries, as power and privilege passed first to the successful eighteenth-century merchants and then to the industrial entrepreneurs of the nineteenth century. The most prosperous of these, however, bought themselves country estates in an attempt to achieve the social status to match their wealth. The nineteenth century also saw a spread of the public-school system in Britain, partly a result of the desire of successful industrialists

---

[1] *Upper class* is taken to mean the group that exercised social power and adopted the aristocratic tradition of manners and sensibility. By the nineteenth century, however, many of the group found their origins in successful entrepreneurs of the industrial revolution.

[2] Compare the puritan ethic, in which work on this earth was taken as evidence of being one of God's elect.

[3] B.A. degrees were classified according to average grades achieved in the final comprehensive examination: alpha would gain a "first," beta a "second," and so on.

1888

THE HEIGHT OF MASHERDOM

'Well, ta-ta, Old Man! My People are waiting up for me, you know!'

'Why, don't you carry a Latch-key?'

'Carry a Latch-key! Not I! A Latch-key'd spoil any *feller's* figure!'

The importance to the gentleman of not spoiling the line of his clothes; satirized in this late-19th century cartoon.

Reproduced by permission of Punch.

to turn their sons into gentlemen.[4] Just as the educational system in the United States was responsible for turning the sons and daughters of European immigrants into good Americans, with the sense of values that entailed, so the British public school took up, preserved, and spread the gentleman's code derived from the seventeenth century.

Though changed in external detail over the years, the sensibility remained intact to be inculcated within the sons of those who gained power through the sweat of their brow—or at least through clever investment! Privilege could now be attained through effort, but when passed on it had to be cloaked in the mask of innate superiority, earned not by labor but by divine right of birth. The gentlemanly manner had such significantly trivial manifestations as the wearing of a pocket handkerchief—it should have a slightly careless appearance, not too precisely achieved—and the leaving undone of the bottom button of the waistcoat to give the look of correct casualness—not too contrived, not too exact.[5] Only deep red carnations were worn with a dinner jacket; pens should never be seen in the breast pocket of a jacket (this would suggest that work was more important than the line of the clothes), and a gentleman was

[4] The public school is the equivalent of the American prep school, a private, fee-paying institution.

[5] This was a later development, said to have been an imitation of Edward VII, who, ironically, became too corpulent to do up the final button.

never seen carrying a parcel—the presumption being that there were servants divinely ordained to do this.

There are a myriad of external expressions of this code of cultivated ease, urbanity, and indolence, but the important fact for the actor is to understand and assume the sensibility. This will enable him to display the essence of the manner rather than attempt to imitate the detail. Display of upper-class manner has been a consistent element in the English drama, and was still apparent in the 1950s, as witnessed by Kenneth Tynan who spoke of "tact, understatement and charm," as part of the "gentleman code which held much of the West End theatre in curious thrall."[6] This should have been no surprise for in the early 1950s two thirds of the entrants to British theatre schools came from the public schools and had been exposed to the code of manners, which then required no effort from them to translate onto the stage in comedy of manners, or the more anemic form, the drawing-room comedy.

Social Mores and Attitudes. Apart from the more general presumptions discussed above, there are certain specific values that tend to be common to all comedies of manners and reveal the prime concerns of the social coterie. The importance of the ownership of land has already been mentioned. It was first a source of income at a time before commercial interests predominated, and then a mark of social standing for the successful merchant. However, if it was important to own land, it was equally important not to live entirely in the country. In the seventeenth century, society was essentially court-oriented, and to live in the country was by definition to be an unfashionable clod. One of the most famous Restoration comedies, *The Country Wife*, deals with an old rake, who has retired to the country because he can no longer stand the

---

[6] Kenneth Tynan, *Tynan on Theatre*, Harmondsworth, Middlesex: Penguin Books, 1964, p. 26.

competition of London society, and his innocent, country-bred wife, who is quickly both captivated and corrupted by the lascivious manner of the town. Again, in Act IV of *The Way of the World*, Millamant tells us: "I nauseate walking; 'tis a country diversion; I loathe the country."

As both communications and facilities improved, the country gradually became acceptable as a place of weekend retreat. However, London remained the center of the social season and, increasingly, of commercial enterprise, which, as it enjoyed greater power in the land, gained more social acceptability. The interview between Lady Bracknell and John Worthing in Act I of Wilde's *The Importance of Being Earnest* bears witness to the consistency of the attitudes still operating in the upper-class society of the late nineteenth century. With regard to land, Lady Bracknell acknowledges the position it still affords, but this is tempered by the difficulties created by the land and death duties imposed by a gradually democratizing society. A country house *is* important, but a town house is *crucial*. As Lady Bracknell says: "A girl with a simple, unspoiled nature like Gwendolen could hardly be expected to reside in the country." This is a splendid piece of comedy-of-manners writing. Wilde takes the Romantic nineteenth-century associations of the country—simple, unspoiled nature—and stands them on their head to comment on the social attitudes of the day.

Wilde is also instructive upon the necessity of being well born, though Lady Bracknell first deals with the economic matters that had priority in society matches, where the real aim was to join breeding with land or money. The satire here is so broad as to reach farce proportions when John admits to being found (in a handbag) rather than born, and attempts to compensate by specifying the particular railway line where it happened. Lady Bracknell thunders that "the line is immaterial." Again a fine piece of manners comedy by Wilde, as in society marriages the particular "line" of a family was often very important.

Land, town versus country, marriage and birth are still the concerns of comedy of manners after more than two centuries. The amateur sensibility is equally evident. Lady Bracknell does not approve of anything that tampers with natural ignorance, a satirical comment on the upper classes' divine right to govern by instinct rather than knowledge and effort. Although the play contains some satire on the idea of love in marriage—Gwendolen being able to marry John only if his name was in fact Ernest—both it and Sheridan's *The School for Scandal* (which otherwise takes a similar perspective on upper-class society) have a sentimentalized attitude towards male-female relationships, compared with that of the seventeenth-century comedies. The court society of Charles II took a somewhat Hobbesian view of life: man was a creature of his animal passions and instincts, the amoral pursuit of pleasure was the true aim of existence, and he who could laugh at life most wittily was the winner in life's ephemeral and somewhat cynical stakes. Thus, carnal pleasure was highly prized and wenching was the great sport of the day. As it was necessary for most young aristocrats to marry in order to protect or increase their estates (or to gain enough of a fortune to be able to pursue the hedonistic life without working for it), marriage was a contract and love did not enter into it. Nor was there the real possibility of divorce. So, under the necessary mask of marriage, both men and women pursued each other sexually for amusement and cursory gratification. It was a game, like cards, horse racing, or going to the theatre. He who won with the least effort and most wit was the model to be respected.

If women were for company in bed, and a witty woman more prized than a dull one, for companionship man sought the company of his fellows: at cards, in the hostelries, and in other social situations in that male-dominated society. The values of comedies of manners reflect this sensibility well into the twentieth century. Under the nineteenth-century mask of moral respectability men locked themselves away from their wives in clubs, and frequented bordellos rather than engaging in the open sexual pursuit of the seventeenth century—the manner had changed but the sensibility remained. The male-oriented presumptions were subscribed to and supported by the Lady Bracknells of their day, who achieved their own power and influence by insisting that the mores were upheld and making sure the male matched his own presumptions.

The first breakdown of these presumptions may be seen in the plays of Noel Coward, written when women had achieved some measure of social and political emancipation after the First World War. The society Coward depicts and satirizes is attempting to reject the manners and mores handed down to it and then discover some way of navigating in the shifting social seas of its time. In many ways the general sensibility was a throwback to the seventeenth-century Restoration period. The romantic sentimentality present in intervening comedies of manners had given way to a more mordant, bittersweet sense of life that reflected ambivalence towards the "restoration" of the good life after the fears and deprivations of the war. A hedonism was abroad that, though neither as savage nor as urbane as at the court of Charles II, placed a frenetic emphasis upon indulging in earthly pleasures and throwing off the restrictive moral mask of the Victorian period. The social ambit was now essentially professional middle class, still desperately clinging to a gentlemanly manner while dealing with drugs, divorce, and homosexuality. The surface gloss hid unease; the casual manner betrayed uncertainty. Comedy of manners would in the future have to reflect a different kind of social mask—the faceless face of an increasingly classless society.

Realism of the Day. Possibly the most difficult problem for a young actor approaching comedy of manners is the tradition of artificiality that has grown up around its performance, and that the language and form of the text may seem to encourage. All too often performances replace manner with mannerism and style with affectation—actors impose an artificial gloss upon the play to compensate for their inability to recognize the truth in it. The influence of naturalism upon theatre has been very strong in the twentieth century, leading to a received attitude that theatre must be "truthful." The philosophy runs like this: truth is what comes naturally, therefore acting must be natural and not artificial, and any form of drama that seems to demand behavior other than what is the actor's own is to be treated with suspicion and a lot of surface gimmickry.

Such an approach has been reinforced by the naturalistic nature of TV and film acting (an ever increasing part of the actor's livelihood) and by the neo-romantic sensibility that demands sincerity in all walks of life—spontaneous emotional reaction and display being regarded as superior to all forms of role playing. But as we have seen, sincerity was regarded as a lapse of good taste in the seventeenth century. A handbook for courtiers of the day suggested: "We must be eternally on our guard not only against those who surround us, but likewise against ourselves . . . there is more wit than people imagine in concealing one's mind."[7] The assumption of a polite manner, the concealing of one's emotions—both not to embarrass others and to maintain a cool rationality that enabled one to prosper in the world's affairs—was part of the reality of the court circle in the Restoration period. For more than two hundred years such a sensibility continued to underlie the gentlemanly code of manners of the British upper classes, manifested still in the effortless and urbane superiority on which those classes prided themselves as late as the 1920s and 1930s.

It is not for the actor either to impose his own sensibility upon a period or to dismiss comedies of manners as unrealistic when what appears to be artificial behavior was the very reality of the time. There is more than

[7] Chevalier de Chetarde, *Instructions for a Young Nobleman* (London: Bentley & Magnus, 1683), p. 39.

one possibility of natural and truthful behavior—it can be a question of perspective. Truth for the actor must be that of the event in which he is involved. An actor is not required to present truth as he feels it, but to motivate action truthfully in terms of the demands of the characters represented. With comedies of manners the external attitudes are a true reflection of the inner sensibility, a flavor of which we have tried to give in the previous sections.

Language and Wit. Part of the seeming artificiality of comedy of manners lies in the nature of the language, and it is important to recognize the part played by conversation in the life style of the upper stratum of society. In the seventeenth century Richelieu suggested that "nothing is more important in the commerce of life than to please in conversation." Conversation is the principal means of human communication, and in a leisured society it is refined into an art. Much of the social round—at court, at the theatre, in eating houses and hostelries—depended upon the exercise of language. To those who did not work, time was not of the essence; one could dwell over food and other pleasures. Today the result of our work-ethic, technological society is the fast-food joint—a quick hamburger and let's get on with making money. The English habit of afternoon tea and the French of lingering over lunch and dinner, to enjoy both the food and the conversation that goes with it, are perhaps the last vestiges of the leisured sensibility, the privilege of a class that did not have to trouble with the detail of making a living.

Thus, in the seventeenth century, and in the social training deriving from it, a person would be judged and accepted as much by the ability to turn a phrase as by the turn of the calf, the arrangement of a cravat, or the handling of a teacup. Conversation was a medium for intellectual display. It had the advantage of involving no emotional contact, no revealing of the self other than what was projected as part of the social mask. At the same time, it facilitated display of superiority of mind and cosmopolitan education. In the seventeenth century, brilliant conversation led to preferment at court, and in later centuries to appearing at the dinner tables of the aristocracy. Before radio, television, film, or the novel, theatre was the principal medium of entertainment, and what better arena for the display of verbal wit? The seventeenth-century courtier went to the theatre as a place of amusement where he would see and hear the manner of his society wittily displayed. In his turn the witty playwright would be accepted at court—an example of the true integrity of the comedy of manners, where the social and theatrical masks become one and the same.

In the fullest sense, wit was more than just the exercise of epigrammatical language. It implied a complete intellectual superiority evinced equally in turning the jeweled and amusing phrase and cuckolding some lesser mortal. Horner in *The Country Wife* is a fine example of active wit. What is more amusing in a time of sexual conquest than to achieve your aim by pretending to be impotent—turning the going sensibility upon its head and making it work for you? The wit was a man who always came out on top by dint of innate superiority. No apparent effort was involved in this; it was part of that amateur sensibility of taking life as a game that one always wins with consummate ease.

Costume. What an actor in a comedy of manners now calls his costume was simply everyday clothing to the society of the time. The relationship becomes more exact if it is appreciated that the costume the actor adopts as part of his character mask was, in its time, just as much of a mask for the individual who wore it. Our clothing is probably the most immediate and obvious manner in which we present ourselves to others. It is our social mask with which we define our external self and conceal what we do not

wish to be seen. By definition, therefore, the nature of a costume will be highly indicative of the nature of a period and should be regarded by the actor not as a strange encumbrance to be overcome, but as a crucial aid to revealing the sensibility of the social group. Clothing has the social utility of making it immediately possible to identify a member of the same social group and exclude or make fun of those who worked too hard at belonging and carried manner to an extreme—as Sir Fopling Flutter in *The Man of Mode*. Perhaps the least subtle form of social identification was reached in the twentieth century, when, as a function of the influence of the public school on British upper-class society, the wearing of the "old school tie" became an evident badge of belonging and acceptability.

In the Restoration period the clothing mask was influenced by the discrete opulence of a wealthy leisured class, the sexual acquisitiveness of the time, and the concealment of both physical blemish and emotion. The emphasis was upon bodily adornment—silks and laces, frills and curls—and the female bosom and the male leg were titillatingly revealed for carnal attraction. The stage, though mirroring life, went even further and by creating breeches parts for actresses enabled them to show that part of their body the social mask concealed. Here the theatre nicely performs its function of showing the true appetite beneath the mask. As cleanliness was not a particular virtue of the age, it was compensated for by powder and makeup. This had the further advantage of disguising the ravages often caused by smallpox and the other "pox" of the time. A perfect mask sensibility is shown by the use of beauty patches, first to conceal pockmarks and then simply for adornment's sake. The heavily made-up face tended, of course, to be somewhat inexpressive—a dispassionate mask that revealed little emotion. This concealment of emotion continued to be a hallmark of the upper-class Englishman long after the male had ceased to wear

Seventeenth-century male costume; note especially the high heels, muff, and snuff-taking attitude.

Victoria and Albert Museum, London; Crown copyright.

makeup, and is testified to by the expression "stiff upper lip" associated with the cliché English character down into the twentieth century.

Clothes, as both mask and mirror, have always reflected social attitudes and needs. Cole Porter was suggesting in the 1920s that a glimpse of Victorian stocking was shocking, but now "anything goes." Today the further physical and moral emancipation of women is indicated by the universal bikini.

Men's clothing became less formal and more functional as pure idleness gave way to professional occupations. Women's clothing took a leap into equality in the 1920s when political emancipation brought a measure of social emancipation with it. Female clothing became boyishly oriented. The woman disguised her hips and breast, wore short hair, and affected cigarette smoking in long holders. The cigarette holder was, of course, as much a prop as the fans of the earlier cen-

Seventeenth-century female costume; note peeping toe, fan, and mask.

Victoria and Albert Museum, London; Crown copyright.

turies. It allowed of elegant gesture and betrayed its mask function in keeping the unpleasant smoky reality of the cigarette away from the smoker's face. The contemporary vogue for dark glasses is the equivalent of the seventeenth-century vizard mask. The padded brassieres of the 1940s, the bustles of the 1880s, and the padded male calves of the Restoration all show the continuity of the costume mask in indicating the sensibility of a time.

Man has constantly sought to personalize himself. Even today, when class distinctions and elite social groups are regarded as unacceptable, the sensibility they manifested is still in evidence. In the United States, which has always prided itself upon being a classless society without the formal external distinctions that are the stuff of the comedy of manners, the term "class" has become common parlance. To have "class" is defined more in individual than group terms, and

1922
GLORINDA

Artist's impression of female costume and posture in the early 1920s.

Reproduced by permission of Punch.

can be taken to mean anything from having your own teeth at sixty-five to that indefinable sense of self or style that sets Jackie Onassis apart from her fellow (lesser?) mortals. "Class" wherever applied is still a positive distinction, used with grudging approval.

Privilege, leisure, a sense of superiority, and a distinctive set of group manners and mores: if these are some of the necessary qualities of the social groups about which comedy of manners is written, it is conceivable that aspects of youth culture, and particularly that of the student, is the true focus for such comedy. The young actor

might, through a study of this contemporary example, gain direct understanding of how sensibility and manner are related. Without unduly overstressing the point, it can be seen that students have more leisure, or at least flexibility in work; are economically subsidized, or at least do not have adult financial responsibilities; tend to have a more progressive attitude in sexual, social, and political matters, and regard this attitude as superior to any other; live in closely related groups and denote their common sensibility in clothing and manner.

Modern student sensibility is antiestablishment or upper-class. The radical inversion of social attributes, created in part by the spread of "sincerity," has made it obligatory to associate with the aspiration of minority groups, the poor, and the working class. Thus, clothing is required to be functional, casual, giving no indication of self-conscious display or wasteful extravagance. The aim is free expression, as far removed as possible from the sense of uniformity of the middle-class social mask—the gray flannel suit, or the pin stripe and bowler hat. But what do we find? An almost universal uniformity in denim. This should preferably look faded and old to the degree where, in order that the right mask should be displayed, old clothes can be more expensive to buy than new. Patched clothes also indicate poverty. Thus, patches become part of the contemporary costume—but expensive patches sewn onto new or deliberately aged clothes. The external form of identity may be reinforced by the wearing of Granny glasses and the use of special handclasps, all part of a manner that signifies that members of the group enjoy a particular sensibility. They belong to a select or "alternative" society, opposed to any form of social masks, but readily identifiable by its clothes, speech, and physical manner.

Although the sense of human values of the late-twentieth-century student is far re-

Marsha Mason in Noel Coward's 1930 play *Private Lives*. Note calculated ease and boyish charm.

American Conservatory Theatre, San Francisco.

moved from that of the Restoration courtier, the special nature of the student's life and community gives rise to a sensibility that still finds external manifestation in a very particular social mask and manner. The connection between mask and manner is as direct as in the seventeenth century and can as easily lead to superficial imitation. Rigidity of mask or the adoption of mask without meaning lends itself as readily today to the comment and satire of comedy of manners as anything written by Wycherley, Sheridan, or Wilde.

Space and Social Settings. Comedies of manners take place within two physical environments—the actual space of the theatres of their time and the social setting portrayed within the play. An understanding of the social setting is of more value to the contemporary actor concerned with the sen-

sibility of the period, but a brief examination of theatrical space will throw some of the structural elements of the plays into clearer perspective. Perspective was, indeed, one of the fundamental visual elements of the Restoration theatre, creating a realistic illusion by means of raked stages and series of painted flats leading up to a backdrop. A representation of St. James's Park created in this way would have seemed as much a miracle of naturalism to the audience of its day as Antoine's use of real sides of beef on stage was to appear two centuries later. The perspective effect gave a central focus to the action, and this was reinforced by an apron that enabled the actor to get very close to the audience downstage center, where the best light was to be found. The sense of pictorial realism with a central thrust towards the audience was completed by the proscenium arch, which framed the scene and created the effect of a picture of the times. The apron and the downstage focus facilitated both direct address and asides to the audience, whose presence was accepted as an integral part of the event: they were after all the same social group as the characters upon the stage. Indeed, in the seventeenth century spectators sat upon the stage itself and spent much time staging their own social performances in the pit.

The settings depicted on stage were the locales of the social round of the day: bou-

doirs, eating houses, and outdoor meeting places such as the royal parks. The furniture was sparse and formally placed, which put the focus upon language and the physical manner of the actor. This sense of space, elegance, and simplicity is fundamental to the comedy of manners. Although the apron disappeared in the eighteenth century and the sparse perspective stage gave way to the more fully realized elegance of the Victorian drawingroom (as the nineteenth century im-

Baroque formality of the English seventeenth century seen in the drawing room of Wilton House.

Countrylife.

Baroque quality of living space recapitulated in the theatre: Operhaus, Bayreuth. Note perspective scenery and large, open stage area.

Verlag Georg D. W. Callwey.

posed its heavier and more opulent sensibility), comedies of manner were still highly pictorial and audience-focused. The theatrical space of such drama must always allow for easy and elegant movement. There must be room for the sweep of costume and the formality of manner that demands a certain social distance between characters. The space should be light, bright, and uncluttered, providing scope for the curving flow of action and the total, effortless command of both social and stage space the actor must achieve.

Character and Social Masks. In the seventeenth century and well into the nineteenth—before the age of psychological naturalism—characters in plays were described and regarded as *dramatis personae:* masks of the drama. Characters were there to serve the action of the play, not the other way around. The playwright's total idea was important, not individual character detail. This was especially the case with comedy of manners, whose function was to reflect the nature of a social group. In these plays character is not gradually revealed to us. We are given a clear

The lighter but still formal living space of the eighteenth century, reflected in the drawing room of Syon House, England.

Countrylife.

indication, from the start, of the role the character plays in the society of his time, and therefore in the working out of the action of the play.

In the seventeenth and eighteenth centuries the very name of the character underlined his principal personality trait and function within the play. The Horners, Sullens, Petulants, Frails, Pliants, Tattles, and Wishforts of the time tell any actor what the spine of his character has to be. Even as late as Wilde, this eponymous principle still operated with the more broadly drawn characters such as Canon Chasuble and Miss Prism in *The Importance of Being Earnest*.

The coterie societies that comedy of manners reflects and passes comment upon are made up of recognizable social types—whether it be the wits, fops, country clods, and testy old husbands of Wycherley's day or the lounge lizards, flappers, and Colonel Blimps of Coward's. The playwrights show them to us dancing their accustomed parts in the "Ronde," going their inevitable way in the social world of their time.

The writer of comedy of manners is not, then, concerned with the psychological depth of any character, but rather with the significant and determinant element of his social mask. This will be based in a social

Strong sense of character mask conveyed by costume, wig, posture, and facial attitude in a production of *The Relapse*.

American Conservatory Theatre, San Francisco.

truth of the time, and the manner and attitude of a particular character will reveal how far he partook of that truth. However, the totality of a character's psyche was not the issue; the significant factor was the part that his mask played in creating a reflection of the total social mask. As society itself, the play may be seen as a large mask made up of many smaller ones, each realized sufficiently to give theatrical life and social relevance to the whole.

PERFORMANCE DEMANDS

Playing the Mask. One of the inherent givens of comedies of manners is the mask nature of character portrayal. The relationship between the creation and playing of a mask and the "truthful" performance of character reality has often confounded the young actor. To restate a point already made, theatre is the communication of the illusion of truth—the mask of truth, if you will. What the actor finds difficult is distinguishing the necessary and discovered truth of the theatrical event from the private truth of his own feelings.

In a comedy of manners the mask is, of course, founded in truth, in the absolute validity of a character's motivations and intentions. But it does not involve a deep exploration of that truth. What we need to know of Horner is that he partakes of the sensibility of the court society of Charles II, and has a dominating drive that reflects an aspect of that society. The final definition of his mask is the way in which he responds to the drive within the constraints of the sensibility. Any deep psychological motivation is irrelevant—it was neither the concern of the playwright nor the interest of the audience. The social motivation, however, is vital and based in complete truth.

Although the actor's task is to understand and completely assimilate the truth of the sensibility and the motivating factors, he must also appreciate the comic intention of the playwright in selecting, heightening, and exaggerating certain aspects of the social situation. The playwright, while reflecting the manners of a society, is also passing comment upon them and taking a particular perspective in the creation of the comic masks. The nature of the comment is always to arouse laughter, even when treating the potentially painful. The actor must be aware of this and not search for deeply felt and painful psychological responses. He should play his mask according to the playwright's truth, so as to reveal the necessary attitudes in the necessary proportion.

The comic comment, however severe, is always good-natured. To take the example of the "testy-old-gentleman" mask, such as Pinchwife, Sir Peter Teazle, or Sir Anthony Absolute, whose social function it was to be cuckolded or thwarted: these characters are all easily angered and fly into rages that are perfectly truthfully motivated—they have good reason from their standpoint. But the

rage is never "real" with any deeply emotional effect upon the audience. If it were it would undermine the comic point of the action, which is to reveal the ridiculous unreasonableness of the character. The rages are exaggerated. These are repressive characters who deserve to be thwarted. They have set themselves up for it, the audience knows this, and it is properly amused when they get what they deserve. The laughter itself is, of course, not without sympathy and recognition of certain human foibles of which the audience could be equally culpable.

Although the audience should have an amused sympathy for a mask of comedy, it should not empathize too deeply with it; that might upset the balance between laughter and pain that comedy is always careful to maintain. There is a scene in *The Way of the World* where Lady Wishfort is repairing her facial mask in order to meet a potential lover. She describes her face as being cracked and "arrantly flayed—I look like an old peeled wall." This is a very funny image, and the sight of this old lady hopelessly trying to repair the ravages of time and present herself like a spring lamb (putting on a mask we know to be cracked) makes a comic mask of the character—a silly, pretentious, predatory, but finally harmless old dame. If we were to examine her situation from another perspective, however, it could be sad and painful.[8] She could appear as a lonely old woman, desperately trying to compete in a world that sets great store on youth and sexual charm and lacking the self-knowledge or ability to come to terms with her situation and grow old gracefully. Comedy is, of course, not unaware of this perspective, but it prefers to laugh rather than weep about the absurdity and fallibility of human nature.

The actor must maintain the comic bal-

[8] It was the adoption of such a perspective that led to the sentimental comedy of the eighteenth century, when the attitude of sincerity prompted pity rather than amusement at the human condition.

ance and, while understanding the human truth of a situation, reveal through his mask the perspective that leads to laughter rather than tears. What is emphasized is the exaggerated nature of the obsession. The total balance of truth is tilted towards the side of comedy, and this disproportion becomes the new truth, the comic reality of the event—the mask. The actor shares this truth with the audience, plays with them within his mask. Both are aware of its exaggeration, that it contains the comic perspective, and there is a complot between them to enjoy the game—to share the agreed reality. The maintenance of an acceptable social mask was a crucial element of comedy of manners. Here the actor takes this truth, and the understanding of the sensibility and attitudes it represents, and shows it to the audience according to the perspective the playwright has placed upon his character. The actor will take and communicate only what is necessary. He makes only those choices that are consistent with the truth of the mask and heighten its effect.

Revealing Tension Between Mask and Appetite. One of the chief ways in which an actor's choices are determined is by the degree of gap between the assumed social mask of his character and the reality of its face. Comedy of manners deals with the mask of a particular social group and the way in which each character relates to the norm and displays a certain aspect of it. For example, part of the social mask of Restoration society was an elegance yet ease of social manner. Thus, much of the humor surrounding the fops or false wits was created by affectation—overdoing the manner—and the lack of self-knowledge that allowed them to assume a superiority that their actions denied. Their mask doesn't quite fit; it is out of balance with the convention of the time, and the actor creates comic tension by the way in which he reveals this solecism.

The playwright may draw the audience's attention to the gap between the assumptions of a mask and its reality by direct verbal comment from another character. He may condemn the character out of his own mouth by failed attempts at wit. More usually, however, the comic tension is revealed in action, which emphasizes the significance of the physical choices an actor makes—the exaggeration of a flourish, the false coyness of the predatory matron.

Comedy tends to deal with human appetites, and comedy of manners deals with the polite veneers with which we cover them. One of the less dangerous appetites, perhaps, is that for food. In *The Importance of Being Earnest* Wilde has invested Algernon Moncrieff with an excessive urge in this direction. He first consumes all of the cucumber sandwiches prepared for Lady Bracknell, and later does the same with John Worthing's muffins. This latter scene contrasts Algy's gluttony with the imperturbable elegance of his manner. He consumes the muffins "calmly," which, as he says, is the only way to eat muffins; otherwise the "butter would probably get on my cuffs." This is an amusing juxtaposition of the necessity for keeping up the outer mask while satisfying the inner appetite. In this particular scene the comic effect is heightened by the emotional crisis that surrounds it, which Algy ignores with superb, self-centered urbanity.

Sometimes the actor may have three levels to juggle with, which gives even greater scope for comic playing. Horner, in *The Country Wife*, wears the mask of impotence over the mask of social manner in order to give play to the reality of his sexual appetite. This is the essence of active wit: to satisfy your appetite by conscious manipulation of the social mask. The comic effect is usually created by the slipping or distortion of the mask to reveal the face, but the playwright will occasionally set up the opposite effect for the actor—revealing the appetite and showing the character masking it. This is the case with Lady Wishfort in the scene described in the previous section. However it

"Imperturbable elegance of manner" as displayed by Algernon Moncrieff in *The Importance of Being Earnest.*

Mark Taper Forum, Los Angeles.

is achieved, the tension between the assumption and the appearance is one of the principal comic devices of the comedy of manners. The degree of a character's deviation from the social norm established on the stage—his lack of self-knowledge or lack of wit—will create the level of humor surrounding a character. This is as true for the "silly asses" of Coward's day as for the false wits of the Restoration. The actor, through his choices, creates the correct degree of comic tension for the truth of his character mask.

Verbal Agility. Wit contained in language is one of the principal elements of comedy of manners. A certain manner of speaking is also one of the distinguishing features of the particular social groups about which comedy of manners is written. The actor has, then, a double demand placed upon him in his handling of the lines. The manner in which the line is spoken becomes an important part of character mask, and the content of the line must also be communicated in such a way as to achieve its inherent comic impact.

The social groups with which comedy of manners concerns itself are highly verbal societies, relying more upon intellectual than emotional communication. During the Restoration this emphasis upon language was institutionalized in the sense that theatre became an extension of the court and a forum for the exercise of that wit, which was an entree to the society of the time. Verbal repartee was not as fatal an exchange as fencing with rapiers, but the tongue could be equally as lethal a weapon in making and destroying reputations.

Though at its height in Restoration comedy, witty exchange is a quality of all comedy of manners right into the twentieth century. The metaphor of fencing with the tongue gives a useful indication of the qualities required of the actor by the lingistic demands of this theatrical form—quickness, lightness, agility, variety, rhythm, and stress are some of the terms that come to mind. Intellectual ability, and therefore superiority, is measured by speed of response. It is not the considered academic reply of philosophical depth that gains recognition, nor language colored by emotional feeling. It is the display of quick verbal reflexes, the consummate and witty employment of the tools of social intercourse—words.

The actor must, then, be able to speak his lines quickly, but, equally, the words must all be clearly heard if the wit is to score its points with the audience. Lip and tongue agility and the use of a variety of head tones to give the correct stress—to point the line—are prime requisites of this acting style. The actor must also be aware of the shape of his lines. Just as the fencer sets up his opponent for the final thrust, so must the actor by his use of rhythm—which communicates the shape of the line—set up the audience to laugh at the right moment.

The art of pointing is to give the crucial part of a line the right stress. Timing is the delivery of that crucial part at the right moment. The actor builds a line by using rhythm so that the audience knows a laugh is coming. He gives them enough time to understand the humor, but not too much to analyze it, and allows expectation to build so that the audience is poised, breath held to laugh at the moment when he hits them with the crucial point of the line. Great players of comedy can sometimes dispense with the audience's intellectual understanding of the line. It is told of Maggie Smith, in a Shakespearean comedy, that she refused to have an arcane and no longer understood word, seemingly crucial for the humor of the line, changed into its modern equivalent, saying she could achieve

the laugh by her delivery of the line. And she did. Her use of rhythm and stress was such that the audience laughed to complete the cycle of comic rhythm built up in them, without entirely understanding the meaning of the line. This point is made simply to reinforce the necessity of rhythm in line delivery, not to discount intellectual clarity. The form and content of the line should be as one.

The demands of comedy reinforce the fact that an actor is playing as much with the audience as with his fellow actors. In comedy the actor needs the audience response, and the verdict is immediate—the audience either laughs or it doesn't. In a comedy of manners much of the response will be to what an actor says (as opposed to farce, where it will be mostly to what he does), and the actor must pay heed to that response. Just as it is pointless for an actor not to deliver humorous lines clearly, so it is pointless for him not to allow the audience to have its laugh. Whereas the audience can watch comic action while laughing, it cannot hear further lines, and this places a particular demand upon the actor in manners comedy: he must have very fast verbal brakes. The pace of the dialogue is brisk. An actor may expect, but he must not anticipate laughter. He must take the line full tilt, then hold when the laugh comes, keep the brakes on until it just begins to fade, and then accelerate away through the end of the laugh into his next line.

If this all sounds somewhat technical—it is. But it is a technique built into the truth of the comic event. An actor in comedy must be aware of his audience. What, after all, is an aside but a taking of the audience into your confidence? The actor expects to hear the audience; if they don't laugh the event has failed. In one sense, then, he is playing for laughs, and uses all the verbal skills suggested above to achieve them. The skills are used not for their own sake, however, but to manifest the truth of the event—the manner, the sensibility, the wit. Technique, his ability to understand all the demands of the event and to communicate its valid essence to the audience, is an essential tool of the total actor.

Sense of Occasion. The verbal and physical masks demanded by comedy of manners communicate that sense of decorous self-display, the doing of the right thing at the right time, that is at the core of the life style of upper-class society. In the Restoration it was the court, theatre, royal parks, and eating houses of the day that were the forum for seeing and being seen. The salons, coffee shops, and spas of the eighteenth century performed a similar purpose. This social round became even more institutionalized in the nineteenth century with the development of the "season." This included racing at Ascot, rowing at Henley, sailing at Cowes, tennis at Wimbledon, and balls both in London and at the great country houses.

The season would start with the presentation at court of the daughters of the upper classes. This was followed by dances at which they and specially selected (for birth, money, and prospects) young men would be allowed to perform ritualized mating ceremonies. The cermonies would continue through the social round of the season, and each occasion would require a special costume, the correct mask for the event: morning dress at Ascot; white suits and blazers at Henley; flowered hats and dresses at Wimbledon. Thus would the nature of the occasion be defined and its ritual celebrated with strawberries and cream at Wimbledon and champagne picnics at Oxford for Eights Week (the annual university rowing races).

The identification of people by their clothing and maintaining class distinction in this way goes back to the butts of Restoration comedy: the countryman who did not wear the latest fashion, or the false wit who wore it too obviously. The importance of the correct mask for a given occasion presumes the wealth to afford it and the manner to wear it well and take the right part in the ritual. Such distinctions reinforced the exclusive and

hierarchical nature of the social system built upon the aristocratic traditions and sensibility handed down from the seventeenth century. By the late nineteenth century, though, those who partook of the sensibility and most strongly reinforced its rituals were likely to be the grandsons and granddaughters of successful Victorian entrepreneurs born, as Lady Bracknell put it, in "the purple of commerce." Just as marriage had a financial basis in the seventeenth century, so the prime function of the season two hundred years later was to join wealth with wealth, or wealth with privilege: to rehearse, extend, and reinforce the power structure of the ruling classes.

A sense of occasion, then, surrounds all the relationships of the social groups with which comedy of manners concerns itself. It is the unspoken affirmation of the fact that a function of the social round is to confirm the values and sensibility of that particular class structure—to check, as it were, the correctness of the mask. The fact of being on parade, of displaying the right mask, is not denied by the pretense of not wearing a mask at all. It is the same kind of art disguising art that is fundamental to the actor's craft. This particular demand of comedy of manners gives the actor a double opportunity—to play at playing—which makes it a theatrical exercise of great potential.

PLAYING THE STYLE

Physical Flair. The physical mask, comprising deportment, clothing, and gesture, is the most immediate and significant mark of distinction among the social groups who have been the subject of comedy of manners. This outer manner reveals an inner sensibility, and although the detail changed between the seventeenth and twentieth centuries, the underlying sense of life remains fairly constant. One of the principal tasks of the actor is to reveal this sensibility in action within the etiquette of the time. A sense of formality and

The upright yet relaxed physical bearing of the eighteenth-century British nobleman seen in this portrait of John, sixth Earl of Mar and Kellie. Note especially the leg position, the hands, and the child's exact recapitulation of the adult manner.

Courtesy of the Earl of Mar and Kellie.

precision combined with grace and ease; the performing of an elaborate social ritual with studied nonchalance; the achievement of an art of movement that disguises the artifice of its attainment—these are some of the fundamental qualities of an upper-class social group, and are revealed in its distinctive physical manner.

Uprightness of stance and posture is a basic feature. Standing upright is a learned behavior for the human being. Slouching or standing loosely is perhaps closer to an un-masked manner. The distinctive upright posture of the upper-class physicality has certain functions: it inhibits emotional display; shows elegant clothing to the best advantage; betrays the assumption of looking down upon, and therefore manifests superiority; and bears witness to particular kinds of training given to an upper-class—from the poise to dance in the French manner in the seventeenth century, to the military officer drill given to public-school boys in the nineteenth.

Clothing both reflects and reinforces the manner of an age. The elaborate clothing and formality of the Restoration put great emphasis upon the male stance. The display of the leg became part of the male sexual attractiveness of a consciously virile age. To "make a leg" the male stood with the weight essentially on the back leg, the front leg advanced and turned out at about ninety degrees, the heel of the front foot pointing to the instep of the rear. This is, of course, the basic third position in ballet, and bears witness to the fact that physical etiquette was taught by ballet masters. As a result of this, most male stances in the seventeenth and eighteenth centuries were some variation of the first, third, and fourth ballet positions. (See figures on pages 129 and 130.)

The fullness and stiffness of the males' upper-body clothing in the seventeenth century mean that arms were held away from the body, which made possible the displaying of lace cuffs, handkerchiefs, and ornate canes and rings. The weight of ribbons and layers of fabric led to a swaggering elegance that allowed the male to carry and dominate his costume—it had to appear comfortable. Some of the apparently mannered gestures of the seventeenth century were a natural function of the costume—the flick of the head to keep the hair off the shoulders; the flick of the wrist to keep the lace off the hand

This painting of a group of eighteenth-century English gentlemen shows the calculatedly casual bearing.

Tooth Galleries, London.

and draw attention to it; the erect, open stride for balancing firmly on high heels.

The main distinction in male attitude in the eighteenth century was that it lacked the precise courtly formality of the preceding age. A leg was still made but with less sexual consciousness, and the arms and hands were never allowed to hang at the sides of the body—that posture was fit only for merchants and servants. So, the gentleman rested his hand on his sword, on his hip, or tucked inside his waistcoat, the top of which was left unbuttoned.

In sitting the eighteenth-century male adopted a pose of elegant nonchalance. Chairs were used as props, and to avoid formality asymmetrical positions were taken: the gentleman seldom sat erect in the center of a chair but reclined to the left or right on the arm, one leg resting lightly on the other knee. If the chair had no arms the male might straddle it with arms resting on the back.

We cannot overemphasize the quality of ease with which the manner was carried off. To a young man today, with his jeans, T-shirt, slip-on shoes, and loose hair, flopping in furniture is natural and comfortable. For an eighteenth-century gentleman this would be not only painful but expensive: his silk stockings would run, his bodice stiffening would cut into his body; his breeches would split, cravate come undone, and wig be

A Club of Artists shows the wide range of leg and hand positions adopted by eighteenth-century gentlemen.

National Portrait Gallery, England.

Compte Robert de Montesquieu displays the quietly elegant sophistication that was the manifestation of the gentlemanly tradition in the late nineteenth century.

Musée du Louvre, Paris.

pushed awry. Precisely in order to be comfortable and feel at ease he had to adopt an attitude that seems uneasy and artificial today. It is the actor's task to make that attitude look absolutely natural.

The sense of gentlemanly nonchalance and studied ease carried down into the nineteenth and twentieth centuries. Though clothing became less elaborate in a more work-oriented society, it was still well tailored and gave a strong contour to the body. Starched collars insured the head was held high, continuing the attitude of aristocratic deportment handed down the centuries. Within this frame the gentleman still carried himself with careful carelessness—flicking the wrist to display a flash of cuff and jeweled links; hitching the trouser to prevent bagging at the knee; carrying a handkerchief in his jacket sleeve, and casually in the breast pocket; cigarette held negligently between index and first finger as he lolled cross-legged in sofa or armchair.

The female manner was equally a reflection of its sensibility and time. In the seventeenth century, women walked as if doing a small stepped dance. Dresses had stiffly corseted bodices cut low to reveal the breast and shoulders. This display was heightened by the deep curtsies of the time and coyly concealed by the fans, whose function was equally to provoke: fluttering and flirtatious,

they revealed the feelings they pretended to mask. Sweeping curves, with the dress held just off the ground, and graceful poses characterized the women's movements, the hint of license always present beneath the air of formal reticence.

The eighteenth-century woman partook of a somewhat more consciously cultivated manner. Affected by bourgeois wealth and a more sentimental than sexual mask, she moved as a ship in full sail, balancing elaborate hair styles. Fans were large and more exquisite, used for display of wealth as an adjunct to dress, as much as for flirtation. The nineteenth-century woman had to swim inside a sea of petticoats, subordinate in a male-dominated society and locked within a moral code that regarded sex for women as, at best, a rather unfortunate method of procreation. Stiffly correct, she displayed the demure manner expected of the weaker sex. Far from the flirtatious prop of the seventeenth

Cigarette held negligently, Richard Johnson lolls gracefully in a production of *Private Lives*. Note careful casualness of handkerchief, ascot, and leg position.

National Theatre, London

1928

He: 'So you're just back from Pontresina? Nice place.'
She: 'Glorious!'
He: 'Go to St. Moritz? Nice place.'
She: 'Marvellous!'
He: 'And Davos? Nice place.'
She: 'Ripping!'
He: 'Had a good time?'
She: 'Divine!'
He (after deep thought): 'Do you know, Mildred, you're just the sort of girl
a man can talk to.'

The emancipated woman of the 1920s aped the male posture.

Reproduced by permission of Punch.

century, her fan is now a security blanket to
ward off the fetid air or glances of overheated
males.

After the 1914–18 war the emancipated
woman strode out of her petticoats into the
freedom of shorter skirts and male trousers.
She could now cross her legs and ape the
lounging manner of her male friends while
elegantly smoking a cigarette. As the final
breakdown of aristocratic and neoclassical attitudes is approached, the underlying social
presumptions of the upperclass are now
manifested in a manner much more equal for
men and women: the feminine ideal is now
much closer to the masculine.

Nuts and Bolts. Once again we are going to
give some details of courtesies, not because
we believe anyone in the audience will be able
to judge their precise correctness or, finally,
care, but because the courtesies create the

physical expression of the sensibility and, more importantly, help the actor to get a better physical sense of the social manner and relationships of the time. **It is the quality and understanding of manner rather than the detail that is important and, beyond that, the way in which the social manner is particularized in terms of character.**

Seventeenth-Century Bow. The hat is swept off with the right hand and transferred to the left. The right foot slides forward a step, feet turned out, both legs straight. The body inclines forward from the waist, spine and neck straight. Both knees bend outwards, the front leg kept straighter than the rear, which takes most of the body weight; feet stay flat on the ground. The right arm sweeps forward and down to the ground. On rising the hand is kissed to the person saluted, the weight comes onto the front foot, and third position is adopted.

Eighteenth-Century Bow. Variations on bows began to proliferate. A general-purpose bow is as follows: the right foot is taken to the side, with the weight on it, leaving the left foot resting on the toe. The hat is removed and taken to the side, and the back is inclined. As the body comes up the left foot comes behind the right into fourth position.

Later Bows. Just as the eighteenth-century bow is simpler than the bow of the earlier century, so the bow becomes more and more simplified through the nineteenth century to the early twentieth. The bow was taken with both heels together and the body bent from the waist. The degree of bend lessened throughout the period until, in the comedies of Coward in the 1930s, it is barely more than an inclination of the head, together with a handshake.

Seventeenth-Century Curtsy. A step is taken to either side, to draw attention to the curtsier; the foot is then brought back to the other foot, heels touching. The knees are bent smoothly and slightly outwards, the body inclined a little forward with arms falling naturally to the side. Depending upon the depth of the curtsy, the heels remain on the ground or are raised slightly.

Eighteenth-Century Curtsy. As with bows there were variations of curtsies. The most respectful was similar to that of the seventeenth century. A more everyday curtsy, somewhat lighter in feeling, was made by sliding one foot forward into fourth position, bending the back knee, then without bending the body rising onto the front leg. This curtsy could be oriented to right or left, and taken without pausing in a walk.

Later Salutations. In formal society the curtsy continued to be used until the early twentieth century, with more or less formal use of the eighteenth-century curtsy. After the First World War the emancipated woman began to shake hands and incline the head like the male in his salutation. Variations on this were the giving of both hands, the extending of one hand palm down, or the directly outstretched hand as the male—depending upon the formality of the occasion, the degree of friendliness, and the level of emancipation of the woman. Whereas a man would always shake hands standing, a woman could remain seated to give her hand to a man, or to a woman who was younger or her social inferior.

Taking Snuff. A highly distinctive male gesture of the seventeenth and eighteenth centuries, it is performed essentially in the following manner: the box is held in finger and thumb to display its jewels; the top is tapped to get the snuff off the inside lid—it is too expensive to waste; it is inserted with finger and thumb to get well up the nose; any spill is dusted off the costume with the handkerchief to prevent stains. There are perfectly good economic or practical motivations for each of the actions. The way in

17ᵗʰ CENTURY BOW

17ᵗʰ CENTURY CURTSEY

Detail of seventeenth-century bow and curtsy.

Line drawings by ClaireMarie Verheyen.

Note: Percentage figures by foot positions equal distribution of body weight.

Detail of eighteenth-century bow.

Line drawing by ClaireMarie Verheyen.

which these actions are performed makes snufftaking part of the social manner of the day, and an element of mask upon which judgments are made. Excessive display denoted the fop, sneezing afterwards the unskilled clod. The only change in the eighteenth century was that the snuff was put in the indentation behind the thumb on the back of the hand, and sniffed into the nostril. This was regarded as less coarse than sticking the thumb and finger up the nose.

The Language of the Fan. The main female prop of the seventeenth and eighteenth centuries, the fan had the practical functions of cooling, shielding the face from fire, and wafting away flies. More importantly, though, it was used as a tool of social intercourse. The fan punctuated a story, beckoned a gentleman across a room. Weaving, twisting, snapping, rising, falling, the fan spoke subtleties in the language of love and private emotion. There were accepted

conventions. The tip of the fan touched to the lips meant "Hush"; to the right cheek, "Yes"; to the left cheek, "No"; and to the nose, "I do not trust you." Yawning behind the fan meant "You bore me"; pointing the fan horizontally to the heart, "You have my love"; hiding the eyes behind the open fan also conveyed love; brushing the open fan towards a person was dismissive. As none of these gestures would be understood today it makes more sense for actors to make up their own personal language, taking the original conventions as examples.

Taking Tay. The drinking of chocolate or coffee, and later tea, was one of the new social rituals of the eighteenth century. Served in delicate china from the newly developing ceramics industry, it became an exercise in effortlessly artful poses: saucers cradled in the palm; cups enfolded with all five fingers, or taken by the handle with thumb, index, and middle finger and raised to the lips with little finger delicately extended. Above all, the

Elegance of manner when taking refreshment.

Residenzmuseum München.

cups should never be seized, or the impression given that drinking was a serious matter.

Exploring the Style. More important than aping any precise detail, the actor should physically understand the social manner and adapt it to the nature of his character. There is all the difference in the world between assimilating a strange manner and adopting a superficial artifice. All the social airs and graces may be played with to illustrate the character mask. The fops or "dandies" of the Restoration were given to extreme behavior. By exaggeration of physical manner an actor has a basis for such a character: overplay the ballet positions; overflourish the bow; flick the head too abruptly to make the curls bounce; peep over muffs; toy with ribbons.

Apply the playwright's clues—Sir Jasper Fidget may perform the social manner with a finicky quality. Discover how a strong mask attitude will affect the way the character walks, sits, bows, or plays with the fan. Explore the possibilities of too much cuff lace or the slipping of padding on male calves. Take the style as far as it will go: lean into it to discover where your character finds his balance. Style should be consistent, but it need not be archaically correct. Nor should it be blandly homogenous—each character will play its particular part in the subtle shadings of the social milieu. The manner should not restrict or strait-jacket the characters; it should arise from the way in which they perceive and confront it.

We have by no means exhausted the conventional mannerisms of the periods, nor would it be possible or useful to do so. We firmly believe that understanding the sensibility is more important than rote learning of detail. No costume will look right on an actress who is fighting the physical demands it makes on her, who, rather than assimilating the social attitudes that gave rise to it is still, in her mind, drooping her shoulders, sagging her bosom, and taking jean-clad contemporary strides. As Yves St. Laurent has said: "What is right in a dress is the woman wearing it." Correctness of attitude is more important than correctness or minute replication of external detail.

We have tried to convey both the intellectual and physical understanding of social manner. We believe that the integration of these two aspects, practiced through the ideas already given and the exercises in the next section, will create a true sense of the event on stage, and engage the audience more than any shallow display of arcane mannerisms.

EXERCISES, GAMES, TECHNIQUES

Patterning Space. Use furniture or blocks to create various ground plans within your space. This will demand particular patterns of movement from the players, who are asked to move through the space at different speeds. It is well to start with slow speeds and build up to a swiftness that is just short of running. Players must not touch any of the furniture as they move on their toes, glide, skate, walk with a rhythmical stride, and so on. As the speeds and types of movement can be varied, so can the shape of the space be altered to provide different patterns. The exercise can be extended, with teams entering from different sides and avoiding each other as well as the physical objects. Ultimately the space can be filled with players performing the task in any combination of speeds and movement.

To this basic exercise may be added any number of elaborations concerned with control and balance. The players can be asked to move with books on their heads; balancing tennis balls in teaspoons; as waiters in a restaurant with trays of crockery and dishes. Extensions can be attached to the players' waists to make their judgment of space more acute, or some may wear rehearsal skirts. The exercise may be turned into individual and team competitions as long as the emphasis does not fall upon the competition rather than the objective of the exercises: controlled, balanced movement combined with ease, agility, and awareness of space relationships. To win is not simply to arrive first, but to do so having fulfilled the demands of the exercise.

Conversations in Space. This extends the previous exercise into making statements with patterns of physical movement. Again, use furniture or blocks to create different spaces. The players are now required to communicate with each other through their movement. The exercise is best begun in pairs, but may be developed to include several players. Although the exercise lends itself to any number of situations (such as quarrels and outwitting), a good starting point for a pair is the flirtation—the mating dance often found in comedy of manners. Players must express this without speaking or touching the partner. The various encouragements, avoidances, carnal desires, and distastes are communicated by movement alone.

An interesting extension of this exercise is to perform it as detailed above, then perform it again, this time allowing the players to express their intentions in any physical manner they wish. Physical contact and full expression of feeling are encouraged—including vocal noises, but not words. After this the original exercise is repeated, and players will then feel a much greater sense of the physical tension between their desires and emotions and the mask of social form through which they must express them. The space may be adapted to the different environmental demands of the comedy of manners, ranging from the open spaces and sparse furnishings of the Restoration, to later comedies, where players are likely to sit more and adopt positions relating to furniture.

Plumage. An exercise related to posture and mask, based upon the adoption of bird physicalities. The player is asked to choose a bird of brilliant plumage and to experiment slowly with the adoption of its posture and manner of self-display. This is first done individually and then developed into an aviary situation in which birds display themselves to each other. The exercise may be extended into courting dances, and a whole range of attractions and responses can be developed through physical display. A broader range of birds may then be introduced, some of greater and some of lesser plumage. The objectives of the exercise now become discovering the pecking order and also attracting a satisfactory mate in competition with the other birds. A range of levels may be introduced into the workshop space to provide perches and enable positions of dominance to be taken up. Although this exercise is concerned chiefly with projection of the physical mask, it also introduces the idea of differing postures—those of individual birds—within the central notion of self-display. All birds may display their plumage equally well, but the nature of the bird will determine the individual manner of the performance.

Preening. This exercise is done in front of a mirror. The player first of all removes his outer clothing, returning himself to a close approximation of a "bare, forked animal," and takes a moment to become acquainted with

his own fundamental physicality and the possibilities of movement it allows. He then slowly adopts the costume mask of, say, the seventeenth or eighteenth century. As he puts on each item he carefully examines what it does to his body, both in restricting or restructuring movement and in embellishing his appearance. He may try items several ways to make sure they are right, and he must enquire just what "right" means in this context. What is the function of each item, and why is he wearing it—both as an actor and as a seventeenth- or eighteenth-century individual? What, for example, constitutes a well-tied cravate,[9] and what is it meant to say about the wearer? Slowly the player builds up, understands, and assimilates his costume mask, aware of the impression it is intended to make. For the normative character in a play this impression is of course instinctive, but it is important that the player understand it both physically and intellectually.

Once the norm is understood, the player may adopt different personas with various degrees of aberration. The exercise may be done with different costume styles and include the practicing of poses and the use of props before the mirror. It may also be done with another player assisting in the dressing—most upper-class persons would have valets and maids to assist them—and helping the first player to examine and criticize the self he is building.

On Parade. A fairly formal exercise for the practice of physical manner. The players should form two ranks, down the center of which each passes in turn, acknowledging the others by means of a bow, curtsy, or other salutation such as kissing hands. The player saluted should respond in like manner. Canes and hats should be used in the exercise, which may be repeated to include an attitude with

[9] Beau Brummel, the eighteenth-century cynosure of fashion, was said to have thrown away fifty cravates on one occasion until one seemed right.

the salutation. Here the player will perform the salutation in correct manner, but with it show a particular feeling towards the person addressed, such as respect, distaste, love, or boredom.

An extension of the exercise is to choose a particular physical setting—park, court, theatre—and have a group of players explore the demands of greeting each other within these spaces and how relationships may be developed in this manner. This will introduce the further problems of sitting and standing, and connect with the conversations-in-space exercise. While one group of players is performing this task another may watch, and, at a signal from the group leader, the first players will freeze in whatever attitude they have adopted at that moment. The watching group will then examine and discuss the "photographic still" for its sense of physical correctness and communication both of general sensibility and particular attitude. This provides the performing group with a useful guide as to how far its intentions are being communicated in action.

Model Show. This is a good early workshop exercise for dealing with the mask and movement demands of comedy of manners. It is not geared to achieving any specific period manner, but generally to helping the player get out of his "normal" physicality and enjoy the idea of dressing up and display. Gather together as many extravagant pieces of clothing and costume props as possible—scarves, hats, boas, bits of colorful cloth, shoes, ornaments—from which the players will improvise costumes for a "high-fashion" show. Set up a situation with a ramp along which models parade to display their costumes, and around which sits the audience of those players not modeling at that moment. Have a commentator describe the nature and utility of each costume—players can take turns at this—and encourage the audience to ask questions of the models regarding the

costumes, examine them, and generally express approval or disinterest.

The exercise usually generates a high level of interest, enthusiasm, and imagination. The generic style of the costumes is likely to be eclectic and contemporary camp, which is fine, for its main purpose is to break the actor out of his sweat-shirt, jeans, and flat-shoes sensibility. The players must be encouraged to take their costumes, however outrageous, quite seriously and to use as a presentational image that air of languidly dynamic cool that is the hallmark of the high-fashion model.

Party Time. An extension of the previous exercise. It is based on setting up a series of parties that allow the player to discover both the common sensibility beneath the external manner of upper-class societies and the different detail by which that manner is manifested. It is best to start from the player's own experience. Have him dress up for a contemporary party, and examine why he adopted certain clothing and how that clothing and the fact of being at a party made him alter his social manner. From here move back in time to, say, a cocktail party in the 1920s, a nineteenth-century reception, an eighteenth-century salon, and finally a court levee in the Restoration period. Use as many costumes and prop simulations as are available, and let the player choose whatever he feels is necessary for the specific occasion. It is also useful to let the players change the settings for each new occasion, making them directly confront the physical demands of the environment.

The exercise should be done twice. First hold a discussion at the end of each party, analyzing the discoveries the players made about each new physical mask and its relationship to the physical manner. The second time the exercise should be allowed to flow as much as possible, one party leading into the next with no definite break. Final discussion should focus on the way the manner of each period was adjusted to the particular environment while the underlying social sensibility remained the same.

A Day in the Life of . . . This exercise examines any one of the periods dealt with in "Party Time" in greater depth and detail. It also integrates background materials (from the sources mentioned at the beginning of the chapter) with what has been learned about inner sensibility and the social mask in action. Though of necessity selective, it simulates a typical day in the life of a principal character of comedy of manners. It will give players a more complete flavor of the time and the experience of continuously presenting a social mask in different situations. Here is one possible outline of a day in the life of a Restoration gentleman:

11 A.M.	Rose. Performed toilet, assisted by valet. Received fencing master (or dancing master, shoemaker, etc.). Wrote, read poetry.
12:30 P.M.	Received friends and repaired for dinner to Sun Tavern in the City. Traveled by hackney coach. Ate stewed carp, a chicken, tansy pudding, neats tongues, and cheese.
3 P.M.	Went to the play; sat in pit or on the stage; spent time ogling the ladies in the boxes and talking back to the actors. Or went to a cockfight, played bowls, or real tennis.
7 P.M.	Walked down the Mall through St. James's Park, bowing to the ladies. Drank sillabub and ate cheesecake at the gate.
8 P.M.	Supper at Locket's on lamb, pigeons, anchovies, and tarts. Drank burgundy; then brandy later while playing cards at friends' lodgings in Whitehall—whist, ombre, basset.
1 A.M.	Took chair to mistress's house. Retired.

Again, the precision of the detail is not as important in this exercise as the sense of life style—the social round, the pursuit of pleasure, the sense of occasion, the incestuous nature of relationships in a small elite circle.[10]

Instant Character. This is a useful general exercise based upon the immediate assumption of a physical mask. Many of the characters in comedy of manners have a strong obsessive trait, which is suggested by their name and provides the basis for their mask. In this context, players are asked to concentrate upon an attitude and allow this to become a strong, one-dimensional relationship of emotion and physicality. This may be done in two ways. The mental attitude may be the catalyst, as in the case of such characters as Petulant, Sullen, and Sparkish. Here the player, by concentrating upon the idea of petulance, sullenness, or whatever, will discover a facial attitude that matches it. This can be taken further into a posture, a walk, and finally a complete physical mask derived from the mental image. In the opposite case, with such characters as Fidget, Snake, and Clumsey, it is the physical manner that is given, and by playing a strong physical identity the player will be able to discover a corresponding inner attitude. The exercise is, of course, simply a tool to encourage physical imagination and the playing of a strong physical mask with clarity and attack. In performance such a character mask will be informed by all the understanding of social manner and sensibility the player's background work will have given him. This will

---

[10] Worth noting here is the relationship with servants. This was usually civil, and sometimes familiar. Indeed, in the nineteenth century the nanny or butler was often better known to the child than the parent. This always presumed an unspoken sense of knowing one's place. As a Victorian hymn put it:

> The Rich man in his castle
> The poor man at his gate.
> God made them high or lowly
> Each born to his estate.

add that subtlety and variety that creates the sense of realism within the demands of the truth of the event.

Tongue Twisters. A few verbal exercises that may be useful in sharpening the lip and tongue agility so necessary for the playing of comedy of manners. First speak them as rote exercises, concentrating upon the absolute clarity of each syllable and then of each word. Then gradually increase the speed of speaking, without sacrificing clarity, until your optimum combination of speed and clarity is reached.

In Tooting two tutors astute
Tried to toot to a Duke on a flute.
But duets so gruelling
End only in duelling,
When tutors astute toot the flute.

The actuary's honorary secretary showed her extraordinary
literary superiority by working literally solitarily in the
library particularly regularly during February.

With blade, with bloody blameful blade, he bravely broached his
boiling bloody breast.

Peter Piper picked a peck of pickled peppers, a peck of pickled
peppers Peter Piper picked. If Peter Piper picked a peck of
pickled peppers, where's that peck of pickled peppers Peter Piper
picked?

She sells sea shells on the sea shore; the shells she sells are
sea shells for sure. If she sells sea shells on the sea shore,
I'm sure she sells sea-shore shells.

Julia was actually due to be married to the Duke of Turin on the
first Tuesday in June, dressed in her superb jewels. When the day

duly arrived, Julia's mature duenna could not produce the jewels.
Julia felt suicidal, for the Duke, persuant to his promise, had
dutifully started a ducal serenade with a superfluous but celes-
tially tuneful Tudor tune played on lutes and flutes.

When the players have gained some skill with the individual tongue twisters, interest may be added by using them as the basis for group work:

Players pass the exercise around a circle, taking a word each.
Two players hold a conversation, with the exercises taking up the words when they wish.
Two or more players use the exercises to hold conversations based upon a particular situation—for example, a love scene, a quarrel, or selling insurance.

To gain a strong sense of the repartee nature of the dialogue in comedy of manners, players may be given sticks (with padded ends) with which they duel, using the lines from the verbal exercises in conjunction with the thrust and parry. This game can be extended into the use of actual dialogue from a play. The stick-play now emphasizes the rhythm of the line and the physical attack of the words.

Other useful verbal exercises may be found in the prologues from Restoration comedies, such as Congreve's *The Old Bachelor* and *The Way of the World*, and the patter songs from Gilbert and Sullivan operas, such as "Commander of the King's Navy" from *H.M.S. Pinafore* and "Model of a Modern Major-General" from *The Pirates of Penzance*.

SUGGESTED READINGS

BRACHER, FREDERICK, ed., *Letters of Sir George Etherege*. Berkeley: University of California Press, 1974.

BRYANT, ARTHUR, *The England of Charles II.* London: Longmans, Green, 1935.

HENSHAW, N. S., *Graphic Sources for a Modern Approach to the Acting of Restoration Comedy.* Ph.D. dissertation. University of Pittsburgh, 1967.

HOLLAND, NORMAN, *The First Modern Comedies.* Cambridge, Mass.: Harvard University Press, 1959.

LOFTIS, JOHN, ed., *Restoration Drama.* New York: Oxford University Press, 1970.

SEYLER, ATHENE, and STEPHEN HAGGARD, *The Craft of Comedy.* New York: Theatre Arts Books, 1946.

SWEDENBERG, H.T., JR., ed., *England in the Restoration and Early EighteenthCentury.* Berkeley: University of California Press, 1973.

WILDEBLOOD, JOAN, and PETER BRINSON, *The Polite Society.* New York: Oxford University Press, 1965.

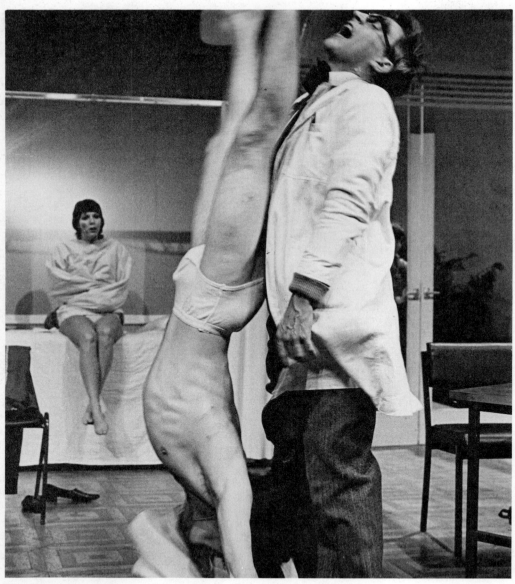

chapter 5

"What the Butler Saw."

Citizens' Theatre Company, Glasgow.

Farce

BACKGROUND

General. Farce probably gets its name from the French *farcir*—to stuff: farce was used as stuffing for other theatrical performances (also, as a form, it is itself stuffed full of business and comic ingenuity). The term came into use in France in the fifteenth century. From that time farce gained increasing significance as a dramatic genre until it achieved a peak in nineteenth-century France—with Labiche and Feydeau—and in England with Pinero. However, as a popular form under other names farce goes back to the very roots of Greek dramatic performance and shows markedly consistent features throughout the long history of drama. The consistency of these features suggests either the continuation of a tradition over more than two thousand years, or that farce finds its dynamic in certain eternal human qualities that tend to remanifest themselves in the same way, irrespective of time or fashion.

Basically, farce is a particular expression of or perspective on life that at times finds itself fully fleshed out in dramatic form as a play. At other times it may appear as part of a dramatic event: for emotional or rhythmical contrast in a serious drama or tragedy (the porter's scene in *Macbeth*, for example); as a more robust and physical element in comedy (the watch scene in *Much Ado About Nothing*); or as a short event in any forum of popular entertainment, from fairgrounds to circuses and vaudeville shows.

Popular appeal and physical activity are probably the two distinguishing features of farce. This could also be said of public hangings in the eighteenth century, so it must be added that farce was intended to entertain and provoke laughter. (Alas, this might also be said of public hangings, which suggests

that one of the sources of human laughter is the discomfort of others—a point to which we shall return.) We are, briefly, going to trace the development of farce from its popular roots in order to identify some of its salient features. Special attention will be paid to a form of drama called commedia dell'arte, which was essentially farcical in perspective and structure and thus provides a useful skeletal basis for an understanding of farce playing.

Historical. The roots of farce are probably to be found in the kind of mimic plays with which primitive peoples celebrated the return of spring, with all its associations of seed sowing, fertility, and renewal of life. Eating, drinking, playing, and copulating are expressions of fundamental human needs—representations of the life force at its most primitive level. The Greek festival of Dionysus, with its ritual invocations of the wine god and his spirit of fertility, provided opportunity for letting down the hair, enjoying freedom from the usual restraints of any social group, and making fun of local authority figures—even the gods themselves. Early revelers in this manner were the Dorian Greeks, whose burlesque playlets may well have been a source for the later, more sophisticated comedies of Aristophanes in the fifth-century-B.C. Athenian celebration of the Dionysia.

Whether Aristophanes consciously imitated the Megarean farces, as they are now called, or whether similar human drives gave rise to similar responses is irrelevant for our purpose. What is significant is the use of masks and phallus in these early plays, and the similarity of human types and attitudes they depicted. The phallus suggests the basic common denominator of sex—a driving force behind most instances of farce—and the similarity of the basic set of masks (i.e., characters) shows the common characteristics of social hierarchies where farce finds the stuff of its humor. Although Aristophanes' comedies were much more sophisticated in plot and in their satirical, political comment than the Megarean farces, they still involved a good deal of physical and sexual humor and included, among a wider range of characters, doctors, soldiers, comic slaves, old men, and old women—the very masks that were found in the early farce plays.

Greek New Comedy tended to take over the masks of its predecessors and add a sentimental love interest in the form of a young man and young woman; the humor became less physical and intrigue more significant. But when we move on to Rome we find

Bawdy physicality of old Greek comedy actors.

Antiken Museum, Berlin.

another basic farce form, possibly influenced by the pre-Aristophanic Greek form—the Atellan farce. This, again, was a masked play whose basic characters—a buffoon, a pedant, a type of soldier, and an old man—bore close resemblance to the Greek stock characters and were played in the vulgar, physical manner of the Megarean type. When we come to Plautus in the third century B.C., the various primitive farce forms and their more sophisticated derivations are brought together in a set of character types, situations, comic business, and physical style of playing that typify farce sensibility and provide a model of the form. It is no surprise that Plautan farces are based upon love intrigue, seduction, and money, and that the character types include young lovers, miserly and impotent old men, pimps, swaggering soldiers, and both stupid and cunning slaves—all the consistent elements of farce's historical evolution.

We are going to trace the lineage of farce through the Middle Ages, the sixteenth-century form of commedia dell'arte, to the bourgeois farce of the nineteenth and twentieth centuries, and draw attention to its consistent elements so that we may make valid generalizations in our later discussion. Having seen that what works as an approach to Plautus works also for Feydeau (accepting the difference in given circumstances), the actor should be able to make his own adaptations and connections with any given play.

After Plautus the actor in the Roman theatre became highly unpopular with the moralistic, nascent Christian church. As we have suggested, there is a certain phallic energy at the root of all farce, and pagan peoples, however sophisticated, were willing to accept the fact and expression of sexuality, with its attendant bawdiness and vulgarity, as a necessary part of human experience. But in the Christian church sex somehow became bound up with original sin, and immaculate conceptions were preferred to fertility rites. So, out went the actors into the wilderness of excommunication, to be classed with thieves and sturdy beggars for the next millenium.

It is difficult for tragedy to survive in the wilderness, but popular theatrical forms such as farce can. Based on stock characters and human foibles that are common to any geographical situation, farce requires mainly physical skills and improvisation, and thrives upon the fairground arts of juggling, tumbling, singing, and dancing. It can also be performed on the back of a cart in any marketplace; on an inn-room table; or in the great hall of a medieval mansion. Thus it was that small groups of itinerant actors under many names—clowns, skops, jongleurs, goliards, minstrels, farceurs, cabotins—kept popular drama alive for one thousand years. The drama itself took many names—folk drama, mummings, sotties, drolls, interludes, and "farces"—but however performed and under whatever name, popular drama was based upon similar situations dealing with stealing or hiding money, sexual intrigue, deception, trickery, and practical joking of all kinds. The characters in the dramas took local forms, but were all some variation of a cunning or stupid peasant or servant, tricky lawyer, voluptuous priest, clever and sexually potent young man, randy matron, impotent and miserly husband. These were all thrown together and mixed up in a bawdy, physical intrigue or romp. We still find them today, less robust, watered down, geared to the needs and sensibility of a late-twentieth-century bourgeois, capitalist society, but little changed in stock situation and type—on television, in situation comedies.

Farce, seen as the physicalization of a human need to let down the hair and enjoy a holiday from social restrictions, also found expression during the Middle Ages within the bosom of moral authority—the Christian church itself. Despite the church's attempts to enforce a sober morality over its flock, strong farcical and physical elements found their way into the religious mystery and miracle plays.[1] The mocking of authority and

sobriety—which goes all the way back to early Greek fertility rites—also burst forth in quasi-pagan festivities such as shrovetide carnivals, fashings, May Day festivities, and the Feast of the Ass (or known also as the Feast of Fools). These festivals, farcical in spirit and often in manner, kept alive an earthbound secularity—a day off from the moral rigor of preparing for the life to come. At Beauvais in France during the twelfth-century Feast of Fools, an ass would be escorted up the knave of the cathedral while a bawdy "prose of the ass" was sung. Censing would be done with black puddings and sausage, and the "mass" would be concluded not with an "amen" but with three asses' brays. The goliards, the traveling minstrel scholars of the thirteenth century, were essentially "dropouts" from the restrictive moral environment of the medieval universities—which were religious foundations. In their songs and verses they propounded an antiauthoritarian, antiacademic attitude: one must keep a balance against the ascetic view of life, remembering the needs of the flesh as well as those of the mind and spirit. One of their songs might be taken from a Greek fertility rite, in its free praise of the libido:

> To my mind all gravity is a grave subjection;
> Sweeter far than honey are jokes and free affection.
> All that Venus bids me do, do I with erection;
> For she n'er in heart of man, dwelt with dull dejection.[2]

That the spirit of the goliards is still alive in modern universities may be confirmed by a practice at an Oxford college one of the authors attended in the 1950s. The Sundial Society of the college would meet once a term to eat abstemiously and to read and discuss learned papers in Greek or Latin. World-renowned classical scholars and their brightest students would follow this solemn practice while, in another part of the college, a

---

[1] A fifteenth-century French miracle play described itself as "Miracles de plusiers malades,/En farses pour être moins fades" ("Several miracles of healing the sick, done with farces to be less dull").

[2] Quoted in Nathan Schachner, The Medieval University (London: Allen & Unwin, 1938), p. 366.

club calling itself The Junior Sundial Society would be performing a parallel but somewhat different rite. The Junior Sundial, created essentially to mock the intellectual earnestness of its dignified parent, would meet to eat and drink to excess. Having done this, one of its members would read a paper of a highly pornographic or scatological nature, written upon a roll of toilet paper. The evening would end in as much of an orgy as the scope of an all-male college could afford, and the playing of some kind of practical joke upon one of the college deans.

Adolescent? Sophomoric? Very probably. But hallowed by a tradition going back to the very roots of human existence: the need to recognize and occasionally display sexual energy and other fleshly wants, and the equal need to temper the sublime with the ridiculous, to bring authority within human grasp, to play the fool that we may better understand the sage. All of this is part of the instinct of farce.

After its wanderings through the Middle Ages, the spirit of popular drama and its farcical instinct next found a permanent form in sixteenth-century Italy. Here the commedia dell'arte developed—performed by troupes of about ten actors and based upon a stock set of characters and situations. The characters were identifiable by a facial mask and costume, which hardly varied from troupe to troupe or place to place. The plots were equally defined in structure, and the art of this form of theatre lay in the improvised changes the actors could ring within the givens of their character and the set nature of the plot. It was essentially an actor's theatre: there were no literary overtones. It found its roots and expressed itself through the popular, farcically oriented sensibility that we have shown to be a consistent form of human communication.

It is no surprise, therefore, that the stock characters, or masks, of the commedia should closely resemble those found in the earliest Greek mimes, the Atellan farces, and in Plautus. There is an academic discussion as to whether this shows the continuation of a tradition passed on over one thousand years from the Romans to the Italian Renaissance, or whether it is the self-contained revival of a popular instinct, which found expression in recognizable forms because of the consistency of human nature and its concerns. Either reason suits our purpose, which is to identify certain qualities of the form and character of popular drama as the continuing essence of farce.

The basic commedia masks are an impotent, lecherous, miserly old man—Pantalone; a pompous, lecherous old pedant—Dottore; a swaggering, cowardly, amorous soldier—Capitano; and a couple of tricky servants known as Zanni, who went by various individual names, but usually Arlecchino and Brighella. The troupes also contained young lovers of either sex and the occasional serving maid or older female confidante. The basic plots are young lovers trying to get together, helped by the servants but hindered by the older men—who either forbade it, wanted the girl themselves, wouldn't give the lovers money, or wanted them to marry someone else. The interest is not whether the lovers would make it—they always do—or whether the older masks would be fooled—they always are—but how the servants would trick the old men, and how the old men would be made fools of this time. The characters and plot situations are very similar to those used in the Roman farces. They were simply given the external appearance of an Italian social type of the sixteenth century: Pantalone was recognizably a Venetian merchant; Dottore, a graduate of the University of Bologna. But as misers, lechers, fathers, and so on, they are recognizable as universal human types going back to man's earliest social relationships. As Gertrude Stein might have said: A lecher is a lecher is a lecher; a miser is a miser is a miser.

The commedia dell'arte lasted the best part of two hundred years and influenced the work of Molière, whose plays, written in seventeenth-century France, are sometimes called comedies of character. However, Mo-

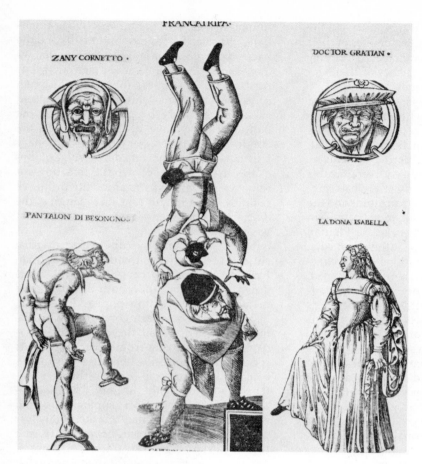

A group of commedia character "masks."

Dover Publications Inc. Reproduced by permission.

lière's work spans a wide spectrum, from satirical plays of considerable literary merit to plays that are unashamedly and brilliantly based upon the tradition of farce characters and intrigue plots. At the simplest level plays such as *The Doctor in Spite of Himself* and *The Knavery of Scapin* are full of tricky servants, mean and lecherous old men, mistaken identities, young lovers, and all the paraphernalia we have come to associate with farce intrigue. Even somewhat more sophisticated plays such as *The Miser* and *The Imaginary Invalid* have a similar formula,

and *Tartuffe*, often regarded as Molière's most brilliant comedy, is not above having a wife seduced on a table beneath which the husband is hiding, or a sassy servant who engages in farcical backchat with her master.

We will look more closely at Molière's farcical genius in a later section. Here, in order to complete our review of farce, we have to move on a couple of centuries to Labiche, Feydeau, and the great French farces of the later nineteenth century. Just as the commedia and Molière, while keeping the inherited stock characters and situations that typified popular farce through the ages, invested the characters with recognizable qualities of their own day, so in the late nineteenth century farce took on the characteristics of that Victorian and bourgeois period.

It is the drawing rooms, the salons, and particularly the hotel bedrooms of the late nineteenth century that are the environments for the intrigues of Labiche and Feydeau. Theatre was now in the period of realism, and the farceurs used entirely recognizable domestic backgrounds for their farcical situations. But if the physical backgrounds and the characters' costumes would not have been familiar to a Roman audience at a Plautan play or an Italian audience at the commedia, the plots and the machinations of the characters would have been instantly recognized. Sex, marriage, and money were the motivating factors of the plot, and the members of the haute bourgeoisie—lawyers, physicians, civil servants, and others with a certain authority and position in society to uphold— were the characters doomed to being made ridiculous. Young lovers did not appear to the same degree in this rather sophisticated and somewhat decadent society: circular intrigues, with everyone chasing everyone else's wife, and the occasional cocotte thrown in for good measure, were the order of the day. But the complications, frustrations, and all the fun of man, the buffoon, chasing his own tail (or phallus) are there. Beneath the now elegant mask of clothing, the stiff collar, and the starched shirt front still beats the heart of the comic satyr, bursting his buttons to get out.

Essence and Function. Why do the same characters or sets of characteristics, the same intrigues, the same situations, the same responses to the same stimuli, keep repeating themselves to maintain the consistency of farce structure over more than two thousand years of theatre history? Essentially because farce takes a particular perspective upon certain unchanging qualities in Man and his relationships. The qualities are the most basic human drives, and the perspective is essentially physical. Farce goes for the belly and the backside. It makes us laugh at the fact that we look funny, or at a disadvantage, with our pants down. Yet three of the five basic human physical functions—shitting, pissing, and fucking—can only be performed with the pants off. We have deliberately used the Anglo-Saxon terms, which our dictionary tells us are "usually considered vulgar," because that is part of what farce does—it removes polite masks to show the primitive realities beneath, and asks us to laugh at the discrepancy between what we show and what we are.

Since Adam and Eve discovered original sin and tried to cover it with fig leaves, man has been constantly caught with his pants down. Farce relies upon both the literal and metaphoric sense of this phrase. The literal, because farce has been concerned with the most primitive of all drives—phallic sex— since the fertility rites from which it traces its roots. Metaphorically, because of farce's concern to debunk all forms of human pretension—to reveal the urgent, primitive reality beneath the most supercilious and sophisticated of human masks. However dignified the human soul, however aspiring the human spirit, both are trapped within and must express themselves through a body that is basically geared to ingesting and excreting through various orifices in a very down-to-earth manner. The romantic tends to become melancholic at the conflict of flesh and spirit; the tragedian kills the body to release and magnify the soul; the farceur makes us laugh at our pretensions so that we may accept ourselves for what we are in the most physical sense: fools of mortals, fated to repeat the comic pattern inherent in human existence, and doomed never to give up trying to escape it. The characters on this human carousel are all pursuing either basic human wants or those that social structures have made desirable: love, sex, food, money, power, glory. They also suffer from the corruptions that the pursuit or possession of these aims has given them: greed, lechery, avarice, vainglory, undue self-esteem, intellectual pomposity. The merry-go-round spins within a closed system of values—social, moral, and economic—that tends to favor those with power and authority.

Farce goes for all pretensions, all masks, and tends to attack in the simplest way, with the kick in the backside or the knock on the head. In the world of realpolitik that farce inhabits, all usually get their just deserts. The power structure of society must be renewed—there is always a need for new virility to preserve the race. Those who get in its way must be outwitted, put in their proper place. To the young and the bold goes sexual fulfillment; to the old and incompetent, frustration; to the clever and agile, an advantage. Factors that tend to paralyze dynamic, to become obstacles that throw society out of balance—power that is petrified, excessive authority, fecundity in the hands of sexual impotence—must be reduced to size and reconciled with society's needs.

Farce deals with the most basic social irritants: interfering mothers-in-law, shrewish wives, impotent husbands, pompous teachers, miserly merchants, arrogant bankers, soldiers, government officials. It pits against them the underdogs, those who have less power but equal human needs: young people in love who can't afford to get married and are forbidden by the social structure to go to bed with each other; servants and others who have to perform the menial functions in life; the poor; the disadvantaged, who have to live by their wits alone; any worthy but socially oppressed figure.

Arrogance always comes before a fall in farce—usually a pratfall. This is normally engineered by the clever underling. Farce has been on the side of the "little man," from the Roman slave to Charlie Chaplin. Chaplin's art in many ways embodies the farce sensibility. He is the downtrodden little everyman, alone against a usually unkind world, who survives on his wits and agility. He is constantly up against the bigger and more powerful—the authority structure in its many forms. His outwitting maneuvers are usually

physical, and just when he believes himself to have gained the advantage, his naive pleasure at his cleverness leads to his own downfall. The advantage gained by all the tricky servants throughout the history of farce is usually short-lived. When they overreach themselves the joke turns on them—any unjustified human pride tends to come before farce's fall. Farce tends to preserve the social balance: it brings the high and low alike back into line when they get above themselves. But Chaplin, like all the clever servants and the eternal resilience of man himself, "picks himself up, dusts himself down, and starts all over again." If tragedy pays tribute to man's indomitable spirit, farce embodies his physical resilience—his enduring capacity to keep on trying. Just as long as he doesn't get too clever for his own good, for then he will assuredly trip over his own feet.

The little man, however, is more usually seen tripping up authority, which practice, together with the ridiculing of sexual taboos, forms the two principal subjects of farce. Breasts, buttocks, phalloi, underwear, bedpans, enemas—all the social "unmentionables" are fair game for farce. Sexual organs and the sexual act are the fundamental human force and the fundamental human taboo. We try to conceal them behind moral strictures and masks of clothing. The "beast with two backs" is the physical reality of the cherubic Cupid (the only word in English that rhymes with "stupid")—a subject for laughter as we hide a sexual function behind a mask of childlike spirituality. If we didn't try to romanticize the sexual act or pretend it doesn't exist, it wouldn't be a subject for laughter. If we didn't have such moral phobias about the body and its functions there would be no need for "streaking" or "throwing moons"—both acts of aggression ("cocking a snook") against the social mores that draw the response of laughter.

If the conscious revealing of the body's sexual and excretory organs is an attack on the moral structure, the unconscious revealing is an act that produces laughter through the embarrassment caused to the victim.

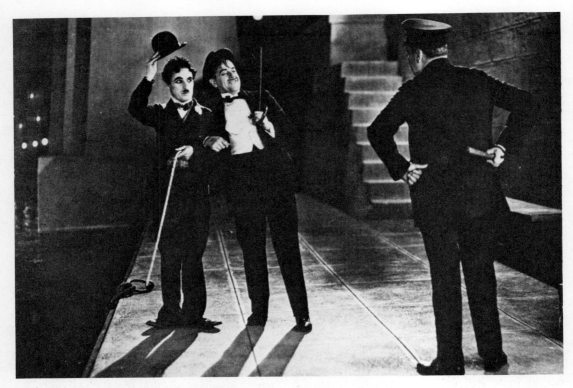

Charlie Chaplin's "little tramp" confronts authority.

Pants falling down, skirts blowing up, and knickers coming down have all been perennial sources of amusement—the revealing of what we try to keep hidden, the slipping of the mask of moral propriety. In 1976 Tom Stoppard wrote a play, *Dirty Linen*, that, although it made some gesture towards satire and intellectual social comment, is essentially a farce. The play is based upon a British parliamentary committee convened to investigate moral standards in public life, every one of whose members seems to have had a clandestine sexual relationship with the committee's secretary, a winsome redhead eponymously named Miss Gotobed. The joke of the play is each member trying to conceal this fact from every other member, and all members trying to conceal all facts from the public. Pairs of French knickers (panties) keep turning up in the most unlikely places—

briefcases, desk drawers, parcels—at the most inopportune times. Finally, the one member of the committee who seemed to be innocent and was about to explode the cover-up himself falls victim to Miss Gotobed's inexorable charms, and is left wiping his brow with a pair of the inevitable knickers, which have somehow found their way into his breast pocket.

The whole play revolves around sex and masks. The knickers symbolize the sexual act and constantly confront the politicians, who try to maintain their masks of propriety in the face of the evidence. The title of the play, *Dirty Linen*, is a metaphor with many sexual layers. Not to wash one's dirty linen in public is an old adage for keeping one's affairs private. Sexual affairs should, people hope, be kept private too. Sexual affairs also tend to soil bed linen, which, like sex, is best kept out of the public eye. Washing linen is one of the practical realities (like sex) of human existence, and soiled linen finds its way into many farces: Pantalone, in *The Three Cuckolds*, is stuffed into a basket of dirty linen, as is Falstaff in *The Merry Wives of Windsor*, and Feydeau's hotel proprietors count their soiled linen as a reminder of the practical reality of the sexual game.

Farce uses laughter—the belly laugh, not the intellectual snicker of less robust forms of comedy—to confront us with the reality of our sexual drives and taboos, and of our social power structures. Laughter has been described as the sudden release of repressed energy that has been performing the function of restraining forbidden desires—keeping antisocial elements away from consciousness. This energy is often sexual and potentially aggressive. It goes back again to the orgiastic joking of the Dionysian fertility rites. These festivities gave play to two

human impulses—to pleasure and self-indulgence, and to aggression and hostility. The Dionysian rites were a festive, hopeful invocation of fertility and its attendant physical pleasure and at the same time an aggressive desire to drive away undesirable social elements and restrictions—famine, hostile neighbors, the repressive acts of authoritarian gods.

The laughter produced by farce is, then, essentially healthful and therapeutic. It is full of pleasure at the recognition of human creative potential, and cathartic in the sense of purging certain repressed insticts—releasing anxieties associated with necessary social impingements upon our personal freedoms. There is, indeed, something orgiastic and destructive about the nature of farce, but in this sense it is a kind of safety valve for the survival of society. Freud, whose theory of laughter as the release of repressed energy was mentioned above,

Mariette Hartley in anxious dishabille watches her pantless bed partner adopt an aggressive manner in *Chemin de Fer*.

Mark Taper Forum, Los Angeles.

suggested in his *Civilization and its Discontents*[3] that man buys his social and cultural structures at the price of frustration. Dreams, fantasies, and farces are the means by which man lives with his frustrations, acting them out and purging them before they lead to madness and anarchy. Marriage, for example, is a necessary social mechanism—providing emotional stability and a secure environment for bringing up children—but it may be said not to satisfy human sexual curiosity or need for variety. Thus the inevitability of dirty jokes, bedroom farce, and mother-in-law gags. Playing out one's fantasies or empathizing with them on stage is a form of imitative magic, a wish fulfillment like that of primitive man, who wore the mask of the animal or enemy he

wished to kill or keep away from him. And the wearing of masks has long been associated with the playing of farce. The very dynamic of farce may be said to be the interplay between the facade—the mask of civilization—and the face of primitive instinct beneath. In the playing of farce the primitive energy must always be present beneath the sophisticated facade.

The energy is potentially aggressive and destructive. It embodies the desire to hit out at what we cannot control, or what excessively controls us. We inhabit a dangerous world, living on the brink of catastrophe in a seemingly irrational universe while trying to operate in a reasonable manner. Farce both enshrines unreason—accepts the primitive impulse beneath the civilized manner—and

The aggression of farce is well illustrated by Laurel and Hardy.

[3] Sigmund Freud, *Civilization and its Discontents*, trans. James Strachey (New York: Norton, 1962).

allows us to work off the destructive repressions that too much reason creates. From the Roman theatre through the Feast of Fools to the Marx brothers, farce has led the revolt against oppressive reason and the attack upon society's sacred cows. It has incorporated the urge to destroy what we cannot understand or operate within. In a Marx brothers movie, Harpo is seen leaning against a wall. Enter cop, who inevitably asks if Harpo is holding up the wall; Harpo nods assent. The cop moves him on and—inevitably—the wall falls down.

In another Marx brothers movie Groucho is asked why Harpo is tearing up a book. He replies: "He is angry because he can't read." We are often angry because of things we cannot do, or because of our insecurities at the difficulty of functioning in a complicated world. So farce lets us enjoy a fantasy of breaking things up—it often involves the destruction of everyday artifacts. It also reassures us by letting us laugh at the comic antagonist. We feel superior to him, are amused by his misfortunes, congratulate ourselves upon being less stupid—indeed, vicariously associate with the clever character who seems to be able to win out against the world. But we aren't allowed to feel too superior. The tricky servant often gets caught by his own cleverness, and the custard pie, after having made the rounds, comes back to land in our own face.

Farce is sometimes criticized for pandering to our "baser" instincts—for encouraging our hostility and indulging a pleasure at the humiliation and suffering of others, which Bernard Shaw thought of as the "beastliest" element in human nature. But this is really the sensibility of a puritanical reformer who refuses to accept people as they are. It misses the point of farce as an accommodation to certain human realities; ignores our efforts to come to terms with our bodies' cravings, restrictive environments, and moral conventions; and discounts the necessity of a sense of humor to our survival—enabling us to laugh at the frustrations and inhibitions that might otherwise destroy us.

The moralizing sentiment also misses the point that farce is essentially amoral. It neither seeks to pass moral comment nor deliberately attempts to avoid it. It is an improbable game based upon probable premises. It shows us how man contrives to escape after being caught in predicaments of his own making. It does this so the world may continue safely upon its way, as it did before the outburst of primitive energy caused the disturbance. This is not the moral solution sought by comedy and tragedy. Farce is a somewhat conservative form that affirms and accommodates to reality.

Being conservative in essence, farce displays few conversions. The characters may be sobered by misfortune, but they leave pretty much as they came in. There is loss of face and embarrassment, but there are no permanent defeats and disasters—death is not a serious threat. Farce is a holiday, a celebration, a day off from responsibilities, that enables us to put up with the rest of the year. And no one really gets hurt. That is one reason we can afford to laugh with impunity at the misfortunes of the characters—we know it's a game. Dogs in films, when they are "attacking," give the game away by wagging their tails—they are "playing" at being fierce and hurting someone. So is the farceur.

Certain elements of farce are sometimes called slapstick. The essence of the slapstick is the essence of farce itself—exaggerated noise and effect, but no real pain.[4] Farce has the appearance of reality, but is distanced from the audience by the manner of its performance. It mustn't be allowed to come too close to the audience's feelings, or become a subject for intellectual appraisal. That is why it goes for the direct, physical response—the belly and the backside. It mustn't allow sentiment. In Shakespeare's *Twelfth Night*, a play that incorporates strong commedia and farce elements, Malvolio, whose very name means "ill will," was intended as a comic butt, an obstacle character, overly ambitious and lacking

---

[4] The slapstick is a kind of paddle split down the middle so the two halves come together with a sharp noise when used to strike someone.

in self-knowledge—a puritan killjoy in a rather catholic play. But in an English production a few years ago Malvolio was played for sympathy. He was a well-meaning, industrious member of a lower class, anxious to advance himself, whose only failing (and that because of lack of opportunity) was lack of breeding. He appeared, therefore, to be ill used by feckless and idle members of an upper class, who wished to keep him in his place. As a consequence of this interpretation the play wasn't funny. In farce the comic butts are meant to be laughed at. We may sympathize with their predicaments as we are laughing, but we can never pity them, or the play is lost. The playing of farce is a robust exercise, but at the same time very delicate. The farceur treads a fine line.

INTRINSIC DEMANDS

Form. Farce celebrates the eternal, ritualistic contest of men and women. Not far beneath its civilized or sophisticated surface it is still primitive in its quest for self-preservation, in its aggressive self-assertion. A "gifle," a small slap in the face, is what farce is all about—an involuntary act of aggression or trespass delivered at the moment when instigation, personal desire, and opportune situation meet. Farce ritual requires no real belief. It moves inexorably through layers of situation, achieving a successful whole without essential meaning. Played well and furiously, it draws us into its own logic, creates for us its own sense of truth. It is an essentially theatrical form truly experienced only in performance.

Even a fully developed farce script is still something of a scenario. The outcome will depend a great deal upon the actor's invention within the series of situations given by the author. The English actor Donald Sinden was once having problems working in farce. He mentioned this to Edith Evans, who replied: "Of course. You see, in a farce you don't have

a play to help you." A farce plot is a thread linking comic situations. It is a pretext to pull the strings of human puppets. The playwright raises storms of banter and arrays of traps so that men may be cheated of their desires and revealed in their folly. The basic principles and qualities of farce structure are:

1. Situation: It is a given and not overelaborated. Brevity is a feature of farce—set up a skittle; knock it down; set up another one. Don't ask questions. The situations are basic human and domestic problems: young lovers, marriage, money, parents at cross-purposes with children, servants at cross-purposes with masters. The situations are compounded and create a snowball effect. This is because decisions are made on impulse, not by reflection. The snowball effect is also a form of repetition and exaggeration, two important comic qualities: father hits boy, boy hits servant, servant kicks dog. To round this one off, dog would bite father.

2. Physical action: The situations and the snowball effect lead to chases, avoidances, pratfalls, beatings—hectic physical movement usually ending in some form of disequilibrium: the reduction of dignity or a bringing down to size.

3. Outwitting: Again a function of the situation, which brings about such maneuvers as disguising, hiding, impersonations, mistaken identities—all different forms of mask play.

4. Obstacles: These are the reasons for the outwittings, and are usually authority characters who have either social, political, or economic power. These characters are reduced, ridiculed, frustrated, reconciled to the necessary social situation, but do not suffer permanent or serious harm.

5. Devices: Farce employs, in physical form, the gamut of comic devices. We have already mentioned repetition and exaggeration. Then there is inversion—servants dominating masters—a reversal of the norm. This is part of the topsy-turvy world of farce—the holiday from reason. Incongruities are a prime farce device: small hats on large heads, too tight trousers, and almost any kind of physical abnormality—especially large noses, cross-eyes, and missing teeth.

Farce structure calls for briskness and quick rhythms. There is no time for reflection. Coincidences, however unlikely, are never questioned. It is all somewhat improbable and exaggerated, but it is, finally, based upon observed human truth, upon man's attempted inhumanity to man, which is accepted, laughed at, and reconciled to the everyday necessities of living. And, like all the best jokes, farce knows when to stop—it comes to a quick end after the punch line.

Form at Work. To put some flesh on the above outline, and to show both how the structure works in practice and how consistent it has been over the history of farce, we are going to look briefly at the workings of plays by Plautus, Molière, and Feydeau, and a commedia scenario. Plautus's *The Pot of Gold* concerns a poor old man who finds a pot of gold, then gloats over it in a miserly fashion while still pleading poverty. He has a daughter who, unknown to the father, has been seduced by an impoverished young man. The plot involves getting the young man married to the girl before she has the baby. Obstacles to this are the young man's poverty, the father's miserliness, and a wealthy neighbor (who just happens to be the young man's uncle) who wants to marry the girl. That is all very simply said and very simply done, for the play actually revolves around the father's attempts to stop anyone knowing he has the pot of gold stashed away. Inevitably he gives himself away, by overcautiousness, to a clever servant who belongs to the young man. Equally inevitably the servant overreaches himself by telling his master how clever he has been. The young man returns the gold to the father and gets the gold as well as the girl.

The play is essentially an essay on the absurd lengths to which the father goes to conceal his gold. He is constantly running back into the house to make sure it is still there, or moving it to ever more ridiculous

hiding places. He constantly believes his servants are cheating him, which leads to chases and beatings and "miser" gags from the servants: "He ties a bag over his mouth at night so as not to lose his breath"; "He had his hands manicured, collected the nail clippings and took them home." But most of the humor is manifested in physical terms—such as the miser, suspicious that a servant has got his gold, asking to see his "third" hand just to make sure. Repetition and exaggeration are the main comic devices.

The "third-hand" gag was, in fact, used by Molière in his play *The Miser*, which is based upon the Plautine theme. Molière elaborates the idea by doubling the number of lovers and putting them at cross-purposes. He also has the miser, Harpagon, as a suitor for the girl, Marianne, whom his son wants to marry. There are a couple of comic servants who cause Harpagon endless trouble by such "extravagances" as wanting food for his horses and money to buy food for his guests. There is a procuress who traces her descent directly from the Roman farces, and another old man whose function is to produce a totally improbable happy ending. But then plot is not what Molière's play is about, any more than was Plautus's or, indeed, any farce. The play is a series of comic confrontations based upon the situation that Harpagon is an obstacle to all the lovers getting together—through being a rival to his son and not wanting to part with money for his daughter's dowry. The play is set in late-seventeenth-century France, and the characters are recognizable as Frenchmen of their day. But beneath their periwigs, Harpagon's attire as a bourgeois merchant, and the servants rig as seventeenth-century coachmen or cooks lie the same human types with the same reactions to the same situations that form the eternal "stuffing" of farce: sex and money provide the stimuli to comic action. Only adultery is needed to complete the unholy trinity of farce action, and adultery provides the dynamic of the last two plays whose structure we are going to look at.

We have suggested that the commedia dell'arte is farce in skeletal form. All the actors had to go on was the scenario, the outline of the plot. Within this they had their repertoire of gags (lazzi), a complete sense of how their character (mask) would operate in any given situation, and a great sense of ensemble playing and improvisation that enabled them to develop and elaborate comic situations within the loose shape of any given plot outline. Farce plays, though using similar plots, situations, and characters, are more fully developed in a written form than the commedia; there is less, if any, scope for verbal improvisation, but still tremendous scope for comic imagination, both in line delivery and physical humor within the more strictly determined situations.

Leon Katz has taken a commedia scenario, *The Three Cuckolds*,[5] and fleshed it out into a farce play, using the kind of devices, comic business, and development of situation that might have been expected of commedia actors. The plot outline has three simple premises: one is a sexual *ronde* with three old men after each other's wives; the second is a young man after one of the old men's wives; third, there is a comic mask of the tricky servant type, who will do anything for anybody for a meal. The play is full of set pieces—which would have been improvisations in the original. The tricky servant is, at one time or another, a doctor, a dentist, and a woman—all in the cause of getting the women the lovers they want and, hopefully, food as his reward. There is a running gag about the bad breath of one of the old men (Pantalone), which sets up a farcical tooth-pulling scene. This does nothing to advance the action, but is simply there for its coarse, physical humor and to bring discomfort to Pantalone. The doctor scene is at the expense of one of the other old men, who is impotent and is told by the "doctor" that his wife is to have a baby. This is all to enable a lover to be smuggled into his house in the baby basket. And so it goes. The outcome is that all the men discover that their lusts and pretensions have rebounded upon their own heads—they have all been made fools and cuckolds—and they are better off accepting things as they are, trying to live in peace with their own wives. The tricky servant, Arlecchino, never gets his meal, but he consoles himself with the thought that if he were ever well fed he would lose all his energy and cleverness. The moralizing at the end of the play is added by Katz. But it is within the implicit spirit of farce. We have suggested that farce restores balance, reinforces the status quo after a romp through the lusts and fantasies of the human appetite. It never makes this explicit—there is no epilogue or direct verbal sententiousness such as Katz gives us—but the point has probably hit home—somewhere below the belt.

Feydeau's farce *Le Dindon* (*Sauce for the Goose*[6]) is also predicated upon the oldest game in town—the quest for illicit sexual adventure. Set in an elegant bourgeois environment in late-nineteenth-century Paris, it starts with a bang—a married woman is pursued by a would-be seducer into her own drawing room. Unknown to the seducer, the woman is married to a friend of his, and, sure enough, in comes the husband. (Feydeau has been quoted as saying that a basic principle of his structure is that when any two characters should on no account come together, he throws them at each other as soon as possible.) The game is discovered, but the husband treats it as a joke and reveals that the seducer has a wife. The seducer claims the wife is hundreds of miles away and crippled with rheumatism. Inevitably, shortly afterwards she walks into the room in sprightly fashion—but not before another potential lover of the wife has arrived. The women, essentially, are trying to remain chaste—the moral double standard has them in its grip—although they may have a lot of inner urges. But, they agree that if they find their husbands in the act of being unfaithful, they will

---

[5] Leon Katz, *The Three Cuckolds*, in *The Classic Theatre*, Vol. 1 (New York: Doubleday, 1958).

[6] Georges Feydeau, *Sauce for the Goose*, trans. Peter Meyer (London: British Broadcasting Corporation, 1974).

Drawing-room elegance of the nineteenth century "farcified" by the actor's body positions, in this American Conservatory Theatre production of *A Flea in Her Ear*.

Photo by Hank Kranzler.

pay them back in kind. Hence the play's title: what is sauce for the goose is sauce for the gander—inverted as befitting a farce!

Not only do farce plots lose all force in the telling, but they also are far too complicated to be understood when recapitulated. So we shall simply go on to illustrate a few of the elements of the play that are age-old farce mechanisms, adapted to the nineteenth-century milieu. It is the second act, set in a hotel bedroom, where all the plot complications come together. By this time Feydeau has managed to achieve three pairs of potential infidelities, all obligingly going to happen in the same room. He then adds to the melee a cocotte, who has been the mistress of the one unmarried man in the play, and an old couple who are celebrating their wedding anniver-

sary and have been given the wrong room. The old couple have essentially nothing to do with the plot—they are there to provide extra physical humor and comic business. The old lady, for example, is deaf. She can "hear" people only when they don't speak aloud—then she seems able to read their lips. The old man is an ex–army officer who is pompous, lecherous, and gets hold of the wrong end of every stick. By the time Feydeau is finished with the bedroom scene he has bells under the mattress to ring when the adulterous couples are in bed; husbands and wives, who constantly just miss seeing each other, hidden behind every door in the room; and the wrong people getting into bed with each other. Finally he contrives to have the police arrive, and the scene ends with everyone chasing after

153

and struggling with everyone else, round and round the room.

The play ends with no one actually committing adultery at all. The only couple who sleep together are the unmarried man and the cocotte. Everyone has been made to look foolish, but all are reconciled. The only one who really loses is the original seducer, who describes his situation in a speech at the end of the play that is worth quoting because of the way it illustrates Feydeau's genius for arranging complicated relationships:

> I'm in the most appalling mess. Two cases of adultery—which I didn't commit. Caught by a husband I don't know, with a wife I don't know. Caught by my own wife, with the same woman I don't know . . . A quarrel with my wife. The woman I don't know arrives this morning and tells me in a German accent I owe her reparation, complicated by the man I don't know taking the law into his own hands. Worries, lawsuits, scandals, the lot. (pp. 105–106)

Nothing really has changed at the end of the play. The social balance has been restored and a lot of prosperous citizens—lawyers, soldiers, merchants—have been made to look foolish. One might presume the play to suggest obliquely that if you set out to commit adultery you will end up looking foolish and infinitely complicate your life, so it probably isn't worth it. The play doesn't say: "It's wrong." The original seducer may have learned a lesson and take pause for a while, but one doubts he will entirely give up his lecherous ways. Anyway, whatever he does or doesn't is, finally, irrelevant to the play—once the game is done and the joke over. Fantasies are best left as fantasies, and laughed at from the comfort of a darkened auditorium.

We have already suggested that the farceur walks a fine line, and some of Feydeau's situations put that to the test. He shows the petty deceits, the interminable wranglings, the trivial catastrophes in the domestic lives of men and women held together by habit alone. Did Feydeau not make them perform before his brilliant distorting mirror, which grotesquely exaggerates and sets them in humorous relief, they would be characters from Strindberg. Indeed, the plays have the

force, the inexorable outcome, and sometimes the violence of tragedies. There is a sense of inevitability about them. But whereas tragedy gives its heroes time to bemoan their fate and ourselves time to consider it, Feydeau denies this to his characters. They are constantly occupied trying to avoid, and setting up for themselves, the next catastrophe. Farce is like mechanical toys gone berserk in a practical-jokes and novelty shop.

Before leaving the discussion of farce form we should say a final word on the difference between farce and other forms of comedy. We have suggested there is a comic continuum and there are no hard-and-fast distinctions. In *The Importance of Being Earnest* we have a mixture of farce situation with a veneer of witty manner. Sheridan and Goldsmith also used farce techniques within comedies of manners. So it is not always a question of this is farce and that is comedy, but instead this situation, these rhythms, this set-piece structure requires this approach rather than that one. As a rule of thumb, farce will have more intrigues per minute than comedy. It will have less metaphor, symbolism, and literary artifacts in general. In farce the situation tends to control the characters. Comedy allows characters a rapport with the audience in unfolding the situation for them. Comedy characters are thus more developed; they have some insights and feelings. The audience has more time to involve itself with the characters in a comedy; it is not just the detached observer of a farcical strategy. Whereas farce gives you a day off to help reconcile you to things as they are, comedy will try to expose shortcomings in the hope of a better possibility. The hymen—young lovers marrying at the end of comedy—has a romantic potentiality for living happily ever afterwards. Farce knows they probably won't, but will help them make the best of it. Farce is more improbable, aggressive, exaggerated, mechanical, and physically oriented. It moves shallowly across the surface of human reality. It avoids cynicism and sentimentality. It is always festive, playful; it has made a compact with the audience to make fun of the world.

(a)

Maccus (a), a Greek farce character; a Commedia Zanni (b), and a servant from a modern production of *The Miser* (c) show the continuity of comic mask characters over three thousand years of theatre.

Maccus, The Metropolitan Museum of Art, Rogers Fund, 1912; Zanni, Dover Publications, Inc.; The Miser, Mark Taper Forum, Los Angeles.

(b)

(c)

Character Masks. We have already traced the evolution and consistency of character types, or masks, from farce's earliest roots to the sophisticated expressions of Feydeau. Here we are going to underline the essential characteristics of these types so the actor may have a simple and clear idea of how character operates in farce.

Character is stated, not examined. It is illustrated by an abundance of verbal gestures or physical actions that show different aspects of the same character traits. The character is motivated by basic human drives—sex, food, self-preservation—not by subtle and individual psychological qualities. Farce is not remotely concerned with why a character happens to be a miser or a lecher. It deals with the surface facts and relies upon its audience's recognition and understanding of basic human motivations. Farce also moves too quickly for the audience to be concerned with subtextual implications or complex psyches. The character is to a great degree the author's puppet, whose strings are pulled according to the requirements of the situation. The characters tend to be blinded by self-conceit, unaware of their deficiencies, one-dimensionally motivated; often resourceful and ingenious, they produce only immediate and temporary solutions to their problems. Lacking in insight and foresight, the characters have their shortcomings exaggerated for comic purposes.

A character's responses to a situation will be as mechanical as his attitudes are rigid. His lack of flexibility will prevent him from adapting to changes in circumstances in any other than an impulsive way. Because they don't examine the results of their actions, the characters are trapped within the improbable logic of extreme solutions. Acting and reacting blindly, they are swept along by the impetus of events. But their mental fixation produces its own logic so that the character, in however exaggerated and abandoned a manner, will always behave consistently within his improbable world. Because of this consistency, and the fact that the character mask is based, however remotely, in observed human truth, the audience will accept the im-

Physically athletic activity of commedia Zanni and Pantalone (on right).

Dover Publications Inc., by permission.

probabilities and exaggerations as part of the logic, the "reality" of the event.[7]

Farce characters are what they seem and do what they are expected to do. The interest lies in the situation and the number of ways the playwright and actor can physically illustrate the quality of the mask. To take the commedia masks as an example: Pantalone, in whatever form, will have all the contradic-tions of senility. He is an impotent old man who has economic power and authority in the community, yet chases after young women and throws childish tantrums when thwarted by his servants. He is miserly yet loves display, crafty but rash, old yet lustful, benevolent and irate. It is these qualities the audience will expect from the Pantalone figure, and it is these qualities upon which the

Hume Cronyn, as Harpagon in *The Miser*, shows a Pantalone-based character.

Mark Taper Forum, Los Angeles.

[7] It is interesting to note, in the context of the reality an audience will accept, that the most farcical character on TV, Mork, of "Mork and Mindy," is made a nonhuman so that his absurd behavior may be acceptable to the audience of a highly realistic medium.

actor must exercise his physical imagination to create the character. The Dottore is basically pedantic, pompous, loquacious, and a muddler. The same exercise may be done for all the commedia characters. How the qualities are manifested in any given situation is up to the actor.

In many ways the basic principle of farce is two-person confrontation: he who kicks the backside and he whose backside is kicked. This, of course, is also the basis of that eternal comic artifact—the double act. The comic servants, or Zanni, in commedia are part of this tradition. One tends to be clever, sharp, the trickster; the other, pleasantly dull-witted but with a kind of native cunning. They are constantly in confrontation with one of the other masks, either kicking backsides or get-

ting their own backsides kicked. The tradition has had some notable representatives in the twentieth century: Laurel and Hardy, the Marx brothers, W. C. Fields, and Charlie Chaplin. Each of these had his mask: unchanging clothes, character traits, reactions. What changed were the situations and circumstances. And so it has always been with the characters in farce, whether in Greek mime form, the commedia, silent movies, or the fully developed, sophisticated plays of Feydeau.

Modern farce, such as written by Feydeau, tends to have a patina of realism over the mechanical structure. This is because its settings are of a recognizably middle-class nature and the characters are evidently members of contemporary social classes and pro-

Physical knockabout in a production of *Charley's Aunt* by the American Conservatory Theatre, San Francisco.
Photo by Hank Kranzler.

fessions. The masks are not as rigid as in commedia, but the essence is the same. Beneath the urbane, everyday manner of the characters in a Feydeau play lie the obsessive and frenetic drives that have catalyzed the masks of farce from the beginnings of drama. They may not get chased with slapsticks, but they get boxed on the ears and hit with umbrellas and canes. And although nobody's backside actually gets kicked—being too improbable in the sophisticated environment—many ways are found to reduce the dignity and upset the equilibrium of the foolish characters. To give a very simple example: in *Sauce for the Goose* the wife gives the would-be lover, kneeling in supplication before her, a push and, sure enough, he lands on his backside on the floor—just as the husband comes in. They may be dressed differently, they may adopt a different social manner, but not far beneath the surface of the magistrates, bankers, lawyers, lechers, and buffoons of modern farces beat the hearts of the Pantalones and Dottores of the commedia—and all their forefathers stretching back to the small Greek town of Megara two thousand years before.

Space/Settings. As farce belongs to no specific historical period, it has not been written with a particular space or setting in mind. It uses pretty much what it finds and ties its antics to the stage conventions of a given time. Because it usually deals with middle-rank authority figures and their families, it has a domestic environment, taking place in or in front of some form of house or home. Roman farces used the conventional set structure of their time, and usually took place on a street in front of two or three houses, with further exits leading to the town and to the country. Commedia tended to have similar settings, either in its more primitive and portable form on a platform stage in front of a curtain or, later, in the proscenium-oriented stages of the Italian and French sixteenth and seventeenth centuries. Molière used stages with settings both in front of and

inside houses, and Feydeau used the nineteenth-century proscenium stage in which to set his salons, restaurants, and hotel bedrooms of the French *fin de siècle*.

More important than the details of particular settings are the demands made upon space by the structure and sensibility of farce. What environment does it need to work within? It needs room for physical action yet a sense of compression and intensification. As the shape of farce tends to be both circuitous and erratic, the space must allow for chases and in-and-out movements—it must channel the actor's physical efforts by providing exits and obstacles. There must also be opportunities for the characters to hide from one another, to avoid one another, and to surprise each other. Finally, as farce is a game, there must be paraphernalia for play: traps, obstacles, objects—the adult variation of the children's playground and sandlot.

The Roman stage provided its farces with up to five different exits: plenty of scope for "shell games" and the mazelike pursuits of farce activity. In keeping with this tradition, the modern farce is unlikely to have less than four or five doors in a set, plus windows that may be looked in, jumped out of, or gotten stuck in halfway. The doors are, of course, a kind of mask. They conceal what is going on: characters hide their presence and their illicit intentions behind them. Doors are also to be escaped through—the most dynamic form of concealment is disappearance. Initially, commedia stages were smaller and simpler: exits behind each side of the curtain and, possibly, off the side of the stage platform. But the stage was essentially a base for the activities of the actors—and their one-to-one confrontations, their individual-set-piece improvisations, their tumbling and acrobatics. The plots of commedia were less complex, the environments less sophisticated, and the world a simpler place than in a modern farce.

The compression and intensity created by the small size of a commedia stage is achieved by the clutter of a modern farce set. We live much more in a world of things, an age of technology. Appurtenances form part of the realistic environment of a modern farce, and provide much of the opportunity for farcical action. We are trapped by the physical world we have created, as well as the physical desires we have inherited. The acrobatic tricks of the commedia Zannis, which were exhibited for their skill alone, have today become falls out of chairs, over sofas, through windows; trips over rugs, our own feet; slips on banana skins. The essential physical function is the same but translated into a modern environment. In the farce of the silent movies and the mid-twentieth-century drama, horseplay includes motor-cars, conveyor belts, electrical equipment—all the clockwork "slapsticks" of a modern technological society that can go berserk themselves or drive us crazy through our inability to control them. Computers are the ultimate authority figure.

Molière took farce characters off the streets and into the bourgeois drawing rooms at the time when farce itself was entering the court theatres. He endowed the traditional masks of farce with characteristics of the seventeenth-century Frenchman and created situations within the domestic milieus of his time. The farce writers of the nineteenth and twentieth centuries did the same. They used recognizably everyday settings in which the totally improbable takes place. These normal social arenas—drawing rooms, restaurants, bedrooms—become the scenes of the downfall of their inhabitants. The mask slips, the private act becomes public: the pants, metaphorically and sometimes actually, fall down. The cluttered, tightly constructed, space-limiting nature of modern farce settings force confrontations that might not otherwise occur. Characters may frequently hide, but seldom escape altogether, and it is a platitude of psychology that confined creatures become frustrated and consequently more aggressive. The furnishings themselves create a tangled web that entraps the victims. Doors won't open, windows won't shut, ties or coattails catch in cupboard drawers, rugs slip from under us, beds collapse on top of us. All of this plays its part in the chaotic working of a seemingly normal environment: that cross between an obstacle course, a maze, and a children's playground that is the physical world of farce.

Costume/Properties. Costume is always a form of mask, and seldom more so than in farce. We have already mentioned the physical masks that formed part of farce conventions from the Greeks through to the commedia. These costume conventions, such as the *phalloi*, can both show the connection with the orgasmic roots of farce and enable the audience immediately to recognize a character. The costumes may be conventional but they are not arbitrary; they originate in some kind of human social truth. Pantalone's traditional commedia costume derives from the dress of a sixteenth-century Venetian merchant. Dottore wore the academic dress of a graduate of the University of Bologna. Perhaps the best example of truth becoming tradition is the costume of Arlecchino (Harlequin). As a poor servant he could not afford decent clothing, so he wore rags with many patches. Over a period of time this was conventionalized into the costume with its multicolored lozenges that is so recognizable today.

Costume and manner become synonymous. The mask may no longer be physical, but the character is immediately identifiable by his actions and reactions, and fulfills his expected function in the structure of the farce. In fact, the great modern descendants of the classical tricky slaves and the commedia Zannis wore an easily identifiable costume mask that is equally a part of their character. Chaplin's tramp outfit and the unchanging clothing worn by Laurel and Hardy, W. C. Fields, Harold Lloyd, and the Marx brothers are totally identified with the consistent character of their wearers. It's interesting to note that the costumes of most of these characters are based upon the accepted wear of the successful bourgeois, from the end of

The well-known "mask" of W. C. Fields, created by costume and physical manner.

the nineteenth century up through the middle of the twentieth: top hat or bowler hat; frock coat or shorter black jacket; waistcoat, collar, and tie; plain gray or striped trousers; gloves, walking sticks, umbrellas. The costumes, of course, don't quite fit the farceurs; they are shabby or worn incorrectly. Such incongruity reinforces the fundamental farcicality of finding upper-class costumes on deadbeat characters. The characters pretend a dignity they don't have. The mask has a double effect: it tells us what they are and how we may expect them to react. Because we associate a particular manner with the costume, it defines the character—Chaplin *is* the tramp.

At the same time, the faded or ill-fitting dignity of the clothing reminds us of what the character would like to be, or sees himself as. This creates the comic gap between mask and reality.

This comic gap finds its part in the effect of modern farce plays. Feydeau's characters wore the proper clothing for persons of their rank in the late nineteenth century. Just as Stoppard's politicians and civil servants in *Dirty Linen* are locked into the pin-striped suits and stiff collars still expected of public figures in late-twentieth-century England. These costume masks set up a series of identifications and expectations—dignity, propriety, authority—that farce sets out to break down and reveal the truth beneath. As with the commedia masks, it is the difference between what "ought" to be expected of the character—given his age, social position, and so forth—and what "is" to be expected of the character when the pressure of farce situations makes the masks slip—or lets the pants fall down.

There is always a tension between mask and appetite, between what the clothing allows and what the character wants. Collars are too high and too tight to allow the characters, comfortably, to chase in and out of doors. Trousers are too tight to allow them, comfortably, to climb out of windows. Hats and ties begin to slip under pressure of physical activity. Shoes or socks get lost or put on the wrong feet; shoelaces get tied together and trip one up. Trousers get put on back to front, and articles of ladies' underwear find their way into gentlemen's pockets in mistake for handkerchiefs. The physical elegance of the dignified bourgeois must constantly be readjusted, as it slips to reveal the impulsive child or instinctual animal below the well-dressed facade.

Incongruity is, then, one of the chief characteristics of farce costuming—either because the costume doesn't fit the character or the character doesn't live up to the costume. If the costume isn't too big, too small, too tight, too loose for the character, then the character will be too manic, too childish, too weak, too lecherous, or too stupid for the costume.

Before leaving costuming we should mention the function of properties in farce action. Here, another fundamental comic quality comes into play—exaggeration. Unusually large properties are standard in farce. They sometimes serve to reinforce character traits; such are the miserly Pantalone's overlarge keys or the Dottore's voluminous books or the braggart warrior's double-size sword. Often they are geared to human discomfort or organic functions—huge enemas, enormous syringes, vast dental instruments. Everyday artifacts of discomfort, or items we would like

to hide, are made larger and more visible. Medical pills become the size of golf balls, or, if one is trying to keep within the bounds of "reality," an improbable number of "normal"-size pills are stuffed down a patient's throat. Surgical operations take place with carpentry saws, hammers, chisels, and an incredible amount of intestinal tubing and lurid-looking organs are "removed" from the sufferer. The very first exaggerated farce property was probably the Greek phallus, which outdid in size even the most optimistic male fantasy. Exaggeration, like incongruity, is comic in its improbability and serves to distance discomfort or pain. We know no dentist would use such pliers, no surgeon such a syringe, no nurse such a needle, so we can laugh at the victim's discomfort while the action lances our own fears of such things happening to us.

Language. Like everything else about it, the language of farce is active. Unlike romantic comedy and comedy of manners, it contains little in the way of literary conceits. Farce doesn't have the time to stop for wordplay. Nor does it make the intellectual appeal necessary for the appreciation of puns, epigrams, verbal wit, or elaboration of whatever kind. Farce language works mostly in structures and rhythms. The joke is contained in the way the verbal situation is built, not in the content of the language. It functions in terms of character and situation by illustrating character in action rather than describing it, and by creating verbal traps.

The basic rhythm of farce tends to be stichomythic. Short, sharp sentences create a strong, vigorous pace and a sense of confrontation. Occasionally there will be longer set-piece speeches, sometimes for the purpose of exposition, or to let the audience watch the thought process of a comic victim as he tries to think his way out of a situation and invariably becomes more entangled in the web of deceit. Set-piece speeches were quite common in commedia. They were in fact the stock in trade of every mask character. Known as *concetti*, they were the verbal equivalent of the comic business, *lazzi*, and used whenever opportunity occurred or occasion demanded. Outside of these conventions the verbal rhythm of farce is short and vivacious.

Molière contains some excellent examples of verbal structures used to illustrate masks of character. In *The Miser* there is a situation in which Harpagon is going to marry off his young daughter to an old man she doesn't want, because the old man will take her without a dowry. Another character is trying to dissuade him from this, but to every argument Harpagon makes the same response: "But, without a dowry." He says it five times in succession, and is clearly incapable of hearing any argument to the contrary. This is an illustration of his obsession with money—his mask of miserliness. The comic device used is that of repetition, and the humor is contained not in the content of what Harpagon says, but in the structure of his responses. Somewhat later in the same play there is an example of the set-piece speech. Harpagon discovers someone has run off with his cashbox. His reaction is completely exaggerated, but totally in keeping with his mask as an obsessive miser. In his frenzy he tries to arrest himself, claims he has been murdered, and threatens to hang the whole audience uless they confess.

It has been said that the ability to speak is the basis of human civilization—it distinguishes man from the other animals. Under the pressures to which farce subjects its characters the ability to communicate tends to break down. This shatters another social mask, for we use speech as much to conceal our real intentions as to reveal them. We use it as a mask of meaning. Under pressure the logic of speech disintegrates, and the ensuing incoherence is often more truly revealing of basic desires. The force of emotion will be too much for words, but farce's characters still try to communicate in normal social terms, which sets up all kinds of comic situations. Harpagon is so overcome with the thought of not having to pay a dowry that all he can do is

repeat the phrase—revealing himself for the miser he is. He is so overcome with the loss of his money that all logic leaves him; he can only shout out the first and most extravagant threats that come to him.

Incoherence, the breakdown of the logic of communication, leads to incomprehensibility and misunderstanding. And this is the stuff of further farcical situations. We have already mentioned the deaf character in *Sauce for the Goose*, who could hear only when her husband mouthed silent words at her. Feydeau also introduced a character with a cleft palate into his play *A Flea in Her Ear*. The breakdown of the normal means of communication helps to throw social relationships into chaos. In the middle of chaos we often truly reveal ourselves for what we are. By using language in this way farce thus achieves two of its chief aims: to keep people in touch with the human reality behind the social mask, and to laugh at their attempts to keep the mask in place.

Appeal. In 1671 Dryden was complaining, in the introduction to his play *An Evening's Love*, that farces usually appealed more to audiences than did comedies. This was a terrible admission from a great neoclassical playwright and critic, for until quite recently, in academic and critical eyes farce was regarded either as not truly a dramatic form at all or as certainly the lowest form of drama. But that very lowness has ensured its perennial success. Its roots go deeper into human nature than almost any other dramatic form. It has survived all assaults because of the depths of those roots—the fundamental appeal to popular sensibility. It incorporates all the elements of popular entertainment: clowning, trickery, physical jokes, bawdiness, risk, energy.

If "lowness" means popular appeal, it also suggests where that appeal is directed: below the belt. Essentially physical, it is based in all those drives, functions, and appetites that reside between the navel and the kneecap. In case man gets too inflated an opinion of himself, it reminds him that he is "no better than he should be." Farce keeps humanity honest. It is essentially ambivalent in its viewpoint; aware that man is neither angel nor devil, it helps him walk the tightrope between heaven and hell. Farce breaks down the facade of civilization in order to preserve it. It cracks the encrusted mask of human dignity to allow the basic resilience of the race to reassert itself. It both destroys and preserves: demolishing overrationality and rationalizing chaos, just as its form, apparently chaotic, is highly disciplined and structured.

PERFORMANCE DEMANDS

Character Mask. Character in farce is not a psychological construct; it is made up of essentially physical qualities. Even if farce took time to concern itself with motivation sinisterly rooted in Oedipal or Electra complexes, the audience wouldn't. It hasn't come to see why the characters act the way they do, but to see what happens to them when they do—that is where the interest lies. Characters do not change, and reveal subtleties or hidden depths. It is the situations that change, while the characters go right on—crashing into them, plunging through them, or bouncing off them. The character is like a pinball in a machine: he is fired into the game and everyone watches excitedly to see what holes he falls into, what lights he turns on, how many points he scores before he returns, after a bruising circuit, back to the starting point.

The problem for an actor with a farce character is not finding out what mixture of parental genetic structure or what environmental influence makes the character act in a particular way. It's a lot simpler: why does the playwright want him to act this way, and what absolutely basic and universal human drives has he given the character to make sure it does? In other words, to revert to the pinball metaphor, the actor needs to know what kind of pinball, what kind of machine, and how hard he is fired. The actor finds the answers in the play's structure—which tells him what the situations are, and what part his character plays in those situations—and also in his own imagination, based upon his observance of human action—this shows him how many ways he can make his character fulfill the role the playwright has given it. Put simplistically, if the playwright wants him to bump into the furniture, the actor must find various amusing ways of doing this within the reality of his mask. The actor needs to discover what the playwright tells him about his character: he is a lawyer, a lecher, a would-be seducer of his friends' wives; he has a great belief in rationality, as befits his profession, yet cannot control his sexual drive; he has a public position to keep up, befitting a prosperous Parisian of the late nineteenth century; he would have himself seen as a man of precise distinction and cultivated taste. One could go on, but there is already enough for the imaginative actor to go to work. What are the physical rhythms of such an individual—how might he walk, carry his head, look down his nose, adjust his pince-nez, brush off his coat sleeves, swagger his cane? Would he have a long, sharp legal nose; stoop shoulders; lascivious lips that he moistens with his tongue; an eye for female rather than legal forms? Rhythms, mannerisms, deformities, physical quirks—all of these form part of the mask of the farce character. Groucho Marx, Charlie Chaplin, and Jacques Tatti all had distinctive walks and bodily rhythms, just as W. C. Fields and Laurel and Hardy had their mannerisms with cigars, fingers, and bowler hats.[8]

The mask is based upon a selected and heightened physical reality. It is then brought into confrontation with the plot situations that have been specifically created by the playwright to reveal it in the most ridiculous light. In the case of our lawyer/ lecher the situations will encourage the mechanistic im-

---

[8] Monty Python—almost a modern commedia troupe—has a sketch called "Department of Funny Walks."

pulses of his sexual lusts and, by frustrating them, exaggerate the inherent conflict in his mask between the propriety of the rational, legal scion of society and the primitive instincts of the lecherous old goat.

So the actor, having determined what his character would be like, then discovers what it would do when confronted with the traps and snares of the situation. The rigid mental attitudes, automatic responses, impulsive reactions to primitive drives show the mask in action. While attempting to keep up the mask of rationality and upholding the law, our lawyer character will be seen leaping into beds that collapse on top of him, falling over furniture in his haste to escape, tiptoeing from bedrooms with his trousers in his hand. How he does all this, what his responses are in physical terms, is for the actor to create from his imagination and physical agility. The responses will be consistent with the mask built by the actor—for they are the mask in action. The mask of a farce character may be improbable, but it is consistent. It will be consistently improbable in its reaction to situations. Once built, the mask is recognized by the audience in terms of its external manner and physical reactions. It will create certain expectations in the audience—even if these are expectations of improbability—which must then be fulfilled. If Chaplin or Fields had reacted differently from the associations of their masks, the audience would have felt cheated, would not have believed them, and the humor would have been lost. (Chaplin was less successful in his later movies, when he tried to move away from the mask associated with him.) Once the level of truth of an event has been established, the audience will believe it—however improbable—as long as it is consistently carried through.

In a sense the actor in farce will have two objectives to play. There will be the very simple one-dimensional objective of his character: "I want to seduce my neighbor's wife"; "I want to hide the fact I am wealthy"; "I want everyone to think I am a sick person."

Then there will be the actor's objective: "I want to reveal the rigidity, the one-dimensionality, the impulsive response of my character's mask as amusingly as possible within the situations the playwright has given me."

The playwright has done most of the work for the actor, if only he will recognize the clues. Not only has the playwright set up his situations so that they will be in direct confrontation with the character masks, but he has given the strong, simple outlines of the mask itself. In some instances this goes as far as giving the character a mask name. Many of Plautus's characters bear names that indicate their mask responses. Commedia is not only based upon a set of physical masks with consistent names, but the responses expected of these masks are completely conventionalized. Shakespeare and Molière, with their Malvolios, Aguecheeks, Belches, Fleurants, Dorantes, De Bonnefois, and Jourdains, used the eponymous principle. Even a modern playwright such as Stoppard names Miss Gotobed as a very obvious indication of the lady's function in his *Dirty Linen*, and in the same play has a character ironically called French—because he is trying hard to be anything but the anglicized conception of the gallic sexual attitudes.

The farce actor must approach performance with absolute seriousness. He must never show that he is aware of how ridiculously his character is acting. Be willing to make a fool of yourself as an actor, but don't show that you know your character is a fool. There is a desperate gravity behind the mask—an attempt to keep the situation normal despite the chaos happening all around. The farce character presumes the audience to be full of individuals like himself. He is not self-critical or aware. He believes the audience to be on his side, sympathizing with his predicament.

Farce is a constant struggle, doomed to inevitable defeat, to maintain the balance of normality. The more the characters get involved with a situation, the more erratic, childlike, primitive they become. The civilized adult mask cannot withstand the intensity of the situation. Farce characters are never more appealing to an audience than when they behave like children. It is a wish fulfillment, a release from restrictive adult responsibilities. An actor must be able to cope with the erratic behavior, the swiftly changing moods of farce: childlike tantrums and sunny charm follow rapidly upon each other.

There is no time for change of motivation, only for change of physical response—an immediate reaction to a changing situation. As with everything in farce, this must be done with a delicacy that heightens the effect of the chaos. The farce actor must be able to "float like a butterfly, sting like a bee," to have that delicacy of touch without which his clockwork toy of a character would either smash itself to pieces or go spinning off into space.

Humor revealed through physical energy and agility in this scene from *Hotel Paradiso*.

American Conservatory Theatre, San Francisco.

Movement. Farce is full of a restless vigor. The jokes are physical, revealed in activity. Acting in farce requires the energy and fortitude of a laborer combined with the physical agility of a tap dancer. The primitive energy at the very roots of farce, which catalyzed the sexual rites from which it sprung, is constantly there beneath the civilized facade. It drives the action at a manic pace. The pace is fast for many reasons: the impulsive drives just mentioned; the characters' constant attempts to avoid disaster (danger either lurks behind every door, or one must get behind a door to avoid danger); the fact that the characters are always either avoiding or trying to catch up with something—like uncertain jugglers, they are constantly toppling forward to keep up with the balls. For farce characters there is no future. They are creatures of the moment, of the body's impulses, not the active intellect—they do not think out consequences. The fast pace also distances the situation—no "real" human being acts like that—while leaving the audience no time to reflect upon the improbabilities. The fast pace heightens the seemingly uncontrollable chaos, adds a sense of frenzy, daring, and danger, allows more disasters to happen per minute.

There can be no gaps in farce action or the actors will be left hanging in midair. There is no infrastructure to support them, only the energy of the moment, which must be kept coming—like hot air keeping up balloons. The devil himself is in farce rhythm. The actor seems to be dragged along behind a runaway horse, but he must, in fact, be keeping a tight rein. The physical space and structure of farce requires discipline, control, agility, precision. The actor must be able to move at speed through physical clutter: in and out of doors, around furniture. He must be able to turn on a dime and change his manner in the wink of an eye to match a new situation. Chaos is always highly organized to produce the appropriate comic effect—chaos per se is not funny. Without discipline

chaos could produce physical injury. Actors must seem to take and give physical punishment; the hitting, falling over furniture, and bumping into each other has to be carefully controlled. Equally, the freedom to improvise in farce must be within a carefully respected set pattern. Finally, farce is a clockwork mechanism that requires as strong ensemble playing as individual imagination.

Movement is, then, quick, light, balanced, flexible. It contains more energy and is exaggerated more than its "real"-life equivalent. Movement always tends to be in conflict with the character's attempt to keep up his mask—retain his dignity, elegance, or whatever—and with intelligent response to a situation. The character's body moves more quickly than his brain. Acting on unthinking impulses, the body often seems to want to go in all directions at once. The impulse to escape, to find any solution, sends arms and legs in different directions. The French farceur Jacques Tatti is a splendid example of this technique. In films such as *M. Hulot's Holiday* he is always looking in one direction and moving in another; legs seem to go in opposing directions and arms somewhere else again. This extends to all he does. He plays table tennis like a ballet dancer, exaggerating and conventionalizing the reality of table-tennis movements into a curious, comic dance.

Such use of exaggerated gesture is another fundamental element of farce movement. Gestures are quicker, larger, more frenetic than the life gestures upon which they are based. Running will be done with elongated strides; beating with large arm movements; expression of surprise can send the eyebrows through the hat brim, or the chin down to the chest. But none of these is sustained. Brevity, as much as speed, is a quality of farce. The gesture or expression makes its point and then the action moves on. There is no time allowed for consideration of the situation or for emotion or feeling to take over. Gesture is based upon a human response, expresses a feeling, but does not

Acrobatic aggression from Charlie Chaplin produces humor through physical imagination.

contain emotion. The incongruous juxtapositions, mechanical confusions, staccato repetitions, brisk reversals, and violent directness of farce all call for short, sharp, quick rhythms punctuated by laughter, not thought. In its movement and gesture farce is true to its origins and employs the speed, energy, physical variety, and broad gesture required to hold the attention of popular audiences throughout the history of theatre.

We have been talking about farce movement as one, and indeed the basic principles are universal. But, perhaps as a footnote, we should mention the particular qualities of commedia. Because of its use of actual masks and its highly improvisational nature, commedia is the most physically oriented,

free wheeling, and broadly played form of farcical theatre. Commedia does not have to keep up the realistic patina of modern farce. Based in a distant reality, the masks now exist in a historical vacuum; they are there to play their part in the comic game of human greed, lust, aggression, pomposity, cunning, and romance that commedia presents in all its absurdities. Each mask can be played to its comic hilt. Pantalone may be old and impotent, but he is still capable of extraordinary physical feats in defense of his money. His speed and agility do not have to take into account his age. Part of the farcical humor is to see what the old decrepit can do when his fixed interests are threatened. And this sets up more opportunities for exaggerated pantings

Lightness and delicacy combined with incongruous physicality create the humor in this scene from *Chemin de Fer*.

Mark Taper Forum, Los Angeles.

and wheezings when the frenetic chase is over. Motivation is even less important in commedia than in other forms of farce. The mask is all. Arlecchino will tumble and perform acrobatics because that is expected of him—he doesn't need a chair to fall over. The servants will be beaten and return beatings with the slapstick, because that is what happens when commedia masks confront each other. Business can be improvised to whatever level and length the audience will accept. As long as they are consistent among the members of the troupe, gestures and movements may be as exaggerated as the rela-tionship with the audience demands and allows. The difference between the physical performance of commedia and more modern forms of farce is a question of degree. The essential farce qualities are common; it is the level of exaggeration, improbability, and physical emphasis—given the differences in costume, setting, and so forth—that demarks the form.

Verbal Manner. The qualities required by farce movement apply equally to speech. Energy, speed, agility of vocal delivery are as much a part of the clockwork mechanism of situation and character as is the movement to which it must be related.

Responses are quick, stichomythic. Characters blurt out unthinking replies—there is no pause for thought process. A pause in farce is physical—a gesture of astonishment or speechlessness. The concern is not with subtext, but with direct action. Verbal manner can be a part of the character mask. The playwright may call for a particular character to have a harelip, a stammer, or a cleft palate in order to use incomprehensibility to complicate a situation. The actor himself may discover that a lisp, an accent, a plummy voice, or a squeaky voice fits the mask of character he is creating. The physical rhythms and mannerisms of a character are likely to be reflected in his pattern of speech.

Whatever the verbal mask, it will have to communicate the linguistic structure of the play. Farce relies little upon verbal wit. It has no time for conceits or contrivances that do not either further the plot situation or, like a physical gesture, reveal aspects of character. Such jokes as there are in farce tend to be one-liners. The gassy stuff is given a quick shake, the cork pops out of the bottle, and is quickly stuffed back in again. There is no slow escape of air such as might be found in a comedy of manners. It is not the content of the lines that produces humor, but rather the structure. The actor must be very aware of how lines are built, and not just his—the development of a verbal gag may take place over several shared lines. The actor is frequently either setting up or completing a verbal structure. We have already used the example of the exchange between Harpagon and Valère in *The Miser* over the question of Harpagon's daughter's dowry. While Valère is giving Harpagon all kinds of reasons why she shouldn't be married off to a rich old man, all Harpagon can do is say "But without a dowry" five or six times. Here Valère is setting up and Harpagon topping. Harpagon must discover changes in inflection and intensity so that each identical line is slightly different in delivery, while rising to the final climax.

The Harpagon–Valère exchange is based upon repetition. This is frequently employed in farce verbal structure, as are those other standbys of comic form—exaggeration and incongruity. Farce requires as great a variety of verbal as of physical manner. It will not be the subtle pointing of comedy, the ability to ease through the labyrinths of epigram, or the coloring of poetic images. It is more the use of a wide range of vocal sounds in an endless number of ways. In farce the tongue is not so much a sword or scalpel as a slapstick. A quick glance at the stage directions in a Feydeau farce shows the following words: "hoarse"; "apoplectic"; "with hollow laugh"; "screaming"; "outraged"; "babbling." The gamut of human vocal capacity is called upon—and at the extreme edges of the range. Cries of anguish, pain, hysterical laughter—everything from the deepest stomach bellow to the highest headnote shriek punctuate farce action. The voices of the characters form an orchestral percussion section, building the action, underlining the responses of characters, and giving a resounding impact to climaxes. Farce is as full of sound as of fury—both, in the end, signifying little.

Physical Imagination. This section might be subtitled "Lots of *Lazzi*." Elaboration of situations and playing out of character mask is achieved most often by physical business. Indeed, it is usually developed out of the confrontation of the mask and the situation. However exaggerated and improbable, business should be discovered in the action of the play through the physical imagination of the actors. Commedia is a slight exception to this in that there are a lot of set piece gags that arise more directly out of the mask conventions. Although these don't directly further the situation or illuminate character, they are consistent with what a particular mask may be expected to do. Some examples of this are the *lazzi* associated with Arlecchino: the catching-and-eating-the-fly gag; the brick that is a "sample" of the house he can build;

the water in the cheeks that inevitably gets spat on someone; covering the head like an ostrich to hide from someone—and getting kicked in the backside. These would be introduced into a scenario, at an appropriate time, over and over again and still get their laugh—in fact, familiarity and expectation would heighten the response.

In more sophisticated farces that make a gesture towards surface realism, some tenuous motivation for business is best found in the character–situation conflict. Here, business will usually arise out of the character's attempt to operate within the world of "things." Impedimenta are a prerequisite of the farceur. If there is a step, he can trip over it—the comedian probably won't, and the tragedian musn't. The technology of the modern world, which we are constantly struggling to control, is the perfect stuff of farce business—the electric beater that covers you with egg, the vacuum that sucks off your undershorts, the pull-down bed that traps you in the wall. The more unnecessary the technology, the more absurd the effect. Woody Allen uses "things" to comic effect in his films. *Play it Again Sam* has an uncontrollable bathroom cabinet that spews its contents all over him. It also has records that jump out of their sheaths and sail across the room like frisbees. This is all geared to undercut the nonchalant self-image Allen was trying to build. While he is attempting to appear suave and Bogart-like the pills and records and "things" that surround him all conspire to undermine his dignity—as does the sofa that he attempts to vault lightly into, only to end up on his backside on the floor. The mask of flair ends up as the reality of gaucherie.

Farce business may be loosely divided into two types: general undermining and discomfiture gags, very loosely connected with character; and business connected more directly with character and situation, though improbable by "real" standards. Business of the first type includes sitting on hats, tripping on rugs, slipping on banana skins, and slapstick of all kinds. Slapstick is a metaphor for a basic, impulsive human response—hitting. It is an essential part of farce vocabulary, as it shows authority, releases aggression, and gives discomfort. Someone's dignity gets undermined. The modern equivalent of the original commedia slapstick is the pie in the face. Usually in the face of "authority," it is a basic *lazzi* for reducing dignity. It makes a great show and doesn't cause real hurt. Variants of this include Chaplin's use of a water hose: inadvertently he stands on it—no water; he gets off to look down the spout—water in the face.

Business illustrating character and situation may be highly exaggerated, but it tends to be less purely physical than basic slapstick. There was a very fine example of this in a production of *The Miser* by the Guthrie Theatre. Harpagon had agreed to give a ring to the girl he was courting. When taken from his finger it was attached by a long piece of elasticized string, so it whizzed straight back. This was repeated three times until finally one of the servants cut the thread. In the same play, but a different production, during a conversation between Harpagon and one of his servants the servant kept lighting a candle—which Harpagon kept, thriftily, blowing out. More subtly, in a production of *The Importance of Being Earnest* Algernon and Cicely meet in the garden. Cicely has been watering with a small can; Algy is infatuated with her and, unable to clasp her hands, clasps the spout of the can. The charming delicacy of the situation made the phallic overtones of the business even more amusing.

The actor discovers business by imaginatively exploring all the possibilities of the situations his character is involved in. The actor should not be tentative; he plays his mask for all it is worth and confronts the obstacles as strongly and as variously as possible. His costume and properties afford further opportunities for business. The costume is both part of the character mask, with exaggerated attributes to explore, and may itself become an obstacle when the character is put in certain situations. Walking sticks can be tripped over, caught in doors or on table legs.

Shoelaces are to be constantly untied, cuff links to fall into soup or catch in women's hair. Trousers are too tight to allow easy maneuver. The whole costume mask comes undone under pressure and has to be continually readjusted. Whatever the business may be, and however brilliantly imagined, the farceur should always keep these principles in mind: it should have some connection, however tenuous, with the action; it should be as simple as possible; and the effect should be immediately comprehensible to the audience.

Playing for Real. One of the problems in playing farce—especially for an actor brought up on psychological realism—is the degree of improbability of the situation and the character reactions. Though at a more exaggerated level, the solution to playing farce is the same as for any theatrical style—learning to play the play and not to impose the actor's own idea of outside reality upon it. Discovering and communicating the inherent reality of the text will communicate the believable truth of the event. If an actor plays his mask at the level of exaggeration demanded by the plot situations, and does this consistently, the audience will totally accept the level of improbability and will not question it in terms of a reality outside the play. In other words, the audience is quite prepared to play its part in the theatrical game if the actor shows it what that part is.

Farce masks and situations are based in truth. However exaggerated, the roots of farce action go down into the deepest part of the human self and feed upon the most fundamental drives and instincts. Even commedia, which is almost entirely a game today, with no patina of surface reality, is based upon those intrigues and desires that have been motivating man since the temptation of Eve. Commedia is, of course, distanced by costume, mask, and historicity, and has the modern function of a kind of live puppet or Punch and Judy show. Just as puppets and Punch and Judy work for young children, so do

modern farces still have an appeal for young adults. One might think that the social freedom and sexual sophistication of young adults would have defused, or rendered simply stupid, many of the situations upon which farce is based. What is all the fuss about sex? Such urgency and difficulty about getting into someone's bed might seem curious or trivial to a generation for whom "musical beds" is a not uncommon party game. But they are still aware of fundamental human frustrations and instincts, and the improbability of people going to such absurd lengths for gratification adds a further distance to the event. It can be enjoyed for its gamelike or "unreal" qualities.

The idea of distance is important to the acceptance of the farce effect. The improbability of the situations and the exaggeration of the responses add to that distance. The audience operates on two levels: it accepts what is going on on stage—the truth of the event—but if asked, it would say it certainly didn't believe that such things "really" happen to people. Thus the audience enjoys the outrage but removes itself from the consequences. It therefore permits itself to laugh, because the pain and discomfort are not "really" real. The high level of pace, energy, and exaggeration in farce contributes to this necessary abstraction of effect. We know no human being could withstand such knocking about and come up smiling—so it's a big joke. We know that being caught in another woman's bedroom isn't going to lead to the legal agony of alimony and property settlements—so we can release our fear of this by laughing at someone else's loss of face.

The level of improbability, external energy, physical aggression, and exaggeration will determine the farcical level of a performance. The right level of exaggerated response is important. In *The Miser*, the scene in which Harpagon discovers his money box is stolen must be done with enormous manic energy and exaggeration of gesture. Harpagon's miserliness is *so* great that he catches and arrests himself in his frenzy. If the actor's manner is less than extreme the scene can become too dark, too painful, and consequently not funny. It has been done that way, and the whole effect of the play is altered. It was not Molière's intention to show the agonized psyche of an unfortunate victim of theft, but the comic responses of a miserly old pantaloon who had brought the well-deserved disaster upon himself. How do we know this? From the text. The exaggerated reactions of Harpagon—arresting himself, then the whole audience, and hanging himself—and the hysterical rhythms of the speech, tell the actor how it should be played.

A game, a joke, a structure of exaggerations and improbabilities farce may be, but it is entirely serious for the actor. No matter how ludicrous the situation, it must be played with total absorption, concentration, and commitment. The hellbent desperation of the character about things that finally aren't all that important must be absolutely total. Farce must never be self-conscious or aware of itself. When the laughs come, don't milk them. Don't overelaborate, nudge the audience in the ribs, show it you know how funny you are. Play the ridiculous seriously—play for real.

Sense of Occasion. This really brings us full circle, back to the roots we spoke of at the beginning of the chapter. For those roots inform the whole sensibility of farce. It is not souls or psyches that are at risk in farce, but bellies and backsides—human relationship at a very basic level. Deriving from orgiastic celebration, farce has an essentially popular appeal at a simple physical level. Farce is above all alive—at the cost of crudity, improbability, indecency. It is the life force having a holiday from reason, restraint, and moral stricture. Eat, drink, be merry; fornicate; smash up the furniture; unpin society's hair—for tomorrow it's back to the same spouse and the nine-to-five routine.

The actor makes a compact with the audience to be ridiculous and play the fool. It is a festival of fools in which no one gets hurt or loses more than a little face, and possibly their pants. The actor plays out the audience's fantasies for it, while the audience cheers him on and laughs at this surrogate for its own fallible humanity. Though playing his part entirely seriously, the actor must be aware of the fun of the occasion. He is playing a game with and for the audience: teasing it, pulling the rug out from under it, letting it teeter, deliciously, on the brink of disaster. In farce, above all theatrical occasions, the actor is aware of the audience's presence through the strong, physical response of laughter. Accepting this, riding on it while not being carried away by it, helps the actor to sustain the energy, exuberance, and physical playfulness that is such a crucial part of farce performance—and connects modern shenanigans in bourgeois drawing rooms directly with the earliest wellsprings of the comic spirit.

PLAYING THE STYLE

Much of what we are dealing with in this section doesn't work well on paper, especially highly practical techniques such as falling or intangible qualities such as timing, which are to some degree instinctive. We recognize this problem but are offering some nuts and bolts in the hope of giving the student an understanding of the structure behind certain techniques, and a stronger basis for his approach to the practical aspects of farce playing.

Joke Structure. Most jokes result from the setting up of an expectation that is then unfulfilled, or whose associations in the listener's mind are departed from. In his essay on the comic, Freud quotes the following story: A marquis at the court of Louis XIV entered his wife's bedroom to find her having sex with a bishop. The marquis calmly went to the window and started to bless people in the street. "What are you doing?" cried his anguished wife. "Monseigneur is performing my function," replied the marquis, "so I am performing his." The joke is based upon a departure from the normal expectation of reaction to adultery. We have:

1. fact of adultery
2. expectation of normal response
3. unfulfillment or inversion of expectation

It is essentially a threefold process: the tension of expectation mounts, but never reaches its expected climax because it is exploded by the marquis's unexpected reaction. This cuts off the logical development of the situation and debunks our dramatic expectations, and the tension explodes in laughter.

To take another well-known dramatic situation involving adultery, from Shakespeare's *Othello:* here tension increases with the expectation of a jealous reaction to adultery until Othello does kill Desdemona—a tragic climax that releases tension in a tearful catharsis. The adultery situation is a joke rather than tragedy when two irreconcilable associations collide and then quickly explode the tension before its logical emotional climax.

Another joke made out of a tragic situation concerns the woman who told her friend she was having problems with her young son—she had taken him to a psychiatrist who said he had an Oedipus complex. "Don't you worry," said her friend, "He'll be all right just as long as he's a good boy and loves his Mommy." Here, again, two logics are clashing—the reasonable assumption that if the boy is good and loves his parents other matters are less important, which collides with the specific logic of Freudian psychiatry. The joke may be seen in the light of the tragic logic of the Oedipus myth.

An audience must have enough information—in this case, knowledge of what an Oedipus complex is—to be able to make an association. At the same time, it musn't have so much information that it can foresee the outcome—this removes the element of surprise. A joke proceeds in jumps, leaving logical gaps that the audience has just enough time to fill in, but not enough time to reflect

upon and become involved with understanding the logic. For example, a pedant is funny: his pedagogical compulsion collides with the futility of his practical influence. But the compulsive neurotic isn't funny, if we have enough time to attempt to understand his problem, enter his logic.

A joke, then, is the collision of two mutually incompatible logics that produces a flash point, a new, surprising result. The success of the joke will depend upon:

1. originality: it must be able to create surprise.
2. information: the listener must be able to make the association.
3. simplification: overelaboration undermines the build of tension.
4. emphasis: exaggeration of crucial elements and elimination of the irrelevant.
5. economy: this is not the same as brevity; it is spacing the impetus so that the audience gets time to fill in the gaps, but not enough to examine the logic.

Practical jokes appeal to a more primitive part of ourselves and produce the farce belly laugh rather than the comedy-of-manners knowing smile or gentle laughter. Most physical humor is based upon discomfiture—in itself a primitive response. Like verbal humor it operates on the 1-2-3 principle: pompous teacher sits on thumbtack; here is a direct association of two opposing logics—public-mask and private-part clashes. The surprise is physically manifested by a jump in the air, which coincides with the observer's laugh.

Finally, we are going to look at possibly the world's oldest gag in order to illustrate the 1-2-3 principle as it relates to the "double-act" situation. "Why did the chicken cross the road?" If the response is "to get to the other side," there is no joke. An absolute, if trivial, logic is asserted: the chicken could not cross the road without getting to the other side. Thus, when the question is posed the listener expects some new information, some logic other than the given. So, "I don't know" is the response. Then the joke comes through the absurd affirmation of the obvious as the unexpected. "I don't know" is essential to the joke. It is the necessary step 2, which enables 3 to be funny.

The double act works on this principle:

1. The comic sets up.
2. The straight man responds.
3. The comic tops off.

Gags tend to work in 3, 5, 7, etc. On the even beats there is a balance, the assertion of a norm that is not funny. The 1-2-3 principle can probably be related to the Hegelian dialectical form:

thesis: setting up a proposition
antithesis: a response that is within the same logic but incompatible
synthesis: a new idea or way of looking at the logic that is surprising or funny.

The thesis and antithesis are usually the opposition of mutually incompatible human choices: wish fulfillment versus shouldn't be found out; pants off for adultery versus musn't be caught with pants down.[9]

Takes. Takes are a physical way of topping—showing surprise. They are based upon a nonimmediate realization that both adds to the observer's anticipation and increases the degree of surprise. A double take is a delayed recognition in passing: a look is taken at what should be surprising, but there is no immediate reaction; there is a return to normal focus; then the realization hits like a thunderbolt with a double-quick return to take another look, followed by surprise. A double take may be made into a triple by splitting the suddenness of realization: first look brings no reaction; somewhat quicker second look, some reaction; lightening-quick third look as realization finally hits. The take is a technique for building up extra comic ten-

sion—the audience gets to enjoy the same situation twice or three times, and is titillated by the anticipated realization of surprise.

As opposed to the quickness of the take, the slow burn extends the dawning of realization and shares it with the audience. It is usually a response to some kind of put-down—like a balloon deflation. When he worked with Gracie Allen, George Burns used the slow burn to suggest: "What can you do?" "Would you believe that?" Jack Benny's burn usually meant "How did I come to fall for that again?" The deadpan is a slow burn without the burn—it lets the audience do all the filling in, taking the reaction the deadpan consciously refuses to reveal. The subtler the reaction, the less of a physical sign given to the audience, the more difficult is the technique. The deadpan is the most extreme form of "playing against" or "doing less," a technique that gives great focus and clarity to an action but treads a fine line between highly comic emotionlessness and simple lack of reaction.

Slapping and Falling Techniques. Ideally, a farce actor should take some instruction in tumbling and falling. Short of that, we are giving a few techniques that will help the actor with the physical-contact part of farce performance.

Slapping. The first technique requires the receiver of the slap to be closed to the audience. The slapper sets up the hit, which he pulls just on contact. The receiver times his reaction with the blow, moving his head (say) sharply and at the same time clapping his hands together, in the closed position, to make the sound of contact. The second technique is possibly better, as it doesn't require the slapper to pull his blow. The receiver should again be turned away from the audience, with his right palm (for a right-handed slap) placed open at the point of contact—say, beneath the jaw. The slapper takes a good swing and hits the open palm of the receiver. At this moment the receiver

[9] We are grateful to Raye Birk of the American Conservatory Theatre for discussing with us some of the concepts examined in this section.

takes a physical reaction. Timing and trust in the partner are all-important, and slapping requires a lot of rehearsal.

Falling. An introduction to falling that also serves as an ensemble/trust exercise is to have six or eight players standing opposite each other with arms linked to form a bed. The other players in turn run and leap into the bed of arms made by the catchers. They are lifted and tossed by this human cradle. A variation on this is to have the group of catchers at the side of a table. Each player in turn falls off the table into the catcher's arms. This should first be done falling forward so that confidence can be gained, but finally it should be a backwards fall into the group. Falls can be practiced with two partners. It is best to use a tumbling mat in the first instance. A good introduction to individual falls is to have a catcher standing behind the faller. The faller begins with short falls, being caught under the shoulders by the catcher. Gradually the fall distance is increased until the faller is caught just short of the ground. Finally the faller goes solo, breaking the fall with backside and forearms just as he touches the ground.

Pratfalls. The most common and comic form of farce fall. The backside is the most cushioned part of the body on which to fall, and most undignified human associations are centered in it. Thus, a pratfall is the technically safest way of achieving the greatest undercutting of human dignity. The fall should be practiced as suggested above, and highly controlled. However, the effect of the fall must be exaggerated—the arms flung up and the legs flung out much more than the dynamics of the fall require. The best ratio is the smallest actual fall done with the largest possible effect.

Heel Slips. A controlled way of falling down a stair or off a level is to place the tip of a heel on the edge of the step and put on weight until the heel slips and a stumbling effect is achieved.

Toe Trip. Perhaps the oldest technical stumble in the farce book. This is induced by catching the toe of the rear foot against the heel of the leading foot during a walk. The resulting forward falling momentum can be a simple stumble; an actual fall on the face; a clinging on to someone for support; knocking that someone over; both persons falling over a chair, and so on depending on how far the gag is to be taken.

Exploring the Situation. In our discussion of character mask we suggested some ways of exploring the comic potential of the farce mask. Humor will arise when the drives of the mask come into conflict with the action obstacles provided by the playwright. For example, in the basic "getting-your-pants-off-to-commit-adultery" farce situation, how will the mask character go about it: Nervously? Arrogantly? Carelessly? The intensity of the drive in conflict with the potential insecurities of the situation creates tremendous opportunities for revealing character in action—and farce action at that. Are the fingers too nervous to handle the zip, with the result that the pants are pushed over the hip, where they stick? Is the force of desire so great that it breaks the zip halfway down, caught in the shirt—so the shirt and pants have to come off as one piece. Perhaps a shoe won't untie, so, with one trouser leg off, the would-be Casanova is hopping around in his shirttails, foot in hand, looking anything but a lover.

The possibilities are just as great if the couple are disturbed and the man has to redress in a hurry. Again problems with the zip; getting a foot in the wrong trouser leg; getting both feet in one leg; getting the trousers on back to front. We have only looked at one costume prop—trousers—and one situation, and the possibilities for comic invention are endless. To take the gag further, the actor can explore how many ways he can trip over a trouser leg, and then involve falling on chairs, which break, or on the bed, which collapses. The degree of invention will depend upon taking a situation to its extremity, pushing the action to find where its edge of gravity is. Successful comic invention requires willingness to risk.

It is possible to take any permutation of situation, mask, and action and develop exercises for discovering comic business. One last example: A young man and woman are sitting on a sofa; they are tentative boyfriend and girlfriend. He is embarrassed by sexual physicality, but has a strong physical urge for her that he is trying to disguise—and he gets an erection. How does he deal with this? Try to cover it with a cushion? Try to cross his legs over it? Turn his lower body away while still facing her? Try to back out to the bathroom? Again, the possibilities are endless. What is needed for farce invention is a strong, simple sense of mask—tentative young man; a strong drive—erection; an obstacle—embarrassment; and a situation that allows for exploration—sofa and cushions. The lust, or intention, will always be extreme in order to support farce's physical exaggeration. But the mask is always based on a simple truth, which is revealed in action not explored psychologically. We are not interested in the young man's psyche—simply how he will deal with the situation.

EXERCISES, GAMES, TECHNIQUES

High-Energy Games. It is useful to begin any workshop or rehearsal for farce with games that require high energy, agility, maneuverability, such as the variants of tag. It is always best to begin with the familiar, so start with a game of basic tag: one player is IT while the other players have to avoid being tagged. Once tagged, a player becomes IT. The game can then be played with everyone having to adopt a funny walk or run—some exaggerated movement rhythm different from their norm. While the basic tag is going on, players can be required to change their

rhythm on a drumbeat or handclap. For farce purposes the space in which tag is played can be complicated by putting obstacles—chairs, boxes, tables—within it. Players have to maneuver around these while playing the game—anyone who touches an obstacle immediately becomes IT.

Three Deep is another good energy, physical-control game. Players form two circles, one immediately behind the other, so that players are standing two deep. Two players are outside the circle. One chases the other around the outside of the circle until he either catches him, when the situation is reversed— the chaser becomes the chasee—or the chasee moves into the circle and stands in front of one of the twosomes, making it three deep. When this happens the rear member of the group becomes the chasee, and must immediately set off around the outside of the circle either until he is tagged, or until he darts into the circle and stands in front of a twosome when the rear member becomes chasee, and so on.

Dropping the Handkerchief is a somewhat similar game. Players form one circle. One player walks around the outside of the circle with a handkerchief. At some juncture he drops this at the heels of one of the players in the circle. This player must pick up the handkerchief and chase the other player around the circle, attempting to tag him before he, the player who dropped the handkerchief, can get back into the space of the chaser. If tagged the handkerchief dropper continues, dropping the handkerchief at another pair of heels. If he gets to the empty space the game continues with the new dropper. The trick to this game is nonchalance on the part of the dropper and alertness on the part of the players in the circle. It can lead to a lot of amusement at the expense of players who don't realize the handkerchief is at their heels.

Spin the Platter. Players sit in a large circle and number off. One player is in the middle with a tin plate (plastic will do). He spins the plate and before it stops spinning calls out a number. The player called has to catch the plate before it starts to fall. If he fails he pays a forfeit; if he succeeds the spinner pays a forfeit. Forfeits are either removing a piece of clothing, taking a swat on the backside with a slapstick, or performing a funny action named by the group. Whoever paid the forfeit continues as the spinner, and so the game goes on. This is a good ensemble, getting-to-know-you game, as well as one that encourages alertness, precision in handling props, and that willingness to make a fool of oneself that is so important to the farce actor.

Touch-Me-Not. Players stand in a circle about the size of a boxing ring. Two players are in the middle. Each has to try and touch the other's back. They may use the whole of the circle, but may not leave it, nor may they touch any other part of their opponent's body (some arm contact is inevitable). Play best of three "hits." Whoever wins takes on the next player. This is a good game for alertness, physical imagination, agility, and finesse. It also encourages concentration on and response to every move made by the person you are playing with.

Slapstick Games. Hitting and physical contact is a fundamental part of the farce sensibility. In all the games set out below, the slapstick is a rolled-up newspaper, which produces no real pain but great effect.

Slapstick Tag. This is a simple introduction to slapstick activity. Any tag game may be played using the slapstick instead of the hand for tagging.

Slap in the Bucket. Players sit in a circle. One player has a slapstick. In the middle of the circle is a bucket. The player with the slapstick walks around the outside of the circle, gently tapping players with the slap-

stick. Finally he gives one player a hearty swat, then runs to the center of the circle to put the slapstick in the bucket. The player who has been hit tries to get the slapstick out of the bucket and swat his assailant in return before he, the assailant, can reach the smitten player's place. If he succeeds, then he must return the slapstick to the bucket and return to his place before the original assailant can get the slapstick and hit him once more. This continues until one player reaches the empty place without being hit. The player left with the slapstick goes around the circle tapping players, finally hitting one, and so the game goes on. This, again, is a game that produces a high level of energy and amusement. It is also good for quick reactions and physical control. There will be a tendency for players to toss the slapstick carelessly into the bucket—whereupon it will fall out and they will be in physical jeopardy, having to put it back in with the smitten player standing on top of them ready to grab and strike. Players learn that haste is not the same as quickness with control.

Slap on the Back is a variation of the preceding game. Players sit in a circle, eyes closed, hands open behind their backs. One player walks around the circle and places the slapstick in one of the open hands. The player who has received the slapstick proceeds to beat one of the players next to him, who has to run around the circle, attempting to avoid the beating, and back to his place. The game continues with the holder of the slapstick going around the circle and placing the weapon in another pair of hands.

Master-Slave is a slapstick game that calls for a simple situation in which a slave or servant is given instructions by a master to perform a task, such as cleaning up a room. While appearing to perform the task, the slave finds various ways to make fun of the master. Pulling faces, making obscene gestures, hiding the dust under the carpet; the possibilities for this are endless. However, the slave musn't be caught at his joking; if he is, he gets beaten with the slapstick. The game may be elaborated by having a series of masters, or supervisors, come in, each superior to the one before. The game now is for all subordinates to poke fun at or score points off those above them—with resultant beatings if they are caught. This game lets the players explore structures of repression as well as the double mask of being both oppressor and victim.

Pecking Order. This is a sophistication of the master-slave game and explores the playing of dominance or submission—which is present in all comic relationships. Set up a situation between two players, such as a librarian and book borrower. Ask them to improvise a conversation in which each tries to be superior to the other. For example:

A: I see you're taking out *The Idiot.*
B: Yes. I've read the rest of Dostoevski.
A: Yes. *The Idiot* is my favorite; I've read it several times.
B: In Russian?
A: No—German, French, Spanish, and Italian are my best languages.
B: Oh yes? My brother is professor of romance languages at Harvard.

And so on. Now reverse the aim so that each tries to be submissive:

A: Gosh, I see you're reading Dostoevski.
B: Only in translation.
A: I couldn't get through that.
B: Well, I only really look at the pictures.

And so on.

Many relationships can be explored in this way: man and wife; manager and secretary; student and professor; waiter and customer. One of the oldest known gags is:

Customer: Waiter, there's a fly in my soup.
Waiter: Well, it can't drink much.

Here the waiter, who is a low-status character, plays dominance. This is often the case with servants in comedy: there is humor in the contrast between the social status of the character and the status he presumes to play. (Chaplin played low status and brought everyone down to his level.) The game shows the strong connection between the assumption of status and the assumption of body attitudes. The player portraying dominance will stand or sit straighter, maintain eye contact, keep the body still. The submissive player will tend to small movements, weak gestures, and stooped postures. An understanding of these physical responses is valuable in the creation of character mask.

An amusing variation of this exercise is to have players insult each other while playing the scenes. For example:

Cop: You went through that light, dummy.
Driver: Dummy! It isn't working, jerk.
Cop: Jerk! That means an extra ticket, crud-eyes.
Driver: Crud-eyes! I bet you wish you could write, meat-face.

It is important for each insult to be repeated with a sense of outrage and incredulity—this involves players totally in the scene. Coach players to concentrate on the action of the scene so that the insults add to it but do not dominate. This exercise, again, helps players to accept being made a fool of on stage, keeps energy flow at a high level between players, and often helps "bound" or uptight players to relax and play with greater freedom.

Chase and Obstacle Games. The function of chase and obstacle exercises is to gain expertise in swift movement with control and agility. The ability to move quickly and precisely through a cluttered or convoluted space must become second nature to a farceur, so that his concentration in performance may be upon the action he is performing—not upon moving around the set. The following games and exercises should be played within increasingly more sophisticated spaces: start with a simple slalom made of chairs; make this into a maze; create a less formal obstacle course with objects to go over and under, as well as around; add furniture and freestanding doors if available, finally creating a complete dummy set.

Skipping. A simple but excellent exercise for keeping players light on their feet. May be done through the slalom individually, then as a team competition.

Musical Maze. Players move through the maze to different musical rhythms and speeds: march tunes, jazz, disco, waltzes, minuets. Ask players to do this in double time, and with different body rhythms and walks. To do this as if in ballet toeshoes is a good exercise.

Obstacle Slap. One player pursues another through the slalom, maze, or obstacle course with a slapstick. If either player touches any of the obstacles, the other player gets a free slap at him. Reverse the players.

Silent Movies. Using the maze, obstacle course, or dummy set, one player is the thief, the others (up to whatever number is reasonable in the available space) are the cops. All have slapsticks and the object is for the cops to catch and beat up the thief. The thief, in his turn, tries to avoid, outwit, and hit back at the cops. The cops should have hats—papier-mâché derbies are good—that are too small for them and that they must keep on at all times. No one is allowed to catch hold of anyone; nor must it become a simple beating match—the thief must try to avoid the cops, not slug it out with them. This can be done with different rhythms, including the stiff-legged, double-time movement of the silent movies—the Keystone Cops. This game can become as elaborate as space and props will allow.

Attacking Space. This takes place within a dummy set containing as much household paraphernalia as possible. Within the set are two players. One is entertaining the other to tea or cocktails, with the ultimate objective of seduction. However, an air of propriety must be maintained at all times. Three or four other players cause chaos. They move chairs from under the two players; pull carpets from beneath their feet; bang them with doors; knock over glasses; hit them with cushions; even walk in on them as unexpected visitors. The would-be seducer must try to restore order and maintain his mask of unconcerned politeness throughout all this—while tidying cushions, closing doors, cleaning off tea spills, and so forth. The chaos-causing players must be ignored, unless they actually enter the scene as a visitor—someone coming to read the gas meter, for example. This is an excellent exercise for developing imagination with properties and maintaining the mask under pressure. Care must be taken that the chaos is organized—just enough disruption happening at any one time.

Clothing and Property Games. The maintaining of the physical mask of clothing under pressure or the use of the costume and properties for comic business is an important part of a farce player's technique.

Difficulty with Objects. Players should sit in a circle. In the middle is a heap of everyday objects: cigarette lighter, can opener, corkscrew, compact, zipped handbag, and so on. Players in turn take one of the objects, perform a short activity illustrating its normal use, then redo the activity, this time having a problem that leads to a comic reaction.

Funny Dressing. Players are again in a circle. In the middle is a pile of clothing. In turn players take two or three articles and dress with them as comically as their imagination allows, producing misbuttoned clothes; zippers that won't work or catch parts of the body; both legs in one trouser leg; shoes on wrong feet; jackets inside out, back to front, arms can't find sleeves. An exercise for physical skill and imagination.

Ruining an Entrance. Players sit in a semicircle with a freestanding door facing them. In turn the players make an entrance through the door, and then redo the entrance to make it as physically comic as possible: the door hits them in the back and sends them on their faces; clothes catch in the door; the doorknob comes off; they drop their handbag, which spills. Again, practice in physical imagination.

Keeping Face. A set of clothing put together with velcro is required for this exercise. One player dresses in the clothes, which, whether male or female, should be a full set; none of the clothing or chase exercises can validly be played in jeans and a T-shirt. The player is put in a social situation— a cocktail party, tea party, giving a public lecture. While he is playing his part in this, two or three other players try to remove parts of his clothing; a tie, a vest, unbuttoning the trousers, pulling off the skirt, blouse, etc. The first player must continue with the social action while repairing the clothing mask, maintaining a straight face and his composure. This can be done as a competition with two players. Points are taken off for breaking composure or losing concentration, and added for the most respectable clothing mask at the end of, say, three minutes. The player with the most points wins.

Quick-Change Artists. Players are in two teams. The first player in each team has a full set of clothes over shorts and a T-shirt. Lengths of two-by-four lead to two other sets of clothing. At "Go," the players have to walk on tiptoe across the two-by-four, undress, redress in the new clothes, and walk back again to their team, whereupon the next player goes. If a player falls off the two-by-four or is incorrectly dressed, he has to go back and start again. The exercise teaches quickness, control, and composure under pressure.

Amazing Dressing. This is a combination of the previous game with "Obstacle Slap." One player is given several articles of clothing: shoes, shirt, tie, pants, skirts, women's stockings, underskirts, and so on. This player has to put these on while being chased through a maze, or obstacle course, by another player with a slapstick—this second player is handicapped by having his ankles tied together with a one-foot piece of rope. Any time the dresser hits the obstacles or fails to get a piece of clothing on he gets an extra slap from the pursuer.

Character/Mask Exercises

Animal Attitudes. This is a very basic and widely used exercise in actor training. It is especially useful for farce, and particularly for commedia characterization. Players are asked to pick any animal. They then walk around the workshop space, keeping the image of the animal in mind and exploring the basic rhythms and movement qualities of its life style. Players should be coached to take their time and explore the possibilities fully: "Where is the center of energy?" "How does it hold its head?" "Does it dart? Flow? Trot?" The idea is not to imitate the animal but to assume its essential movement qualities.

Players are then coached to take the essential qualities and to build the mask of a human character from this, using the rhythms, energy centers, and patterns of movement. Players should not get too sophisticated—two or three absolutely basic characteristics are all that is required. Players are then coached to play with these masks, exaggerating rhythms and movements, to discover the comic possibilities in physical action. The mask will finally be simply and clearly defined—recognizably human, but with exaggerated qualities deriving from its animal base. When the character mask is set, games can be played in character: frisbee, tumbling, or any of the chase games given above.

Exaggerated Essences. This exercise has a structure similar to that of the previous exercise, but the starting point is a quality or attitude. Players are asked to take a quality such as miserliness, gluttony, or pomposity and work with it to discover what physical response they find in their body, what rhythms, what physical attitudes, what disposal of energies are suggested by these qualities. Again players should be coached to take their time, repeating the idea to themselves and using whatever images come to mind, until the body gradually takes the quality upon itself. Having discovered the outline of the mask, players are coached to play with it, exaggerating aspects of movements, gestures, rhythms, and so forth, to explore the comic possibilities. What will be achieved is a series of gestures and physical attitudes that illustrate the particular quality the player started with, and at the same time give a broadly defined character.

Deformities. Another exercise is based upon the use of physical qualities to create character masks. Players should walk about the workshop space with an easy consciousness of their own physical rhythms and energy center, achieving a comfortable neutrality. Players are then coached to adopt various abnormalities: their legs become two feet longer; their feet double in size; their arms touch the floor; their nose is a foot long. Each time they adopt the physical deformity they are coached to explore what it does to their body rhythm, posture, energy center, etc. Players should return to neutral between each abnormality. After exploring various abnormalities and the rhythms associated with them, players are coached to build a character mask by adopting two or three of the physical attributes they discovered when exploring the deformities. This should be done gradually,

one at a time, until a strong, integrated physical outline of character is created.

Mechanical Toys. Players work in pairs. One player decides what toy he wishes to make of his partner. The choices should be distinctive—for example, a clown, trapeze artist, tin soldier, witch, circus strong man, or lion tamer. The toy maker then "whitewashes" his partner with his hands to remove all traces of his real self, and proceeds to "paint" with his hands the characteristics of the toy upon his partner's body. This should be done slowly, carefully, and precisely. The partner who is being painted should close his eyes and follow very carefully the brush strokes of the toy maker, assimilating the feel of what is being done to him. In about eighty-five percent of the cases in which concentration is good by both partners, the partner being painted gains a correct impression of what is being done to him. When the toy maker is finished he winds up the toy, which then walks about in a mechanical fashion and performs the actions its nature would suggest. The toy maker can alter the speed of the toy by the way in which he winds it up. Finally he should overwind it, and the toy can go berserk, performing its actions in a highly exaggerated manner at a crazy speed. Partners then change places.

Id and Ego. Players work in threes. One player is placed in some social situation of temptation. Food, money, fulfillment of sexual desires are the basic aims of this player. The other two players follow him around, one at either ear. One of these players is the superego or conscience; the other is the id or primitive drive. Throughout the acting out of the improvised scene, the id encourages the player in his desires while the superego points out the consequences of any act. This game is also easily applicable to work on a text, and sets up the tension between the mask of propriety a character may wish to keep up, and the pursuit of his desires in any situation. The player achieves an experience of the opposing pulls from which all farce characters suffer: what I should like to do versus what I am supposed to do. It is this conflict that creates much of the compressed hyper-energy of farce playing.

Slapstick Shakespeare. This exercise can be used to pull all the techniques of the farce player together. A player, or players, take any well-known scene or soliloquy from Shakespeare and make it farcical. The scene should be from a tragedy—the balcony scene in *Romeo and Juliet*, Lady Macbeth sleepwalking, Hamlet and the gravediggers. It is first done straight. Then the players employ all the tricks at their disposal to make it farcical: awkward entrances, problems with props and clothing, the use of chases and beatings. Players should not get away from the action of the scene; it should be played through, but changed in style to create the farce effect. This exercise provides a good basis for discussion, in hard and direct terms, as to what precise elements of playing made the scene farcical—what succeeded, what failed, and why.

SUGGESTED READINGS

BEARE, W., *The Roman Stage.* London: Methuen, 1950.

BENTLEY, ERIC, "The Psychology of Farce," in *Let's Get a Divorce and Other Plays.* New York: Hill & Wang, 1958.

BLITSTEIN, ELMER, *Comedy in Action.* Durham, N. C.: Duke University Press, 1964.

CORNFORD, F. M., *The Origin of Attic Comedy.* London: Edward Arnold, 1914.

DUCHARTE, PIERRE LOUIS, *The Italian Comedy.* New York: Dover, 1966.

DUCKWORTH, GEORGE, *The Nature of Roman Comedy.* Princeton, N. J.: Princeton University Press, 1962.

FEIBLEMAN, JAMES, *In Praise of Comedy.* New York: Russell & Russell, 1962.

KOESTLER, ARTHUR, *The Act of Creation.* London: Pan Books, 1975.

MADDEN, DAVID, *Harlequin's Stick, Charlie's Cane.* Bowling Green: Popular Press, 1975.

MOORE, WILL G., *Molière.* Oxford: Oxford University Press, 1949.

NICOLL, ALLARDYCE, *The World of Harlequin.* Cambridge: Cambridge University Press, 1963.

OREGLIA, GIACOMO, *The Commedia dell'Arte.* New York: Hill & Wang, 1968.

The books by Ducharte, Oreglia, and Nicoll cited above are also excellent visual sources. For commedia the paintings of Callot and Watteau are useful, and for character illustrations of the nineteenth and early twentieth centuries the following may be referred to: the sketches of Max Beerbohm; the cartoons of Spy (to be found in *Vanity Fair*); and the cartoons of Gill in *La Lune*, (published in Paris in the late nineteenth century).

part III

PLAYING CONTEMPORARY DRAMA

The most influential trends in the second half of the twentieth century have been Absurd, Brechtian or epic, and Artaudian theatre. These forms share a common sensibility in breaking out of the narrow and detailed representational confines of naturalistic theatre—the dominant genre of the preceding seventy-five years.

Nineteenth-century theatre was preoccupied with the problems of economic man—the bourgeois in an industrial society. This was followed in the twentieth century by microscopic examination of psychological man—that intense concern with the inner self that marked the dead end of the humanistic tradition. The process of self-consciousness that began in the Renaissance and led on to the Enlightenment ended by examining itself out of all values and leaving man in a world devoid of purpose. God, science, material progress—all seemed to have failed, leaving a vacuum filled with existential angst. What mid-twentieth-century man seemed to be lacking was any sense of deep human purpose, an authenticity, something with which to fill the vacuum of self in a meaningless universe.

The main theatrical forms responded to this situation with different solutions. The absurd could suggest no panacea for human ills, but rather an end to placebos of all kinds: an acceptance of the reality of human existence, however harsh; an accommodation to the truth of nothingness so that man may live positively with it. Brecht's answer to the wasted self of post-romantic disillusionment was to define man in his socioeconomic identity and create a new purpose—a political ethic based upon the religion of Marxism. Artaud was a neoromantic who wished to cleanse the discontents of bourgeois civilization by getting man back in touch with his basic instincts: an antirational, holistic perception of life in which man's true self is revealed through a confrontation with his deepest nature.

While each form evinced a particular response to the existential problem, the three are connected by an underlying similarity in theatrical sensibility. Breaking away from realistic effects and the concern with individual psychology and character minutiae of naturalistic theatre, they returned emphasis to a broader conception of dramatic action. Dealing with larger issues found a response in larger gesture and more total physical involvement. Characters were not made up of small individual traits but once again functioned as *dramatis personae*. The quality of communication became more presentational; there was a return to a fundamental sense of mask and play, which connects contemporary theatre with the classical forms already discussed.

While identifying three major trends in the second half of the twentieth century, we acknowledge the existence of other forms that attempted to mirror the fragmentation of contemporary life and reflect the search for meaning. We do touch upon transformational theatre, and some of the qualities and techniques we discuss under the absurd apply to Pinter, who tends to combine qualities of absurdism with naturalism—the existential threat made manifest in a salt cellar, and human futility encompassed in a journey to Sidcup. But we do not deal directly with Pinter or, for example, with happenings and performance art which are more individualistic responses than identifiable forms: their style is almost a refutation of style.

Our approach to contemporary theatre—as throughout the book—is to deal with the significant and identifiable stylistic modes without attempting to give a recipe for every distinction within them. We believe that a performer, once able to work with the salient characteristics of a style, can then make his own adaptations to particular demands within it.

chapter 6

Peggy Ashcroft in the British National Theatre production of *Happy Days*.

National Theatre, London.

The Absurd

BACKGROUND

Historical. Our discussion of the actor and style of performance began with Greek theatre. Here we found a highly religious, god-oriented society with a strong sense of ethical values. Theatre was a dialogue between man and God, performed by larger-than-life characters before an audience of the whole citizenry. The time of Sophocles and Socrates saw the birth of intellectual curiosity, the dawn of rationalism; man, with his eyes upon Olympus, was laying the foundations of the "glories of Western civilization."

In the course of the next two thousand years man was to put himself on a par with the gods as master of the universe. Judaism made man the favored of the Creator; Christianity went further and had man visited and saved by God's own son. Chosen by God, guided by commandments inscribed on marble plaques, nourished by reason, man was "number one" in the major league. He lived in a world of essential truths, knowable by reason. Descartes showed that by exercise of mind man—originally created in his maker's image—could re-create the world in his *own* image. Isaac Newton made this philosophical thought into a scientific fact; industrial capitalism did the rest. From the eighteenth to the twentieth century progress was the touchstone, progress was inevitable, and progress was good.

However, even while man was achieving this self-proclaimed perfection and manifesting his superiority as the chosen ruler of the universe, the inevitable truths and certitudes upon which his claim was founded were being pared away. Copernicus and Galileo showed that the earth, far from being the center of the universe, was an insignificant planet going nowhere in particular in an undefined space. Darwin destroyed the lovely thought that we were a special race, created by divinity and ordained to rule over lesser species with whom we had no biological connection. Suddenly we are second cousin to the orangutan. Our hair falls out; our teeth rot; our bodies decay—we are far from being divine.

Shortly after man had his comeuppance, God got his. Nietzsche baldly stated that God was dead, and, with all due acknowledgment to believers, functionally we live today in a world without a godhead. But if not divinely guided, at least we had reason—until Freud. Rather than creatures who could know all and control our universe by exercise of mind, we now see ourselves as driven by deeply subconscious desires and sexual urges, of which we are but dimly aware and find hard to control. "I think, therefore I am" becomes "I lust, therefore I am": man's knowable self is no more a fixed or certain place than the earth or, indeed, the universe itself, for Einstein, the latest in the litany of man's disillusionment, showed that everything is relative. The universe is not rationally organized; there are no "hitching posts in space." Everything around us, including ourselves, is volatile.[1]

The upshot of this is that today we have neither god-given truths nor man-given truths. Scientists who had replaced God as the truthgiver now admit that they can at best describe phenomena—not understand them. Neither causality nor determinism is inherent in nature; what we have is the "ultimate unpredictability of things."

The "essential truths" that had served man for two thousand years were found to have no other basis than that someone believed them. We no longer lived in a mean-

---

[1] We are indebted to Robert Cohen for some of the images in the foregoing discussion.

ingful, explicable world. Nietzsche's Zarathustra officially proclaimed God dead in 1883. For a long time before that, however, His function was gradually being taken over by man s rational faculty and the substitute religions of nationalism, Marxism, and scientific progress. Then came the First World War, and shortly afterwards the Second. We finally discover what man's scientific achievements and patent religions mean: the gassing of six million Jews, the destruction of human life with metallic, technological efficiency, and, of course, the final achievement, the possibility of total destruction—the nuclear bomb.

For all man's strivings, all his achievements, all his romantic hopes and belief in ultimate freedom and perfectability—nothing works. Not God, humanism, or science. Man exists in a metaphysical void. Ionesco, one of the leading playwrights of the mid-twentieth century, said: "I really have the feeling that life is nightmarish, that it is painful, unendurable as a bad dream. Just glance around you: wars, catastrophes, disasters, hatreds and persecutions, death awaiting on every side. It is horrible, it is Absurd."[2]

In the midst of the material wealth he has accumulated and the technological triumphs of air travel, television, and computers, man feels estranged from God, nature, and his own self. The questions are still there but the answers have failed. As Yeats said in "The Second Coming": "things fall apart; the centre cannot hold; mere anarchy is loosed upon the world." In this situation the search for ultimate meaning turned in upon man himself. Not any attributes or essences, but the fact of his existence was to define him.

This is basically the drift of existentialism—a philosophy evolved in France in the 1940s and associated with the names of Sartre and Camus. Underlying this philosophy is the idea that nothing has a fixed, determined, and knowable existence. Even

[2] Eugene Ionesco, *Fragments of a Journal*, trans. Jean Stewart, New York: Grove Press, 1968, p. 35.

Guernica, Picasso's nightmare impression of the twentieth-century human condition.

Collection, The Museum of Modern Art, New York, Picasso, Pablo, Guernica (1937, May-early June). Oil on canvas, 11' 5½" × 25' 5¾". On extended loan to the Museum of Modern Art, New York, from the estate of the artist; recently returned to Spain.

if existence were knowable the knowledge would be incommunicable. There is no objective "human nature": man is what he makes of himself; he is defined by his actions and choices as he goes along. There is no fixed character; man is an existent in a situation. In himself man is nothing. Our sense of being is informed by our experience of an alien, inexplicable world in which we live in isolation from other beings. Aware that life has no larger meaning, man exists in a void. This emptiness, meaninglessness is the experience of the absurd.

"Absurd" means out of harmony with reason and propriety. What man seeks is some measure of happiness in a reasonable and predictable world. What he seems to get is unhappiness in a chaotic and unpredictable one. Devoid of purpose, cut off from religious, metaphysical, and spiritual roots, betrayed by reason, man is lost—all his actions become useless, senseless, absurd. At the root of all consciousness is *le néant*: the void. Man cannot know himself, yet he is doomed to dwell upon that lack of knowledge. Descartes has come full circle: "I am not—therefore I think."

Aesthetic. What is the function of art in an absurd world? It is, as ever, to reflect the reality of man's existence. With the absurd, the nature of that reality has changed, and it is no longer possible to accept art forms based upon concepts that have lost their validity. In a world where it was possible to know moral laws, to perceive ultimate values, where there was certainty about the place and purpose of man, the function of art was scientific: to portray events and objects as they existed in external reality. But with the bankruptcy of reason and logic, and the admission by science that all is relative and finally inexplicable, the logic of realism with its rational structure no longer reflected the true, logicless, irrational, discontinuous, noncoherent reality of the human condition. So, from the end of the nineteenth century the search in art was for new forms more

nearly representing the situation of the human spirit in this logicless world.

Cubism, futurism, surrealism, dada were all part of the attempt to discover the true nature of existence in a world in which traditional values had disintegrated and from which the light of reason is missing, a world where man is left groping around in the ruins—in the dark. The surrealists looked for a reality beyond or deeper than the surface reality of external forms. They believed that the artist's vision—his evocative imagination—brought man closer to the fundamental truth of existence than the realists' "slice of life." They used the grotesque, the fantastical, the nonsensical, the stuff of dreams to liberate the human mind from its dependence upon rational forms and social conventions. Accepting the unreality of external appearances, they looked for the spontaneous gesture, however illogical or incoherent, that truly represented man's deepest inner response to his condition.

Dada went even further than surrealism. It took the logic of an illogical, formless, meaningless world to its anarchistic ultimate: "Our symbol was nothingness, a vacuum, a void," said George Grosz. Dada ridiculed the whole concept of taste and form; how could there be any fixed criteria in a constantly changing world? Tristan Tzara said: "Dada is everything; Dada doubts everything. The real Dadas are against Dada." While Dada was theoretically constructive—in destroying all old forms so that new forms more truly representative of man's contemporary condition might be discovered—in practice it was closer to a series of childish pranks played among the ruins of nineteenth-century values. Dada could not win; it could do no more than reinforce the absurdity of the situation: if one acknowledges no rules, then how can anyone win? So the amusing but finally trivial and futile game goes on forever in a shapeless void, until the players tire of it or die. This is the absurd's sense of life itself.

Being formless and abstract, dada and surrealism were more aesthetic influences than new forms. As such, they touched art, music, dance, and finally theatre, which, being sophisticated, cooperative, and social, tends to respond more slowly to new influences than more individualistic art forms. At the end of the nineteenth century, Strindberg, who had mastered the realistic form, found it too limited to express the deeper anxieties of mankind. In his dream plays he presented the illogic of the subconscious, the dis-connected truths of fantasy, attempting to find a dramatic shape for the essentially formless. At the same time Alfred Jarry, in his *Ubu* plays, made an attack upon comfortable boulevard realism and bourgeois sensibility, presenting grotesque, surrealistic figures who matched the cruelty and absurdity of the universe with the incoherence and imbecility of their own lives. Jarry's use of masks and exaggerated gesture, his dis-

Robert Morgan's costumes for *Ubu Roi*. Note the grotesqueness and the clownlike facial mask combined with military costume pieces and weaponry.

regard for verisimilitude in character or setting, makes him a direct forerunner of absurd theatre.

The questioning of the nature of reality was carried forward in the 1920s by Luigi Pirandello. His plays had a realistic patina, but made use of the fact that theatre is an illusion of reality to ask what was reality and what illusion. With this question Pirandello reinforced the idea that truth was endlessly relative, and character endlessly unknowable. This essentially existentialist idea was also the basis for the plays of Jean-Paul Sartre and Albert Camus, who in the 1940s propounded the tenets of existential philosophy in plays with basically traditional forms. Although the philosophical ideas and sensibility of Sartre and Camus have been highly influential in the development of absurd theatre, their plays are less significant, in that they use essentially rational forms and knowable characters to deny the validity of rationality or the possibility of knowledge.

It was the 1950s that saw the development of a dramatic form capable of giving an audience a true experience of the absurd condition of man: the theatre of the absurd showed man as having no large purposes in life. Habit and material possessions limit his freedom; the inadequacy of language prevents communication of inner reality. Man no longer has a nature proper to himself. He is, at best, the sum of his actions, confronting the ethical and spiritual void in which he is doomed to pass his trivial existence.

Theatre of the absurd did not use traditional plot structure with conflict and vertical progression. It borrowed some of the effects of surrealism to express irrationality—persons with three noses, no heads, turning into rhinoceroses or floating through the air—but did not cultivate such effects for shock value; it used them as a necessary part of the form.

The absurd is not a theatre of events. Nor does it attempt logically to describe or explain any philosophical position—this would be a contradiction in terms. It gives its audience an "experience" of the absurd condition. It dethrones the primacy of language and logic to get at a truer reality beneath. One should not ask of absurd theatre, "What is it about?" or, "What is going to happen?" The question more properly is, "What is the felt experience communicated through rhythms, sounds and images?"

While the dramatists of the absurd recognize that the confrontation of man s true condition is a bitter and despairing prospect, they believe that such a recognition is essential if man is to live with this situation and not surround himself with pretended answers, pretended purposes. Ironically, absurdity is the only ground upon which man's understanding can be secure. One of Samuel Beckett's favorite expressions is that "nothing is more real than nothing." There is also a Zen proverb that claims:

> The denying of reality is the asserting of it;
> And the asserting of emptiness is the denying of it.

Though the acceptance of le néant, nothingness, is a seemingly negative experience, the approach of the dramatists of the absurd is, finally, positive. The playwright confronts the audience with the experience of absurdity in order that they may be freed from dogma, illusion, and superstition, come to terms with their true reality, and thus find the power to act. Absurd theatre castigates lives that are aimless and unaware, senseless and mechanical. It does this in order to make man conscious of true reality and face, in a positive way, the great absolutes of time and death. Or, as a contemporary man with an acute sense of the absurd, Woody Allen, put it in his movie *Sleeper:* "Solutions don't work. I believe in sex and death—two experiences that come once in a lifetime!"

Absurd theatre is to some degree a catchall category. The playwrights included under the heading used a variety of approaches to communicate their sense of the absurd condition of man's life. Not all the attributes of absurd style are to be found at all times in all the plays of all the playwrights. Samuel Beckett presents the most perfect integration of form, content, and sensibility. He is the classic exponent of the absurd, and has the most refined and all-embracing sense of what absurdity is. He, together with Eugene Ionesco, who belongs also to the tradition of French farce, will be the prime focus of our discussion. Much of what we have to say will apply specifically to what is likely to be the classic corpus of absurd theatre: Beckett's *Waiting for Godot, Endgame, Happy Days, Play,* and *Krapp's Last Tape* and Ionesco's *The Lesson, The Bald Soprano, The Chairs, The Future Is in Eggs,* and *Jack, or the Submission.* It will also apply selectively to the plays of Adamov, Genet (who also owes allegiance to Artaud—see Chapter 8), and Albee (*The American Dream* and *The Sandbox*). We are not dealing here with Harold Pinter, whose plays both have a realistic patina and are laws unto themselves. Our aim is to discuss the range of aesthetic and technical demands of absurd theatre and show how the absurd sensibility is manifested in physical terms. Actors will then be better able to identify those elements that are applicable to their work on any particular play, and make appropriate choices.

INTRINSIC DEMANDS

Form. "Nothing happens, nobody comes, nobody goes, it's awful," says one of Beckett's characters in *Waiting for Godot.* This play has also been described as one in which "nothing happens—twice." The absurd theatre tends not to have any of the structural characteristics of well-made drama. There are no neatly plotted crises and climaxes, no discoveries and reversals to keep the audience on the edge of their seats, hardly any events as such, and no vertical plotting towards a grand climax and denouement. Nor do the plays have the conventional three-act structure, which presumes a beginning, middle, and end. The absurd is not logical and linear; it does not deal in tidy plots and

clockwork formulas. In a formless, relativistic world drama must reflect the inconclusiveness and lack of solutions that are the pattern of our daily lives.

The problem for the absurdist playwright was how to reconcile the inherently irrational and formless quality of the absurd with the structural requirements of theatre—that is, how not to make the error of Sartre and Camus and contradict the content with the form. The answer was to do away with concentration upon content and detail—not to discuss or describe, but to embrace the audience with the experience of absurdity. That experience is essentially circular and repetitious. Life without meaning cannot have a focus or move directly towards some objective. It doesn't "go on" so much as repeat itself. A circular structure communicates the lack of real progress or resolution. The circle of the play's action describes both the sense of infinity—a circle goes on forever—and circumscription—you get nowhere, and might as well be in a cage. The sensation of nothingness is that of total possibility—no restriction—and total futility at the same time: "Nothing to be done," which is the first line of *Waiting for Godot.* A circle equals 0, which equals nothing.

In a world of no purpose or determined values, everything operates on a flat plane of equal insignificance. As with the flattening of pictorial space in cubist art and the flattening of time in the modern novel, so in absurd drama there is a flattening out of form. Man is no longer an aspiring creature, moving upwards towards ever greater achievement; he is either chasing his tail on the flat plane of existence or moving downwards towards disintegration and decay. The form of absurd drama tends to be either circular and repetitious, as with Beckett's *Godot* and *Play* and Ionesco's *The Bald Soprano* and *The Lesson,* or a declining spiral into futility and dissolution, as in *Endgame, Krapp's Last Tape, The Chairs,* and *The Future Is in Eggs.* In a world in which all events are equally meaningless there can be only one climax—and that is the negative one of death: "This is the way the world ends, not with a bang but a whimper.''

Absurd drama is not concerned with the representation of events, the telling of a story, or the depiction of a character as much as the presentation of individuals within a situation in such a way as to communicate their experience of existence. The plays tend to be many-layered poetic images that have to be intuited in depth rather than rationally followed through a linear development in time. The situation is full of activity, none of which, however, changes the situation in the least. The plays are stuffed with the trivia of daily existence and employ theatrical effects in a wholesale manner—circus clowning, music-hall backchat, farce, ritual—to show the endless and futile ways in which man attempts to fill the vacuum of his existence. The case is never argued; it is presented through concrete images of the absurd in action. Man is seen as an actor in a cosmic farce. With no accepted values all experience is equally serious, equally ludicrous. Ionesco: "It all comes to the same thing—comic and tragic are two aspects of the same situation; it is now hard to distinguish one from the other."[3] Laughter tempers the reality of despair and makes comedy the bedfellow of pathos.

Language. The use of a circular and repetitious form communicates the lack of ontological meaning in life. The approach to language in absurd theatre both reinforces that quality and, specifically, shows that language is not equipped to express knowledge or to define the meaningless. Language, the supremely rational structure, is often used as the final distinguishing feature between man and other animals, whose responses are more instinctual than logical. However, the mid-twentieth century saw rational language come to a dead end in logical positivism. Language was seen to have no value in defining the essential properties of existence; it

was reduced to such profound assertions as "green is green." To make a "true statement" was to be redundant. By definition language could not express the inexpressible and was thus reduced to making trivial statements or, worse, to masking true experience beneath rhetoric.

The playwrights of the absurd, especially Ionesco, felt that language, like logic (which is concerned purely with its own form), was irrelevant to existential problems, as it could express nothing outside of itself. Words, having no profound meaning, become interchangeable objects.[4] Language is depersonalizing and automatic. The more we trust language and involve ourselves with its formality, the less of our real human substance we touch. Thus we find in Ionesco a derision of language: vacuous discussions about unimportant matters; nonsense phrases; meaningless association of words—the destruction of language; or its use as automatic response to match the automatic behavior of the characters. Often language breaks down entirely: in *The Lesson* and *The Bald Soprano* there is a climactic paroxysm whose intensity of feeling language cannot convey; in *The Chairs* the "message" that is to be communicated is given to a deaf-mute—there is no meaning, or if there is, it cannot be communicated.

Although Ionesco uses language in a gestural manner—that is, to express an idea (such as the futility of language!) by its total pattern or impact rather than its rational meaning—he is not as consciously poetic as Beckett. Beckett, equally aware of the rational limitations of language, used the gamut of its melodic, rhythmical, and asso-

---

[3] Quoted by Richard Schechner, *Three Aspects of Ionesco's Theatre.* Unpublished dissertation, Tulane University, 1962.

[4] This inherent meaninglessness of words has been compounded by the way in which media advertising has used language to make an impact rather than to convey meaning. Some years ago when one of us first came to California we passed a huge roadside sign: "Carpinteria—the world's safest beach." Being unaccustomed to the hyperbole of American advertising we naively thought, "Isn't that interesting; UNESCO or some agency must have done a survey, and here we are at the world's safest beach." It was only later we realized the phrase was as meaningless as "the world's finest coffee," razor blades, bathroom scourer, or any other of the vacuous claims of modern advertising.

ciative potential—as well as silence—to produce an essentially poetic dialogue whose meaning lies not in its content as much as in its shape. The language here is at one with the form in its all-embracing, imagistic impact, rather than displaying any logical structure or intellectual force. Beckett's dialogue is almost a dance of words—its choreography matches the careful physical choreography of his movement. There are strong rhythmic progressions, or "canters"; comic patterns of stichomythia; pathetic duets. The meaning is found in the experience of the sound and tone, the patter and the silence, the rush of words and the absence of content.

Specific qualities of the language include simplicity and brevity of sentence structure and spareness of statement. The simplicity of the line, surrounded by empty space, underlines the starkness of the situation. The spareness of the statement gives it a profundity in that it allows of many meanings and yet does not define any of them. The frequent use of pauses isolates words, just as space isolates characters. The silences both make the audience aware of infinity (silence is always a felt presence in tragedies—"The rest is silence") and point where language is useless in expressing the ultimate feeling. Then, again, speech often occurs because silence is unbearable. To say anything (which is to say nothing) is better than the embarrassment of silence—just as individuals who do not know each other well will talk to disguise the fact of basic lack of communication.

Lack of communication is also shown by the use of comic stichomythia. Characters follow their own train of thought, and what seems to be a conversation is a set of parallels that can be amusingly contradictory:

Didi: You're right. We're inexhaustible.
Gogo: It's so we won't think.
Didi: We have that excuse.
Gogo: It's so we won't hear.
Didi: We have our reasons.

Stichomythia can also be used for pathos, a poetic duet, shared as is the misery. The preceding dialogue modulates into:

Gogo: All the dead voices.
Didi: They make a noise like wings.
Gogo: Like leaves.
Didi: Like sand.
Gogo: Like leaves.
            (*Silence*)

Didi: They all speak together.
Gogo: Each one to itself.
            (*Silence*)

Didi: Rather they whisper.
Gogo: They rustle.
Didi: They murmur.
Gogo: They rustle.[5]

In a poetic statement like this, character is of course irrelevant. The parts in the duet are interchangeable—it is the total impression that touches the audience. While speaking of language in relation to character, we should note that the brevity of lines—the abrupt exchange of trivialities—tends to give an unsustained quality to the characters and to isolate them from the situation. Beckett in particular will frequently have a character act in direct contrast to the expressed intention of the dialogue. This further weakens language, as it is seen not to represent any real communication and loses dramatic force.

The use of rhythm, repetitions, greetings, and pleasantries lends a ritualistic quality to many of the plays of the absurd. This in its turn reinforces the sense of aimless continuity: the situation seems to be part of eternity, to have been going on forever without changing. This illusion of progress without any forward movement is carried further by the use of word games and cross talk that,

[5] Samuel Beckett, *Waiting for Godot* (New York: Grove Press, 1954), p. 40.

like the physical games played by the characters, end in themselves—passing time without gaining on it.

Finally, language is used to undercut sentiment, to give an ironic edge to the situation and prevent indulgence in pathos. Beckett does this with the apposition of phrases: "Embrace me"—"You stink of garlic"; "He's crying"—"Then he's living"; "He's bleeding"—"It's a good sign." Beckett and Ionesco both use scatological words and play on words. These bring the whole situation down to earth: we are creatures dominated not by our minds but by our bodies—we can live without thought, but not without defecating.

Having recognized the limitation of language in conveying intellectual meaning, the absurdist playwrights used it to express the experience of the absurd in both poetic and practical terms. On the one hand their language communicates by rhythm, shape, and sound; it embraces the audience in an almost lyrical manner. On the other hand it becomes gestural, forming a direct relationship with the techniques of mime, comedy, and slapstick farce. By these means the playwrights, while dethroning the rational, everyday function of language, infinitely expand its capacity to convey meaning.

Space. For absurd theatre the term *space* has more than usual significance. In theatrical terms space is taken to be where the actors perform, but it is usually identified with *setting*, which is how that space has been filled in order to create an identifiable background or environment for the play. As the absurd is occupied with a sense of nothingness, emptiness, and void, space itself becomes a concrete fact: no matter what is put in it, an all-embracing sense of vacuum is the true environment of the play.

For the absurd, the stage, which had been reduced by realism to a one-to-one representation of a small "slice of life," returned to its earlier image as a metaphor for the world itself. The quintessential absurdist stage is stripped down to its bare minimum, with man reduced to his questioning, existential stance as a "bare, forked animal" in the middle. Simple, stark—this is the stage of *Waiting for Godot*. It is a symbol of the naked void that disregards, almost self-consciously, the material paraphernalia of the realistic stage and its presumption that some action of import can take place. *Godot*'s space is defined by two axes—the horizontal road and the vertical tree. The rest is empty wasteland (recalling T. S. Eliot). It is the simplest possible human definition: we stand on the earth.

The quality of this theatrical image itself conveys the experience of absurdity. Space equals vacuum equals nothingness. All man's attempts—his aimless searches—to define himself by fixing his position in the void are doomed to failure. If he knew who he was he might discover where; if he knew where he might discover who. We are everywhere and nowhere at the same time—either at the lonely, unspecified crossroads of Beckett, or in the isolated rooms of Ionesco (or Pinter, whose sensibility touches the absurd in its nonreferential character). The world or a room: it is finally the same thing; both are contained spaces, empty of meaning. One of the essential qualities of the absurd is a double sense of space as both infinite—nothingness can have no bounds—and totally confining: nothingness is impenetrable, and man feels small and isolated in the space he himself occupies. The universe is contained within a grain of sand, and has as much significance.

If Beckett's characters are not in the visible wasteland, they are buried up to their necks in sand, or in coffins, or in the unspecified limbo of the room in *Endgame*. In whatever situation, Beckett's space conveys a sense of oppressive emptiness filled with inexpressible meaning. Ionesco's space is more cluttered but the feeling is the same: impenetrable meaning, created by a wall of "things." The setting for *The Chairs* is the best example of this: a room full of empty chairs—clutter and yet vacuum at the same time. The chairs, addressed by the two char-

Two American soldiers stare at the holocaust at Gardelagen, where one thousand Jews were burned. A combination of this image with clowns in a circus ring gives a strong sense of the spatial sensibility of Absurd theatre; compare *Waiting for Godot*.

Margaret Bourke-White, LIFE Magazine, © 1945, Time, Inc.

acters as if they were occupied, stand for the emptiness of actual human presence in everyday life: even when people are present this adds no definable meaning to life. Material "things" are important to Ionesco, as they take the place of living. Men live through objects, which take over their lives until they become objects themselves. This victory of the material, antispiritual forces leaves humanity as a parade of puppets, mechanically walking in aimless, banal circles amongst the lifeless clutter of their empty rooms. Whatever the specific setting, it is what the fact of space says rather than what space is made to represent that gives atmospheric quality to absurdist theatre.

Time. Some years ago one of the authors went to Australia. We flew westward toward an ever fleeing dawn, a twenty-one-hour journey in continual darkness. On the way we crossed the international date line, and a stewardess told us we had "lost" a day but would pick it up on the way back. There was a nonsensical feeling of putting twenty-four hours in a suitcase, to be taken out for future use. It made one realize the absurdity of regarding time as something that can be altered by turning the hands on a watch. Time is simply a man-made convenience for measuring our movement through space—that other immeasurable concept! There we are, sitting in this black void for twenty-one hours, according to a watch, with no sense of motion but simply a roaring in the ears. Then we get off the plane and are told we are in Australia, and it is two days later. It was all impossible to grasp, irrational and immeasurable—absurd.

We in the Western world have a tremendous preoccupation with time. The concern for the temporal is in many ways the disease of modern industrialized man. In the Middle Ages man's horizon was the eternal: life was a continuous movement toward oneness with an ineffable spirit. For modern man time equals money. There is an anecdote about a businessman who was extremely happy when the supersonic Concorde jet came into service. Extolling this to a Chinese friend, he said: "Now I can fly from New York to London in four less hours." To which the Chinese replied: "How nice. But what do you do with the time saved?"

"What do you do with the time saved?" To the businessman this was a stupid question. The answer was various: make more money; make another appointment; make a bunny in a Playboy Club. To the Chinese from a different tradition, the occupation with time—especially the saving of it—was amusing and absurd. Time is a flow; it cannot be saved; it cannot even be grasped. It simply has to be accepted and lived. But we in the West have not been in the habit of doing this. We have tried to define, rationalize, and harness time to give our lives structure and meaning. We are always looking optimistically toward tomorrow: "I love ya tomorrow, you're always a day away." We defraud ourselves by pretending there is something (better) yet to come and give ourselves hope through this false expectation of futurity. As long as we were locked inside our man-made system, things were reasonably fine—we made money, gave internal significance to the trivia of our lives. But once we stepped outside that system and applied our puny logic to the explanation of larger purposes—to define time and space, to calculate our existence, to assess the sum of things in terms of thought—then we put ourselves in the position of being absurd.

In Beckett's plays there is always an interminable twilight—time is constantly dying, but goes on. Time is a hemorrhage of existence. We dwell in a vague present whose limits can be expanded or contracted without affecting its significance. Time is eternal, yet passes in a flash. One instant contains a life: "We are born above a grave," says Didi, "the light flashes and is extinguished." "What time is it?" asks Hamm. "The same as usual," replies Clov. The double sense of time, a crucial part of the sensibility of the absurd, gives existence its quality of comic pathos. It is pathetic because human striving is directed towards infinity, and attempting to identify man with the infinite is the supreme achievement of pathos. It is comic because such striving is self-contradictory. Seen pathetically, a second has infinite value; comically, ten thousand years are an instant of tomfoolery.

The sense of timelessness, or the logical absurdity of time, is found in the internal repetitiousness and circular structure of many of the plays of the absurd—plays that end where they begin, or begin over again. This aimless continuity is the playing out in dramatic terms of the myth of Sisyphus (which Camus used as the subject of one of his existential essays). Sisyphus was condemned to Hades, where he was to spend an interminable afterlife pushing a stone up a hill, only to see it roll back down each time it reached the top. Human purposes are no longer judged by the gods; the absurd now places the afterlife upon this earth—hell has become other people, as Sartre suggested in his play *Huis Clos (No Exit)*. Time is the oppressive force that both stretches endlessly before us and yet is gone in the very instant we try to live it.

Character/Mask. One of our premises is that the forms art takes at any particular time tend to depict that period's image of man. This is true of the Greek, Renaissance, eighteenth, and nineteenth-century periods, in which persons were represented in painting and sculpture as having different backgrounds, attitudes, expressions, clothing, and relationships to the world, but were always recognizably human in form. Modern art and sculpture have been concerned with destroying this traditional "realistic" image of man. Painting contorted man's external shape the better to reveal his inner self, or depicted human experience as a noninterpretable abstraction. Figures in modern sculpture are frequently endowed with holes where significant parts of their bodies would be—indications of the void within man, and the void man is in.

Against such an aesthetic background it is no surprise to find absurd theatre representing formlessness, its characters abstractions of human attitudes. **Characters do not represent any man in particular as much as mankind in general.** They are not there for self-revelation, but demonstrate or symbolize human properties. They have an objective quality: Ionesco's exaggeration and Beckett's intensity achieve distance in their work. Characters are no longer masks of gods and heroes but are still macrocosmic in a smaller spiritual universe. They are masks of man more than individuals, no longer, like the Greeks, larger than life—for the world we inhabit is the democratic one of small men— but larger than "reality." The characters are exaggerated; their situations are intensified; they are invested with the mythology of the circus, vaudeville, Guignol. All this is to suggest larger truths about the human condition, truths that have to be experienced. Facts are limited and may be known: realism deals in facts. The absurd deals in truth.

Beckett's tramps, *clochards*, and down-and-outs represent the inalienable part of man, which transcends social, political, and ideological details. These characters are negligible if identified with any attitudes or class of people less than mankind itself. We are told little about the background of the characters—like man's own origins, they are shrouded in mystery. Any attempt to treat them as "real" individuals reduces their impact. They are there to "be." They have no future and no past. What they do is what

they are. To determine their "character" one looks to the structure and language of the plays, in which it is deeply imbedded. **The plays are not about anyone; they are about everyman.** Everyman can have no "character" in our limited psychological sense—it is a function of the total experience of the play.

As an example: Some critics have suggested that Didi and Gogo in *Waiting for Godot* must be intelligent and educated men because of the literary and biblical references they make. This is to commit the naturalistic fallacy: to look at them as real persons instead of part of the structure of Beckett's play. Beckett (indeed, an educated and intelligent man) uses references because they are part of man's mythology and create the kind of texture and feeling he is trying to communicate. Didi and Gogo may or may not be educated—it is irrelevant to the play. Although one of the many layers of meaning in the play may be concerned with the bankruptcy of man's intellect, to play Didi and Gogo simply as intellectuals fallen on hard times reduces the play's size.

For Ionesco too there is no idea of character as a knowable, irreducible essence. If man can choose himself anew at each moment of existence, then any fixed idea of character is inadmissable. Thus, Ionesco's characters tend to be interchangeable. They no longer think or feel individually; they have become mechanistic extensions of a norm. The old man and old woman in *The Chairs* have some resemblance to Didi and Gogo in their futile attempts to remember a dim past, but they are more mechanistic, showing Ionesco's penchant for farce—a more typically French form than the music hall that Beckett uses. None of Ionesco's characters has any real identity or anything to say. The people in *The Bald Soprano* are social puppets, and *The Lesson* is full of increasingly hysterical gibberish. The characters are pathetically farcical, for their mechanical existence denies individuality; they wind their way through incoherence, vacuity, anonymity.

Double Act. One of the features of characters in absurd drama is that they often come in pairs, like vaudeville or music-hall comedians. Ionesco uses this structure in *The Lesson* and *The Chairs*, Genet in *The Maids* and to some degree *The Balcony*. Most notably, however, it is Beckett who, with Hamm and Clov, Nagg and Nell, Didi and Gogo, and Pozzo and Lucky, uses mutually dependent pairs of characters to make universal statements. The pairs tend to be complementary, making up between them in a kind of yin-yang fashion a total human construct. Didi and Gogo, for example, operate on three levels of relationship. On the comedic level they are a double act, with Didi tending to be the straight man and Gogo the banana. Their cross talk and a lot of the physical gags have the rhythms of this relationship. On the human level they have the qualities of an old married couple. They have a mutual dependence they wish they could reject: like most human relationships they don't quite work together, but neither could they live apart. Third, and embracing the other two levels, they **create one macro-human character— a mask of mankind itself.** Didi tends to be the thinker, representing mind and intellect. Gogo is more prosaic and earthbound, emphasizing body and instinct.

As with the use of space and time in Beckett's work, so with the use of character there is a complete integration of the mask into the structure and atmosphere of the play. Without an awareness of all the levels upon which character operates, and of its function as part of the total construct of absurd theatre, an actor will make the mistake of examining his character with a microscope and inevitably reduce its size and the suprahuman impact of the play.

Costume. Costume reinforces the mask. Obviously all costuming says something about the character wearing it, but the nature of character in absurd theatre means that **costume defines not so much the individual as what the character represents.** Costume tends to be either nonspecific or a highly specific cliché. Beckett's characters, being of the everyman nature, are largely nonspecific in costuming; it is important that they be so, as highly distinctive costuming would reduce universal qualities. Hamm, Clov, Lucky, and Krapp all wear indeterminate clothing that, if suggestive of anything, has the quality of the thrift store in the poorer district of any modern city. Even the generally accepted dress of Didi and Gogo—the tramp's outfit—is said to have been a happy accident, stemming from the mind of Roger Blin, the first director of the play. In some respects the tramp is the perfect icon for Beckett's work, carrying as it does overtones of Chaplin and Laurel and Hardy as well as the generalized sense of the lonely wanderer on the brink of decay who is still trying to make a living.

The costumes used by Ionesco and Genet say equally little about the individuals wearing them, but are more specifically clichés. The married couples in *The Bald Soprano*, for example, could be interchangeably dressed in "typically" British middle-class clothes while the costumes of the maid and fire chief are defined by their functions. School costume and academic dress are called for in *The Lesson*, and *The Balcony* takes the cliché costume to its ultimate in making the statement that power resides in appearances— whether it be bishop, general, or police chief. The mask is all.

Summary. As the term absurd theatre is something of a catchall, including a range of techniques not all applicable to all the playwrights included under the heading (although they share a common sensibility), it might be useful to conclude our discussion of intrinsic demands by reviewing the common features and pointing out some of the individual properties of Beckett, Ionesco, and Genet.

Whereas Beckett deals with the problem of existence from a universal perspective, Ionesco takes a less cosmic approach, employing the French tradition of domestic farce to make his statement about the meaningless, mechanistic nature of life. Both see life as purposeless tedium in a hostile universe. For Beckett the hostility is that of absence, uncaring, vacuum. Ionesco finds it more concretely menacing: his characters are surrounded and harried by hostile matter. Both tend to use the circular form with minimum development, but Ionesco is more preoccupied with breakdown of meaningful forms, and his structure often recapitulates disintegration, plunging into chaos. Beckett conveys the experience of endless waiting and futility.

Both deal in essences rather than psychology, and employ amplified, theatrical images of life. Ionesco exaggerates the character and situation; Beckett works more from outside, using rhythms and silences to magnify the meaning of his poetic images. Ionesco is more social than Beckett. His people are lonely in crowded situations—at home, at a party, at their places of work. They are isolated by society from a true experience of life. Beckett's people are isolated by their existing in the void. Beckett creates an absolute that is a minus quality, a concrete silence, a meaningful absence of meaning.

Genet shares the absence of a defined character, and motivation. He concentrates on situation rather than narrative plot, and equally dismisses the intellectual content of language. Language for Genet is incantatory. In a world of dream, myth, and fantasy, language does not communicate so much as embrace; it conjures up essences. Genet, like Beckett, wishes to transmit an experience rather than make a statement. His sense of the world is that of a black mass—religiosity turned on its head. The pursuit of the abject is done with saintly devotion. Logic is inverted. If there is no reality, then fantasy must be pursued with rational fervor. Genet's world is a house of mirrors: prison, brothel, bedroom. Christ said: "My father's house has many mansions." For Genet this is a house of illusion filled with sexual fantasies. Dealing with explicit make-believe, Genet questions reality and underlines the absurdity of our role playing. His double acts in *The Maids*, *The Balcony*, and *Death-watch* are master/slave relationships, explored in a fantasy world of sexual games. Sharing the absurd's belief in no supervening moral structure and the absence of any "reality"—be it of character or of the visible world—Genet equates sin with purity and creates characters that are reflections in a mirror, dreams within a dream.

PERFORMANCE DEMANDS

Movement. We have already suggested that the form and the action of the absurd tends toward the circular, so it will be no surprise to discover that basic movement patterns reinforce this. As there is no forward progress to be made, **the only possible movement is circular**—around the perimeter of the space—**or repetitive**—back and forth across the lateral plane. Nothing leads anywhere, but we go about our business just the same, as if there were some purpose. Thus, the actor will move with a purposeful futility. The circular and repetitive patterns are invested with an urgency as if they might achieve something, but always end where they began. The actor doesn't drag himself around, self-consciously burdened with despair; he performs the absurdly repetitive rituals of movement with a heightened energy that further underlines their futility. Equally, when the movement ends nowhere and stops, the stillness reinforces the vast emptiness of time and space surrounding the characters. Statis is an important characteristic of the absurd, which Beckett, especially, uses to the full. "Let's go." They don't move. Where is there to go, and for what reason? Yet at times movement is necessary both to alleviate the boredom and to attempt to prove the fact that one is there—wherever "there" may be. The alternation of movement and stillness in repetitive patterns lends a ritualistic quality to the event, and gives Beckett his embracing atmosphere of what has been called "immortal inertia."

Although movement in absurd theatre is not extended or exaggerated in size, neither is it naturalistic. Movement has great precision and clarity; it is outlined in such a way as to give it a heightened impact in the frame of space. The effect is achieved by giving every movement a defined beginning, middle, and end—no small, imprecise movements; nothing loose; no blurring of the physical image by swaying and shuffling. When a movement is over the actor stops, and there is an instant of absolute stillness

and clarity before another movement is begun. This is not a consciously mechanistic effect (except occasionally in the case of Ionesco—see below); it is a disciplined contour to movement that lends it a super-reality without becoming puppetlike.

In absurd theatre it is space and time that lie heavily upon the stage, not the action. The action is filled with the trivial "busyness" of our day-to-day lives. There is a briskness and variety of pace and rhythm. The basic rhythm is, of course, the unchang-

Trivial activity in the midst of inner and outer vacuum is captured by Peggy Ashcroft in Beckett's *Happy Days*.

National Theatre, London.

ing flow of time, but within this are determined little attacks—Beckett's canters—upon the impassive pace. The actor's basic movement goes against the constant rhythmical flow—not heavy and oppressive, but rather quick and light; not on the toes, like farce, but a flat-footed dexterity.

Pain, decay, and age are part of the atmosphere of the absurd, but more a manifestation of the physical mask of a character than a constant feature of his movement. The bend of the knee, stoop of shoulders, general set of the body will create the necessary image of pain or decrepitude, but it should not be overindulged as a constant obstacle to an actor's movement. The rhythms and total images of the play are the issue, not the physical suffering of any one character. Didi's bladder, Gogo's feet, Clov's inability to sit, the age of the old couple in *The Chairs*—these are part of the fabric of the play, constants we aren't particularly aware of until the playwright chooses to use them for specific action. The general pattern and quality of movement should manifest the necessary pace and rhythms required by the action. It would, once again, be committing the naturalistic fallacy for an actor to say the old couple are in their nineties, or Gogo has bad feet, so they can't move briskly—they are often required to by the play. **To belabor character detail is to flatten and reduce the size of the characters.**

Adaptation for Ionesco. Although much of what we have said will apply to Ionesco, he belongs to the tradition of French farce and has a more domestic environment for his plays. Both factors affect the quality of movement in his work. Ionesco employs some of the conscious automatism of the farce character. More than a clarity or precision of outline, Ionesco can border on the mechanical. The Martins and Smiths in *The Bald Soprano* are meant to create an image of the meaningless fatuity of bourgeois life. They are puppets manipulated by reverence for social convention. Without giving the characters

the stiff, clockwork quality of the puppet, the actor can achieve the effect by an overprecision of movement. This not only underlines the strict adherence to social convention, but adds a mechanical quality without destroying the human base. The quality of overprecision is applicable to most of Ionesco's characters, as are the circular patterns of their movement. The old couple in *The Chairs* move in a futile manner through space. In and out of the doors and around the empty clutter of the chairs they perform the double-circle, figure-eight pattern of the farce shell game. If they stop, Ionesco asks that their eyes, heads, and hands continue to go around like a wound-up toy. Similarly, the professor in *The Lesson* is in perpetual motion—wheeling in circles and spinning like a top increasingly out of control. Repetitious gestures reinforce the gibberish of his speech to show his lack of flexibility and programmed acceptance of linguistic absurdity. Ionesco uses many farce techniques, but places them within an atmosphere of conscious futility. Farce has some, however insular, purpose: there is a highly complex plot that keeps the characters on their toes chasing or avoiding something. The absurd has no such plot or purpose. Ionesco places his farce techniques in the void, to destroy meaning, to show life itself as a hollow farce.

Hyperconcentration. Concentration is a necessary attribute of all acting. It keeps the actor aware of the action; it creates one-hundred-percent focused energy; it allows of immediate reaction; and it has a compelling power that draws the audience's attention. In the absurd it is more than just a necessary technique—it is part of the physical style. In the pauses of Beckett's work the actors do not sit passively—they sit actively. When they look into space it is not a vacant look but an intense stare—at nothing. The time in the pauses is not empty; it is filled by intense concentration that makes the vacuum of space a felt presence for the audience. Effort for no reward; energy wasted in the void; futile activity followed by interminable waiting—this is the essential dichotomy of the absurd.

The inverse ratio of effort to result is clearly illustrated at the beginning of *Waiting for Godot.* Gogo spends several minutes of concentrated effort trying to take off his boot. Beckett gives such directions as "tears at his boot" and "with supreme effort succeeds in pulling off his boot." Having done this he discovers nothing (which could have hurt him) inside, and stares "sightlessly" before him—**tremendous effort for no return** and in the end an attitude of concentrated stasis. "Sightlessly" is a carefully chosen term. The eyes of a blind person have a great intensity, which comes from the concentration of the person locked within his own space. The sense of being trapped within his private space, despite the vastness of the space surrounding him, is a necessary quality of the absurd character, and is achieved by hyperconcentration.

Intensity of effort, followed by intensity of stillness, produces compression and futility. Concentration makes time appear to stand still, to become a concrete quality, to weigh down upon character and audience alike. Bursts of intense energy followed by total collapse: like the labor of an elephant to give birth to a gnat, they create a disparity that is comic, a sense of futility that is absurd. The impossible task is never quite completed—the task that is life itself. As Hamm says: "moment upon moment, pattering down, like the millet grains of that old Greek, and all life long you wait for that to mount up to a life." Living is like endlessly dividing and subdividing a grain of sand, and the smaller it gets the more concentration it requires. By his use of concentration, by making it an intensely felt force, the actor creates the intangible but absolutely necessary atmosphere surrounding absurd drama.

Business/Gesture. Intensity of concentration is present in all business and gesture. It lends a heightened energy and clarity to the physical activity that achieves the larger-than-reality effect. **Much of the business in Beckett's plays is a form of child's play.** If there is no final, objective reality, existence becomes a kind of game, and one way to accept this is to approach existence on its own terms, consciously using games to fill time. Beckett's characters approach their game playing with the innocent enthusiasm of children and with a child's concentration and total commitment to the moment.

The sense of game playing carries over into business, which is derived from the activity and gestures of everyday life. These gestures of normality have a particular manner of presentation, a consciousness of performance that has the effect of ritualizing them and giving them larger significance. The plays are full of gestures of looking, shaking, tapping, feeling, smelling, embracing, recoiling, brooding, searching with nose to the ground, agitated pacing, bouncing entrances. Each gesture is filled with heightened energy and concentration, which produces an outline in the emptiness of space yet underlines its inadequacy, its ultimate futility. When they think, the characters don't simply sit quietly, they adopt thinking attitudes; they show that they are thinking, as if that will help to give the activity some meaning. They don't simply greet each other, they fall into each other's arms. They don't simply look into hats or boots, they peer with great concentration. All of this energetic occupation with trivia, with moments of glee, hope, excitement about everyday events, is an attempt to light up an empty existence, to fill the stillness and the vacuum that surrounds them, and to which they always return.

Clowning. Absurd characters have the awkward dignity of the circus clown as he parades around the ring before tripping over his feet and falling on his face or backside—and then getting up and carrying on. It is a parody of the average lifetime: there are existential resonances in every fall, every excitement, every brooding silence. It is important for the ac-

Heightened, concentrated gesture and comedic physical mask
seen in this production of *Waiting for Godot*.

Guthrie Theatre.

tor to recognize the elements of clowning, vaudeville, and farce in absurd drama, to accept the pattern of gags and comic set pieces for what they are, and not to try to make them "believable" within the context of some character structure or "realistic" conception of action. They are believable within the total metaphor of the play. No one asks if a circus clown is believable. The proper questions are Is he funny? Is he sad? Does he affect you? We accept the structure of the event. On a simple level the clown entertains us; on a deeper level he touches us, says something about our humanity in ways of which we are aware but may not be able to define. So with the sensibility of the absurd. The actor must approach each moment of action upon its own terms, recognizing its function in the larger whole that the playwright has conceived. Only in this way will the full dimensions of the absurd be communicated to an audience.

Ionesco and Linguistic Absurdity. We have mainly been discussing Beckett because, as we have already stated, his sense of the absurd is the most total. But the approach to business and gesture applies equally to Ionesco, if understood within the context of Ionesco's greater concern with linguistic absurdity. Ionesco reveals the inability of language to express meaning by using language to undermine itself. Many of his effects, both comic and absurd, are achieved by revealing the disparity between language's presumed ability to communicate and its obvious lack of real meaning. Rhythms and patterns of language are used gesturally and to create comic business. Repetitions, circularities, redundancies are the verbal techiques Ionesco employs to make his point.

When Ionesco does use physical business it tends to be secondary and to reinforce his linguistic games. The actor should recognize that clues for physical manner will be found in the language structure. The professor in *The Lesson*, the old couple in *The Chairs*, the bourgeois couples in *The Bald Soprano* all have very particular verbal rhythms that demand supporting patterns of gesture. The language should not be approached as if it were naturalistic speech. It has a surface realism that is a necessary part of Ionesco's point—to lead us into believing that because the language has a "normal" structure it must be meaningful. He then undermines our assumption by showing the meaning to be redundant or tautological. But beneath this surface realism the language has a structure and rhythm that are poetic; if felt by the actor, they lead him to the physical gesture and images that illustrate the total meaning of the play.

Mask/Character. The nature of the mask of character is implicit in what has been said about movement and gesture. The physical patterns and images created by the characters in the space define their function. The plays are not concerned with the lives of individuals or stories about what is happening to them. The plays are conveying an experience of what it is like to be men in a particular ontological environment. It is the arrangement of physical patterns, images, rhythms—the sounds and signs in space and time—that communicates this experience to the audience. This is done partly through the agency of the characters, but it is not done through an examination or revelation of individual personalities.

The characters are not discrete individuals; they are parts of the larger metaphor, which has universal, not particular, resonances. The plays tend to take the form of a series of duets—the yin-yang quality we spoke of earlier. Even *Krapp's Last Tape* has this structure: Krapp is involved in a duet with his younger self. The duets form one mask of relationship with many levels, encompassing the range of human experience: parent/child, husband/wife, master/slave, youth/age, body/mind, comic/pathetic. The characters operate at as many and as different levels as the action demands. The actor must discover what part of the relationship is his at any one time and respond to this stimulus.

Although the character is recognizably human in form, he is not closely defined as a personality: he has metaphysical significance, but little psychological content. Background details are irrelevant to Didi, Gogo, Hamm, Clov, the professor, Pozzo, the Smiths, and the Martins (who can't, themselves, remember who they are). The very ambivalence and uncertainty are part of the atmosphere of the absurd. Too many specifics reduce to earth characters who have also to connect with space and time. In a world in which no knowledge is possible, a character cannot have internal definition—the self is in constant flux in the changing flow of time. Didi asks Gogo if the "same lot" beat him. He replies: "The same. I don't know?" In such a world motives cannot be precise, and responses are arbitrary, determined by the demands of the situation.

The comedic/pathetic double act of Hamm and Clov in *Endgame.*
Note Clove (on the right) and his mask of hopeless yearning. Also
compare his physicality with the illustration of the concentration-
camp survivor.

American Conservatory Theatre, San Fransicso.

Characters relate through space, objects, activity, rituals—through the situation rather than directly and emotionally.

In creating the mask, the actor has all the resources of the text: the rhythms, patterns, gestures, and business called for by the playwright. He will discover recurrent details that create a form for the character in the situation: Didi's walk, pensive attitudes, and paternal manner towards Gogo; Clov's walk, volatility, bursts of activity, and clowning; the professor's agitation, repetitiousness, lecherousness, and verbal pomposity. All of these qualities and many more are part of the play's givens and fuel for the actor's imagination. Such particulars may be heightened to form a functional outline for the character—his mask.

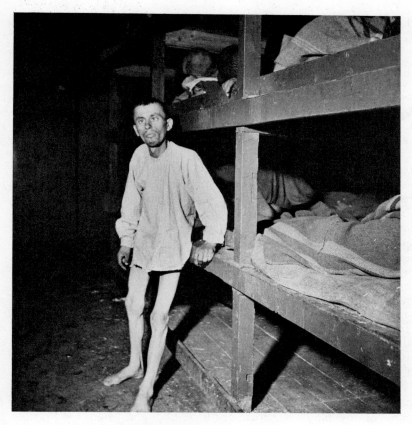

A survivor of the concentration camp at Buchenwald.

Margaret Bourke-White, LIFE Magazine, © 1945 Time, Inc.

Truth of the Mask. The mask is played flexibly and truthfully from moment to moment. Truthfully here means with the necessary value for the communication of the action. It does not mean indulgence in pain, despair, or any of the ongoing properties of the character when they are not the focus of the immediate action. Such elements may represent the outline or form of the mask, but how that outline is fleshed out will depend upon the given demands of the action. Didi's walk (due to some kind of prostate problem, if the actor needs to put a name to it) is part of his mask and also of the fabric of the play: it indicates man's decaying functions. The

audience accepts Didi's problem and needs to be consciously aware of it only when it directly affects the action—at which time the playwright will have written it into the rhythms. The problem may be used to give a quality of pathos to the play—but Didi is not consistently a pathetic character.

The mask is not a psychologically developed individual, but neither is it a lifeless cardboard construct. It is the selected and heightened outline of the attributes the character must have in order to play its part in the action at any moment. In this way the particular truth, or style, of the playwright's intention will be communicated to the audience—in this instance, the comic/pathetic sense of life's absurdity.

Vocal Delivery. There is a danger that the actor will attempt to force meaning on the meaningless. We are used to making apparent sense when we speak, and it is difficult for the actor to accept that the meaning of a play lies in the lack of surface meaning. **Lines should not be overexamined, searched for subtext.** There is not a cryptic meaning beneath the line as much as a broader resonance that surrounds it—**a supratext,** in fact. For example, in *Waiting for Godot* lines such as "I don't know" respond on the surface to a particular question, but the effect of the answer should be existential, and delivery should communicate the broader meaning: "We have never known anything." Again, Gogo constantly responds to Didi's "We're waiting for Godot" with "Ah!" It has been suggested by critics that this exclamation should be given different values—as it would be if a normal comic structure were involved—but this seems to work against the function of the lines in conveying the total meaning of the play. Rather than making sense, the "Ah!" is somewhat like a simple expulsion of breath. It does not indicate recognition of the situation, or understanding; it is simply acceptance, unexamined, of Didi's response. The repetition of "Ah!" in the same manner with the same lack of significance reinforces the empty repetitiveness of the situation.

The same lack of true meaning behind the words applies to Ionesco. Ionesco's characters use language to fill the vacuum at the core of their existence. There is a surface quality of meaning, a concerned facade, that covers the emptiness beneath. The characters have an overly polite, programmed response; an overinsistence upon meaning contrasts with the actual lack of content in what they are saying (just as in our own lives we have a tendency to agree the harder when

we don't understand what is being said to us). In *The Bald Soprano* the characters don't examine what they are saying or really listen to what is being said. The Martins are not aware of the absurdity of their discovery that they are man and wife. They are politely unemotional; even their expressions of surprise carry no sense of surprise behind them. Similarly, in *The Lesson* the professor's nonsense has to be spoken as if containing meaning, but with the quality of a tape-recorded speech: a button has been pushed, language is spilling out, but it seems to have neither meaning nor connection with a human being. The language controls the speaker.

In the absurd the significance of language is not in any meaning, but in the patterns of speech, the rhythms, inflections, and especially the way in which sound is related to silence. The use of builds and undercuts shows unfulfilled expectation; the monotonous circularity of life is evidenced by the verbal repetitions. The patterns of language are not geared to giving significance to any individual. They are part of the construct of the joint masks, and often take the form of duets: Didi and Gogo; the Martins with their duet of recognition; the Smiths with the saga of Bobby Watson and the tongue-clicking punctuation; the student with her "toothache" counterpoint to the professor's speeches. The language of the absurd must be approached as a poetic structure—for its function as part of the total statement of the plays rather than for specific content or conversational qualities.

Sense of Occasion.

> Man that is born of woman is of few days,
> And full of trouble.
> He cometh forth like a flower,
> And is cut down.
> He fleeth also as a shadow,
> And continueth not.

There is a strong sense of religiosity about the absurd. We have mentioned the ritual nature of Genet and his black mass. Beckett too lends a deeply ritualistic quality to his work, and extrapolates a universal atmosphere from the trivia of the mundane. Even Ionesco—despite his more domestically based concerns and his focus upon language—creates a supervening atmosphere of meaningless absurdity that strongly challenges the audience's sense of existential purpose.

The response to the absurd theatre is not simply didactic, emotional, or psychological; it is an aesthetic totality, an experience that both defies and is reduced by analysis. It is challenging and liberating, bringing the audience face to face with its fears, its false hopes, its very existence, in order to produce a new, deeper sense of reality and accommodation to the true nature of life. In this sense the absurd is not negative but optimistic.

It is important for the actor to recognize the positive side of the absurd, to give full rein to the childlike quality of enthusiasm, the humor, and the constant recognition of play. Beckett's characters especially are conscious of playing, of themselves as acting a part. Hamm's first words are "Me to play." Clov asks what there is to keep him here, to which Hamm responds: "The dialogue." Clov says, "Let's stop playing," to receive the decided answer from Hamm: "Never." That "Never" says much about the attitude of the characters and the general sensibility. Man is trapped in some futile experience, but he carries on. It is part of his dignity; it defines his selfhood. Man is an actor in the cosmic farce. Just as the actors on the stage form parts of a larger whole, so the actors and the audience complement each other in sharing not just the theatrical event but the all-embracing experience of what it means to be alive on "this bitch of an earth." To be alive, to share, to commiserate, to laugh at, to accommodate to—the actor must be aware of this communion, must realize that while he plays the human event he creates larger vibrations. He is part of the eternal poetry of existence—the messenger of the gods in a godless world.

EXERCISES, GAMES, TECHNIQUES

Because of the basic preoccupation with time and space, workshops in the absurd cannot be hurried. The experience of void and endless time is something the actor must be allowed to develop. The leader of the workshop must be constantly attentive to the actors so that the exploration of time and waiting is positive, and the actors should not be allowed simply to become bored with the exercise. Subtle side coaching to maintain the actor's focus and concentration will be necessary in many of the exercises.

Space/Time Exercises.

Leading the Blind. This well-known "trust" exercise is a good starting point. Players pair off. One is blindfolded and then led around for twenty minutes or so, experiencing the nature of nonvisible space and examining the tactile qualities of any objects that may be encountered. It is important that this exercise not be hurried, so that the blindfolded player develops both an experience of space and confidence in his ability to move within it. Partners then change places. When all the players have experienced being led around blindfolded, all should then be seated, blindfolded, within a large, completely empty indoor space. All are then asked to explore this barren space, at any speed, in any way they wish. They should try to avoid contact with other players. At intervals coach to change position: those who have been walking should sit and shuffle, or crawl; those who have been exploring lower space should become aware of the upper space. Continue the exercise until all players have explored the total perimeter of the space and have moved in several different ways through the inner vacuum.

Blindman's Bluff. Players scatter throughout an empty space. One player is blindfolded. All move around the space until the blind man claps his hands. All freeze. The blindman is allowed three paces to find a player. If he does so he must try to identify the player by feeling his clothing and face. If he correctly identifies, they change places. If not, the game continues with the same blindman.

Moving Knock. All players are blindfolded and scatter throughout empty space. The leader of the workshop knocks on certain parts of the walls or floor or ceiling. The players have to make their way toward the knock. Just before any reach, the knock is made elsewhere. When some players catch on to what is happening they may simply give up. This is fine, but they must sit completely still and do nothing until the exercise is over.

Hunt the Thimble. This game is played in a cluttered space with a lot of furniture and props. While the players are outside the space the leader hides a thimble. The players return and search for it. Repeat the game, this time in a darkened space. Then repeat the game in an almost darkened space, but this time don't put the thimble anywhere! When the game is called off, discuss the nature of the frustration felt by the players when unable to find the thimble. What did they instinctively feel like doing?

Vacuum. Players sit anywhere in the space. Have them do a deep breathing exercise for two or three minutes and then "drain" by consciously allowing tension to move to lower part of the body, where a plug

is pulled and all tension drained out. Now ask players to concentrate upon some small object—a stain on the floor, a crack in the wall, the tip of a shoe or foot—until their mind is cleared of all other ideas and finally that object itself loses any meaning and becomes simply an inanimate "thing." This is a difficult exercise. One of the most difficult problems man has is just to "be," like a child or an animal. Coach quietly for the maintaining of active concentration, so that the players gain an experience of the meaninglessness of "stain" or "crack"—its complete lack of real connection with the object they are staring at. Ultimately the players will find that they lose all sense of a context and become aware of the isolation of themselves in an undefinable environment.

Effort/Frustration Exercises. Players scatter throughout a space containing various children's play objects, such as balls, hoops, skipping ropes, and bats, and use the props to play at children's games (or games that don't need props, such as hopscotch and tumbling). Coach them to put as much energy as possible into their play. Then, on a handclap have them stop dead, drop whatever they are doing, and go into the vacuum exercise. On another handclap they begin another activity at high speed. The rhythm of this exercise alternates between high-energy activity and complete stasis. Coach for total concentration; don't let the playing of the games have a lot of surface energy but little deep concentration: the energy must be highly focused. Repeat the exercise; this time make the game-playing take place in pairs and the focus of the stasis some small part of the partner's clothing or body.

Sisyphus.

a. Players are given small heaps of sand, which they have to move, grain by grain, to another place.

b. Players are given a piece of soft wood which they have to reduce to the smallest splinters possible.

c. Players are given a large piece of paper, which has to be torn into pieces, mixed up, and then put together again.

d. Another version of exercise *c* is to give a group of players a large jigsaw puzzle to put together—the puzzle will have three or four pieces missing.

e. Players are given another piece of paper, which has to be divided in half, then in half again, and so on into microscopic pieces.

f. Break the players into groups of two or three. Ask a group of players to arrange twenty or thirty chairs in a particular fashion in the space. When they are halfway through their task, have another group begin to rearrange the chairs in a different pattern. When the first group has arranged the chairs, they must go back and put the rearranged chairs into their original pattern—and so on.

Still Frame. Players select some small, usable object such as a pack of cigarettes, box of matches, camera, or compact. Players now perform a simple action involving the object: taking a cigarette and putting it in the mouth; lighting a match; powdering the face. The action is repeated, the player breaking it into as many individual completed actions as possible. For example, putting the cigarette into the mouth involves grasping the cigarette, taking it from the pack, turning it towards the mouth, opening the mouth, putting in the cigarette, closing the mouth. Each of these actions has a clear beginning, middle, and end. The player should call out "begin" as an action commences and "end" when it is completed. Having done this, the player repeats the whole action a third time, this time silently but as swiftly as possible, maintaining a flow but still with a clear sense of each individual action. This is an excellent exercise for precision in all acting work, but it is especially useful in the absurd, as it will outline each detail and seem to give actions a heightened intensity and size.

No-Sense Exercises.

Roundalay.

a. Players sit in a circle. One player starts a conversation with the person on his right, making completely trivial or redundant statements, which must be said as if they were of surprising import—for example, "When people fall over they are no longer in an upright position." The person to whom this is said must pick up on it and make a statement to the player on his right, such as "Upright people go to church on Mondays as well as Sunday." This continues around the circle. There will be a tendency at first for some players to giggle or be self-consciously funny—coach for absolute seriousness.

b. Players pair off. Each pair chooses a theme for conversation. The theme is then discussed, but only proverbs or clichés may be used.

Broken Record. This may be played around a circle or in pairs. Choose a convoluted and opaque paragraph from a textbook on linguistics, psychology, or sociology. A player now reads this mumbo jumbo as if it were part of a course on a record. At intervals the leader of the workshop or the partner claps his hands and the previous phrase has to be repeated as if the record were stuck, until a further handclap allows the player to continue. A tape recorder rather than a record player may be used. In this instance it should be played in pairs. One player reads the information as if he were a tape recorder. The partner makes adjustments to the recording—changing speeds, stopping and starting, reversing—by pressing or twiddling "knobs" on the player. Partners change places. This is a good exercise for conveying the "disembodied" or potentially mechanical nature of speech.

What Life? Players tell the story of their life to an empty auditorium. Make a serious attempt to interest the empty seats in what is being said. A variation on this exercise is to have players seated in a circle. One player is in the center. All lights are turned off. The player in the center now relates his life story. At any juncture players in the circle may question the storyteller about the details of what he is saying and make him justify his assertions—"prove" that events did in fact take place. The exercise should not be allowed to become chaotic, with interruptions every other second. Coach players to pick significant occurrences to question closely upon. The questions coming from disembodied voices out of the darkness can lead players seriously to doubt "facts" about their past that they have taken for granted. The impossibility of verifying past events is brought strongly home.

Mechanical Men. Players choose a character with a mechanical attitude or function: TV car salesman, door-to-door salesman, worker on a production belt, supermarket check-out clerk. Each player does a small improvisation illustrating the character, and then repeats two or three times, each time performing the function more quickly until it is like a speeded-up film track. The player then performs the improvisation at "normal" speed. This performance will have the quality of a heightened reality as it will retain some of the precision and pace of the preceding performances. *Note:* The mechanical exercises in Chapter 5 will also be useful here.

Body and Mind. Players pair off. Jointly they are one human mask: one player is the body, the other the mind. Choose a number of situations for the mask to respond to: sitting in a cafe noticing a good-looking man/woman—should one approach, and how; on a diet at a party with masses of food; late at night but haven't finished a paper due the following day. The body and mind players voice aloud their reactions to the situation: what the body instinctively would do, what reason advises. Try to establish a dialogue, not ignore the other voice. Try to integrate the differing responses; make the dialogue a duet so that

finally the mask acts as one person, aware of his double consciousness.

Married Couples. Another joint-mask exercise. Players are paired: man and wife, long-time roommates, or whatever! There has to be a presumption of a long association. A series of domestic problems, situations, are set up. Ultimately the pair has the same interest in achieving a solution, but they can take many different views of the same situation. Coach the players to reminisce about the past, talk in parallel, argue their point of view, and finally come to an acceptable solution to the problem or accept the situation as it stands.

Godot Game. This is an extended improvisation, pulling together some of the previous exercises. It is particularly useful for rehearsing the techniques and assimilating the atmosphere necessary for the performance of Beckett's work. Required is a large, empty workshop space and lights on a dimmer or rheostat. Begin by creating the environment of a children's playground. Coach players to take part in high-energy games, individually and with partners. After some time, when the rhythms of the environment are well established, bring down the lights slightly and suggest to the players that it is beginning to get dark and a little cold, and they should think of going home. Now coach for the idea that they cannot find the way out of the playground; it becomes darker, colder; it begins to rain; they search but cannot find the way home. This is an important part of the exercise as it establishes the atmosphere for much of the rest of it. Take time over it. Coach hard until you feel all of the players are committed to the situation and experiencing the dark, cold, and frustration. Bring down the lights to a mere twilight; introduce the concept of hunger—painful hunger. The players are tired, cold, lost, with the pain of hunger in their stomachs. Players will react to this differently. Some will cry, shout out, thrash around. Let them. Coach that it isn't going to make any difference. Coach the players to accept the situation—not to forget and ignore it, but to accept it. Coach for stillness, awareness of the dark, empty space; no knowledge of how to get out. Take out the lights completely. It is night. Players have to find the best way of passing the night. Most will curl up in a fetal postion or try to hide in corners of the space—a very basic, primitive reaction. Let the night be at least fifteen minutes of absolutely dark solitude. Occasionally remind the players, quietly, of the hunger, cold, solitariness. Bring up the lights very slowly for morning. Coach the players to examine themselves—they are the only persons they can clearly see—to examine fingers, toes, hair; to determine their own reality. Coach then for discovering ways to pass the endless time. There is no release: they must accept the moment and find ways of filling it. Then, as the lights come further up, coach to discover one other person; to relate silently; to find ways to help each other pass the time. Players will rub each other's backs, massage feet, pick lint off each other, play leapfrog. Coach again for hunger, solitude, emptiness, now letting the pairs of players support each other in the situation.

Getting out of the improvisation without breaking the mood is difficult. A good way is to coach for weariness, sleep. Then introduce sunshine, warmth. The players will relax. Go into a deep-breathing exercise and conclude with a vigorous shakeout. The exercise should take up to two hours. When it works completely it gives players a strong sense of an existential angst and void, the importance of basic creature comforts, and

the way in which a dependence relationship develops with another person.

SUGGESTED READINGS

BARRETT, WILLIAM, *Irrational Man.* New York: Doubleday, 1958.

BIGSBY, C. W. E., *Dada and Surrealism.* London: Methuen, 1972.

ELIOPULUS. JAMES, *Samuel Beckett's Dramatic Language.* The Hague: Mouton, 1965.

ESSLIN, MARTIN, *The Theatre of the Absurd.* New York: Doubleday, 1961.

——————— , ed., *Samuel Beckett.* Englewood Cliffs, N. J.: Prentice-Hall, Spectrum Books, 1965.

FLETCHER, JOHN, *Samuel Beckett's Art.* New York: Barnes and Noble, 1967.

GUICHARNAUD, JACQUES, *Modern French Theatre.* New Haven: Yale University Press, 1967.

HAYMAN, RONALD, *Eugene Ionesco.* New York: Frederick Ungar, 1976.

JOLIVET, REGIS, *Sartre: The Theology of the Absurd.* New York: Newman Press, 1965.

PRONKO, LEONARD, *Avant-Garde: The Experimental Theatre.* Berkeley: University of California Press, 1965.

SCHECHNER, RICHARD, *Three Aspects of Ionesco's Theatre.* Ph.D. dissertation, Tulane University, 1962.

WILLIAMS, RAYMOND, *Drama From Ibsen to Brecht.* Oxford: Oxford University Press, 1969.

chapter 7

Helene Weigel as Mother Courage.

Brecht and Epic Theater

BACKGROUND

Personal. In 1883 Nietzsche's Zarathustra announced to the world that God was dead. In 1914 German machine guns annihilated the heroically futile panache of the charging Hungarian cavalry. Between this triumph of scientific rationalism over faith and scientific technology over romantic chivalry was born Bertolt Brecht. With the soul of a nineteenth-century romantic poet and a mind conscious of the mechanistic materialism of the twentieth century, Brecht was to form a permanent dialectic of his life. From the first he was aware of the irrational and compulsive drives of his inner self and the rational need to accommodate to the social conditions that determined the world he inhabited. He recognized the conflict between the romantic idealization of man's spirit and the physiological reality of his animal nature. The character of Brecht's theatre reflects his lifelong attempt to balance emotion with reason, poetic instinct with scientific discipline.

While still a young man, Brecht had his medical studies interrupted by the First World War, into which he was drafted as a medical orderly. The traumatic experience of witnessing the senseless slaughter of human beings and attempting to repair mutilated bodies left a permanent impression upon Brecht. He became a fanatical pacifist, violently opposed to those international political forces (which he identified with capitalism) that for their own economic profit could send men into such carnage. More than this, his war experience reinforced Brecht's sense of despair and cynicism at the gap between man's aspirations and his physical circumstances. He rejected incipient sentimentality to search for a creed that would bring some sense of purpose and hope to a corrupt and senseless world.

In 1918, at the age of twenty, Brecht found himself in a world that had denied God and had seen romanticism to be a hopeless gesture. He was living in a defeated country that was morally and economically bankrupt and had no sense of purpose; in a political climate ripe for fascism, and a spiritual climate of despair. The defeat of France in 1940 gave rise to that sense of existential angst in which the absurd theatre flourished. Equally, for a generation of Germans, the defeat of 1918 and its consequences fired both anger at man's condition and a strong sense of need for social and political change. Brecht's answer, as we shall see, was the creed of Marxism. But before he reached that belief he wrote a play, *Baal*, which typified the cynical and despairing start of his progress from poetry and putrefaction, through political didacticism and social mechanics, to the epic or "dialectical" theatre of his mature years.

Baal, written in 1918, has the episodic structure of Brecht's later work, but is filled with youthful disgust at man's inability either to control his own lust and greed or to influence the world around him. The play is filled with images of drifting and decay. Man is seen as an excremental creature whose aspirations are mocked by animal instincts and physical decline. Here, as in his play *Edward II*, Brecht identifies human nature with physical nature; the plays are full of savage landscapes, slime, rot, and self-indulgence. We are as little able to change nature as to control our own.

This anarchical, nihilistic Brecht begins to discover a possible solution to the decadent purposelessness of man's condition in his play *Man Is Man*, written in 1925. Here there is still the sense that man is no more than man (with the negative connotations of that fact), but the lack of a defined individuality is now turned to profit: man can be remade into any

215

Two cartoons by George Grosz depict the sense of disgust and despair at man's inhumanity to man that was shared by Brecht after the First World War. Note too the strong gestic masks of the soldiers, and the total gestus created by the horseman of the apocalypse. (For discussion of gestus, see page 224.)

Nicholson and Watson.

model that particular social conditions may require. The possibility of social engineering (with all that suggests, both in terms of "superman" and brainwashing) was a turning point in Brecht's rejection of his youthful nihilism and his movement towards social awareness and didacticism.

It was after writing *Man Is Man* that Brecht turned to a study of Marxism. This led to the writing of his most overtly political plays: *St. Joan of the Stockyards, The Measures Taken, The Exception and the Rule,* and *The Mother,* all written between 1929 and 1932. In these plays he perfects both the didactic nature and the dialectical structure of his epic theatre. The plays of his maturity—of which the best known are *Mother Courage, The Good Woman of Setzuan,* and *The Caucasian*

Chalk Circle—keep the moralistic nature and the epic structure of the earlier plays, but allow his instinctive poetic nature more scope. These later plays are more free-flowing and have less direct didactic impact: Marxism and romanticism, individualism and collectivism, rational skepticism and myth, are blended. The pessimism of Brecht's youth is balanced by the optimism he found through the Marxist creed. This dialectical position enabled him to say in the epilogue to one of his last plays—*The Good Woman of Setzuan*—"There must, there must, there's got to be a way."

Aesthetic. The artistic climate in which Brecht grew up was that of the early-twentieth-century avant garde. This was the period of dada, cubism, surrealism (discussed in the previous chapter) and the wholesale attack upon the form and sensibility of nineteenth-century bourgeois art in both its romantic and naturalistic manifestation. It was also the period of expressionism, aimed at creating artistic images of man's inner feelings, thoughts, and fantasies. In theatrical terms expressionism used multiple scenes, having no rational connection to recapitulate the fluid, nonlogical sequence of thought and dreams. It was theme- or idea-centered, as opposed to the plot- or conflict-centered nature of the "well-made" play. In its themes, expressionism also shared in the social and political revolt against bourgeois sensibility that was at the root of the artistic avant garde.

Brecht accepted the revolutionary sensibility of the theatre of his time. He rejected the staple diet of nineteenth-century German theatre—bombastic classics, photographic realism, drawing-room comedy—as "culinary" theatre, to be consumed for emotional titillation or after-dinner entertainment. Like Stanislavski, he reacted against the empty rant of the romantic acting style and sought after a more "truthful" theatre. But whereas Stanislavski's truth was an emotional and psychological one that led him to become the great exponent of naturalism, Brecht's was a sociopolitical truth that led *him* to reject naturalism and romanticism alike.

In simplistic terms, the revolt against nineteenth-century theatre took two forms. The first was naturalistic, aimed at the presentation of life in every truthful detail, not excluding the ugly existence of the oppressed social classes. The second form was aesthetic, and appealed to those who thought that art should be more than any detailed representation of life. Brecht, though influenced by these two forms, was not satisfied with either. Aesthetic forms were for him too far removed from reality, but he also believed that an imitation of life, in whatever naturalistic detail, was purely formalistic if it

did not consciously deal with social and political realities in such a way as to achieve some betterment of the human condition.

A form of theatre that more nearly approximated Brecht's intention was that of Erwin Piscator, who regarded the theatre as an instrument for the political education of the masses. It was a theatre of minimal literary content, often compiled simply of newspaper reports or documentary material. Piscator would use graphs, captions, projections, and newsreel and film sequences to convey the political or sociological background to the play. The propaganda inference was drawn by choruses, on stage or in the auditorium, singing or speaking the political point so the audience couldn't miss it.

From Piscator Brecht took the technological structure and political focus of his theatre, and from expressionism he took the episodic form. His themes were not to be the inner-directed and Freudian ones of the expressionists. He rejected these psychological concerns as he rejected the emotional focus of what he termed the "Aristotelian" theatre of vertical plot progression and cathartic climax. The aesthetic of Brecht's theatre was to show and demonstrate the economic, social, and political condition of man.

Political. Brecht's sensitivity and intelligence would not let him tolerate the stupidity of mindless patriotism, the hollow veneer of bourgeois society, and the crude vulgarity of what he took to be the capitalist system. His denial of most of the current values of his day left him at first in an existential void, filled only by despair at a human condition governed by aimless and irrationally impersonal forces. Brecht needed a core of positive belief, and this was afforded by Marxism. His answer to *le néant* was not to see it as absurd, but to fill it with the vision of a new, progressive man.

To the anarchical side of Brecht, which had seen the world without sense or purpose, the Marxist concept of a dynamic pattern in human history—the inevitability of the class struggle and progress towards the victory of the proletariat—came as both a relief and a worthwhile cause. Life was no longer static and incapable of being influenced by human endeavor. All causes, all effects, all relationships are dynamic and therefore susceptible to improvement. History was not written by an unkind and unknowable fate; it was the outcome of human struggles, and the laws governing these were known. This scientific and rational explanation of life gave Brecht a firm foothold among what had been the shifting sands of an aimless existence. He clung to his newfound belief and determinedly rejected psychological or emotional explanations for man's behavior—a principle that was to have a crucial effect upon the nature of his theatre.

Marxist Dialectic. It was not only the scientific certitude of Marxism that appealed to Brecht, but also the dramatic quality of the Hegelian dialectic upon which it was based. The coexistence of opposites, the merging of thesis and antithesis, the fact that order cannot be conceived without disorder—in a word, dynamic ambiguity—was for Brecht the ironic essence of drama. The dialectical sense runs throughout his theatre: the actor who impersonates the character, yet remains himself; the stage that represents reality, yet remains a stage; the characters who are themselves, yet can be made into something else.

The dialectic also gave Brecht his integrated form. Following Hegel, Marxism believed that content determined form. Forms are historically determined by the kind of content they have to embody. Thus, the nature of a country's economic structure determines the form of its social, political, and cultural identity. The political intention of Brecht's theatre must, therefore, determine and be dynamically related to its form. More than this, the politically engaged nature of Marxist art (it must be involved in the crea-

tion of a Socialist society) rejects empathic illusion (which Brecht associated with Aristotelian theatre), so that the audience will not mistake the symbols and images it receives for realities. Here is the basis for Brecht's objectivity of presentation—or "alienation" effect.

Marxism provided Brecht with a strong sense of purpose; an optimistic political faith susceptible of scientific proof; a political content that matched his theatrical form; and the triumph of rational thought over romantic sentimentality. Yet the poet survived. Perhaps the most important dialectic of all, that between the politician and the poet, remained a constant feature of Brecht's life and was to be acknowledged in one of his poems:

I am the most practical of all my brethren—
And my head comes first of all!
My brethren were cruel, I am the cruellest—
And I weep in the night.[1]

Theoretical. Alienation, otherwise known as "distancing," and in German *Verfremdungseffekt*, is possibly the most important, and most misconstrued, part of Brecht's dramatic theory. It is directly related both to the political intention of his theatre and to his sense of "Aristotelian" theatre. Dramatic theatre (to which he opposed his concept of epic theatre) based upon Aristotelian principles was for Brecht a way of fooling people into the acceptance of their condition. With its plot-centered structure moving towards a climax and catharsis that sucked the audience into emotional empathy with the action, this "dramatic" theatre drugged the audience with feelings, anesthetized its critical faculties, and obscured the true nature of its condition with highly colored illusions of reality. The function of Brecht's theatre was political, and had to be viewed with a critical objectivity: "I have feelings only when I have

---

[1] Quoted by Martin Esslin, *Brecht: A Choice of Evils* (London: Methuen, 1965), p. 227.

a headache, never when I am writing: for then I think."[2] Brecht also rejected the Aristotelian idea of a common humanity with a collective response to the emotions in a play—a human spirit, timeless and unchanging. He took the Marxist position that emotions have a class basis: the form they take is historical and specific, not universal. Along with this Brecht objected to the tradition of fatalism in drama—man as a pawn in the hands of unchanging fates. He believed that tragic protagonists are victimized by social conditions of economic origin; these are harsh, but changeable. Man can remake those circumstances of life that cause people to fear and pity one another.

Brecht did not reject the place of emotion in human life and in theatre. Nor did he exclude pleasure and entertainment as a function of theatre. But the pleasure was not to be gained through meretricious and narcotic emotional self-indulgence. It was to be a more intellectual pleasure, of the kind experienced when one successfully solves a mathematical problem or understands the causes and circumstances of some human event. It was not emotion per se that Brecht excluded, but the empathy that it produces. Empathy: giving oneself up to the emotions of a theatrical occasion; sharing the emotional state of the character to the degree that his emotions become "real" and erase all consciousness that one is at a theatrical event. It was to this that Brecht objected. For in this condition man has suspended his capacity for critical judgment of the social reality behind the emotional state.

Alienation Breaks Empathy. It was toward the breaking of empathy that Brecht directed his alienation effect. The function of the effect is not, as has sometimes been interpreted, to attack or offend the audience. Brecht wants his audience to be at one with the event, in

[2] *Ibid.,* p. 201.

such a way that the interaction raises its critical consciousness. The actors share their ideas and attitudes with the audience in order that it may come to perceive true social and political reality. A critical attitude is not a negative one; it is socially active and practical. Alienation has the function of freeing socially conditioned phenomena from the stamp of familiarity. To see your mother as "a man's wife" is to achieve an alienation. Alienation draws attention to the familiar by showing it in a new light. It makes something special out of the ordinary.

In the theatre, alienation prevents empathy by breaking the dramatic illusion that what the audience is witnessing is a form of "real" life. The audience must be reminded that it is in a theatre, that the play is not a seamless whole but constructed of many parts, and that those parts must be kept independently visible so the audience may reflect upon the way in which the events are represented. As Brecht put it in the preface to *St. Joan of the Stockyards:* "The intention is to exhibit not only the actions, but the manner in which they are subjected to the processes of theatre."

The theatrical principle of alienation ties in, once again, with Marxist doctrine. *Entfremdung* is the estrangement felt by the worker in a capitalist society who can only sell his labor, and not participate directly in the economic control of the society. The need Brecht saw for alienation (estrangement) was related to a critical objectivity about the complex social and political ramifications of capitalist society. Rather than accepting conditions as inevitable, they must be viewed with critical remove, a scientific capacity to see beneath the surface of things, or to regain the experience of the first perception. Brecht was to express this in his poems for the *Messingkauf Dialogues:*

O joy of beginning. O early morning.
First grass. O first page of the book,
Long awaited, the surprise of it.
And the first spray of water

on a sweaty face.
The clean, cool shirt.
O beginning of love,
O beginning of work.
And first puff of smoke,
filling the lungs. And you too,
New idea.[3]

Epic versus Dramatic. The achievement of alienation underlies Brecht's whole theory of epic theatre. Brecht set out the theory, comparing it with dramatic theatre, in a note to his *Mahagonny*. It will be useful to quote it in full before commenting upon it. *(See Table below.)*

The point here is not the extent to which Brecht was right in his assessment of dramatic

or Aristotelian structure, but how the whole theory of epic theatre is geared towards the creation of the alienation effect: the keeping of a critical remove on the part of the audience that enables it to consider the social content of theatrical action and to make decisions about it in political terms. Epic theatre moves in an episodic manner. As far ago as 1797 the German playwright Schiller suggested that such a structure enabled the spectator to consider the action at his own pace, and not become sucked into the restless emotional evolution of the plot.[5] While making a thematic whole, each episode of the epic is complete in itself, illustrating one specific aspect of the totality. The spectator can reflect upon this, as he is not anxious to press on to discover how the story ends. There is no story

DRAMATIC THEATRE	EPIC THEATRE
plot	narrative
involves the spectator	makes the spectator an observer
wears down his capacity for action	but arouses his capacity to action
provides him with sensations	forces him to take decisions
experience	view of the world
suggestion	argument
instinctive feelings preserved	brought to the point of recognition
spectator shares the experience	spectator studies the experience
human being is taken for granted	human being subjected to inquiry
he is unalterable	he is able to alter
eyes on the finish	eyes on the course
one scene makes another	each scene for itself
growth	montage
linear development	in curves
evolutionary determinism	jumps
man as a fixed point	man as a process
thought determines being	social being determines thought
feeling	reason[4]

[3] From BRECHT ON THEATRE, edited and translated by John Willett. Copyright © 1957, 1963 and 1964 by Suhrkamp Verlag Frankfurt Am Main. This translation and notes © 1964 by John Willett. Reprinted by permission of Hill and Wang (a divi-

sion of Farrar, Straus and Giroux, Inc.).

[4] *Ibid.*, p. 37.

[5] *Ibid.*, p. 210.

in a plot sense. Epic theatre is about the social condition of man; it reports and comments upon various aspects of that condition. It is only the nuclear form of epic theatre that can embrace such a comprehensive task.

One last point of theory. Brecht insisted upon the historification of his theatre—the setting of its events in the past. This was again in the cause of alienation. Historification will shut off the conditioning forces of society and allow the audience to sit back and critically consider events placed in the past. However, these events will have significant connections with its present circumstances.

Purposes. As Brecht was developing his theory of epic theatre in the mid 1920s, it was reinforced by the current principle of *neue sachlichkeit*—new objectivity, or matter-of-factness. Aspects of this were the functional aesthetics of the Bauhaus, the emphasis upon reportage and documentary, and the abolition of upper-case letters. It was the age of scientific utilitarianism, and artists wanted to be social engineers. This tied in strongly with Brecht's own sense of theatre's purpose. The sacrifice of the audience's intelligence to its dreams and fantasies, the appeal to emotion rather than to reason was unworthy of a scientific theatre. Theatre must associate with the most progressive currents in society, and use its influence, like social engineers, to create a better human environment—and thus a better man. Marxism, scientific functionalism, and behaviorism all came together to give Brecht's theatre its strong focus on social mechanics. His first really didactic play, *A Man's a Man*, contains these lines:

You can do with a human being what you will.
Take him apart like a car, rebuild him bit by bit.[6]

In exile in Denmark, Brecht exhorted working-class actors first to change them-

[6] From the Grove Press edition, edited by Eric Bentley (New York, 1964), p. 160.

selves and then to show the world as it really is—made by men and open to men's improvements. Brecht did not exclude feelings, insights, and impulses from his theatre, but wished to employ them primarily to change the whole field of human relationships. For Brecht, the author, actor, and director are producers, like any other maker of social produce, and they operate in a concrete world of scientific data—not a world of abstract creativity. The produce—the play—is not a reflection of, but a reflection *on*, social reality. It should show that character and action are historically determined and subject to change. The spectator sees man the way he is not because fate is the way it is, but because social conditions are the way they are. A new man, not socially or economically oppressed, is needed, and theatre should demonstrate the possibility of his achievement.

The purpose of epic theatre, then, was:

to make the spectator a critical observer who must make decisions.

to present the world as an object and to do this through dialectical demonstration.

to focus on the process, not the outcome of the play.

to explore the social determinism of the individual, showing the historical nature of human misfortune, the changeable order of nature, and the manipulability of man and his environment.

It was a social and scientific theatre. Brecht accommodated his personal dialectic—the pull between a sensitive nature and a rational intellect—to the sociopolitical dialectic of Marxism. Rather than allow his youthful, romantic despair to take him along the existential and metaphysical path of the absurdists, he found a positive focus in concentrating upon concrete social problems, which the scientific basis of Marxism held to be capable of solution. Brecht has been described as a passer-by of our time who lived for the future, a scientist, a poet without incense who sawed gently at our social nerves.

INTRINSIC DEMANDS

Form. Brecht used the term *epic* for his theatre in the German sense of the word: a narrative not tied to time. This he opposed to *tragic* or Aristotelian form, which was geared to a strongly focused action and more unified time and place. *Epic* did not necessarily have the connotation of a heroic scale, but simply the idea of a loosely linked series of events. We have already suggested that the episodic form this sense of epic gave to Brecht's theatre was related to expressionism—without that movement's highly colored emotional quality—but it also found its sensibility in older forms of theatre. The morality tradition, which saw man as process rather than character, had a similar sense of direct address with a moral theme and abstract use of time and place. The Elizabethan drama and the German playwrights Büchner and Wedekind used a dynamic, sequential episodic structure. The broad canvas of the Elizabethan theatre was well fitted to Brecht's concept of the Marxist dialectic: argument, clash, confrontation—a running sequence of actions in which each issue is plain.

Again, the epic form resembles a Homeric narrative. *Mother Courage* in particular is not unlike the *Odyssey*, with its twelve independent scenes, the journey of its central character, a wagon taking the place of Ulysses' ship, and the battlefields of Sweden and Germany equaling the plains of Troy. Within this form Brecht draws liberally from fairy tales, clown traditions (such as the German folk figure, Hans Wurst), and the British authors Kipling, Gay, and Dickens. Indeed, like Shakespeare, he used whatever suited his needs to create a nuclear form moving on several levels of time, space, and narrative at once. What resulted was a clear, coolly delineated chain of events presenting a body of evidence from which sociopolitical lessons might be drawn in a detached and lucid manner.

The episodic structure, calculated to break the audience's emotional continuity and thus its empathy, had a strongly dialectical basis.

The thesis-antithesis structure of an argument was present in the relationship of scenes. This was most evident in Brecht's didactic plays (or *Lehrstücke*), but was also present in his later parables. We are going to look briefly at the structure of a play from the period.

Epic Form—An Early Example. *The Exception and the Rule* is one of Brecht's most famous didactic plays. It is in nine episodes, and deals with a German merchant somewhere in Asia who is making a difficult journey through uncharted deserts to beat his competitors to an oil concession. He has with him a guide, and a coolie as porter. The first episode illustrates the merchant's harsh, exploiting attitude towards his companions—his philosophy of winning at all costs. In the second episode the merchant realizes he can't win on his own, so out of self-interest he appears to change his attitude. He is friendly to the guide in the third episode, but failing to win him over and realizing the coolie can act as guide and carry the goods as well, he dismisses him. A constant dialectic of attitude is taking place, showing the changing faces of self-interest and exploitation.

Episodes four through seven continue the dialectical quality of the play: the more the coolie shows himself intelligent, useful, and willing to serve the merchant, the more the merchant mistrusts and fears him. There is a splendid irony when the coolie pitches a tent for the merchant to sleep in, but the merchant fears he will be attacked in the night and stays awake while the coolie calmly sleeps. Finally, when they have run out of water, the coolie makes a gesture to share his bottle with the merchant, but the merchant's mistrust is such he thinks the coolie is trying to kill him with a stone, and he shoots him. The final scene is in a courtroom—the dramatic yet factual and dispassionate nature of legal proceedings was one of Brecht's favorite models. The merchant is tried for killing the coolie, but the judgment is a neat dialectical irony. The merchant is acquitted be-

222

cause after all he had done to the coolie he had no reason to expect kindness from him, and had every reason to think the coolie would kill him—thus, he acted in self-defense. The didactic moral of the play is that, the way the world is now oriented, kind and humane actions lead to death, and conscious exploitation to success. The audience is asked to recognize this and—the last line of the play—"do something about it."

A Later Example. *The Exception and the Rule,* being geared entirely toward didactic ends, is a highly refined example of the dialectical structure of Brecht's work, to the exclusion of the more sweeping, poetic qualities of his later writing. But running through the broad palette of his mature epic drama is a strong structural spine of a dialectical nature that gives the plays a clear sociopolitical focus. *The Good Woman of Setzuan* is an example of this. Written in ten episodes, it is a parable-cum-fairy tale about three gods who come down to earth in a Chinese city looking for "good" people. The only person who will give them shelter is the local prostitute Shen Te—an immediate assertion of true goodness being found in a woman regarded as "bad" by society's morality. The play then goes on to explore the dialectic between the attempt to be good and the need to make a living in contemporary social conditions. This is done through the central conceit of the play: Shen Te becomes a split person, pretending to become her cousin, Shui Ta, who is her temperamental opposite—a tough, rational businessman. Each episode of the play gives a different perspective upon this central theme, and the episodes contrast with each other to show the problems Shen Te's "goodness" gets her into, followed by the hard-nosed actions of Shui Ta sorting the problems out.

The dialectical theme of the play is clearly delineated in each episode and constantly brought to the audience's attention. Shen Te, as her own loving, sympathetic self, finds it impossible to operate in the world, whereas the somewhat ruthless, hardheaded Shui Ta actually brings about more "good" in the world's terms than she does. Nor are the gods any help. Having found some goodness in the world, they are happy enough to leave things as they are—the implication being, of course, that man must change himself. Shen Te is left in pretty much the position she started in—to be good and yet survive tears a

A strong, physical scenic gestus created by actors in *The Measures Taken.*

Mark Taper Forum, Los Angeles.

person in two. Brecht has stated the thesis and the antithesis; he leaves the audience to find the synthesis, saying, "It is for you to find a way, my friends, you write the happy ending to the play."

Gestus. The strong didactic purpose in a dialectical form is present to some degree in all of Brecht's work, and provides actors with a firm basis for their performance. Their function is not the creation of emotional response in the audience but the presentation of a clearly defined sociopolitical theme. The theme is demonstrated in dialectical action, which provides the actor with that relation-ship of opposites his approach to his character must embody. That each episode is complete in itself, as well a forming part of the nuclear whole, gives each scene a well-defined action and purpose that Brecht called a *gest* or *gestus*. In essence, a gestus is a refined and firmly outlined physical representation of the thematic idea. Each scene has its gestus, as well as each character—the scenic gestus and character gestus must reinforce each other.

The episodic structure is an alienation factor, disrupting the creation of a build of emotional empathy in the audience. It will also have this function for the actor. Episodes do not build in emotional intensity;

A scream of despair at the human condition, from the painting by Edvard Munch.

The Scream by Edvard Munch, 1893. Reproduced by permission of the National Gallery, Oslo.

Mother Courage reacts to the loss of her son, in the New York Public Theatre production.

Photo by Martha Swope.

they simply add further evidence and throw a new perspective upon the theme. The emotional rhythms of the play tend to be even, with a narrative rather than a climactic quality. Even does not mean unvaried or uninteresting, but simply a lack of intense emotional moments. Where Brecht's work at times might seem to lend itself to emotional display, the actor should play against it. Perhaps the most famous example of this is the moment in *Mother Courage* when the title character is shown the bullet-riddled body of her son Swiss Cheese. Helene Weigel, playing Mother Courage, turned away from the body and uttered a totally silent scream: a perfect example of gestus, true to the Brechtian sensibility.

Space. The use of space both accommodates and reinforces the epic qualities of the plays. It allows for episodic change and a wide sweep of events—being essentially unlocalized and unspecific, after the tradition both of the medieval stage and the Elizabethan theatre. There is no attempt to create any realistic illusion. Everything about the staging is practical and utilitarian, revealing a sensibility based upon the spare didacticism of the classroom or lecture hall and the earthy dynamic of the boxing ring. These environments support the function of Brecht's theatre as an arena in which a dialectical action is fought out for the education of the spectators. In the context of dialectical space, it is interesting to note that

Brecht's own theatre, Theater am Schiff-bauerdamm, was an ornate bourgeois theatre in which pragmatical Marxist drama was presented—an immediate visual dialectic of a new order unfolding within the framework of the old. The theatre is also situated in Berlin—a city divided against itself.

In his conscious undermining of illusion Brecht did not attempt to disguise any of the theatrical apparatus of his stage. His lights were ungelled, and the instruments shown hanging on their pipes. Scaffolding was often employed rather than solid scenery. The whole use of scenic space advertised that this was not an imitation of life; this was a theatre, and one that was an intellectual workshop. The direct relationship among the epic form, the didactic intention, and the spatial dynamics of the theatre was rein-forced by Brecht's use of screens, titles, pro-jections, slides—all the technological para-phernalia of a scientific age. Items that today would be known as teaching aids are used by Brecht to serve the didactic purpose of his theatre. Breaking illusion meant, for Brecht, alienating emotional empathy to produce in the audience the critically engaged attitude of the student or of the spectator at a sporting event who is judging the quality of the play and the technical expertise of the players.

Scenic Gestus. The space is a classroom, the set is a teaching aid, and the actor is an instructor. While playing its part as an alienating factor space is also, crucially, being used to demonstrate the theme of the play. This is done by use of the scenic gestus. The action of the scene, as performed by the ac-tors, should directly relate to and be rein-forced by spatial environment. The set doesn't just provide a background to the ac-tor; it must present the play's thematic concern. To take a simple example: episode eight of *The Good Woman of Setzuan* takes place in a tobacco factory where the workers are being exploited. Here the actors might perform in a mechanical manner, with somewhat clockwork gestures, so that the sum total of their movements creates the necessary scenic effect—a tobacco factory—and at the same time makes the statement that factory workers are regarded as nonhuman artifacts by the capitalist system. This is a scenic gestus in which the scenic structure, the actor's performance, and the thematic statement become one.

Brecht's use of space for his production of *Mother Courage* is perhaps a perfect exam-ple of a gestus running throughout the play. Mother Courage's wagon is on a turntable, moving in the direction opposite that of the actors. This gives the appearance of move-ment through time and space—a neat solu-tion to the changing locations in the play—but in fact the audience is also aware that the wagon is moving but not getting anywhere, despite the effort by the pullers, who are Mother Courage's sons. The action is actu-ally a declining one, for at the end of the play Mother Courage's children are all lost or dead and she, left alone, harnesses herself like an animal to the wagon. The thematic idea is that Mother Courage stupidly serves the warmongering capitalist system that kills off all of value in her life and gives her nothing in return. This is illustrated by the scenic gestus: her children yoked to the wagon (which contains the goods she sells) getting nowhere in spatial terms until finally only she is left, still pulling the wagon with her declining brute strength—and still going nowhere, except to her own death.

The simplicity, spareness, and utilitarian quality of the space in epic theatre empha-sizes the play's narrative and the actors. The acting, closely related as it is to the setting, must have a similar clarity, strength, and reserve. Nothing can be wasted; nothing must be overdone; there is nothing to hide behind. The social sinews of the play are as cleanly revealed as the scaffolding of the set and the musculature of the acting. In a final dialectic, this simplicity does not reduce the size of the theme or narrow the impact of time and space. Rather it allows for mythic

Brechtian scenic space in a production of *The Caucasian Chalk Circle*. Note visible lighting instruments, screens and projections, and the sparseness and simplicity of the set.

overtones, as in parable, fable, and epic legend. As Eric Bentley noted,[7] Brecht set his *Caucasian Chalk Circle* in Transcaucasia, the place where Asia and Europe meet; where Prometheus was chained to his rock; where Jason found the Golden Fleece; and where both Genghis Kahn and Tamerlane wrought havoc with their armies.

Costume and Properties. Though Brecht didn't operate on any kind of realistic premise in his use of space, he took extreme care that costumes and properties create the cor-

rect socioeconomic impression. Simplicity and selectivity were, again, two principles on which he operated, but to these were added a strong functional and utilitarian sense. His production of *Antigone* used sackcloth and cotton for the costumes, with inserts of leather—workmanlike materials with tactile qualities. The colors were deep browns, reds, and grays—the colors of earth, blood, and granite. Brecht wished each scene, or episode, of his plays to have a basic tonal gestus. This developed with the play to underscore the total gestus, or thematic idea. Costumes had to show the evidence of wear, and the props were not realistic but in fact real. Brecht would have them made not by theatre technicians but by actual craftsmen,

[7] Bertolt Brecht, *Parables for the Theatre*, trans. Eric Bentley (Harmondsworth, Middlesex: Penguin, 1966), preface.

or he would use objects that had been in daily use in real life. One of his poems shows his sensibility in this area:

Of all works my favorite
are those which show usage.
The copper vessels with bumps and dented
  edges.
The knives and forks whose wooden handles
  are
worn down by many hands.[8]

This flowed from Brecht's pragmatical romanticism. The simple, well-worn human artifact appealed to his sense of man's dignity and aspirations seen in a social and historical context. He was as careful over the correct use of properties as he was of the correct performance of work on stage: scenes of building, cooking, mending, and other basic human tasks had to be done with workmanlike accuracy. Work, the economic produce of labor, was, after all, at the basis of Marxist philosophy.

Brecht's emphasis upon the correct detail of costuming and properties was due to their direct social and economic function within his theatre. Settings can be simple, func-

Hair, mustache, hands, and walk create basic character gestus for Arturo Ui in this production of *The Resistible Rise of Arturo Ui.*

Guthrie Theatre.

[8] John Willett and Ralph Manheim, eds., in BERTOLT BRECHT POEMS, 1913-1956, trans. by John Willett. "Volumes 3 & 4 of 'Gedichte': © Copyright Suhrkamp Verlag Frankfurt am Main 1961." Reproduced by permission of Methuen, Inc. From the estate of Bertolt Brecht.

tional, and highly selective and still create the necessary historical background, the atmosphere of epic, myth, or parable. But costumes and properties create the play's reference point in the present—the socioeconomic reality. They must, therefore, be authentic so that the audience may relate directly to the attitudes of a character and submit them to valid criticism.

As props and costumes relate so specifically to character, the way in which they are worn or used can make them part of a character's gestus. The wearing of a cloth cap can be a strong gestus indicating a worker—just as a bowler hat can suggest the bourgeoisie. In *A Man's a Man*, guns denote both military and phallic oppression. In *The Resistible Rise of Arturo Ui*—which transfers to Chicago the story of the rise to power of Adolf Hitler—a mustache and a particular manner of wearing the hair are enough of a gestus to identify the leading character. In this way makeup can play its part in creating both character mask and gestus. In his production of *Edward II*, Brecht asked the question "What do soldiers do in battle?" Someone suggested: "They are afraid." Brecht gave his soldiers chalk white faces in a brilliant gestic sense of the scene.

Mask as Gestus. A deathly white face is virtually a mask, and Brecht was given to the use of physical masks, especially in his earlier plays. He was influenced in this by the use of mask in Oriental theatre, which created a broad yet controlled style of playing in which small emotional or psychological detail was discounted. A mask thus becomes an alienation factor and at the same time an absolute indication of character attitude—a strong, simple, if unsubtle, gestus. A mask leaves an actor in no doubt of the objective nature of the character he is "wearing."

Music and Song. Brecht uses music and song—which appear in virtually all of his plays—for the same two basic purposes that underlie the dynamics of the rest of his theatrical form: alienation and gestus. There is never any attempt to disguise the music or use it in an atmospheric or "incidental" way to create emotional mood. The musicians are on stage in full view of the audience, as much a part of the setting as the lights. The nature of the music is also calculated to break any empathic response from the audience. It is functional music, never lyrical except when passing a comment upon lyricism, as in *The Threepenny Opera*, where the most tender love song described the attachment of a pimp and his whore—a dialectic between form and content.

The songs punctuate the action of the play and reinforce the theme. There is no pretense—as in musicals or operetta—that the action is continuing from speaking into singing. The action stops for the song—thus reinforcing the alienation effect—and the song passes comment upon the action in a gestic manner. Thus, the song becomes a part of the total gestus of the scene, while adding a perspective to the action that leaves the audience in no doubt as to the correct critical position it should take. The songs range from the most aggressively didactic, as the "Song of the Courts" in *The Exception and the Rule*:

The law courts will give the vultures food-
    aplenty.
Thither fly the killers. The tormentors
Will be safe there. And there
The thieves hide the loot they call profit. . . .[9]

to the more ironic song of Mother Courage:

Sabres and swords are hard to swallow:
First you must give men beer to drink.
Then they can face what is to follow—
But let 'em swim before they sink!

[9] *The Measures Taken* and other Lehrstücke, Bertolt Brecht. From *The Exception and the Rule*, trans. Ralph Manheim, (London: Eyre Methuen, Ltd. 1977). p. 52. Translation copyright © 1977 by Stefan S. Brecht, DIE AUSNAHME UND DIE REGEL (The Exception and the Rule). Copyright 1957 by Suhrkamp Verlag, Berlin. Reprinted by permission from Random House.

Christians awake! The winter's gone!
The snows depart, the dead sleep on.
And though you may not long survive
Get out of bed and look alive![10]

To heighten the alienation effect and project the ironic nature of their content, the songs are consciously unmelodic. They are acted rather than sung. The singer is a reporter of the verse, tending not to follow the melody but to speak against the music, setting up a dialectic that creates a strong aural impression on the audience. The audience is not lulled by the music, but made to sit up and take notice of the gestic content.

Language. The linguistic form of Brecht's theatre, as befitting the title *epic*, is suited to the telling of a story. But this narrative quality, although not geared to the creation of emotional response, is a highly dramatic one, compounded out of many elements Brecht borrowed and refined over the progression of his work—from its early opulent and decadent poetry, through the austere didacticism of the *Lehrstücke*, to the final eclectic but highly integrated epic form.

Brecht was a poet and songwriter before he became a playwright—a poet of the streets and cabarets whose verse had a light and satirical quality and owed much of its simplicity and directness to the tradition of Anglo-Saxon ballads. This was the basis of his whole sense of language. There was a roughness and irregularity, a carelessness that yet gave a unique sense of character—not unlike the work of Woody Guthrie and Bob Dylan and the folk and protest singers of the 1960s. He drew on street songs, sentimental "pop," the *Barrack-Room Ballads* of Kipling, cabaret lyrics, biblical syntax,

---

[10] *Mother Courage and Her Children*, trans. Eric Bentley (London: Eyre Methuen Ltd., 1972), p. 4. Translation copyright © 1955, 1959, 1961, 1962 by Eric Bentley; original work published as *Mütter Courage und ihre Kinder* copyright 1949 by Suhrkamp Verlag vormals J. Fischer, Frankfurt/Main.

and the sweeping unrhymed verse of the Elizabethans. He refined this mixture to the bone, cutting out anything that did not speak to the essence of the theme. The result was a richly textured yet dry, chopped-off linguistic style with a syncopated rhythm—clarity and precision with an inherently dialectical sense of contradiction built into the language. It is full of contrasted half-sentences, parallelisms, inversions. Prose moves into heightened prose or irregular verse. Blank verse and prose alternate. The whole narrative pattern is interspersed with songs.

The language had to do three things: be intelligible to the ears of a proletarian audience; convey the underlying gestus—the essential attitude of the character; and avoid the creation of emotional empathy in the audience. Lyricism, undue embellishment, and rhetorical passion had no part in epic theatre. A narrative style and asymmetrical verse form allowed for both the didactic aim and a poetic impact that kept the audience off balance with its rhythms rather than lulling them to sleep. For Brecht, language was theatrical insofar as it correctly presented the attitude (gestus) of the person speaking it. Everything in his theatre is geared to the presentation of the social theme of the play. The setting makes a thematic statement; the scene/episode has a gestic core; the character has his gestus; and the language—as conveying the theme and used by the character—will have gestic qualities that fit these purposes.

A simple narrative style; an asymmetrical sense of rhythm; an ironic, dialectical content; a refined poetic eclecticism; and a clear, direct thematic focus—these are the elements the actor must encompass when dealing with the language of Brecht's plays.

Didacticism. Together with alienation and a strong sense of dialectic, the educational function—what today would be called the raising of the audience's social consciousness—was a consistent feature of Brecht's work. His theatre was a political instrument whose purpose was not to describe human nature but to change it. In this he was following Marx's dictum: "The philosophers have interpreted the world; the point, however, is to change it." The human condition has been created by people and can be changed by people, but only if they are taught to take nothing for granted, to view everything with a critical eye—the scientific skepticism that underlies the alienation principle.

Didacticism is overtly or implicitly present in all of Brecht's work, and an actor will be unable to perform validly in his theatre without recognizing this. The *Lehrstücke* contain the most explicit instructions to the audience. The opening of *The Exception and the Rule* states:

Examine carefully the behaviour of these people.
Find it surprising though not unusual
Inexplicable though normal

. . . .

For to say that something is natural
is to regard it as unchangeable.[11]

And as we have already noted, the ending to the play asks the audience to "do something about it." Another famous *Lehrstück*, *The Measures Taken*, specifically sets out the ABC of communism, both within the play and in the final chorus:

The ABC of Communism:
Instructions to the ignorant concerning their condition,
Class-consciousness to the oppressed
And to the class-conscious, practical knowledge of the revolution.

[11] *The Exception and the Rule*, trans. Manheim, p. 37.

. . . .
Taught only by reality can
Reality be changed![12]

Even the parabolic nature of such a play as *The Caucasian Chalk Circle* did not prevent Brecht from giving the play a completely didactic premise: it is acted out to find the answer to an actual political problem.

Mother Courage is perhaps Brecht's most oblique play in the making of its sociopolitical point—mainly because of the audience's tendency to empathize with the indomitable spirit of Mother Courage herself—but its final chorus should leave the audience in no doubt as to the author's intention:

The war takes hold and will not quit.
But though it lasts three generations
We shall get nothing out of it.
Starvation, filth, and cold enslave us.
The army robs us of our pay.
Only a miracle can save us
And miracles have had their day.
Christians awake! The winter's gone!
The snows depart. The dead sleep on.
And though you may not long survive
Get out of bed and look alive![13]

Brecht the Ironist. "And though you may not long survive, get out of bed and look alive!" is typical of the way in which Brecht's didacticism expressed itself. He was, true to the dialectical quality running through his life and work, an optimistic pessimist. He had no illusions about the way in which the world actually worked; he wasn't blind to man's faults and weaknesses. But Marxism taught him that society could be changed and that man's good side would then assert itself. He accepted this because he wanted to believe

[12] *The Measures Taken*, trans. Carl R. Mueller (London: Eyre Methuen Ltd., 1977), p. 34. Translation copyright © 1977 by Stefan S. Brecht DIE MASSNAHME (*The Measures Taken*) copyright 1955 by Suhrkamp Verlag, Berlin.

[13] *Mother Courage*, trans. Bentley, p. 81.

that life had a positive purpose—that it was not merely absurd. However, while engaged in raising people's consciousness so that society would improve, he still had to live in the world as he found it. To do this he assumed an attitude of ironic servility: do not antagonize authority; confuse it with irony. The survivors are the antiheroes, those who bend with the wind so as not to break. Enlightened self-interest and peasant cunning will help the oppressed to survive in a world geared against them. One day social revolution will destroy capitalism and preclude war making, so it is important to survive till that day. Like the Good Soldier Schweik, who avoids death by pretending to comply, or Azdak, the corrupt judge who achieves good by playing the world at its own game—two of Brecht's most engaging characters—Brecht's own stance was a pacifistic and antiheroic one.

A strong flavor of the man comes through in his plays, a didactic purpose that not only preaches Marxist philosophy and the need for a revolution in man's socioeconomic condition, but also teaches the importance of playing for time, waiting for the right moment—and surviving. The grasping of this dialectical and ironic sensibility is important to the actor who wishes to understand Brecht's work: the work of a man who had a Marxist theatre and an Austrian passport; who performed plays in East Germany but published them in West; the anticapitalist who kept a Swiss bank account—the world-acclaimed theatrical practitioner who liked to speak of himself as "Poor Bert Brecht."

PERFORMANCE DEMANDS

Character and Gestus. In epic theatre an actor will build his part from a social perspective. He is not looking for emotional, psychological, or metaphysical motivations for action, but for the social gist of his part. Brecht was not concerned with (indeed, did

not believe in) eternal truths, but rather with the specific social and economic truths of a given period, which condition human behavior at that time. The actor must examine his part carefully to discover the political dialectics of the play, and the function his own character has in the presentation of the theme.

The questions an actor must ask are not Who am I? but What am I? Not Who does this action? but What is this action? It is the action and the consequences of that action in social and economic terms that concern Brecht, not the nature of the psychical self. The question is not Is a capitalist a capitalist *because* he is anally retentive, or sexually impotent? but What is the social effect of his *being* a capitalist? Rather than try to develop an emotional persona for the character, or write up an imaginary biography of his past, an actor should make a skeletal outline of the events and action of the play and underline where his part fits in. Work on a character's strategy—how he adapts to the society he exists in—and his tactics—the way in which he confronts problems and achieves his adaptation. Look for the socially determined insights and impulses and establish the modal points of the character's function in the story. Examine the structural relationship of these points to each other—how they create specific episodes. Discover ways to narrate these episodes so that their social significance is made clear. Ask of the character: What happens to him? How does he respond? What opinions does he express and confront?

The actor should not be too anxious to set his character, or he will lose critical objectivity about it. He should continue to explore, to conjecture about his part throughout the rehearsal period. A useful practice is to swap parts so that the character may be considered from a truly external perspective. Nor should the actor try to build an immediately logical and consistent character. Inconsistent first impressions should be kept, not subsumed into a homogeneous whole.

The gestic idea embodied by George Grosz in this cartoon of the capitalist: cigar, paunch containing his stomach/factory, and stance and closed eyes provide all the comment necessary.

Nicholson and Watson.

Character gestus of downtrodden peasant created by facial mask and posture in this production of *The Measures Taken*.

Mark Taper Forum, Los Angeles.

Just as the play itself has independent and dialectically opposed episodes that constitute a thematic integrity, so a character may be created in a piecemeal fashion that contains certain contradictions but is at one with the thematic focus of the play as a whole. Anything that seems obvious should be questioned.

Creating the Gestus. The basis of physical characterization is gestus. This is both a physical attitude and a point of view. The physicality embodies meaning in a precise, almost hieroglyphic way. The starting point is an external one, not arising from generalized aspects of human behavior, but from those physical elements that will delineate a sociopolitical individual in a specific time, place, and class structure. To take the example of the dialectical character Shen Te/Shui Ta in *The Good Woman of Setzuan:* a change of body rhythm from the shuffling, compliant walk of the exploited woman to the determined stride of the entrepreneur; a change of vocal intonation; plus the change of a chongsam for a business suit will, in very specific yet simple ways, achieve a complete change of character gestus. Strongly defined body rhythms and centers of energy are fundamental to the delineation of character gestus, which should be done as if using a charcoal pencil with firm, selected, economical strokes.

We have already noted that Brecht was influenced by Oriental acting—especially Chinese. It is interesting in the context of the use of gestus to note the tradition of the male actor playing female parts in the Chinese theatre. This lasted for two hundred years—until 1966, when women began to play female roles in the Peking Opera. During the period of the male tradition, the actors attempted not to impersonate women but to present a gestus that created the essence of the female roles. There was a stylized makeup, a wig, a tripping footstep, a certain use of the costume sleeves, and a stylized vocal quality. A. C. Scott, discussing the possible introduction of female actors, says: "Actresses are bound to fall back upon their natural qualities. They cannot sustain the intensity of the actor's symbolism, and little by little realism creeps in."[14] If we substitute gestus for "symbolism" in that quotation, it gives us an interesting comment on the distinction between realistic and epic styles of acting, between impersonating and presenting a character.

Another good example of the creation of character gestus—although a gestus not consciously made for the purpose of social criticism—may be found in the films of Humphrey Bogart, especially *The Maltese Falcon*. Bogart's character creations were all distinguished by certain gestic features: a walk, a hunch of the shoulders, a curl of the lip, a sibilant, almost lisping speech, a coolly dispassionate manner, a hat, and a macintosh. This was the gestus of the antihero of his time—the outsider; the cynical, warm-hearted, ironical tough guy. Never sparing more effort than was necessary; never emotionally self-indulgent; always coolly in control of himself; seemingly at an intellectual remove from what he was doing, Humphrey Bogart could well have been a Brechtian actor. Indeed, one of his fellow actors in *The Maltese Falcon* had worked with Brecht: Peter Lorre played the leading role in *A Man's a Man* and other Brecht productions. Lorre's facial mask, peculiar vocal quality, threateningly cringing manner (a dialectic), and dry, restrained style just hinting at emotion are all typically gestic qualities. In the same way, Sydney Greenstreet's corpulence, panama hat, sweaty forehead, cigar, and oily politeness created the gestus of the capitalist, gentleman crook. These actors all give the impression of being aware of what they are doing. There is a clarity, economy, and intelligence about their work that sug-

---

[14] A. C. Scott, *The Classic Theatre of China* (London: Macmillan, 1957), p. 73.

Humphrey Bogart's well-known character gestus, as seen in *The Maltese Falcon.*

gests they could well be passing comment upon their characters.

A gestus may be the physical (including costume) attributes of a character that project the essential socioeconomic function of the role, or it may be a particular gesture or moment of action that embodies thematic meaning. Whatever it is, it is external and physical. In *A Man's a Man* Peter Lorre used a cosmetic gestus in whitening his face to show that he was afraid, rather than attempting to work with an inner, emotional fear of death. In the final episode of *Mother Courage*, when Helene Weigel in the title role payed the peasants to give her daughter

a decent burial, she took the coins from her purse, then put one back before giving the rest. Her gestus showed Mother Courage's essentially economic outlook towards life: money, her job had come before her children. In a production of *Roundheads and Peakheads*, a play in which the governor is a manipulated puppet, the actor playing the part used puppetlike rhythms as part of his character gestus. And in a brilliant scenic gestus, when the governor was called upon to sign a paper his manipulator moved the paper over the pen held stiffly in the governor's hand—a perfect presentation of the meaning of the scene.

(a)

(b)

Bogart with Peter Lorre (a) and Sydney Greenstreet (b) in *The Maltese Falcon*. Note Lorre's facial mask and Greenstreet's total body gestus.

Whatever form it takes, the gestus should always be related to the total thematic concern of the play. This, as we have suggested, will be embodied by the use of space and the setting of the play, and each episode will have its gestus of action that relates to the whole. In working on and presenting his character, an actor must be aware of the group scenic gestus and the part he plays in it. The presentation of the total statement of the play is more important than any one character—it is very much an ensemble form of playing. The actor must be aware of his relationship to the scenic environment and the action gestus of the scene, while presenting his own character gestus and discovering the gestic actions that relate it to the thematic whole.

Character and Alienation. One of the clichés about Brecht's theatre is that it requires a nonemotional style of acting. Yet no one quite knows what this is. In fact, as every actor is aware, it is impossible to avoid emotion in acting—it is an automatic response to any action or attitude. Brecht himself acknowledged this. The point of distinction about epic acting is that its *prime* function is not the engendering of emotion—either in the actor or in the audience. The purpose of epic acting is to entertain and arouse the critical consciousness of the audience, not to create an emotional empathy with the audience and fool them into taking a realistic approach to the stage illusion. The epic actor does not look for emotion, pump it up, wallow in it. He accepts what is there, controls it, and channels it into the objective playing of the action. Emotion is then externalized and becomes living energy in the presentation of the gestus; it is not held within and subjectively examined. Emotion is thus subjected to criticism, together with the other elements of action, in terms of the socioeconomic theme. Mother Courage is no Lady of the Sorrows; she is deeply flawed in terms of a pathetic heroine. She has the wrong historical and economic sensibility, and the actor should criticize this in her performance, not seek for emotional empathy. When wrong, emotion must be shown as wrong and *alterable*—not as part of the pitiable human condition.

An old theatrical adage is that an actor should have a warm heart but a cool head. The cool head is especially true of epic acting. The actor must not let himself be carried away by his character's emotion so that he cannot have a critical perspective on it. The actor in performance must always play for events, not temperament—play the action, not the emotion. In rehearsal an actor can discover as much about his character's emotional or psychological makeup as is necessary to enable him to build a workable part—to determine the character's actions within the situation and pass valid criticism upon those actions. In performance emotion and psyche are not the prime considerations: the actor is presenting a report upon his character's actions, seen in the socioeconomic perspective of the theme.[15]

Just as there will be some emotion in a performance, so it is impossible for the actor to avoid some identification with his character. And just as the actor attempts to objectify and rechannel the emotion, so he will attempt to alienate himself from—stand outside—his character. The attempt to avoid identification with the character sets up the dialectic of playing in epic theatre. The basic dialectic of acting has always been the relationship between the actor as self and the actor as character. Many positions have been taken on this, and aesthetic arguments abound,[16] but Brecht neither avoided the dialectic nor attempted to reconcile it; he accepted it as the basic approach to his acting style—the actor is himself *and* presents a

---

[15] In a certain sense an actor inevitably comments upon his role by the nature of the choices he makes. It might be useful to the Brechtian actor to think of this process as placed within a political context.

[16] See, for example, William Archer, *Masks or Faces* (New York: Hill & Wang, 1957).

character that he passes comment upon. In the balance between the "otherness" of the character being portrayed and the actor's total, personal commitment to the character, Brecht emphasized "otherness," because criticism of the character's socioeconomic actions was his focus. Stanislavski, on the other hand, stressed the personal, emotional response of the character to a particular situation. Both were aware of the dialectic; both were in search of "truthful" performance; it was their focus that differed.

An Approach to Epic Acting. Brecht, then, was concerned with demonstration rather than empathy, with criticism rather than catharsis. The actor displays his character, quotes his lines, demonstrates the incidents. In dialectical terms the character is the thesis, the actor is the antithesis, and the synthesis is in the audience. Here are a few further specific approaches to epic acting:

1. Read the play more than usual; don't jump into "living" the part.
2. When reading the part take a critical point of view—weigh up the conduct of the character. Be aware of the social responses before you learn the lines.
3. Identify the political focus of the play.
4. Identification with the character may be possible at rehearsal, but only as a method of exploration and observation of the character.
5. In performance don't be transported by your part or try to cast a spell on the audience. The audience's immediate reponse should not be "What a lifelike portrayal."
6. Don't use self-conscious verbal cadences.
7. Don't draw attention away from the actor's report to admiration for his art.
8. Always be aware of where the play is going—what its social "superobjective" is (to adopt a Stanislavskian term).
9. Talk to the audience and demonstrate the character's actions—there is a gestus of "showing" that underlies all the epic actor does.

10. Know what critical response you would like the audience to have. It is the presentation of the character with a critical viewpoint that alienates emotional empathy.

Physical Presentation. "Underplayed overstatement" may be a dialectical way of describing the playing manner of the epic actor: overstatement inasmuch as the nature of gestus will give a heightened clarity to the character and its movement—the dramatic bones are not obscured by psychological flesh; underplayed because of the emotional coolness and reserve with which the character is presented. The uncluttered simplicity of the setting in epic theatre throws the actor into high relief and makes every gesture significant. This makes the observation and selection of gestic detail extremely important, especially in the handling of props and the performance of manual work—elements that give much of the socioeconomic texture to the scenic effect. In rehearsal the actor should listen to and observe his character; be looking for new perspective, unique qualities; be surprised at what he discovers and allow that sense to inform his manner of playing.

When the actor's work is presented to the audience, it should have an elegance, dryness, and objectivity—a practical quality as if a sculptor were discussing where his work should be displayed, not its "meaning" or spirit. There will be an ease that has been achieved through effort, a deliberateness that is the result of conscious choice. Brecht suggested images of achievement through leisurely effort:

> As a river wears down its banks;
> An earthquake shakes the ground with a
>   relaxed hand;
> A fire devours in comfort.[17]

It is important for the actor in epic theatre to know the difference between strong and

[17] Quoted by John Willett in *The Theatre of Bertolt Brecht.*

Dynamic coolness of gestic manner in a production of *The Seven Deadly Sins.*
Citizens' Theatre Company, Glasgow.

crude, relaxed and loose, quick and hurried, imaginative and distracting, thought out and concocted, deep-felt and emotional, passionate and uncontrolled. The first set of adjectives apply to Brecht's theatre. There is no indulgence in bombast or intensity, but a basic irony of playing: "quick, light, strong," as Brecht himself reminded his actors in his final note to them, written as they undertook their British tour in 1956.

The essential qualities of physical presentation will also be found in the vocal manner of epic theatre, with the added demands of the variety of vocal forms Brecht employs. The actor should take each form on its own terms, not try to blur the distinctions among them. Prose, verse, blank verse, chorus speaking, and song are all used by Brecht for consciously rhythmic, gestic, and alienating pur-

poses. The actor must be aware of the purpose of each form and adapt his manner of presentation to it. We have already suggested that the singing form is not melody but rather a speaking against the music that almost alienates the rhythm. Similarly, speeches must be examined for their gestic content. Frequently there will be an ironic comment upon the character, as when in *Mother Courage* the chaplain says: "I was so scared I almost broke out in prayer." And the officer has the line "I don't trust him; we're friends." An actor must discover where it is necessary to alienate the speech, to achieve a gestic comment by the manner of presentation. If the contemporary expression "I have to get my shit together" is said in a polite, distant manner, it is immediately alienated and thrown into critical relief. Similarly, the well-known song "Let's all go barmy, let's join the army" from *The Threepenny Opera* should be sung in such a way as to make the aggressive words ridiculous and laughable, not frightening to the audience.

The actor should not be concerned with giving his character a consistent manner of vocal presentation—the manner will be determined by the gestic demands of the play. The consistency appears in the total pattern of the event. As with everything else in epic theatre, the performance as a whole reveals in a nuclear manner the consistent thematic concern of the play.

Sense of Occasion. There is always the danger in speaking of the necessary didactic purpose and emotional remove of Brecht's theatre that all sense of its function as entertainment—to provide pleasure—will be lost. But Brecht, though holding firm to his desire for raising the political consciousness of his audience, never took himself too seriously. He believed that theatre was a form of game, that it was essentially superfluous—but that the superfluous gave life significance, that nothing needed less justification than pleasure, and that the highest form of pleasure came through learning—expanding one's human horizons. Brecht was not a sober-sided Marxist intellectual. He was a man of sly humor and vital energy who was aware of all the pleasures and temptations of the flesh and spent much of his life trying to reconcile and discipline (though not purge) them with an austere political life style. Brecht was poet and playwright before he was politician.

It is true that an actor performing Brecht must understand the political intent of his theatre: it is an exercise in formalism to do a Brecht play without a grasp of the social reality being presented. It is equally true that the classroom is joined by the sporting arena and the cabaret as formative images in

Brecht's work. Music, song, sleight of hand, ironic humor, and conviviality are as much teaching aids as the posters, placards, filmstrips, and litany of alienation effects. The didactic intention is present; to fulfill this the audience must be able to criticize the social reality being presented to it in a dispassionate manner. But the audience is certainly not to be alienated from the actors or prevented from enjoying itself. Audience and actors are on the same side—that of humanity. They are part of the family of social man—observing and criticizing; sharing ideas, attitudes, feelings, and responses; but above all enjoying a pleasurable, entertaining, edifying, social occasion.

EXERCISES, GAMES, TECHNIQUES

Rehearsal Techniques. Brecht himself suggested various ways to approach epic acting:

1. transposing the actions and remarks of the character into the third person
2. transposing the action into the past
3. speaking the stage directions

Thus, a piece of action in rehearsal might go as follows: "Mother Courage slowly got down from her wagon, walked over to the officer, looked at him and said, . . ."

Using the third person and the past tense enables the actor to achieve the right attitude of distance from the action. Putting the action in the past allows the actor to look at his words and make judgments on them. Speaking the stage directions in the third person has the effect of alienating them from the text itself.

These techniques may be varied and elaborated upon. The stage manager can call out the stage directions or narrate the action as the actor moves through it: "So then Mother Courage wearily sat down, took her daughter Kattrin's hand, and waited for the soldiers to bring in the stretcher bearing the body covered with a sheet." The actor may use the third-person alienation technique and add a comment upon the action—the kind of critical comment that the gestus should convey: "He stood up weakly, as, due to the soldiers taking the food, he had not eaten for three days, and, facing the officer with bitterness, said, . . ."

Witness Game. This is based on Brecht's own quintessential model for epic acting—the street scene. Set up a situation in which one of the players is relating an incident he has seen to the rest of the group. In Brecht's model the incident was an automobile accident at a street corner, but the possibilities are unlimited. The witness describes and acts out the circumstances of the situation so observers are able to form an opinion. The witness demonstrates the actions of the persons involved in the incident, but does this as himself—there is no attempt to create an illusion or to become emotionally involved. If the witness wants to suggest that someone was angry, he will display the actions of the anger, but not assume the emotion himself. The characters involved in the situation will become known to the observers by their actions, and only those actions that are absolutely necessary to describe the nature of the event. The witness will demonstrate the actions and talk directly to the observers. If he wishes to use props or costume elements it will be for gestic purposes. For example, a crooked hat may suggest that one of the characters was drunk, or a white stick that he was blind.

The object of the witness's demonstration is to show what part each individual played in the incident and enable the observers to form an opinion and fix responsibility. The player who is the witness must always take an objective standpoint, using the "He did" and "He said" construction, so that the observers are aware of both the witness and the person he is demonstrating—the actions and opinions are never merged into one, though the witness may have his own point of view. The game may be placed in a courtroom environment with witnesses, jury, judge, and lawyers. A certain license will be allowed so that witnesses can demonstrate more physically than they would in a court of law, and the jury should be allowed to ask questions.

Storytelling. This has a function similar to that of the previous game. Players should arrange themselves comfortably around the space and focus on the center. One of the players is the storyteller or troubador—if you wish to specify the environment, it can be a medieval hall, a Victorian parlor, a Christmas party, depending upon the nature of the story to be told. The storyteller then narrates the story, with as much acting out of the actions and demonstration of the characters involved as he thinks necessary to entertain and illustrate the theme. Stories from Dickens—such as *The Pickwick Papers* and *A Christmas Carol*—are especially good for this exercise, as are biblical tales such as David and Goliath and the coming of the wise men. A player may also use a historical narrative based upon his own experience.

Players take turns being storyteller, and after each tale the group should discuss the clarity of the narrative: Was there too much detail? Were the characters sufficiently distinguished? Were they overelaborated? How effective were the gestic qualities used? This is a good exercise for maintaining thematic focus, direct communication, imagination, and selectivity of gestus.

Roundalay. This is another exercise used by Brecht. Players sit in a circle. One begins a poem, which is picked up by each of the other players in turn so that it becomes a round. As each player joins in he takes a specific vocal character attitude. Brecht's favorite poem was this one:

> A dog went into the kitchen
> And stole an egg from the cook,
> The cook took his cleaver
> And cut the dog in two.
> The other dogs came in
> And dug him a grave,
> And put on it a headstone
> With the following epitaph:
> A dog went into the kitchen
> Etc.

One player would take the vocal attitude of the dog: he was hungry, he had puppies to feed, he was a petty thief; another player the attitude of the cook; another the grave-digging dogs. There are many possibilities. Nursery rhymes or any poems involving many characters can be used for this exercise.

Machine. This is a very basic acting exercise. Players stand in a circle. One goes into the center and begins a simple and repetitive physical movement. The other players join in, one at a time, adding a movement that relates to those that have gone before, until a machine is created by the bodies and their movements. With inexperienced players the first machines will tend to be vertical and have a lot of arm movement. Coach players to use their whole bodies and every plane of the space. The game should be repeated several times, with sounds added to the movements. The game is excellent as a warm-up, and helps to develop ensemble relationships. Its usefulness for epic acting is that it creates a scenic gestus—the completed machine—out of the sum of the individual gestuses—each player's specific movement. When the players have become adept at the game give them a specific focus for their machine, one having some kind of economic or social significance—a machine for the creation of nuclear energy; a machine for building robots; a machine for political brainwashing. Finally, have the players repeat these machines, asking each player to take a critical attitude towards them, which will be manifested in the way that he performs his gestus. Discuss with the players what adjustments were made from performing a simple movement, to performing it with a specific focus, and then with a critical attitude. This is a very good early exercise, as it helps actors get a clear sense of gestus as the embodiment of meaning in a physical attitude.

Common Task. Players pair off. One of them performs some everyday working task—digging a garden, washing up, changing a tire, changing bed linen. This should last about a couple of minutes, and should focus upon highly specific details. The other player then repeats his partner's performance as accurately as possible. He then repeats it a second time with whatever adjustments necessary to clarify the nature of the task. He may wish to omit some details, add others, change rhythms, and so on. The players then discuss the differences in performance of the task, paying particular attention to accuracy of detail, clarity, and the essential actions. The exercise may be repeated with each player taking a particular social or economic attitude to the task—a trade unionist changing the tire on a Rolls Royce; an out-of-work engineer digging the garden; an impoverished student changing the linen in an expensive hotel. Taking a critical attitude should alter not the basic detail of the task, but the way in which that detail is performed.

Social Mirror. Players pair off and begin a simple mirror exercise, establishing good concentration and exchange of rhythms. When the game is well under way suggest broad characters to the players—housewife, model, truck driver—and let them base their mirror movements upon a physical sense of the gestures and rhythms of such a character. Have the players shake out and change partners every few minutes, to keep them relaxed as well as concentrated and to stimulate their imagination. Continue the game, now giving broad socioeconomic situations as the basis for the mirror movements: energy crisis, gas rationing, motherhood, feminism—whatever happens to be topical. Finally, still within the structure of the mirror exercise, give the players a character type and, when it is reflected in the mirror movements, add a socioeconomic situation. The player will now be presenting a movement gestus of a character, and presenting it in such a way as to reflect that character's attitude toward a socioeconomic situation. The exercise must be watched carefully, as there is a fine line between allowing players time to develop their movements validly and tiring them out due to the intense physical concentration the game requires.

Social Critics. This is an extension of the previous exercise. The players scatter about the space and walk around, focusing upon their own rhythms and energy centers. Coach players to change these rhythms and energies by throwing physical changes at them: they are wearing size-twenty shoes; their ankles are tied together; their head swells to twice its size; their arms become six feet long. When the players are accustomed to making these adjustments, throw them characters who have a specific socioeconomic function in a modern political structure, such as teachers, soldiers, lawyers, policemen, preachers, and physicians. The players now explore the movements, rhythms, and energy centers they associate with these characters, until they achieve a highly selective gestus with which they feel comfortable. Now set up a series of improvisa-

tions that allow the players to confront their character gestus with a situation that demands some critical comment from them. For example: a doctor's office with a patient who has a serious problem but no means of paying the physician's fee; an affirmative-action case about a woman teacher denied tenure—this could involve lawyers, educational administrators, judges, and others. Coach players to keep the focus upon the socioeconomic theme (don't let it wander up emotional blind alleys) and the critical playing of the character gestus.

Social Puppets. The exercise begins as the previous one. Players explore movements, rhythms, and energy centers until they feel comfortable with a character gestus. Players now pair off, and each in turn gives the other instructions—actions to play as his character. The instructions should always be given in the third person, past tense: "The soldier was on a route march"; "The solider was under fire."

This is in keeping with Brecht's own use of the third person in rehearsal and with his demand for the historification of the event. There is a sound logic to this that is crucial to epic acting. In one sense an actor knows he is not a soldier and is not under fire. He is an actor in a rehearsal room or on a stage. If he attempts to *relive* in the present an imaginary event, he will constantly come up against that fact and will have a blurred mixture of self and character. What an actor does is *reenact* in the present a past event in which he had no part, an event that is historically laid to rest. In the present what an actor does is perform in a play: he will show what he has created. Rehearsing and performing exercises in third-person past tense will keep the distinction clear between the actor and his character. The value of this may be proved in the present exercise. Suppose the situation that the soldier has taken a position and is to dig in. Let his partner give this instruction in three different ways: ''Dig in''; ''You were told to dig in''; ''The officer told the soldier to dig in.'' As the order moves from the first-person present to the third-person past, the player/soldier will become more directly related to his space—rather than being on the edge of something ill defined—will relax physically, and will increase his range of movement. He moves from a self-centered, closed position to an other-centered, dynamically extroverted position. His energy is released into his action, which becomes stronger and clearer.

Unmasking. This exercise is done with a series of character masks. Players should begin the exercise by adopting the mask before a mirror and allowing it to be absorbed into their bodies (the technique for this was fully described in the exercise on neutral mask in Chapter 2). When the use of mask is successful, players will discover rhythms, energy centers, and gestures suggested by and appropriate to the mask—in other words, a character gestus deriving from the mask. Players are now asked to unmask and comment upon the attitudes of the mask character they have been presenting. They should do this while holding the mask to one side of their body, so that other players get the impression of the player and the mask as two separate identities, connected by the player's comments To illustrate any comment a player may quickly readopt the mask, present an attitude, then unmask and discuss it. The exercise gives players a strong sense of how the actor, the character gestus, and the concept of commenting upon a character's actions are linked.

Cloning. The exercise is in three parts.

1. Players in turn describe the essential physical qualities of an individual they know, or have seen, while the other players build a character gestus from the description. Players should be coached to reduce their gestus to as few physical attributes as possible.

2. Players scatter around the space and focus upon their own physical rhythms and energy centers. The focus then changes to the other players in the group, and the aim is to clone each other. A player walks behind another player and tries to assume his body rhythms and balance—walk, set of the shoulders, carriage of the head, and so forth. This should be done quickly and economically. As soon as a player has a clear sense of gestus he should move on.

3. Write the names of all players on cards, one to a card. Players pick a card and then have ten minutes to clone the player written on it. Each player works individually, in his own space, to identify, explore, and reduce to an absolute essence the physical properties of his clone. For the game to succeed, players should have known each other for some time. When all the players are ready, the group sits in a circle and each player in turn presents his clone to the group by performing a simple action. The group then has to identify the player being cloned. A successful clone will lead to an immediate and unanimous identification. After each presentation the whole group should discuss the specific attitudes that made the clone identifiable—or why it failed. The best clones will be those created by two or three clearly outlined gestic strokes. In one group with which we have done this exercise there was a trained ballet dancer who always adopted third position when standing at rest. The player who cloned her had noticed this, and using this attitude (gestus) not only immediately identified the person but dissolved the whole group in laughter. The exercise is usually enormous fun for a group, and not only gives excellent practice in the creation of character gestus but helps players to identify their own specific, physical persona and thereby better control it.

SUGGESTED READINGS

BRECHT, BERTOLT, *Antigonemodell* 1948. Berlin: Henschelverlag Kunst und Gesellschaft, 1955.

——————, *The Messingkauf Dialogues*, trans. John Willett. London: Methuen, 1972.

EAGLETON, TERRY, *Marxism and Literary Criticism*. Berkeley: University of California Press, 1976.

ESSLIN, MARTIN, *Brecht: A Choice of Evils*. London: Mercury Books, 1965.

GRAY, RONALD, *Brecht*. London: Oliver & Boyd, 1961.

WEIDELI, WALTER, *The Art of Bertolt Brecht*. New York: New York University Press, 1963.

WILLET, JOHN, *The Theatre of Bertolt Brecht*. London: Methuen, 1967.

——————, ed., *Brecht on Theatre*. New York: Hill & Wang, 1964.

WITT, HUBERT, ed., *Brecht as They Knew Him*. London: Lawrence & Wishart, 1975.

chapter 8

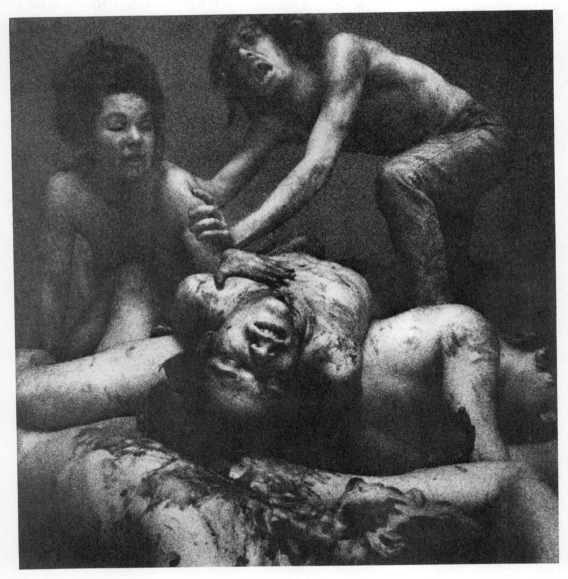

Dionysus in '69.

© *Max Waldman, 1969.*

Artaudian Theatre

BACKGROUND

Identity. Beckett, Brecht, and Artaud were born within ten years of each other, and as such were children of the same cultural environment, subject to similar social influences, and faced with the same existential problem—the absence of deep meaning, the spiritual void of the twentieth century. A difference in personal sensibilities led each to a different solution. Beckett and other playwrights of the absurd made a social/classical response, accepting *le néant* and optimistically continuing to play rational games within the irrational framework of life. Brecht took a political position, hoping to give purpose and meaning to life by changing man's nature through the highly rational and scientific process of the Marxist dialectic.

Artaud's reaction is spiritual and metaphysical: he is the prophet of the irrational or prerational. To some degree that reaction was determined by Artaud's personal inability to conceptualize in a verbally oriented, rational way; it was difficult for him to operate logically in the world around him. Artaud's mind worked in images and thought clusters. He suffered from severe head pains and what were medically described as manifestations of madness. He spent much of his adult life in mental institutions and under the influence of drugs. The inability to think in a Cartesian manner and his highly sensitive poetic nature led Artaud towards a theatre that worked on the nerves and the senses, rejecting the domination of language and intellect. Artaud sought for self-expression through exploration of his inner world and the fantastic and disturbing images he found there. Though a victim of his own mental disturbances and psychic energies, he intuited a sense of life of greater magnitude and intensity than that imprisoned within the logical forms and narrow social structure of twentieth-century society. He attempted to express this through a "theatre of cruelty," but his illness prevented him from carrying out much practical work. It is through his writings that his sense of theatre has had significant influence upon contemporary practitioners, and Artaud has come to be recognized as one of the great prophets and catalysts of the twentieth century.

Romanticism and Revolution. Artaud's sense of life was directly opposed to that created by the rational and scientific tradition of the eighteenth century, which culminated in capitalistic industrial society and the bourgeois culture of the late nineteenth century. With the comforts and technological conveniences of this bourgeois society came its discontents—the absence of eros, of fantasy, of deep feeling and physical expression. The price of civilization was the petrification of man's inner self, his separation from all experience of life in a nonrational, sensual, all-embracing fashion. The theatre Artaud discovered in Paris in the 1920s seemed to represent all the worst values of bourgeois culture. It was a literary theatre dominated by the importance of text.[1] Intellectual, nonphysical, static, and verbal, it was stultified by recitation of dead masterpieces, or trafficked in cheap boulevard entertainment.

---

[1] Nineteenth-century education tended towards textual explication—the dead end of universal literacy. This final triumph of mind and rationality over body and instinct can be dated from Descartes' division of man into a separate body and mind, shortly after the development of print, which reinforced emphasis upon intellect.

Unable to respond to this form of theatre and instinctively opposed to the values it represented, Artaud wanted a "true theatre [which] disturbs the senses' repose, frees the repressed unconscious, incites a revolt."[2] The revolt was as much social as theatrical. Artaud saw theatre as a means of freeing man from his cultural restrictions: to change the form of theatre was to change the life of man. Artaud believed that bourgeois culture had never been at one with life, but had tyrannized it. Theatre must reveal how man's social condition is iniquitous; it must break through the dead encrustation of bourgeois forms that have spiritually and creatively warped and restricted man, to regain touch with the profound poetry, the deepest source, "the obscure root of the scream," from which all true human culture flows.

Artaud's is an essentially revolutionary and romantic spirit. It manifests a desire to return to an idealized past, to a communal, tribal sensibility where man's senses are at one with his surroundings: a prelogical time before our Protestant, capitalist, individualistic ethos analyzed and compartmentalized man and alienated him from his true relationship with the nature both inside him and without. Through theatre Artaud wished to reachieve an authentic human experience, to connect with "the force that through the green fuse drives the flower," to use Nietzsche's term. Artaud is at one with Nietzsche in wishing to release the Dionysian force in man—a unifying, life-giving, celebratory, sexual power too long crushed by the dead hand of industrial civilization. Artaud shared with Nietzsche the spirit of messianic revolt—the will of the poet to play the Messiah, to perceive and transmit dreams from the cosmos. Perhaps the best example of the way in which the social revolutionary and the romantic go hand in hand in Artaud's theatre comes from the opening of *Paradise Now*,

created by the Living Theatre, disciples of the Artaudian sensibility: "I demand everything—total love, an end to all forms of violence and cruelty such as money, hunger, prisons, people doing work they hate. I demand it now."

Cruelty. There might seem to be a contradiction in the Living Theatre, self-avowed disciples of Artaud, demanding an end to cruelty, while Artaud himself took cruelty as the essence of his theatre. But it is the cruelty of social oppression the Living Theatre wishes to root out, which is entirely consistent with the cauterizing nature of the cruelty Artaud perceived. Artaud had little chance to practice his theatre, and his writings, though copious, tend to be abstract and metaphysical. While the precise practical expression of his theatre is subject to interpretation, the aesthetic and purpose of the theatre of cruelty is clear, despite early misinterpretations of the quality and function of "cruelty."

The essential purpose of cruelty is to smash through the veneer of bourgeois civilization to reach an organic, elemental culture. Artaud dismissed the realistic theatre—occupied with the accurate reproduction of life's trivia—and the concept of masterpieces, which he perceived as having a deadening and repressive effect. He felt that all forms of sacred art had been destroyed by bourgeois values and that people were hungry for an experience of the sacred and profane. His theatre would unleash human appetites, express the potentiality of life in its most transcendent form, including love, crime, drugs, war, incest, and revolution. Cruelty, as expressed by Charles Marowitz, one of Artaud's most fervent disciples, is "the exposure of mind, heart and nerve ends to the gruelling truths behind a social reality that deals in psychological crises when it wants to be honest and political evils when it wants to be responsible, but rarely if

---

[2] Antonin Artaud, *The Theatre and Its Double*, trans. Mary Richards (New York: Grove Press, 1958), p. 28.

Detail from *The Garden of Earthly Delights* by Hieronymus Bosch suggests some of the intensely physical and uninhibited images of Artaud.

ever confronts the existential horror behind all psychological and social facades."[3]

Cruelty is above all rigor. It is a metaphysical cruelty—implacable, incandescent, determined and absolute. It is free from hatred and desire for vengeance; it is a pure, detached feeling that is capable of overriding everything else in life. It does not necessarily involve sadism and bloodshed, but it does not shun them if they serve the violent intention of the attack upon the senses. It is the cruelty of man confronting his destiny at the most intense edge of his being. Artaud called for violent physical images to crush and hypnotize the sensibility of the spectators, and suggested actors be like martyrs, burnt alive but still signaling to us through the flames.

[3] Charles Marowitz, *The Act of Being* (London: Secker & Warburg, 1978), p. 147.

A strong sense of the violence, sexuality, and debased religiosity of one aspect of the theatre of cruelty comes through in this production of *No Orchids for Miss Blandish.*

Citizens' Theatre Company, Glasgow.

In a famous image Artaud likened his theatre to a plague that breaks down normal human functions, leads to delirium, visions, strange images, and sends the last of the living howling through the streets committing gratuitous acts against "normal" nature. Like the plague, the theatre must compel men to see themselves as they truly are, without the mask of lies and hypocrisy that obscures the clarity of the senses. Like the plague, cruelty finally achieves a release, an act of sincerity in which man unveils his true self, free from custom and accepted behavior. The release is also a purgation brought about through the intense impact upon the senses made by the physical images of the theatre of cruelty.

His emphasis upon the physical aspects of performance relates Artaud to Meyerhold,[4] but contains a much more apocalyptic sensibility. Artaud was also strongly influenced by the gestural vocabulary of Balinese theatre, which confirmed his belief that theatre's impact should come through physical images, and signs that contained sacred truths. This sense of sacred signs, of the god

[4] Myerhold was the disciple of Stanislavski who emphasized the importance of physical action to an almost gymnastic degree, through his principle of bio-mechanics.

The apocalyptic and physically imagistic quality of Artaud is suggested by this engraving of hell by William Blake.

in the object, let Artaud to his belief in the power of totemism and ritual, and to consider myths containing man's earliest response to the great mysteries of life as a dynamic source of drama.

The aesthetic of the theatre of cruelty:

sought to break through the veneer of bourgeois culture by an intense and rigorous impact.

rejected literary, psychological, and intellectually didactic theatre.

wished to return to a theatre of myth and ritual, as known to ancient cultures.

emphasized dream, fantasy, and archetype.

demanded a new theatrical language of physical signs and hieroglyphs.

created an all-embracing sensual impact and spectacle.

aimed at a therapeutic purgation in the spectator.

Artaud summed up his intention succinctly in talking of his most famous production, *The Cenci:*

My heroes dwell in the realm of cruelty and must be judged outside of good and evil. They are incestuous and sacriligious, they are adulterers, rebels, insurgents and blasphemers. And that cruelty in which the entire work is bathed is not a purely corporal cruelty, but a moral one; it goes to the extremity of instinct and forces the actor to plunge right to the roots of his being so that he leaves the stage exhausted. A cruelty which acts as well upon the spectator and should not allow him to leave the theatre intact, but exhausted, involved; perhaps transformed.[5]

Interpretation and Synthesis. Artaud's is a theatre of self and of self-sacrifice, a journey in search of his own tormented personality. Unable to relate to or function within the social and spiritual restrictions of twentieth-century society, he turned his own quest for ultimate self-expression, for the impossible meaning that lies beneath nature's deepest mysteries, into a ceremonial journey towards knowledge of man's unknowable self. The "martyrs" of his theatre, in the midst of a stage exploding with images and gorged with feeling, signal with intense clarity through the sacrificial flames.

The themes Artaud based his theatre on were the ultimate truths of man's existence: creation, chaos, birth, death, eros. These are the myths man has inherited through his blood and his religions—the very stuff of the human collective unconscious. In specific theatrical terms he suggested reinterpretations of Elizabethan and Jacobean plays ('Tis Pity She's a Whore), romantic melodramas (The Cenci), and the use of biblical stories and those of the Marquis de Sade (note Peter Brook's "theatre of cruelty" production of Peter Weiss's play known in the shortened title as Marat/Sade). Artaud wished to release, in a controlled theatrical environment, the lusts and passions that are mixed with creative energies in the darker corners of man's soul. Vicariously purged of blood-stained instincts, the actor and the audience could pursue a life of peace, freedom, and harmonious creative expression.

Body Over Mind. Artaud's instincts struck their most responsive chord in the 1960s. That decade marked a social, political, and

cultural watershed in its rejection of many of the humanistic, rational, and scientific values handed down by the Renaissance and Enlightenment, and of the repressive economic and social structures that had grown up around them. Capitalism and Christianity seemed to have failed. The existential void had no logical hitching posts, no rational paths. Man had to come to terms with randomness, disorder, and simultaneity, and for a while the perceived solution was to "blow one's mind" and follow the dictates of the body. A physical theatre responded to this need for physical solutions. Fellow feeling, both in a literal meaning of tactile sensation and in its corporate sense of close human relationships, translated into a theatre of sensual communication and ritualized group activity. At the beginning of their Paradise Now members of the Living Theatre moved amongst the audience chanting "I can't take off my clothes," "I can't travel without a passport"—making contact with the audience and ritualistically underlining the restrictions upon man's bodily freedoms of being naked and traveling where he wishes.

The all-embracing physical demands of Artaud's theatre and its antiliterary stance were reinforced by the perceptions of Marshall McLuhan. In his highly influential sociological theses Understanding Media and The Medium is the Message, McLuhan suggested that the worldwide proliferation of media had turned the world into a global village. Post-Renaissance man had been rationalized into using but a part of his sensory capacity, and had hidden feeling beneath intellect and the printed word. But now the imagistic world of film, televison, and visual immediacy could return to man his capacity for a total sensual experience of life in a preliterate, prerational, multi-focused and many-faceted way. Such a thesis is supported by much of what has happened in the broad world of art. Action painting and collages seek the direct involvement of the artist with his work, and the physical impact of op, pop and psychedelic art and, above all, electronic music is designed to arouse, disturb, and possess the spectator/listener and transform him

[5] Antonin Artaud, Oeuvres complètes, Vol. V (Paris: Gallimard, 1964), p. 309; our translation.

and his perception of the world—a "cruelty" of powerful and intense sensation, which equates with Artaud's use of the word.

As befitting a prophet, Artaud was some thirty years before his time and had little opportunity to practice his theatrical intuitions. The meeting point for his instincts and the social forces that would respond to them came in the heady, revolutionary days of the 1960s, when a new sense of life reinforced the need for a new sense of theatre. The radical social and moral attitudes of that decade have now been winnowed out and significant changes absorbed into the mainstream of life. In a similar fashion Artaud's ideas, explored, practiced, and refined by various theatre groups, have come permanently to affect theatre practice with a general Artaudian sensibility—as well as defining a specific form of theatrical event.

Ideas in Action. Artaud's immediate disciples took his ideas in various directions. Perhaps his most famous follower is Jerzy Grotowski, whose Polish Laboratory Theatre developed a series of stringent exercises to support the physical demands of Artaud's theatre, and formulated an aesthetic of the "holy" actor in a "poor" theatre. Grotowski emphasized the self-sacrificing religiosity of Artaud's ethic—his theatre smacked of the self-flagellating abnegation and transcendental emotion of medieval monks. Grotowski's actors were the prime focus of his theatre: everything was stripped away to reveal the actor in an intense confrontation with the great human myths and legends. Through this confrontation the actor would reveal the modern significance of the myth, touching in the process his own deepest self and that of the audience.

Richard Schechner and his Performance Group emphasized the all-embracing "environmental" aspects of Artaud, experimenting with theatrical spaces to include the audience totally as participants in the event. Schechner's theatre was also sensual and tactile, using nudity and physical contact to make moral statements. The Living Theatre

was similar to Schechner in its physical stance, but more aggressive in its social statements and highly tribal in life style. Joseph Chaikin's Open Theatre created its own rituals to comment upon the political and moral problems of contemporary man. It dealt in strong images and symbolic gesture to try to alter the spiritual shape and purpose of social man. Chaikin expressed his purpose as "to shake off the sophistication of our time by which we close ourselves up, to become vulnerable again . . . , become naive, innocent, cultivate our deeper climates—our dread. Only then will we be able to express the attitudes we hold in common with the outside world."[6]

Interpretation of Artaud was not rigid. Peter Brook felt Artaud's ideas could help theatre practitioners to rediscover true Elizabethan relationships linking the private and public worlds, the intimate and the crowded, the secret and the open, the vulgar and the mystical. Not all of Artaud's disciples agreed upon the precise interpretation of his principles. Some took ritual and rites of passage further than he, and explored the shamanistic roots of the actor; others worked physically around and amongst the spectators, whereas Artaud would simply surround them with the total impact. But that his followers shared his basic sense of theatre is witnessed by the names of the more important groups—"Open," "Living," "Performance," "Laboratory."

What we are calling Artaudian theatre is a matter of degree—it is not as much a precise form as a set of attitudes, approaches, aims. Not all the elements we are discussing will be found in any "Artaudian" event at any one time—the exact synthesis will depend upon the aims of the actors and director. But the influence of Artaud, as prophet and catalyst, is so widespread that no modern actor can regard himself as complete without an understanding of his essential sensibility. This will lead him to the choices and adaptations he must make when working within the style.

---

[6] Quoted in Robert Pasolli, *A Book on the Open Theatre* (New York: Bobbs-Merrill, 1970), p. 95.

INTRINSIC DEMANDS

Form. The idea of form—indeed, the whole concept of "intrinsic demands"—works on a set of presumptions that are not as directly applicable to Artaudian theatre as to other more strictly text-oriented kinds. The intrinsic demands and the performance demands of Artaudian theatre are more closely linked, because the actor is more involved in the actual creation of the event. In most theatre there is a literary form that is converted by actors, directors, design artists, and technicians into a physical form. The intrinsic demands of the literary form are those elements that the playwright both consciously and unconsciously introjects in his text and that must be unlocked and revealed by the performing artists through their understanding of the form, sensibility, and values of the text. Given this understanding, the performing artist breathes life into the literary form by the exercise of his imagination and technique.

Because Artaudian theatre is not essentially a literary theatre, the form tends to be the physical shape. The text, score, or scenario of Artaudian theatre usually evolves from a physical form rather than the other way around. Artaudian events can be evolved in different ways. If a text is used, it becomes a pretext—not a literary artifact to be regarded as sacrosanct, but a sounding board or artistic trampoline. Against this the actor tests his responses to the text's deepest impulses and creates a physical form that reflects those responses. The actor is not trying to discover and recapitulate the playwright's precise intentions, but is using the playwright's ideas and intuitions to discover and reveal his own reaction to the deepest purposes of the play. This was the principle Grotowski employed when working on such texts as *Akropolis* and *The Constant Prince;* it was also Richard Schechner's intention in transforming Euripides' *Bacchae* into *Dionysus in '69.* The term for this process is *confrontation.* In speaking of *Akropolis* Grotowski said: "One

structures the montage so that this confrontation can take place. We eliminate those parts of the text that have no importance for us. We did not wish to write a new play, we wished to confront ourselves."[7]

Frequently Artaudian theatre is not developed from a text but from themes, impulses, or ideas that concern the participants. The Open Theatre developed their *Terminal* from an exploration of the concept of death. Conversely, their *Serpent* evolved from an interest in the idea of original creation and original sin—the myth of the Garden of Eden, man's paradise lost. *The Serpent* became a text in collaboration with Jean Claude van-Itallie—a not infrequent method of working whereby a playwright sets down the sound and shape of the theatrical piece as it is originated by the actors in their exploration of impulses and ideas. It is then reconfronted by the actors, and the process continues until all participants are satisfied with what has been produced. This is the essence of physical responses determining a textual form.

With or without a text, the shape of the theatrical event is determined by the directness of the participants' physical responses to the ideas or images being confronted. The concepts are not trivial, and the responses are the deepest and most intense the participants are capable of—clichés are constantly discarded in an attempt to discover profound images that enable the participants to relate to each other and create the form of the event through physical communication.

The form of the event created by the participants' confrontation of the pretext or basic idea is frequently that of a ritual or rite of passage. It is not so much the telling of a story but the exploration of a theme, and one that touches the core of man's identity. The ritual is a search for deep meaning, a rejoicing in naked impulses, and a celebration of the fact of man in all its dimensions. The sacred

---

[7] "Grotowski in Interview," *Tulane Drama Review*, Vol. 13, no. 1 (Fall, 1968), 44.

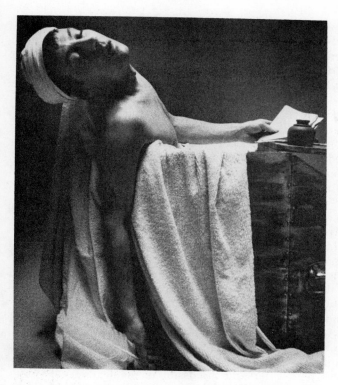

The death of Marat from Peter Brook's Royal Shakespeare Company production. Note the passion and pathos in the ritualistic death, which is staged after the famous painting by David.

© Max Waldman, 1966.

reinforces the profane; there is awe and anger, reverence and defilement. The event is concerned more with process than performance—what happens to the individual as he participates in the movement from one state to another and explores his connection both with other human beings and the forces that surround man's existence. The shape of the event is unlikely to be narrative and logical like a story, but nuclear and imagistic—full of signs and sounds that have an intense significance for the participants. Like the Christian mass with its smell of incense, incantations, symbolic sharing of flesh and blood, and raising of the host, an Artaudian theatrical event physically and spiritually embraces the participants with an intense experience of deep human significance celebrated within a symbolic form.

Actor as Shaman. The return to a search for ritual in theatre equates with the desire of social man to rediscover some sense of unity and communality. Ritual is a formal celebration of a community's identity and faith in itself. Twentieth-century society lacks that sense of faith, and is broken into heterogeneous, self-centered units. The disciples of Artaud attempt to return to the very roots of drama, to bring back communality and combat man's sense of alienation. They wish to rediscover myth and the miraculous, which has been undermined by psychological causations, just as eros has vanished beneath libido to become associated with the dirty, crude, and inelegant instead of the joyfully creative.

Man's earliest rituals were concerned with hunting and sexual activity—with the main events and the cyclical process of man's life. Killing and the restoring of life, nakedness and fertility, the passage from boyhood to manhood, from child to warrior—it is from these that drama takes its preoccupation with violence, love, and death. And it is to these fundamental properties of drama that Artaud wished to return. In such a form of theatre the actor takes on the function of the shaman in those early rites of passage, or the priest in the religious ceremonies that followed them. The actor is a form of priest who builds bridges between the past, himself, and the spectators.[8]

The priest's predecessor, the shaman, conducted the earliest religious ceremonies—the initiation rites of boys at puberty. The reaching of the age of fertility was approached both reverently and ecstatically, befitting a central mystery of life. The shaman was priest and witch doctor; he was in touch with all the spirits, both good and evil, that influenced the community's life. He was the go-between through whom the spirit moved into the audience, transporting both priest and audience with the ecstasy and satisfaction of the event. The shaman connects the different realms of human experience, interprets man to himself, celebrates the ongoing wholeness of the society, and purges it of sickness. The shaman/actor's performance is the revelation of a truth that stands for all. The actor, as descendant of the shaman, was reviled by the established church, which would accept only half of the shamanistic experience—the sentimental celebration of man's potential goodness. The magic, the trickery, the sexual ecstasy was

dismissed The puritanical pursuit of "goodness" finally atrophied man's capacity for total feeling, complete human experience. The priest emasculated the shamanistic spirit and used his spiritual power to whip the Dionysian devil out of man.

The Artaudian actor, as true descendant of the shaman, touches the untouchable, reveals the mysterious, liberates the total spirit. Through the ecstasy of the ceremony man is purged of his darker impulses and the community is cleansed and united. The actor/shaman conducts the rite of passage, which is, to quote the Living Theatre, "a voyage from the many to the one and from the one to the many. It is a spiritual voyage and a political voyage. It is an interior voyage and an exterior voyage for the actors and spectators."[9]

Space. The "voyage," the rite of passage—by whatever description, the theatrical event takes place within space. In the earlier chapters our discussion of the demands of space has been determined either by the theatrical givens of a particular period (for example the architectural nature of the Greek, Elizabethan, or seventeenth-century playhouses), or by the specific form of a play, as in the work of Brecht or Beckett. With Artaudian theatre the space tends not to be either architecturally or textually predetermined, but to be created in accordance with the evolving nature of the event.

Artaud described his sense of staging as "a concrete physical space which asks to be filled and to be given its own concrete language to speak."[10] He suggested that the spectator should be in the center of the space, surrounded by the sights, sounds, and concentrated action of the event. Artaud's own ideas on use of space have been variously interpreted by his followers, but two premises

---

[8] The Latin for priest is *pontifex*, meaning "he who builds bridges."

[9] Julian Beck and Judith Malina, *Paradise Now: A Collective Creation of the Living Theatre* (New York: Random House, 1971), p. 5.

[10] Antonin Artaud, *The Theatre and its Double*, trans. Mary Richards (New York: Grove Press, 1958), p. 37.

seem constant: the audience should be surrounded by the event, and the whole space should be used. Even if a text is being used as a basis for the event, this places no demand for historical accuracy upon the use of space—the demands of period and architectural structure are subordinate to those of actor/audience relationship and physical impact.

Artaudian theatre comes completely out of the proscenium and returns to a medieval, or even pre-Greek quality of staging, bringing theatre full circle and back to its physical roots in ritual whereby space is altered and structured to suit the demands of each particular celebration. Because an open space is concrete yet totally flexible, it can be transformed and articulated to match the shapes and rhythms of the event as it evolves from the responses of the actors. Space never becomes simply an architectural backing to the performance. It is fully involved with the action, affecting and being affected by the

actors: space and impulse, spirit and physical image, movement and characterization are inter-responsive and, evolving together, determine the shape of the event.

Working on this principle, the Performance Group discovered a circular shape for their *Dionysus in '69,* and their *Makbeth* finished up angular, disjointed, and on many levels. Grotowski's company built their setting for *Akropolis* out of stove pipes as the performance proceeded. The shape of an Artaudian performance will also determine the degree of audience participation. How far the audience should be directly involved as participants in the event has been variously interpreted. Artaud seemed to be asking for the audience to be surrounded by the "impact" of the event, but not necessarily for the event to take place amongst the spectators or to include them as participants. One of the points of distinction between ritual and theatre is that ritual includes the whole body

Naked actor in midst of audience during performance of *Dionysus in '69.*

of participants on a more or less equal level, whereas theatre distinguishes between actors and audience and tends to give each a discrete physical space—the spectators are drawn viscerally, emotionally, intellectually into the event, but they are not physically embraced by it or included as direct participants.

Spectator as Participant. To achieve the effect of communality, all-embracing sensibility, and the intense physical impact of "cruelty," Artaud's followers have attempted, to a greater or lesser degree, to use the spectators as participants in the event. Grotowski has solved this problem in the most sophisticated manner—especially in his production of *Faustus*, where the spectators were Faustus's guests at a last supper, sitting around a refectory table while the events leading up to his damnation are related in flashback. In *The Constant Prince* Grotowski again had the spectators surrounding the event, this time as around a bullring or an operating table watching a surgical procedure—the revelation of the actor/character's self—take place. His *Akropolis*, on the other hand, was built and took place amongst the spectators, who became inmates of the concentration camp.

If Grotowski is closest to Artaud in the restraint with which he physically uses audience participation, Richard Schechner takes the concept of involvement much further. Schechner describes his form of theatre as "environmental" to underline the total use of space and the all-embracing nature of the event. The action may take place around, above, behind, below, and among the audience. The experience is totally shared, with body contact taking place between actor and spectator. Spectators may be drawn into and become an integral part of the event. In *Dionysus in '69* spectators took off their clothes and joined naked actors in a ritual celebrating birth, and at the end of the performance ran naked into the streets—thus making the space outside the theatre equiv-

alent with the inner space (and also making a statement about social attitudes towards the body). This is to take Artaudian theatre to its ultimate and attempt to recapitulate predramatic ritual in which all participants are both themselves and actors.

Schechner reinforces the total flexibility of his use of space by employing variable

Audience members engaged in undressing and embracing rituals during a performance of *Dionysus in '69.*

focus—that is, simultaneous actions taking place in different areas of the space. The spectator is involved at different levels and perspectives, and it is not just various sights and sounds with which he is surrounded, but different actions creating a nuclear rather than one-dimensional impression. The multifocal principle is holistic in the tribal sense of many experiences happening at the same time, and is related to McLuhan's tribal-village concept of modern man surrounded by a constantly changing plethora of visual and aural impressions, which he absorbs through all his senses: the experience creates the impact; "the medium is the message." Schechner's principles are perhaps as close to the "happening" as to Artaud, whose sense of embracement was more symbolic and hieroglyphic than directly tactile, and who required a more direct focus for the impact of his "cruelty." But the actor may be exposed to many possible interpretations of Artaudian theatre.

Mise en scène. It is somewhat futile to attempt to discuss costume, lighting, sound—all the effects with which the space is filled—as separate entities. Artaud's intention was that they create an integrated and concrete impact, the *mise en scène*—a dynamic totality of impression that produced the effect of cruelty by the intensity of its assault upon the audience's senses. The actor is in the midst of the *mise en scène*, but not necessarily the most important feature of it. He must be prepared to create sounds, respond to lighting, and wear costumes not in the performance of a specific focused action or as part of the development of a character, but as one of many artifacts geared to making a total impression that may cohere only in the audience's mind. We will discuss below the actor's creation of physical images.

Though he subordinated language to action, Artaud did not dismiss the effect of sound. Inarticulate groans, roars, liturgical chants, folksong, declamation, babblings—

the whole range of human vocal possibility is at the Artaudian actor's disposal. Added to this would be unusual musical instruments capable of new pitches and unbearable noises. The instruments themselves are used as objects—part of the *mise en scène*—and are not separated from the action. Lighting was intended to produce an equally intense impression in the spectator—Artaud was obsessed with red, the color of blood. Threatening, vibrating, penetrating into the audience's mind like blazing arrows, the light, like the sound, should move it to paroxysms of terror, eroticism, anxiety, or love.

Costume, again, will serve the total visual sense of the event, with no restriction in terms of historical accuracy or detail. Although Artaud rejected modern dress because of its limited and specific connotations, costuming has run the gamut from the simplest body coverings, such as T-shirts and leotards, to resplendent and ritualistic dress. The qualities of Artaudian costuming will be body enhancing, timeless, and symbolic: everything from nakedness—the purest and most ritualistic form of body enhancement—to shamanic masks of paint, animal fur, body ornaments and feathers.[11] The Performance Group first used T-shirts in *Dionysus in '69* and then progressed to nakedness. Grotowski used a loincloth for his principal actor in *The Constant Prince* and jute sacks with holes for the actors in *Akropolis*. The function of the costume is not to delimit a situation or specifically define a character—it enhances the total *mise en scène*, reinforcing visual impact and broader meaning.

Light, sound, and costume, together with the plasticity of the actors' bodies, create a mutually supportive and all-embracing *mise en scène.* Images and movements will collide with objects, silences, and aural rhythms and physically surround the spectator, immersing him in a constant but ever changing bath of light, sound, and fantasy to create an in-

[11] The symbolic significance of costuming and properties should be explored, as in American Indian culture, where an eagle feather worn by a shaman symbolized the power of flight.

tense sensual impact—the experience of cruelty.

Hieroglyph. The "signals" through the flames," of which Artaud speaks when discussing the function of the actor, are of an imagistic or hieroglyphic nature. The hieroglyphs, created by the actor's gestures, are not private, psychological, or pantomimic, but of larger symbolic content—metaphysical and archetypal. A hieroglyph is similar to a gestus (which we discussed in the chapter on Brecht), but whereas a gestus may relate directly to external or objective ideas—social, economic, political—a hieroglyph is more metaphysical in its connotations. A hieroglyph relates to spiritual or emotional states or ideas having roots in man's deepest cultural associations—the human "collective unconscious" of which Jung spoke. It is a refinement of intense human essences turned into a physical image.

The hieroglyph will have a poetic rather than a realistic quality. A poetic hieroglyph, played with great intensity, will have far more intense an impact than the literal use of torture. In his production of *Marat/Sade* Peter Brook had Charlotte Corday flagellate de Sade with her hair. This is an essentially Artaudian image, more interesting, more intense in audience impact, and of far broader dramatic significance than any literal whipping of de Sade could be—quite apart from the practical point that no actor could withstand a real whipping throughout the run of a play, and to make a pretense at a "real" whipping is always an inadequate gesture.

Actors' bodies may be used to create collective hieroglyphs such as the womb and vaginal passage created by the Performance Group in *Dionysus in '69*. In this image Dionysus was born through a passageway of naked actors pulsating and groaning in expulsive rhythms. Here the naked body of the mother, the image of birth, and a literal rite of passage is combined in one active hieroglyph compounded of the bodies of many actors who experience the event as individuals and blend their bodies in a group image at the same time. The serpent in the Open Theatre's production of that name was created in a similar manner, a line of actors performing in a serpentine manner to create the image. There was no attempt to imitate a snake, but the qualities of evil and temptation—the serpent's action in the Garden of Eden—were blended into a poetic hieroglyph far more interesting and dynamic than any literal imitation.[12]

The hieroglyphs created by the actors are not played in a random fashion according to the impulse of the moment, but are combined into a score—like a piece of music—that determines the shape of the event. Just as the cruelty called for by Artaud is not literal, neither is the nature of the images. There is a poetic content and a certain symbolic remove about the hieroglyphs, but they are communicated with a great intensity of playing. It is this intense quality of communication, not the nature of the act, that creates the impact of cruelty. There is no contradiction between objectivity of image and intensity of impression. Watch a brilliant moon in a clear, cold, starlit sky: it is removed and objective, yet its all-embracing intensity can be awe-inspiring.

The hieroglyphs must have form and clarity—this calls for disciplined playing. The basic qualities of theatrical performing will apply to Artaudian theatre as to any other style. The Artaudian event is created by the actor—by his impulses and direct confrontation of ideas. The actor has a direct, visceral connection with the event as through an umbilical cord, but in performance his choices are not random—he plays the score of the event that was discovered in its creation. He will reconfront those choices each time he plays the event; he will rediscover and communicate their intensity, but their shape must

---

[12] Note the relationship to the creation of the dragon in the ancient Chinese dance ritual.

Scenic hieroglyph created by actors in Grotowski's *Akropolis.* Note jute-sack costumes and intense facial masks creating a metaphysical image of the concentration-camp experience.

Teatr Laboratorium.

The birth of Dionysus from the Performance Group production.

By permission of Richard Schechner.

be clear and precise, or the event will be a meaningless jumble of emotional pyrotechnics.

PERFORMANCE DEMANDS

Vocal Dynamics. Artaud was not against language per se but against the way in which it dominated the theatre of his time. He felt that all other theatrical qualities were subordinated to rhetoric and the literary expression of the text. The actor was locked into words, and the verbal expression of feeling tended to hide the very thing it was trying to communicate. Language had to become more concrete, have a physical impact, satisfy the sense rather than appeal to the mind.

The voice must be used in unaccustomed ways to express what is normally hidden beneath the patina of polite speech; the information it will convey will be less intellectual, more visceral. The voice must not be limited to the throat and head but be connected with the body. The reserved, word-oriented, intellectual tradition of social relationships and the rhetorical, literary tradition of the theatre meant that ideas remained in and were expressed from the mind. The whole emphasis is upon the head and upper part of the body. The immediate impulse and response, instead of connecting with the breath deep in the solar plexus (the traditional seat of the emotions), is cut off by the mind and filtered through the intellect to come out in words as a pale imitation of the original inspiration.[13] Artaud wished to use words as a concrete means of expression conveying an emotional content arising from every part of the body and impelled by one of the body's two basic rhythms—the powerful pulsing of the lungs.

[13] *Inspiration* literally means the taking in of the breath, which shows the original connection among impulse, breath, and creative feeling.

In technical terms the actor must develop his breathing capacity and control so that he may make as full use as possible of the resonating capacity of the body. He must be aware of diaphragmatic rhythms and connect vocal with physical responses (see the sound and movement exercises below). He must stop "thinking" about his reactions and learn to respond in a more immediate and visceral manner. The actor must get out of the "academic" habit of prejudging his responses because he is afraid to make mistakes. We are taught not to scream and shout—in pleasure or pain—in public. The actor must break down this social barrier and give air to his deepest animal sounds.

Artaudian theatre does not destroy language; it gives it broader and deeper dimensions. The intellectual information of the words is less important than the poetic feeling the sound conveys. In working on a text the actor will discover where clarity of information is important and where concrete vocal sound best conveys the impact of the moment. The text will be reduced to its most essential elements. Indiscriminate howling and groaning are of little value if they do not illustrate action or communicate passion. The Artaudian actor has to be hyperverbally aware, because he must be conscious of the sound beneath the word so that he may give the intention of the word full emotional value. He must make use of the emotive potential of vowels, especially *a*, *o*, and *u*, the piercing quality of *e* and *i*, and the sibilants. The onomatopoeic roots and incantatory rhythms from which our verbal language has evolved create the vocal dynamics of Artaudian theatre, which are strongly and directly connected to bodily impulses as in the earliest predramatic rites and rituals.

Via Negativa. Artaud left no details of an acting process; this has had to be explored by his disciples, such as Chaikin, Schechner, and especially Jerzy Grotowski. It is Grotowski who has given a name to the basic approach of an Artaudian actor—the *via negativa.* This method proceeds by an eradication of blocks and resistances that prevent a performer from fully acting out the impulses he finds within himself when confronting a role. Rather than building up a collection of external attitudes, the actor approaches the part like a sculptor, chipping away to discover the form that exists within the stone. This is consistent with the larger social purpose of Artaud's theatre— breaking down taboos and social masks to touch and reveal a true humanity. It is a one-to-one relationship with the role, a conscious act of self-exploration and revelation catalyzed by the confrontation of self and role.

The willingness to reveal the self, to get behind politeness, good taste, all the social masks, is a fundamental requirement of the actor in Artaudian theatre. With Yeats he

The physical and spiritual intensity of the "holy" actor: Ryszard Cieslak in Grotowski's *The Constant Prince.*

Teatr Laboratorium.

must be willing to reveal the truth, even if it is "sinful" and unattractive:

> I must lie down where all the ladders start
> In the foul rag and bone shop of the heart.[14]

Too many young actors want to appear "sympathetic" and are unwilling to take risks for fear of failure. If, as actors, we are constantly monitoring ourselves, looking for the right result, then only the mind and not the body works and we are limiting our range of choices. The ability to be still and naked, both literally and metaphorically, is a basic starting point for the Artaudian actor. To be still at the core of his self; to have that balance at the center that allows all impulses to flow freely through him; to be stripped of all physical masks that might block the full expression of feeling—this is the goal. It is not easy to achieve. It requires tremendous personal commitment and discipline to achieve the physical and psychical fine tuning this state demands. To take off your clothes and lie down is not to be still and naked. Equally, to perform exaggerated bodily gestures without physical flexibility and control is to deal in awkward self-indulgence. The risk of self-indulgence, always a trap for the actor, is never more present than in the Artaudian form. Self-revelation is a challenge, not an excuse for the easy gesture, the shallow emotion. There is a need for stringency, discipline, detachment; to be carried along on a sentimental flood tide of emotion is to be soft, excessive, unconvincing, and to deal in generalizations that will have no intensity of impact.

There is about the actor in an Artaudian event an air of secular holiness of almost self-flagellating, medieval intensity. He sacrifices himself to the act and by challenging himself confronts others with their own truth. Like the shaman, the actor makes the intangible visible, translates his spiritual ecstasy into practical communication with the audience.

[14] W. B. Yeats, "The Circus Animals' Desertion," in *Last Poems*.

The actor is saying to the audience: see me being spiritually dismembered, see my guts being revealed. The audience participates in the conflict, agony, death, dismemberment at the deepest possible level. Whatever the apparent and superficial meanings of the event, the performer is always trying to contact the audience at the core of its humanity, purging and healing it with his own passion. That passion can be touched and revealed only by the process of *via negativa*—the removal of all blocks that stand in the way of the most direct, simple, and pure response.

Confrontation. Self-revelation is not an egotistical act; it takes place within a focused theatrical context—the confrontation of the text, myth, idea, whatever the impulse for the event may be. The actor uses the object of confrontation as a tool with which to chip away at or penetrate himself to discover his responses. The actor does not "play" Hamlet, or the Constant Prince, he does not build up attributes or adopt any exterior mask; rather, he removes anything that stands in the way of his most intense personal response to the role. The Artaudian actor is not trying to find the detailed and specific responses of a character in terms of any biographical data. It is the total, not the particular, with which he is concerned—instincts and consciousness rather than social and historical detail.

To confront the role is to use it both as trampoline and scalpel. The actor researches the situation with his body. He probes for responses, finds associations, contacts, and relationships, and then uses these as a springboard for confronting the spectator with the hyper-intensity of his discoveries. In rehearsal the performer selects from among his discoveries those responses that create the shape of the event with the greatest intensity and clarity. These become the score of the event, a series of consistently motivated actions. The score is fixed, but does not restrict the actor. In the first place, it is a part of him, created from his own organic responses. Second, it is not rigid—it is rather like two banks of a river between which the actor flows in performance.

The act of performance is a further confrontation. The actor confronts the audience through the score, adjusting to the living moment in the fluid space, and in this final act of self-revelation draws the audience into the event, embraces them with its "cruelty," and leaves them purged and whole.

Physical Imagination. The score is the "signals through the flames"; it is the series of physical gestures, signs, hieroglyphs discovered by the actors in their confrontation of the action. The hieroglyphic gesture carries the sense of the action powerfully to the spectators. Artaudian theatre takes these gestures and pushes them as far as they will go. They have the impact of silent blows, and create a resonance far beyond that of a detailed, realistic, psychological gesture. Forms of common or natural behavior often mask deeper truths. A man who is in touch with his deepest responses often begins to weep and laugh, to dance and sing; he does not behave "normally." He uses rhythmically articulated physical movements to express his elevated state. A hieroglyph expresses just such a response on the part of the actor. It is

Stark simplicity in use of actors' bodies and stage properties to produce highly charged yet cool poetic image in a production of *Chinchilla*.

Citizens' Theatre Company, Glasgow.

not a common gesture such as might be made over a cup of coffee, with a cigarette or a toss of the head. Anger is not a tick of irritation; it is a metaphysical gesture that might disturb the gods.

While the hieroglyph played intensely will draw strong supporting emotion from the body, feeling, as such, is not a dominant requirement of the Artaudian actor. Feeling has no value unless shaped into a communicative image. Feeling without form can be soft, mawkish, sit like a leaden pool upon the stage. A gesture, a sign, a hieroglyph is a statement in itself: it doesn't require the motor power of feeling to register, but when it is played with the intensity demanded of the Artaudian actor, it has the potency of "cruelty" in its impact.

Discovery through the body is the method of the Artaudian actor. Through the process of *via negativa* all that is unnecessary is stripped away so that the body's imagination may react directly to the impulses that result from the actor's confrontation of the action. Inevitably the actor will at first respond with clichés. The social training of many years cannot be quickly overcome. The second stage is likely to be a new set of clichés. They will not be mask social responses, but will still reflect aspects of the actor's self that are personal and idiosyncratic. It is a deeper response the actor must seek, one that finds its roots in the collective iconography, symbology, hagiology of man—the shared unconsciousness that is the evolutionary product of millenia.

The actor will find props useful in his physical exploration. Not the properties of our everyday life, the bric-à-brac of realism such as cups and saucers, cigarettes, glasses, books—the Artaudian actor does not "measure out his life in coffee spoons." The properties have a less specific identity—colored ribbons, staffs, pieces of cloth, nets, ropes, pieces of paper—and may, by the way in which they are used, be given a highly symbolic value, just as the wafer and the wine become the flesh and blood of Christ in the Christian Mass. By the use of gesture the ac-

tor can transform a piece of blue silk into a rippling sea, a stool into an altar, a piece of glass into a teardrop—and by the intensity of his performance the audience is seared by the joy, pain, or fervor of the images he communicates.

Images in Action. One of the difficulties in talking of the Artaudian experience is its essentially physical nature—any description will lose intensity and appear dead upon the written page. Despite this we are going to conclude with some images and hieroglyphs discovered in workshops we have conducted on Artaudian theatre, in the hope that they might further clarify the way in which the actor approaches the Artaudian experience. Two young actors working on the chorus and messenger speeches near the end of *The Bacchae* (roughly lines 1,000-1,100), which describe the death of Pentheus, used ivy leaves, red ribbons, a stepladder, and red paint to create some intensely dramatic images. They approached the spectators from behind and used the words "run, run" from the text to drive them from their seats into the center of the stage space. In the space one of the actors perched on top of the stepladder, garlanded with ivy, as Pentheus hiding in his fir tree. The other actor danced in amongst the spectators, using Euripides' frenzied words to create a great physical excitement. Then she started to shake the stepladder (as Pentheus was shaken from his tree by the Maenads). The shaking had reached hysterical pitch when the actor playing Pentheus fell with a dynamic, acrobatic leap into the audience. The other actor, declaiming Euripides' lines about the Maenads tearing off Pentheus' flesh, now tied red ribbons to various parts of his body—this, in connection with the intensity of the lines, gave an extraordinary effect of strips of bleeding flesh. Finally, as the Maenads scattered the torn body of Pentheus, so the actor ripped the ivy leaves into pieces and threw them amongst the audience. Then she took a bowl of red paint and anointed each member of the audience—an act of primitive communion suggesting that we all are blood brothers and share the guilt for the spilling of our brother's blood.[15]

On another occasion a white sheet was brilliantly used as a symbol throughout an original piece, connecting images and denoting the action of the event. At different times the sheet was a cloak—the removal of which represented a physical stripping and transfer of dominance—a serpent, representing sensuality and threat; a whip, tantalizing and punishing; and a shroud, creating the image of death. It was also used as an umbilical cord and, passing through the crotch of one player to the crotch of another, represented the passage of semen in the sexual act.

In both the instances described above, it was the way in which the actor used the props that created the validity of the images and the largeness and intensity of the playing that produced its powerful effect upon the audience. The Artaudian actor must beware of lack of total commitment; he cannot afford to teeter on the edge of an image. If he holds back and fails to connect viscerally with what he is doing, he will find himself playing an empty attitude rather than a hieroglyphic action. The image may be admired, but it will not have a "cruel" impact. Clarity is also important; a few strong images will have more impact than a lot of busy activity.

Avoid naturalistic detail and voyeurism. Copulation is much less dramatic than its symbolic enactment—it is pornographic rather than erotic. The poetic hieroglyph played with intensity has a larger impact than the literal use of sexuality or bestiality. The Artaudian actor must be able to distinguish between sensuality and mere salacity, between catharsis and nausea. These distinctions are connected to the level of exploration and discovery reached by the actor in his confrontation with the text or idea of the

[15] There is an interesting analogy here with the "blooding" of a new member of a hunt. When the fox has been killed, the new member is smeared with its blood—still today in civilized old England and New England.

event. The deeper the discovery, the more authentic the image and the greater the impact. The rehearsal process is the selection of the appropriate, the demanding, the right gesture. Once discovered this becomes a part of the score—the signs, images, hieroglyphs by which the impact of the event is communicated. The score is structured, disciplined. The spontaneity of the event comes from the manner in which the score, and thus the audience, is reconfronted by the actor. In performance the actor rediscovers his initial impulse and plays out the act of self-revelation with complete sincerity through the articulated score—but now in confrontation with the audience.

Process. In Artaudian theatre the act of performance is never finally completed; it is always in a state of growth, as each event brings a new audience, a new temporal situation, and thus a new set of circumstances to be confronted by the actor. The score does not change, but the confrontation of the score will lead to new discoveries at each performance. The actor should thus avoid the danger of trying to imitate himself, recapture the conditions of a previous performance, or be rigidly focused upon a particular goal. He should concentrate upon opening himself up to the situation, responding to the moment—within the outline of the score.

This sense of performance is allied to the broader sensibility of Artaud, who remarked that some become priests and others practice religion as part of their daily lives. The sense of actor as shaman as priest is very strong in Artaudian theatre, and this relates the process of performance to the process of life itself. Life can never be fixed; experience changes as we live it. As human beings we must never become petrified, but must continue to reexplore ourselves and confront new experiences. Life is not a finished performance. We cannot catch the moment and repeat it; we must learn from the moment and move on. So with Artaudian theatre: performance is part of the process of life, and it is the process—

the reconfrontation and discovery—that is of the essence.

Macrocosmic Mask.

The Artaudian actor does not create an individual mask of character. The mask of the event is all-encompassing; it is the completed, performed score. Each actor confronts his own part of that score and creates the larger mask in cooperation with his fellow actors. The actor does not attempt to disguise his own persona, but neither is he simply performing as himself—he is revealing his responses to the situation in the form of images and hieroglyphs that are larger, more significant than any individual.

An actor normally constructs a mask by discovering and rearranging those elements of himself that fit the character—the audience has an experience of the character through the agency of the actor. The Artaudian actor gives the audience an experience of his (the actor's) self through the way in which he confronts his score of actions. Artaudian acting does not involve the creating of a mask in the normally accepted stage sense. It is, rather, the creation of a score of images and the confrontation of these in performance to discover a set of responses. It is an act of dynamic nakedness: it operates in an area between self and character where the actor's own self is exteriorized and transformed into elements of the total scenic mask (or *mise en scène*) of the production. It is not mimetic; it is both "real"—in that the actor reveals his deepest self—and highly theatricalized—in that the actor's responses are much larger than "real" life, are hieroglyphic in form and metaphysical in value.

Different Masks for Different Styles.

In this last section on character/mask we are going to suggest some rule-of-thumb distinctions among various stylistic approaches to the creation of mask:

1. In the most *naturalistic forms* of acting—film and television—the actor tends to use his own psychological and emotional qualities as those of the character—he makes the mask fit himself. This is really personality acting, a form of selected "being."

2. In most forms of *"realistic" acting* the actor takes on the life of the character. He plays from himself, fits himself to the mask.

3. In *Brechtian acting* the actor creates a mask from himself in a highly selective gestic way and then responds to it, or comments on its actions in his own person. He is both within the mask and outside it.

4. With *Beckett and the absurd* the mask is distinctly individual but with larger-than-life connotations. It is a broad symbol for aspects of the human situation but is recognizable in its specifically human detail. The aspects of the mask are selected so that the playing of them will create the wider resonances of absurd theatre. The mask is larger than the actor but bears his features.

5. *The Artaudian actor* does not have a specific mask. He has a score of actions that he has discovered, and that he confronts in performance. This score is part of the *mise en scène*, the total, macrocosmic mask of action. The actor reveals himself through the total mask.

Sense of Occasion.

The words that come to mind when trying to encapsulate the essential quality of the Artaudian theatrical event have all been used before and are implicit within our discussion: holistic, ritualistic, participatory, intense, all-embracing. The use of total space, the filling of the total space with images and sensations, the tearing away of masks to reach human essences, the confrontation of man with himself as represented in his most deeply rooted myths—all of this suggests the physical and spiritual demands of the Artaudian occasion.

The purpose of the physical impact, the essential function of "cruelty," is therapeutic—to effect a change in the human condition. As the shaman conducted the rites of passage in ancient rituals, so the actor in Artaudian theatre seeks to transport the audience into new levels of consciousness. The actor's intense self-revelation discovers a truth that stands for all and engages the audience in its own act of self-searching and revelation. The actor, through his creation of the images, patterns, and hieroglyphs of a shared humanity, gives himself to the audience and changes both his state and theirs.

In simply technical terms the directness of the spatial relationship between actor and audience allows the actor to include the audience members in the event. They may become peasants, soldiers, the dead, the legions of the damned—whatever the focus of the myth or idea the actor is confronting. Thus, the participation can be physically realized, but the true participation happens at a deeper level: it is an embracement of a spiritual kind. In a way the sensibility of Artaudian theatre brings us full circle: aesthetics and ethics meet as they did in the earliest rituals, and in the Greek theatre, the starting point of our discussion. The essential sense of community, the sharing of the ideal of citizenship underlying the sensibility of the Greek theatrical event is something the Artaudian theatre wishes to recapture. Call it ritual, communion, mass: the core of the event is the actor's and audience's celebration of their common humanity, a celebration that reveals their deepest selves and shares the catharsis as they touch and act out the grace that lives within us all.

EXERCISES, GAMES, TECHNIQUES

An actor's physical instrument should always be well tuned, but never more so than when confronting the demands of Artaudian theatre. Companies such as Grotowski's and Chaikin's spent years in stringent daily physical and vocal training. We cannot pretend to set down such a program on paper. Rather, we are giving a core of basic exercises that will cover the range of demands placed upon the Artaudian performer, while recommending his serious attention to extending his vocal range and capacity and achieving a freedom and supple, tensile responsiveness in his body. It is the technical achievement of the process of *via negativa:* being open to stimuli

and having the physical capacity to respond totally, yet in a disciplined, theatrically oriented way.

Free Flow. These are spinal exercises. The spine carries the nervous system, the flow of bodily impulses. The freer the spine, the more fluid the flow and the fuller and more direct will be the physical response to action. When engaged with the pelvis—the body's center of gravity and balance—the free spine allows the actor to respond with a complete instrument—not just the movement of arms and legs for physical expression and the face for feelings.

Solo Stretch. Sit on the floor, well forward on the pelvis and elongate the spine. Open the legs into as wide a V as possible and place the hands behind the body, fingertips touching the floor. Flex the feet so that the heels come forward. Push the body up off the floor with the fingertips so that it is balanced on fingertips and heels. Point the toes and release the pelvis to the floor. Repeat twice, then return to original position and breathe for one minute. Now walk the hands out in front of the body, stretching forward until the elbows contact the floor and, if possible, the chest contacts the floor between the V of the legs. Sustain this position for one minute. Breathe in, lengthen the spine, and return to original position. Now draw the knees up to the chest and, with the soles of the feet touching each other, let the knees fall to the floor at either side. Take the image of a butterfly for this position. Stretch the knees outwards without bouncing; try to lengthen the chest onto the floor while the knees work outwards at the side. Breathe in, lengthen the spine, and return to original position. Repeat the whole pattern again.

Spinal Walk. Two players stand front to back and breathe in unison. The front player releases his head and chin onto his chest. The rear player touches the top of his partner's head and with two fingers walks the length of the spine from head to tail bone. Wherever the front partner feels the fingers walking he releases forward and will finally be rounded over, arms dangling, experiencing the length and elasticity of his spine. The rear player now slides the palm of his hand three or four times along the length of his partner's spine. With each slide the spine will become more supple. The rear player now walks the two fingers back up the spine, which is lifted in response to the touch. When the front player is upright both players breathe together for a minute. Reverse roles and repeat.

Spinal Float. Two players matched in height and weight stand back to back. One player wraps his elbows under his partner's and bends his knees so that the partner's buttocks rest in the small of his back. Straightening the knees the partner leans forward so that the other player is stretched along his back, legs dangling and spine released. Both players breathe for a while in this position—take an image of floating on water. The under player now takes the other's wrists and they straighten up, once more standing back to back. Reverse roles and repeat. This is a good activity after the rounding exercises, as it takes the spine in the opposite direction.

Monkey Walk. Lie on the stomach, head resting on folded arms. Breathe in, lift the head, and curve the spine into the yoga cobra position. From the cobra lift the pelvis into the air, forming the high point of a triangle with hands on the floor, heels on the floor, and shoulders pulled back to lengthen the spine. Now walk the palms towards the feet, keeping the knees straight. Tap the way up the body with the palms: along thighs, through the stomach, up the chest to the top of the head, and end with arms extended as far as they will go. Reverse the process—down the body, into triangle, into cobra, and back to starting position. Accompany the activity with sound—an ascending note to go up, a descending note to come down. Repeat. Players feel foolish doing this exercise. That's fine; players must be willing to make fools of

themselves to release the deepest impulses. The exercise is a good coordination of pelvis with spine.

Rope Trick. Sit on the floor with knees drawn to chest and arms around them. Elongate the spine. Now roll spine down to the floor until it reaches the small of the back. Roll back to a seated position. Repeat, this time rolling down to middle of back and up again. Finally, roll the entire spine down to the floor; then reverse, tucking the head slightly forward and elongating the spine. Repeat the entire process, taking the image of pulling a rope taut with a partner: release to roll down; pull on the rope to sit up.

The Whip. Stand in a neutral position. Gradually release forward until hanging loosely from the lower spine. Round the pelvis and lift the abdomen to form a curve with the spine. Keep the pelvis in place, and elongate the spine parallel to the floor. Raise the upper spine, making a dip through the lower spine; arch the upper spine. From the arch release into a straight line, release from the straight line into the curve, then release the curve and hang forward. Repeat the process: curve to straight to arch to straight to curve. Take the image of a whip being gently cracked.

Groin Grind. Stand opposite a wall with the arms extended so that the fingertips just touch the wall. Now place palms on the wall—this will make you lean slightly forward. Now bend the arms so that the chest moves forward to touch the wall; this will make the spine concave. Push off the wall so that the spine becomes convex, and return to beginning position. Repeat, this time trying to touch the wall with the groin. Push into convex position and return to start. Repeat the process several times, trying to make fuller contact with the wall each time.

The Cat. This is an exercise popularized by Grotowski, but which originated with

Stanislavski. Lie face down on floor, head on arms. Move into the cobra position, and from here into a triangle by lifting the pelvis into the air with hands and feet on the floor. Circle the torso to the right. Repeat, circling to the left. Release the pelvis towards the floor, then arch back up to the roof. Now extend left leg as far as it will stretch and shake it out. Repeat for right leg. Repeat for left arm, then right arm. Now release knees to floor and slide back into the cobra, and from there into a prone position. Do not force this exercise; it should flow. Taking the image of a cat waking and stretching should help to achieve the exercise.

The Plastique. Stand in a neutral position with the legs comfortably apart, knees slightly bent, pelvis released forward. Isolate the head, drop it forward, return center, drop it back, return center. Now drop right, center, left. Make a complete head roll. Now raise right shoulder, drop, and return to center. Drop shoulder down, lift, and return to center. Roll shoulder in a circular pattern. Repeat process with left shoulder. Isolate the rib cage, bring it forward, return to center; to the right, center; left, center. Isolate the pelvis and repeat the process. Circle with pelvis. Work through the fingers by stretching and releasing. Work through the wrists, pulling them in and away as if pulling taffy. Rotate the elbows; stretch them and pull the shoulders forward. The movements should be taken quickly, and each pattern repeated several times.

Space Concrete. Players walk around the space in a neutral posture, focusing upon the manner in which their bodies confront and make their way through space. Coach players to explore the environment fully with their bodies: to feel it, rub against it, embrace it, listen to it, make contact in as many ways as possible with as much of their body as possible. Now coach players to move through space in as many different rhythms as possible: to run, to roll, to somersault, to glide, to

swim—whatever their physical imagination gives them the impulse to do.

Now, fill the space with as many different physical obstacles as are available: boxes, benches, broken chairs, hurdles, rubber tires—make a maze (it might also be considered a children's playground) out of sizable bric-à-brac. Players now combine the two previous exercises. They move through the maze in a series of different rhythms—rolling, slithering, crawling—while making contact with all of the objects with as much of their bodies as possible. Other players should be accepted as among the spatial objects and explored physically when encountered. Coach players to make sounds expressing their responses to the objects they encounter. This is an excellent exercise for encouraging actors to relate with all their bodies to the total *mise en scène*. It also encourages them not to be afraid of full bodily contact with other players: this comes about as a secondary function of the spatial exploration—the body is regarded as another object, which removes the taboo block from physically encountering other persons.

Sound Concrete. Players sit at random around a space. Within the space are numerous objects with which sound can be produced: sticks, stones, tin cans, empty boxes, and so forth. The players explore the sound potential of these nonmusical "instruments," playing them on the floor, in midair, muted against the body. The body may also be used as a sound instrument—by patting air-filled cheeks, slapping parts of the body with hands or solid objects, clicking with the tongue, using exaggerated breathing. The purpose of the exercise is to get players to understand the possibilities of producing different sounds without the voice or musical instruments—the range of the actor's aural imagination can be enormously broadened.

When the players have gained some facility they should be coached to try rhythms that vary in pace and intensity. Finally, groups of rhythms can be discovered and complete conversations held by exploiting the sound and rhythmical range of the objects and the body.

The Chord. Players stand in a close circle with their arms around each other's shoulders, eyes closed. They listen to and fall into rhythm with the breathing of the player on either side. Players are coached to extend the breathing until it becomes a hum. When this happens the hum will ultimately extend itself into a chord. The chord of breathing will rise and fall, achieving crescendos and dying away in keeping with the basic feeling and rhythm of the group. When the chord has been going for some time it will become quiet. At this juncture coach to listen to individual breathing and finally to open the eyes and drop the arms. The chord (originated by the Open Theatre) is a good ensemble exercise. It also gives players deep contact with one of the body's basic rhythms. While performing the chord there is often a strong sensation of the body falling away, and an almost trancelike state is induced.

Zap. Players form a circle, or two lines opposite each other. One player throws a ball of energy with a particular body movement and sound at another player. The second player must accept the energy, repeat the movement and sound, transform it into his own movement and sound, and zap it at another player. There should be no gap between receiving the energy, performing it, and then transforming it. The game is high-energy and high-pace. Players may need to be coached to use their whole bodies, rather than just arms and legs, in performing the movements. The game is a good warm-up and encourages 360-degree use of physical imagination.

Conductor. This can be played as an extension of "Zap." Players form a circle with one player in the center. The center player performs any kind of rhythmical movement with his body. The other players respond with movements of their own, not imitating the central player but picking up the dynamics of his rhythmical action. He is the conductor, and they are the orchestra. He can change the rhythm and pace at any time, and they should follow. After a short while the conductor offers his rhythm and action to a specific member of the orchestra, who picks it up, moves into the center, and becomes the new conductor. He may now create his own dynamics. The exercise continues until all players have a turn as conductor. An elaboration upon the exercise is to add non-musical sound to the movement, emphasizing the rhythm and connecting physical and vocal impulses.

Tone Poem. This is an extension of "Conductor." Begin that exercise and allow the rhythmical concentration to develop. When the exercise is under way throw various themes at the conductor as a basis for the "music" he is creating. The themes may start simply and allow of imitation—a carousel, an old Ford car, a 747. They should then move into broader essences and abstractions—for example, colors, tastes, and concepts such as imprisonment, revolution, and hatred. Through this exercise the players will find themselves on the way to exploring their basic reactions to metaphysical ideas and to discovering hieroglyphic responses.

Party. Another sound and movement exercise. Set up a simple situation such as a cocktail party, patio party, opening-night party, whatever. Have the players improvise on this situation in a realistic manner for a few minutes. When all the players seem to be into the rhythms of the exercise, continue it without the use of language or simple gesture: players may make nonverbal sounds and gesture with their bodies, but not just with their arms. Players must now find fuller and stronger ways of "conversing" with each other, by creating their own language of sounds and meaningful body movements. Players usually find that their "conversations" become more significant: the trivia of everyday speech disappears with the trivia of everyday gestures.

Backslapping. Players form a ring with two players in the center. The center players must try to touch each other's back with their fingertips. They must not make contact with any other part of the body and must stay within the ring. Whoever first makes three touches is the winner and two other players take over. The game can be played with the winner staying in the ring and taking on all challengers until defeated. The game encourages quickness of response and body flexibility. It can also be used as a warm-up exercise for any highly physical style such as farce. (See chapter 5.)

Phantom Fighting. Players pair off and begin a fight, but without touching each other. All the motions of punching, kicking, butting kneeing, etc., can be gone through, but they must be controlled so that no contact is made. The styles of fighting may be varied: boxing, wrestling, laser swords, street brawling. This is another total-body-involvement game, but it also requires a strong sense of awareness, of playing with another actor. The players can be coached to experience the fight intensely, but the performance of it takes on a ritualistic quality—it is the essence of a fight that is being created by the participants.

Ritual Combat. This exercise (originated by the Performance Group) extends "Phantom Fighting." A circle about twenty feet in diameter is marked out. A player goes to the center of the circle and issues a challenge by means of an aggressive dance. Another player enters the circle and takes up the challenge by performing his dance. The dancers move into combat, which involves sound, aggressive movement, and strong body commitment but no physical contact. Each time a player

"strikes," the other receives the blow. There are no misses—all blows wound. Once wounded, the player carries the wound through the rest of the fight. If one player sustains a broken shoulder he must fight with the other arm. Similarly, a broken leg, or a stomach wound that doubles him up, must be sustained until the end. Because of the totality and intensity of the combat it lasts a brief time—until one player is totally disabled. The winner performs a dance of triumph in which he is joined by half of the remaining players. The other players mourn and carry off the loser. The game combines a ritual structure with a strong sense of body involvement. The ritual structure will be enhanced if carrying off the dead player is made into a ceremonial, with the use of a bier, libations, keening, and so forth. Carrying is an important element of human rituals, from the baby carried to its mother's arms to the final carrying to the place of interment. The act of carrying is far more than simple transportation—it elevates and dignifies, it solaces, it gives over the body to others' care, it sacrifices, it presents, it is an act of love.

Four-Letter Feelings. Players find their own space and begin to improvise upon some basic human function, such as eating. They should start with the most polite form they know— possibly a formal banquet or sophisticated restaurant with the paraphernalia of silver and linen napkins. As they go through the improvisation they should murmur appropriate words such as "dining," "entertaining," "banqueting." Gradually reduce the formality of the situation, doing away with knives, forks, and napkins and using the hands and appropriate words such as "eating" and "chewing." Finally, reduce the act to its basic animal idea, using hands and feet and tearing with the mouth—the words will become "gnaw" and "rip" and finally simple animal sounds. This exercise should be done with all the human functions, at the discretion of the coach and group of players. The willingness to deal with such concepts as fucking and shitting will be a test of the group's ability to get below polite masks and strip away taboos. It is not an exercise that should be attempted by an inexperienced coach with a group that has not learned to have mutual trust. It is an exercise that takes the players back to more dynamic and vivid physical responses—it brings their center of response out of their head into the lower, pelvic part of the body, where it should be. We have learned to wrap up subjects that society finds taboo in polite terminology;[16] we talk of "putting to sleep" when we mean "killing." The sex act is perhaps the strongest taboo, and dealing with it in this exercise produces interesting modulations, which will go through flirting, making love, going to bed, having sex, and finally the ultimate four-letter word and the rhythmical, dynamic, total body response the act presumes.

Lip Sync. This is an exercise that players usually enjoy. Have them choose a piece of rock music by one of the more physically expressive singers (Patti Smith, Rod Stewart, whoever is popular at the time) and perform to it, lip-synchronizing the words. Encourage players to be as physically expressive and sexually outrageous as they wish. It is a good exercise for encouraging bodily engagement and the dropping of masks—especially as some players are inclined to be more free when they feel it is "Patti Smith" doing the action rather than themselves. This is, of course, another form of hiding, but if it serves the purpose of liberating bodily expression, it is often a long step forward for players who have strong social inhibitions.

Encounters. Players pair off and select a simple human relationship, such as boy-friend/girlfriend, cop/crook, teacher/pupil, salesman/customer. Without exchanging ideas the players move around the space exploring the relationship. No words are used and no realistic props. Concentrate on the rhythms of your character, expressing them through space to your partner. A pattern will emerge that expresses the nature of the relationship as both players perceive it. At this stage of the exercise one partner should choose a simple but emotionally strong message to communicate to his partner—for example, "The man you shot died," or "I'm leaving you." Again, no words are to be used; the message is to be communicated through the body movements in the spatial pattern already developed. When the partner senses the nature of the message he replies in a similar manner—with body movement in spatial patterns. With strong concentration and bodily commitment to the exercise, messages can be understood and dynamic conversations held. Some coaching will be needed to channel players away from small, realistic gestures into more deeply seated, engaged movements of the whole body. As players become familiar with the exercise, more complex transactions can take place upon more fundamental issues.

Hieroglyphs. A series of games to help the actor discover and then physically communicate the essential nature of concepts:

Paper Signs. Divide players into two teams. Each team has a drawing pad and a colored crayon. Players in turn take a card from a stack; on the card is written a concept such as pain, sacrifice, or caring. The player now has to draw a hieroglyph of the concept on the pad while the other players try to identify it. Once it is identified another player takes a card, and so on until one team has identified all its concepts. This is an excellent game for getting actors to the core of a concept and choosing the simplest and most dynamic way of conveying its essence. The control is built in: if the other players cannot identify it the hieroglyph is weak.

[16] It is interesting to note that the basic, expressive, simple terms tend to be Anglo-Saxon, closer to the primitive origins of a culture. The complex terms of the English language have mostly a Latin base, brought into the language by the invasion of the more sophisticated Norman civilization.

Contrasts. Players scatter around the space, contacting it in a neutral manner. Within the space are various nonspecific props, such as sticks, ropes, colored ribbons, and pieces of cloth. Number the players and introduce opposing concepts to be explored, such as harmony/discord. Have the odd-numbered players explore one concept, the even numbers the other. Players should work individually and physically at first, responding to an immediate sense of what the concept means to them. The response should be confronted and refined into a hieroglyph—a series of gestures or movements. When the players seem to have discovered their hieroglyph, call out pairs of numbers—one even, one odd—and have these players reveal their hieroglyph to each other, responding to each other's rhythms, confronting the opposite concept, and adjusting so that the two hieroglyphs become one—a hieroglyph that displays the essence of the dichotomy. While working in pairs players may use any of the props around the space. There are many pairs of concepts that work for this exercise: goodness/evil, victory/defeat, truth/falsehood, freedom/restraint, self-interest/sacrifice, and so on. Players should be coached to reject the realistic gestures they first employ and to discover deeper and more broadly meaningful images.

Seven Deadly Sins. Players begin by contacting space in a neutral manner. Introduce the "sin" concepts (gluttony, lust, avarice, envy, pride, sloth, wrath) one at a time. The players should follow their immediate physical response. At first there will be a certain amount of imitation, pantomime—the sticking out of the belly for gluttony, moving slowly for sloth. Coach for an understanding of the full medieval significance of SIN—not contemporary peccadilloes. Coach for a strong visceral reaction, a full body response from the feet up, a total physical exploration. When all players seem to be working at this deep level, coach to refine the physical discoveries into a

rhythmical, disciplined, repetitive image that retains the intensity of feeling at its core. Between work on each concept have the players shake out and resume a neutral walk in space—this is necessary due to the intensity of the work involved. When all the sins have been individually explored, throw them all at the group and allow players to work on one they have a particular response to. After a few minutes' work have the players shake out and sit in a circle. Now each player in turn performs his particular hieroglyph in the center of the circle. The other players don't know the concept, but if the hieroglyph is valid they will soon sense it. As they get the idea they begin to whisper the concept: "lust," "envy," "pride," and so on, in time with the center player's rhythm, encouraging the player to a peak of intensity. The exercise is excellent for achieving a visceral response to ideas and a refined, intensified image based in that response. It quickly reveals clichés and weak, realistic gestures.

The following four games examine the nature of everyday social masks, identifying and revealing the hidden attitudes, censored subjects, and proscribed acts the masks conceal. They have been developed by the authors from an exercise done by the Open Theatre.

What the Butler Saw. Players pair off and improvise upon some private human act, the kind of thing that normally goes on behind closed doors: undressing, seduction, bedroom romps, personal perversions. Each pair in turn then performs their scene for the other players as if those players were looking through a machine in a penny arcade. The scene thus becomes mechanical and jerky-paced, like the series of old film stills it is. The scenes usually produce a great deal of laughter, and by creating a certain distance make players more comfortable with the material they are handling. It is a good way of getting players familiar with delicate areas.

Fantasies. Players split up into groups of about four. In turn each of the players arranges the others in a tableau illustrating a fantasy—profane, morbid, heroic, erotic, whatever has some deep meaning for the player. Then, as in the previous exercise, the tableaux are wound up and act out the fantasy like a penny-arcade machine. Fantasies, as depicted by man in his art, from the earliest cave drawings, are the wellspring of human imagination and are strongly connected to the ritual roots of drama.

Sub Rosa. Players improvise a social event—cocktail party, PTA meeting, presidential inauguration, homecoming ball—with the necessary social decorum and the polite conversation appropriate to the situation. When it is established, the players begin to act out impulses that are normally controlled beneath the social mask: they pick noses, smell armpits, unzip pants, look under dresses, pinch bottoms, giving free physical rein to the instinct of the moment. While they are doing this, however, they continue to make the right small talk and register no surprise at what is going on. The exercise shows in strong relief the difference between our social behavior and our basic instincts.

Taboo. Another game that identifies the unmentionable or unperformable in a social situation—this time exploring how it will break the situation up. Players split up into groups of three. The first group goes into the middle of the work space, and one of the watching players throws a situation at them—doctor's office, professor's study, dentist's waiting room, fashion boutique. The group begins to improvise on the situation, looking for the taboo inherent in the circumstances as they develop—what should not be said or done. At first not very serious faux pas may be produced, but ultimately there will be a taboo revealed that is strong enough to break up the situation. When this has been discovered, the group leaves the

space and another group begins work on a new situation. Sexual taboos tend to be the first to arise, and sometimes on a superficial level. Coaching will produce deeper responses and the exploration of a wider range of taboos.

Cruelty. This is an exercise that pulls all the others together: "Encounters" and "Hieroglyphs" are especially good exercises for leading into it. Players choose a five-to-ten-minute scene from a play—strong classical texts such as *'Tis Pity She's a Whore*, *The White Devil*, and *Titus Andronicus* work best—and explore the text purely in terms of sound to get at the core of the feeling—a quality sometimes hidden by the words. Players will begin by extending vowel sounds and drawing out the words themselves. Coach them to get more deeply in touch with the essential meanings of the scene and discover sounds that may have no specific reference points in the text. Repeat the exercise, this time adding physical gestures—the sounds and gestures should support each other. Again, players will at first simply extend everyday gestures; coach for stronger confrontation of the ideas in the text, to reject clichés and discover clear, powerful images that encapsulate the essential qualities of the scene. As the other exercises lead up to this, it shouldn't be played until near the end of a fairly extensive workshop exploration of the style.

Our two final exercises may be used in working on Artaudian theatre, but have a broader application. As befits the last two exercises in the book, they are concerned with the creation of masks, and may be used to test the actor's quickness and openness of response to an impulse, within the structure of any of the styles we have discussed.

Sixty-Second Commercial. Players perform the exercise individually before the group. The player is given a topic—energy crisis, inflation, sexism—and a style in which to communicate his response to the topic in a sixty-second improvisation. The styles are not just theatrical; start with something lively, such as rock or disco. Styles may include silent-movie, southern-preacher, "jock"—anything, in fact, that has a distinctive quality. Move into theatrical styles—Greek, Absurd, Brecht, and others—once the exercise is under way. It is a quick exercise—ten players can each work on three styles in half an hour. It is a good exercise for testing the players' immediate grasp of the essence of a style.

Transformations. A theatrical style evolved from this exercise, and was formalized especially in the plays of Megan Terry.[17] As a technique it increases an actor's aptitude to seize upon the essence of an idea or a character and reveal it with a few vocal and physical specifics. It shows the actor that "playing" does not necessarily rely upon psychological motivation and logical transitions. The exercise can be started with players walking around the space with a neutral posture. Throw out some easily identified social roles—film star, truck driver, cowboy, football player. The players have thirty seconds to respond to the impulse and create a physical mask of the role. Players should trust their immediate physical impulses and then refine and clarify the rhythms and energies of the mask. After this initial exercise, improvisations, including several players, can be set up. Begin the improvisation in the player's own persona, and when it is established throw out images such as animal, musical instrument, and vegetable and further roles such as air hostess, marine, and professor. The players must maintain the thread of the improvisation while adopting masks based upon the given images. Players

should be coached away from clichés and towards rhythms and energies expressing a more essential response. The exercise makes players extremely aware of their bodies, sharpens physical imagination, and taps subconscious resources—the impulses hidden behind and inhibited by the rational mind.

SUGGESTED READINGS

ARTAUD, ANTONIN, *The Theatre and Its Double*, trans. Mary Richards. New York: Grove Press, 1958.

BENEDETTI, ROBERT L., *Seeming, Being and Becoming*. New York: Drama Book Specialists, 1976.

CHAIKIN, JOSEPH, *The Presence of the Actor*. New York: Atheneum, 1972.

GROTOWSKI, JERZY, *Towards a Poor Theatre*. London: Methuen, 1969.

KNAPP BETTINA L., *Antonin Artaud: Man of Vision*. New York: Avon Books, 1971.

MALPEDE, KAREN, *Three Works by the Open Theater*. New York: Drama Book Specialists, 1974. This is an excellent visual source.

MAROWITZ, CHARLES, *The Act of Being*. London: Secker & Warburg, 1978.

PASOLLI, ROBERT, *A Book on the Open Theater*. New York: Bobbs-Merrill, 1970.

SCHECHNER, RICHARD, *Environmental Theater*. New York: Hawthorn, 1973.

———, *Essays on Performance Theory 1970-1976*. New York: Drama Book Specialists, 1977.

———, *Public Domain*. New York: Bobbs-Merrill, 1969.

SELLIN, ERIC, *The Dramatic Concepts of Antonin Artaud*. Chicago: University of Chicago Press, 1968.

[17]Of this genre are *Viet Rock, Comings and Goings, Keep Tightly Closed In A Cool Dry Place, The Gloaming, Oh My Darling*, and *Calm Down Mother*.

Index

A

Absurd theatre, 184, 186–213
  definition of, 189
  exercises for, 209–13
  intrinsic demands of, 192–200
  performance demands of, 200–9
Achilles, 17
Acoustics, Greek, 22
Action, 3
  activity compared to, 23–24
  in Greek Tragedy, 19, 23–26
    exercise in, 37
  in Shakespearean drama, 79
Action painting, 252
Actors
  in Artaudian theatre, 254, 255–56, 262–65
  as central in Shakespearean theatre, 59, 72
  in epic theatre, 237–38
    rehearsal techniques, 240–41
  in Middle Ages, 140–41
Adamov, Arthur, 192
A day in the life of . . . (exercises), 95, 135
Aeschylus, 15, 19
  Agamemnon, 44
  Oresteia, 25
Agamemnon (Aeschylus), 44
Agon (in Greek drama), 19
Akropolis (Grotowski), 254, 257–59, 261
Albee, Edward, 192
Alexandrine rhythm, 61, 62
Alienation
  Artaudian theatre and, 255–56
  Brecht and, 218–20, 229, 230, 237–38
Allen, Gracie, 175
Allen, Woody, 171, 191
Alliteration in Shakespeare, 66
"Amateur" sensibility, 103
Amazing dressing (game), 181
American Conservatory Theatre, 81, 116, 153, 158, 166, 175*n*
Anapest in Shakespeare, 61, 62, 63
Anderson, M. J., 47
Animal attitudes (exercise), 181–82
Animal mask (exercise), 41
Anthony and Cleopatra (Shakespeare), 66
Antigone (Brecht), 227
Antigone (Sophocles), 25
Antoine, André, 112
Apollo (god), 35
Apron (of stage), 112, 113
Aristocracy, British, 102–8, 121

Aristophanes, 139
  The Birds, 19
  The Clouds, 16
Aristotle, 16, 23, 44
  Brecht's critique of, 217–19, 222
Arnott, P. D., 47
Art
  contemporary "cruelty" of, 252–53
  and contemporary image of man, 197–98
Artaud, Antonin, 184, 247–53
Artaudian theatre, 246–77
  "cruelty" theme in, 247–53, 265–67, 268
    exercise in, 276
  general exercises on, 269–77
  intrinsic demands of, 154–62
  performance demands of, 262–69
Ashcroft, Peggy, 186, 201
Ashland (Ore.) Shakespeare Festival, 55
As You Like It (Shakespeare), 51, 80
Atellan farce, *see* Rome—farce in
Athens, 17
  See also Greece
Audience (spectators)
  in Artaudian theatre, 253, 256–60, 264, 266–69
  in comedy of manners, 120
  direct communication between actors and, 77–78
  in epic theatre, 219–21, 230, 238, 240
  in farce, 165, 173
  Greek, 18–19
  Restoration, 112–13
  for Shakespeare's plays, 52, 57, 74–75, 77–78, 79, 87
Auditoriums, *see* Audience; Space; Stages
Aykroyd, J. W., 97

B

Baal (Brecht), 215
Bacchae, The (Euripides), 16, 21, 25, 41, 42, 44, 254, 266
Backslapping (exercise), 273
Balcony, The (Genet), 199, 200
Bald Soprano, The (Ionesco), 192, 193, 198, 199, 202, 208
Balinese theatre, 250
Ballet, aristocratic stance and, 123
Barrett, William, 213
Basic process of acting, 3
Beare, W., 183
Beauty as truth, 16
Beauty patches, 108
Beauvais (France), 141
Beck, Julian, 256*n*
Beckerman, Bernard, 97